DIVINE SUBJECTIVITY

DIVINE SUBJECTIVITY

UNDERSTANDING HEGEL'S
PHILOSOPHY OF RELIGION

Dale M. Schlitt, O.M.I.

University of Scranton Press
LONDON AND TORONTO: Associated University Presses

All rights reserved. Authorization to photocopy items for internal or personal use, or the internal or personal use of specific clients, is granted by the copyright owner, provided that a base fee of $10.00, plus eight cents per page, per copy is paid directly to the Copyright Clearance Center, 27 Congress street, Salem Massachusetts 01970. [0-940866-11-0 $10.00+8 cents pp. pc.]

B
2949
. R3
S275
1990

Associated University Presses
440 Forsgate Drive
Cranbury, NJ 08512

Associated University Presses
25 Sicilian Avenue
London WC1A 2QH, England

Associated University Presses
P. O. Box 488, Port Credit
Mississauga, Ontario
Canada L5G 4M2

The paper used in this publication meets the requirements of the American National Standard for Permanence of Paper for Printed Library Materials Z39.48-1984.

Library of Congress Cataloging-in-Publications Data

Schlitt, Dale M.
    Divine subjectivity: understanding Hegel's philosophy of religion
    /Dale M. Schlitt.
      p.   cm.
    Includes bibliographical references.
    ISBN 0-940866-11-0 (alk paper)
  1. Hegel, Georg Wilhelm Friedrich. 1770-1831–Contributions in philosophy of religion. 2. Religion–Philosophy–History–19th century. I. Title.
B2949.R3S275   1990   90-33188
200′.1–dc20   CIP

Printed in the United States of America

CONTENTS

ACKNOWLEDGEMENTS   vii
ABBREVIATIONS OF WORKS BY HEGEL   ix
INTRODUCTION   xiii

I.   HEGEL'S PHILOSOPHY OF RELIGION LECTURE TEXTS   1
     1.   NEW EDITIONS – CONTINUING THE HEGEL
          RENAISSANCE   3

II. HEGEL'S TRIPARTITE PHILOSOPHY OF RELIGION   29
     2.   THE CONCEPT OF RELIGION   31
     3.   DETERMINATE RELIGION   67
     4.   THE CONSUMMATE RELIGION   99

III. HEGEL'S RELIGIOUS DIALECTIC OF
     IDENTITY AND DIFFERENCE   131
     5.   IDENTITY AND RELIGION   133
     6.   THE WHOLE TRUTH: TRINITY   171
     7.   INCARNATION AND OTHERNESS   199
     8.   THE KINGDOM OF GOD   271

CONCLUSION   319

BIBLIOGRAPHY   325

INDEX   341

To my sisters and brothers and their families

ACKNOWLEDGEMENTS

Some of the chapters in this volume were written during a sabbatical leave generously granted by my university. During this leave, 1986-1987, Prof. Bernard McGinn and the Institute for the Advanced Study of Religion in the Divinity School of the University of Chicago graciously created an atmosphere conducive to reflection and writing for myself and for other Institute Fellows. The Research Centre of St. Paul University provided funding for my research assistant, Mr. Denis Hurtubise, who carried out his editorial functions with great competence and insight. My religious congregation, the Missionary Oblates of Mary Immaculate, have encouraged my work with generous financial and moral support.

Prof. Dr. Ekkehard Mühlenberg, Göttingen University, deserves my continued thanks for originally directing my attention to Hegel. Prof. Dr. Traugott Koch, Hamburg University, has read earlier versions of several of these chapters and offered valuable suggestions. Prof. Peter C. Hodgson, Vanderbilt University, has shown a passion for understanding Hegel and a careful attention to detail in editing Hegel's philosophy of religion lectures. His research has born rich fruit in the English edition of these lectures. Prof. Hodgson and his translation associates have earned the deep gratitude of those who would like to learn from Hegel. His edition sets a standard for future renderings of Hegel texts in English. I have repeatedly learned from Prof. Hodgson's Introductions to the English edition of Hegel's philosophy of religion lectures, from his published articles, and from his generously offered, timely and wise advice. Dr. Walter Jaeschke, formerly of the Hegel Archives in Bochum and presently at the Schleiermacherforschungsstelle in the Berlin Academy of Sciences, has continued, in the kindest of ways, to provide invaluable assistance. Not only has he helped me to understand Hegel better and kept me abreast of recent research, but he has become a friend in the best German sense of the word. His editorial achievements, articles, and longer studies represent the highest quality Hegel scholarship. They have created for him a special place in the landscape of Hegel research. Thankful as I am to all who have so generously helped me, I must accept responsibility for the understanding of Hegel presented in this volume.

Chapters One to Four of the present volume are revised, reorganized, and somewhat lengthened versions of feature review articles previously published in *The Owl of Minerva*, Biannual Journal of the Hegel Society of America. The original articles appeared in vol. 16 (1984) 69-80, vol. 18 (1987) 179-197, and vol. 19 (1987) 63-83. The slightly revised Chapter Five was originally published as "Hegel on Religion and Identity" in *Église et Théologie* 17 (1986) 195-221. Chapter Six is a slightly revised version of "The Whole Truth: Hegel's Reconceptualization of Trinity," which appeared in *The Owl of Minerva* 15 (1984) 169-182. And Chapter Eight represents a moderate revision of "Hegel on the Kingdom of God," published in *Église et Théologie* 19 (1988) 33-68. Materials from *The Owl of Minerva* are copyright by the Hegel Society of America and are used here with the very generous permission of the editor, Prof. Lawrence Steplevich. Those from *Église et Théologie* are copyright by Saint Paul University, Ottawa, and are included here with the very kind permission of the editor, Prof. Léo Laberge.

St. Paul University/Université Saint-Paul   Dale M. Schlitt
Ottawa, Canada

ABBREVIATIONS OF WORKS BY HEGEL

D   *The Difference between Fichte's and Schelling's System of Philosophy.* Translation of *Differenz des Fichte'schen und Schelling'schen Systems der Philosopie* (see GW 4:1-92) by H. S. Harris and Walter Cerf. Albany: State University of New York Press, 1977.

E   *Enzyklopädie der philosophischen Wissenschaften im Grundrisse.* Third original edition 1830. Philosophische Bibliothek. Vol. 33. Edited by Friedhelm Nicolin and Otto Pöggeler. Hamburg: Felix Meiner, 1969. § = paragraph. R = remark following the numbered paragraph.

FK   *Faith and Knowledge.* Translation of *Glauben und Wissen* (see GW 4:313-414) by Walter Cerf and H. S. Harris. Albany: State University of New York Press, 1977.

GL   *Hegel's Science of Logic.* Translated by A. V. Miller. New York: Humanities, 1969.

GW4   *Gesammelte Werke.* Vol. 4: *Jenaer kritische Schriften.* Edited by Hartmut Buchner and Otto Pöggeler. Hamburg: Felix Meiner, 1968.

GW9   *Gesammelte Werke.* Vol. 9: *Phänomenologie des Geistes.* Edited by Wolfgang Bonsiepen and Reinhard Heede. Hamburg: Felix Meiner, 1980.

GW11   *Gesammelte Werke.* Vol. 11: *Wissenschaft der Logik. Erster Band: Die objektive Logik (1812-1813).* Edited by Friedrich Hogemann and Walter Jaeschke. Hamburg: Felix Meiner, 1978.

GW12   *Gesammelte Werke.* Vol. 12: *Wissenschaft der Logik. Zweiter Band: Die subjektive Logik (1816).* Edited by Friedrich Hogemann and Walter Jaeschke. Hamburg: Felix Meiner, 1981.

GW21   *Gesammelte Werke.* Vol. 21: *Wissenschaft der Logik. Erster Band: Die objektive Logik (1832).* Edited by Friedrich Hogemann and Walter Jaeschke. Hamburg: Felix Meiner, 1985.

L1   *Lectures on the Philosophy of Religion.* Vol. 1: *Introduction and The Concept of Religion.* Edited by Peter C. Hodgson. Translation of materials from V 3 by R. F. Brown, P. C. Hodgson, and J. M. Stewart with the assistance of J. P. Fitzer and H. S. Harris. Berkeley: University of California Press, 1984. "Editorial Introduction" pp. 1-81.

L2   *Lectures on the Philosophy of Religion.* Vol. 2: *Determinate Religion.* Edited by Peter C. Hodgson. Translation of materials from V 4 by R. F. Brown, P. C. Hodgson, and J. M. Stewart with the assistance of H. S. Harris. Berkeley: University of California Press, 1987. "Editorial Introduction" pp. 1-90.

L3   *Lectures on the Philosophy of Religion.* Vol. 3: *The Consummate Religion.* Edited by Peter C. Hodgson. Translation of materials from V 5 by R. F. Brown, P. C. Hodgson, and J. M. Stewart with the assistance of H. S. Harris. Berkeley: University of California Press, 1985. "Editorial Introduction" pp. 1-57.

L4   *Lectures on the Philosophy of Religion.* One-volume edition. *The Lectures of 1827.* Edited by Peter C. Hodgson. Translation of materials from V 3, 4, and 5 by R. F. Brown, P. C. Hodgson, and J. M. Stewart with the assistance of H. S. Harris. Berkeley: University of California Press, 1988. "Editorial Introduction" pp. 1-71.

PM   *Hegel's Philosophy of Mind.* Translation of E, Part Three, by William Wallace. Oxford: Clarendon, 1975. § = paragraph. R = remark following the numbered paragraph.

PN   *Hegel's Philosophy of Nature.* 3 vols. Translation of E, Part Two, by M. J. Petry. New York: Humanities, 1970. § = paragraph. R = remark following the numbered paragraph.

PS   *Phenomenology of Spirit.* Translated by A. V. Miller. New York: Oxford, 1977.

PSS   *Hegel's Philosophy of Subjective Spirit.* Translation of E, the first section of Part Three, by M. J. Petry. Dordrecht: Riedel, 1979. § = paragraph. R = remark following the numbered paragraph.

SL *Hegel's Logic*. Translation of E, Part One, by William Wallace. Oxford: Clarendon, 1975. § = paragraph. R = remark following the numbered paragraph.

V3 *Vorlesungen: Ausgewählte Nachschriften und Manuskripte*. Vol. 3: *Vorlesungen über die Philosophie der Religion. Teil 1: Einleitung. Der Begriff der Religion.* Edited by Walter Jaeschke. Hamburg: Felix Meiner, 1983.

V4 *Vorlesungen: Ausgewählte Nachschriften und Manuskripte*. Vol. 4: *Vorlesungen über die Philosophie der Religion. Teil 2: Die bestimmte Religion. a: Text. b: Anhang.* Edited by Walter Jaeschke. Hamburg: Felix Meiner, 1985.

V5 *Vorlesungen: Ausgewählte Nachschriften und Manuskripte*. Vol. 5: *Vorlesungen über die Philosophie der Religion. Teil 3: Die vollendete Religion.* Edited by Walter Jaeschke. Hamburg: Meiner, 1984.

Hegel's German texts and lecture transcripts found in GW 4, 9, 11, 12, 21 and V 3, 4, and 5 are usually cited by page and text line. In L 1, 2, 3, and 4 the German edition pagination is conveniently indicated in the outer margin of the text. Therefore, unless the English translation of Hegel's texts and lecture transcripts is quoted, generally reference is made only to the German edition of V 3, 4, and 5. The corresponding English translation can easily be found by following the English edition's indication of the German edition pagination. Also, the historical critical *Gesammelte Werke* edition of Hegel's works retains older forms of German spelling used by Hegel. German citations from this edition will retain these spellings. E.g., the modern German *Dasein* is rendered *Daseyn*, and the modern form *dies* is given as *diß*.

INTRODUCTION

Hegel has created a unique philosophy of religion. His is no merely extrinsic effort to reflect on God, on religious consciousness, and on the relation between the two of them. He wanted his philosophy of religion to be the expression of the inner dynamic of spirit. In his philosophy of religion God was to be spirit. So he set about to work out his philosophy of religion as the dialectical development of God. God must be thought not only as substance but as dynamic subject, and thus as spirit.

For many years Hegel struggled to give clearer and more coherent expression to his understanding of God as subject and spirit. He knew that any treatment either of God or of human religious consciousness alone would be one-sided and, therefore, false. He realized that if he related God and the human in a merely external way he would never be able to reconcile the two. He looked again at the religious notion of God and saw in it the potential for expressing a dynamic movement and relationship which would include both divine and human. Hegel fashioned the religious notion of God into a dialectical movement of divine subjectivity. He constantly argued that, for God to be truly infinite, God had to include the finite or the human. His argumentation took the form of a philosophy of religion as the thinking through of the notion of God as spirit. God was to be thought as subject inclusive of the other. And this "thinking through" of the notion of God was, for Hegel, the very development of God as spirit in and through human thinking. In Hegel's philosophy God is a dynamic movement of inclusive divine subjectivity.

Even when we try to speak more generally of Hegel's philosophy of religion, we immediately find ourselves at the very heart of his philosophy. Hegel will not let us remain on the surface. Practically every remark he makes, every argument he proposes, forces us to the very core of his thought – there, where he was concerned with questions of alienation and reconciliation difference, and mediation. Since he followed upon Kant, Fichte, and Schelling, it comes as no surprise that he would quite spontaneously, and quite naturally, formulate a response to these questions in terms of subjectivity.

If we want to understand Hegel's philosophy of religion, we need to formulate a very general or initial understanding of his concept of subjectivity.[1] To understand his view of subjectivity is, in a sense, the burden of our whole study. Still, it will be very useful for us to have available right from the beginning, and in quite preliminary fashion, something of what Hegel means when he speaks of subjectivity.

Hegel recognizes that there is such a thing as "mere subjectivity." We can understand subjectivity to refer simply to the subjective. If we consider the subjective in this more isolating sense, then it is one-sidedly personal. This is, for Hegel, an inadequate understanding of subjectivity. Yet this apparently one-sided instance of being subject can, upon further reflection, be found to have included within itself the notion of the other over against which it is one-sidedly subjective. Initial identity gives rise to difference. But then, of course, this other is itself one-sided when it is considered for itself or in its own right. So we arrive at one-sided understandings of subjectivity and of objectivity. Hegel insists that an adequate thinking through of these instances of subjectivity and of objectivity will lead us to the recognition that they both include one another. With this realization Hegel has led us to see the unity of the two. He has created a notion of inclusive subjectivity. He has proposed the mediation of subjectivity and of objectivity in a higher and more inclusive notion of subjectivity. For Hegel this movement to the inclusive notion of subjectivity is what it means to be true subject or spirit.

Hegel works with this general movement of spirit in his philosophy of religion. He realizes that religion is essentially a movement from finite religious consciousness to God. Religion is the elevation of the finite to the infinite. But he also comes to understand that this, we could say dyadically structured, movement from finite to infinite must be seen in the wider philosophical context of what it presupposes. In other words, Hegel sees that this elevation of the human spirit to God is part of the wider and more inclusive movement of divine subjectivity. We could say that the phenomenological movement from finite to infinite finds its grounding in the dialectical movement from God to us.

Hegel gives this movement of divine subjectivity what can be called a speculative formulation.[2] That is, he argues that the dynamic which underlies and grounds the philosophy of religion is the movement of spirit. He universalizes his general understanding of spirit when he presents God as the true content of philosophy and of religion. God is the initial moment of subjectivity. But then God is the one whose nature it is to be revealed and manifest. God, or as Hegel will say, the divine idea appears in nature and finite spirit. Nature and finite spirit are reconciled with God in and through finite spirit, for, in thinking through opposition or contradiction, finite spirit is thinking through its own being. This thinking through of contradiction is, for Hegel, the dialectical moment. Thinking through contradiction, thinking through "yes" and "no" together, enables finite spirit to see the unity or identity underlying its self-contradictory reality. In so thinking the human is elevated to God. This whole process is the speculative presentation of the dynamic of inclusive divine subjectivity.

Here we have in a nutshell the doubled inner dynamic of Hegel's philosophy of religion. Religion is the elevation from finite to infinite. And when we spell out the philosophy of religion we realize that this elevation takes place within the more inclusive movement of spirit. Hegel has developed a unique, important, and influential philosophy of religion, which is to be understood as a movement of inclusive divine subjectivity. It is a movement of God as spirit.

Whenever we approach Hegel we need to make certain choices. His philosophy, and here I mean in particular his philosophy of religion, is so complex and so rich. In the present study I have decided to work more directly with his overall speculative formulation of God as movement of divine subjectivity. This means I will treat less explicitly of certain notions such as faith or the cosmological proofs for the existence of God, which characterize more what we might call the dyadic movement from finite to infinite. To this extent my analyses will not be as fully representative of what Hegel is doing as they could perhaps be. But, then again, I would propose that, in working with the speculatively formulated movement of God as inclusive divine subjectivity, we are in fact equally attending to the elevation of the human to the divine.

I am suggesting, then, that we can come to understand Hegel's philosophy of religion to the extent that we think of it in terms of a movement of divine subjectivity. Furthermore, I am proposing that it is particularly helpful to approach Hegel's philosophy of religion from the perspective of the speculative formulation of this dialectic of inclusive divine subjectivity. Our goal, then, is to aid in understanding[3] and, consequently, critically appreciating, Hegel's rich and original philosophy of religion.

We will pursue this goal with a certain order and progression in mind. We will work primarily with the newly available texts of his Berlin lectures on the philosophy of religion. Hegel structured these lectures in three parts: The Concept of Religion, Determinate Religion, and The Consummate Religion. The eight chapters of our study follow, in a doubly repeated pattern, the overall structure and sequence of Hegel's own threefold division of the philosophy of religion. Parts One and Two of our study provide the occasion for our first following of the development within Hegel's philosophy of religion. In these Parts One and Two it is our intention progressively to work our way into the complexities of Hegel's thought. In Part Three we will begin again to follow, in a general way, Hegel's threefold division of his philosophy of religion. Here we will pursue more detailed analyses of several of Hegel's presentations of the dynamic movement of divine subjectivity.

In Part One, Chapter One, we will make brief reference to the Hegel renaissance which has continued throughout the twentieth century. This renewed interest in Hegel forms the context for an appreciation of the significance of the new editions of Hegel's lectures on the philosophy of religion. Chapter One opens with a brief summary of the editorial history of Hegel's lecture materials on the philosophy of religion. It continues with a somewhat lengthier discussion of the importance and characteristics of the new three-volume German edition, and of the new three-volume and one-volume English editions. At the end of the chapter we make several observations regarding further research opportunities opened by these new editions.

In Part Two, "Hegel's Tripartite Philosophy of Religion," we proceed in such a way as to reflect the structure and movement of Hegel's own presentation of his philosophy of religion. We want to point out as well that Hegel's various lecture presentations of each of the three parts of his philosophy of religion are now gathered, and separately printed, in one of the three volumes of the German and English editions. Therefore, Chapters Two, Three, and Four are each devoted to a presentation of important aspects of one of the three parts of Hegel's own triply divided philosophy of religion lecture materials. In each of these three chapters the presentation is carried out in three steps. First of all, we introduce the subject matter which Hegel treats in the particular part of his philosophy of religion under consideration. At the same time we present the specific German and English volumes containing that part of his philosophy of religion. Secondly, we analyze selected important aspects of the Hegel materials being treated. Thirdly, at the end of each of these chapters we propose a number of areas for further research. These are areas opened up by the new presentation of the Hegel materials contained in the particular volume being considered. Along with Chapter One, these three chapters help bring us up-to-date on the status of current textual resources. More importantly, they have the perduring value of introducing certain basic characteristics of Hegel's various series of lectures on the philosophy of religion. In addition, they point out a number of questions still being discussed in the area of Hegelian philosophy of religion. The focus and progressive arrangement of these four chapters should help us see how Hegel's philosophy of religion is, indeed, a presentation of inclusive divine subjectivity.

Part Three, "Hegel's Religious Dialectic of Identity and Difference," consists of four chapters. These chapters present both a more detailed overview of the speculatively formulated dynamic of Hegel's thought and analyses of several of the religious themes he interprets. This dynamic and these themes are treated from the overall perspective of Hegel's understanding of the relationship between identity and difference or, more traditionally stated, between the one and the many. They lead us into the heart of Hegel's philosophy of religion. Chapter Five, "Identity and Religion," situates the role of religion in the wider framework of Hegel's systematic thought by studying religion's "function" in Hegel's wider quest for, and understanding of, identity. Chapter Six, "The Whole Truth: Trinity," recapitulates Hegel's dialectical interpretation of Trinity as the dynamic interaction of identity and difference in a movement of inclusive divine subjectivity. Chapter Seven, "Incarnation and Otherness," examines one of the major ways in which Hegel discusses otherness. It looks at the way in which the world and Christ appear as other to and of God. Chapter Eight, "The Kingdom of God," sorts out, in some detail, Hegel's philosophical interpretation of this central religious metaphor throughout the four series of Berlin lectures on the philosophy of religion.

This Part Three will help us see how Hegel works out his philosophy of religion, and especially his philosophy of what he calls the consummate religion, as a post-Kantian reformulation of the relationship between identity and difference. He subsumes the older formulation of the question of the one and the many, or the more modern concern for identity and difference, into a speculatively presented movement of inclusive divine subjectivity. As we will note in the Conclusion to our study, Hegel's is a philosophy of religion before which we cannot remain neutral.

NOTES

[1] On the notion of subjectivity I have found the following particularly helpful: Karl Homann, "Zum Begriff 'Subjektivität' bis 1802," *Archiv für Begriffsgeschichte* 11 (1967) 184-205; Klaus Düsing, *Das Problem der Subjektivität in Hegels Logik, Hegel-Studien*, Beiheft 15 (Bonn: Bouvier, 1976); _____, "Hegels Begriff der Subjektivität in der Logik und in der Philosophie der subjektiven Geistes," in *Hegels philosophische Psychologie. Hegel-Tage Santa Margherita, Hegel-Studien*, Beiheft 19, ed. Dieter Henrich (Bonn: Bouvier, 1979) 201-214; John N. Findlay, "Hegel's Concept of Subjectivity." In *Hegels philosophische Psychologie. Hegel-Tage Santa Margherita. Hegel-Studien*. Beiheft 19 pp. 13-26, Ed. Dieter Henrich. Bonn: Bouvier, 1979; Walter Jaeschke, "Absolute Idee – absolute Subjektivität. Zum Problem der Persönlichkeit Gottes in der Logik und in der Religionsphilosophie," *Zeitschrift für philosophische Forschung* 35 (1981) 385-416.

For bibliography on Hegel's philosophy of religion, in addition to the works indicated in Dale M. Schlitt, *Hegel's Trinitarian Claim. A Critical Reflection* (Leiden: Brill, 1984) 6 n. 31 and 196-197 n. 1, see Falk Wagner, "Bibliographie zu Hegels Religionsphilosophie," in *Die Flucht in den Begriff. Materialien zu Hegels Religionsphilosophie* (Stuttgart: Klett-Cotta, 1982) 309-345; Walter Jaeschke, *Die Religionsphilosophie Hegels* (Darmstadt: Wissenschaftliche Buchgesellschaft, 1983).

[2] On the speculative and the phenomenological in Hegel's philosophy of religion, but from a somewhat different perspective, see the very helpful article by Peter C. Hodgson, "Hegel's Approach to Religion: The Dialectic of Speculation and Phenomenology," *The Journal of Religion* 64 (1984) 158-172. One might profitably compare Hegel's remarks on "speculation" and religion in his 1821 and 1824 lectures. See, for example, V 3:114.119-116.452 (1821) and V 3:55.614-56.646 (1824). In addition to this helpful distinction between speculative and phenomenological there is, from another perspective, a sense in which the speculative is the phenomenological in that the

speculative is the universalized and generalized formulation of the phenomenological move from immediacy to distinction.

3 "Understanding" is generally being used with the standard English meaning of a real or good comprehension of something. The same word is customarily used to translate *Verstand*, which for Hegel means that level of human thinking which distinguishes and divides without seeing the inner unity involved in whatever is being thought. In the present volume the specific context in which "understand" is used will indicate how it is to be understood. See Hodgson, in L 1:56-57.

PART ONE

HEGEL'S PHILOSOPHY OF
RELIGION LECTURE TEXTS

CHAPTER ONE

NEW EDITIONS – CONTINUING

THE HEGEL RENAISSANCE

G. W. F. Hegel. *Vorlesungen: Ausgewählte Nachschriften und Manuskripte.* Vols. 3-5: *Vorlesungen über die Philosophie der Religion. Teil 1: Einleitung. Der Begriff der Religion. Teil 2: Die bestimmte Religion. a: Text. b: Anhang. Teil 3: Die vollendete Religion.* Ed. by Walter Jaeschke. Hamburg: Felix Meiner, 1983, 1985, 1984.

Lectures on the Philosophy of Religion. Vol. 1: *Introduction and the Concept of Religion.* Vol. 2: *Determinate Religion.* Vol. 3: *The Consummate Religion.* Edited by Peter C. Hodgson. Translated by R. F. Brown, P. C. Hodgson and J. M. Stewart with the assistance of J. P. Fitzer (Vol. 1) and H. S. Harris. Berkeley: University of California Press, 1984, 1987, 1985.

Lectures on the Philosophy of Religion. One-volume edition. *The Lectures of 1827.* Edited by Peter C. Hodgson. Translation by R. F. Brown, P. C. Hodgson, and J. M. Stewart with the assistance of H. S. Harris. Berkeley: University of California Press, 1988.

The twentieth-century Hegel Renaissance shows surprising signs of continuing vitality. Already at the beginning of the century two

German volumes, concerning Hegel's early life and writings, marked the beginning of a steadily increasing twentieth-century interest in Hegel's philosophy. Wilhelm Dilthey's *Die Jugendgeschichte Hegels*,[1] a study of the early Hegel, and Hermann Nohl's *Hegels theologische Jugendschriften*,[2] a collection of Hegel's earlier so-called "theological" writings, had great influence especially in Germany, France, and Italy.

We need merely mention a few names and titles to recall the continuing, and growing, interest in Hegel throughout the century. Works such as the Italian Benedetto Croce's *What Is Living and What Is Dead in the Philosophy of Hegel*,[3] the Frenchmen Jean Hyppolite's *Genesis and Structure of Hegel's "Phenomenology of Spirit"*[4] and Alexandre Kojève's *Introduction to the Reading of Hegel*[5] have had great influence within and beyond the borders of their own countries. We could as well recall the Marxist reading by Georg Lukács in *The Young Hegel*[6] and the volume by John N. Findlay, *Hegel. A Re-examination*.[7] Findlay's study was very influential in the generally more analytically oriented English-speaking philosophical world. Interestingly, since at least the 1920's a number of Japanese scholars have shown a great interest in Hegel. Perhaps the easiest way to indicate the increasing twentieth-century interest in Hegel is to point to the thousands of twentieth-century studies identified in Kurt Steinhauer's 894 page *Hegel Bibliography*[8] and to the hundreds of doctoral dissertations written since the early 1960's on Hegel in Germany and especially in the United States and Canada.

It is quite fitting that the twentieth-century Hegel renaissance, which had its origins at least partially in the rediscovery of Hegel's earlier writings on religious subjects, should now, toward the end of the century, be characterized by a flourish of critically edited volumes of Hegel's texts, lecture materials, and auditors' transcripts. But it is especially fitting that the new editions of Hegel's Berlin lectures on the philosophy of religion stand preeminent among these recent editions. Hegel studies, and interest in Hegel in general, have often been linked with the editorial history of the publication of Hegel's writings and of auditors' transcripts.

In this our first chapter we will follow one strand of this interweaving of editions and interest in Hegel, namely, the publication of Hegel's lectures on the philosophy of religion. To some extent, now toward the end of the twentieth century we are following this interweaving from the vantage of its end point and result. For the long, complex editorial history of Hegel's lectures on the philosophy of religion comes, in a sense, now to a happy end with several impressive editions. The final, historical-critical German *Gesammelte Werke* edition will apparently not be completed before the mid-1990's. Nevertheless, the present German text, as critically secured by Walter Jaeschke, Ricardo Ferrara and Peter C. Hodgson, and the translations based on it, provide truly reliable access to Hegel's lectures of 1821, 1824, 1827 and, to a lesser extent, of 1831. The German, English, and Spanish editions have appeared concurrently; French and Italian translations are in preparation.[9] Though all of these editions and translations follow the same general editorial principles, we will here begin our project of understanding Hegel's philosophy of religion by focusing, in a somewhat more technical way, on the German and English editions. We will examine these two editions as follows: 1) their historical context, and here we will need to turn back for a moment to the nineteenth century; 2) a general overview of the new editions; 3) a resume of the way in which the new texts were established; 4) remarks on the English translation; 5) reference to the general indices; and, 6) further research opportunities opened by these editions.

1. *Historical Context*

The editorial history of the German texts of Hegel's lectures on the philosophy of religion and their historical impact have, as mentioned, so far been inextricably intertwined. There are three landmark editions which, in various ways, take on the value of sources for the present editions. Back in the nineteenth century, within less than a year after Hegel's death, Philipp Marheineke had, in 1832, quickly pulled together the first of these editions. This edition has come to be known as the "first Friends Edition."[10] Marheineke integrated auditors' transcripts, but particularly those from Hegel's later and supposedly more mature lecture series. His intention was to produce something between a finished book and the reproduction of a series of lecture transcripts. However, the resultant text, in which the conflated transcripts remained more juxtaposed than truly integrated, gave rise to divergent interpretations concerning Hegel's views on God, pantheism, immortality, and Christ. That such varied thinkers as Göschel and Strauss, Marx and Stahl used this same edition reinforces the editor of the German edition, Walter Jaeschke's, evaluation that this first Friends Edition did not evidence a clear and intentionally one-sided presentation of Hegel's thought.[11]

Many, including members of Hegel's family, pushed for a new edition in the hope that a more representative selection of lecture materials might resolve the question of divergent philosophical interpretations. So in 1840 Markeineke introduced a "second Friends Edition,"[12] which was edited by Bruno Bauer without external constraints. Though Bauer maintained Marheineke's original conception of something between a book and a printing of lecture series,[13] he integrated new material from Hegel's 1821 manuscript. Needless to say, this second Friends Edition failed to resolve conflicting philosophical interpretations of Hegel's thought. Trying to integrate the structurally different 1821 lectures with the more homogeneous later series left the impression of a relatively compact and, consequently, a potentially more influential work. But it also rendered almost impossible the tasks either of deciphering the development of Hegel's thought during the Berlin years or of trying to follow Hegel's argumentation within a given lecture series.[14] The editor of the German edition, Walter Jaeschke, examines, but does not resolve, various contradictory interpretations of Hegel's thought as it is presented in the second Friends Edition. Included among the questions on which Jaeschke comments is whether Hegel might have shifted to the right or to the left during the Berlin years. He concludes that Bauer worked objectively even while, and perhaps precisely because, he was undergoing a conversion from right-wing Hegelianism to atheism. A critical analysis of the two Friends Editions fails to indicate any overall intentional manipulation of the texts themselves.[15]

If we rush on now to the end of the first quarter of the twentieth century, we come to the third of these landmark editions, that of Georg Lasson in 1925.[16] His is the third edition which, in some way, takes on the value of a source for the present late twentieth-century editions of Hegel's philosophy of religion lectures. Lasson had intended to produce a critical edition. He distinguished, with larger print, the text of Hegel's 1821 manuscript from the interwoven transcripts of the later lecture series. However, Lasson's structuring of his edition according to the 1821 manuscript, his at times faulty reading of the manuscript, and his less than acceptable identification of the later lecture transcripts produced anything but a truly critical edition. Nevertheless, given the current text situation, Lasson's edition remains, even today in the last quarter of the twentieth century, the best available basic text for the 1827 lectures.[17]

The fundamental problem with these three previous German editions was their attempt to integrate lecture series which differed in structure, in distribution of content, and in the amount of content included. In the present German, English, and other language editions the editors no longer try to hybridize something between a book and a reproduction of lectures. They no longer try to integrate the four series of lectures. Rather, with these editions they resolve problems inherent in such an integrating approach by returning to the original lecture format. The editors print Hegel's four lecture series separately and sequentially by overall lecture subdivision. They can, therefore, reliably reconstruct the content and flow of the 1821, 1824, and 1827 lectures and, to some extent, also those of the 1831 lectures. Now toward the end of the twentieth century the Hegel Renaissance continues because we can study Hegel's philosophy of religion the way it should be approached and understood. We can read the lectures the way Hegel actually gave them.

The new, we could say, penultimate German edition itself has a history dating back to Jaeschke's 1971 typescript M.A. thesis on the structure and previous editions of Hegel's philosophy of religion lectures. *The Owl of Minerva,* Biannual Journal of the Hegel Society of America, has provided helpful progress reports on the new editions. This is especially true for the period around 1979, when the present series of editions was being more modestly conceived by Peter C. Hodgson as a "study edition" in English, and possibly also in German. Previous English translations proved woefully inadequate both because they were based on either part or all of the conflated Second Friends edition and because the translations themselves were quite flawed. However, by mid-1980 the intended study edition had quickly given way to plans for a full-fledged series of critically secured texts. The result is now a number of editions in several languages. Each of these editions is bound in three volumes and, thus, for the first time published in line with Hegel's own originally intended overall triadic division of the philosophy of religion: Part One: Introduction and The Concept of Religion; Part Two: Determinate Religion; Part Three: The Consummate Religion.[18]

2. General Overview of the New Editions

Both in the German and in the English editions the three volumes of Hegel's philosophy of religion lectures form part of announced ten-volume series of selected manuscripts and transcripts of Hegel's various Berlin lectures. The German edition of the lectures on the philosophy of religion constitutes Volumes Three to Five of the ten-volume German lecture series. It follows a strict editorial principle in not only clearly distinguishing between, but also effectively separating any editorial material from Hegel's manuscript, from other Hegel materials, and from transcripts of his lectures. Editorial information and observations are either gathered into the important general Editorial Preface found at the beginning of Volume Three or placed in the abundant endnotes to each volume and printed in italics. The 77-page Editorial Preface remains the key to these three volumes as a whole. Here the editor has summarized, updated, and corrected earlier published or unpublished material as well as included significant new research on sources for Hegel's philosophy of religion lectures and on these lectures' editorial history. Each of the three volumes presents the sequentially printed 1821 manuscript and transcripts of Hegel's 1824 and 1827 lectures, which are then followed by either supplementary or secondary transmissions of lecture materials and pertinent excerpts from David Friedrich Strauss's reworked transcripts of the 1831 lectures. Each of these German volumes of Hegel's philosophy of religion ends with a series of helpful indices. The fourth volume, containing Part Two or Determinate Religion, also includes an impressive series of indices to the three parts of Hegel's philosophy of religion as a whole. We will refer more explicitly to these general indices below.

The three-volume English edition generally follows the same format as that of the German edition. However, in addition to summarizing some of the content of the German edition's Editorial Preface, the Editorial Introduction to the first volume of the English edition also presents a longer discussion of basic principles of the

English edition as a whole and of the translation of the lecture materials. This Editorial Introduction fulfills an important role analogous to that of the Editorial Preface in the German edition. Of particular interest and importance, the Editorial Introduction to each of the three English volumes includes an extensive analysis of the structure and development of the Hegel lecture materials presented in the particular volume in question. Each Editorial Introduction contains a very helpful diagrammed comparative analysis of the structure of the Hegel lecture materials which are presented in the particular volume being discussed. In contrast with the German edition, in which editorial material is contained in endnotes, the notes in this English edition, whether containing further source materials or providing more editorial information, are conveniently placed at the bottom of the page. They do not generally reproduce the German edition's longer quotations of authors to whom Hegel refers. In a particularly helpful move, the English edition indicates the parallel pagination of the German text in the outside margins. Therefore, in referring to Hegel's lecture materials, we will simply cite the German reference unless either the English edition itself is quoted or footnoted lecture materials have been placed slightly differently in the English edition.

The one-volume English edition contains Hegel's 1827 lectures on the philosophy of religion. In the Preface to this one-volume edition the editor, Peter C. Hodgson, indicates that he chose the 1827 lectures because they are the latest of those which can be fully reconstructed, "are the most clearly organized, and the most accessible to nonspecialists."[19] They are also of a manageable size. In the Editorial Introduction to this one-volume edition the editor presents further new reflections, while also conveniently gathering, and at times reworking, a number of materials from the unabridged three-volume English edition. Among these materials are items such as the list of sources for Hegel's philosophy of religion, augmented comparative outlines of Hegel's four series of lectures on the philosophy of religion, and a very insightful analysis of the text of the 1827 lectures. Of particular interest are the editor's various discussions of, and remarks on, the logical or "deep structure" out of which Hegel interprets religion and the history of religions.[20] This one-volume edition has surely become a most useful, and even necessary, student text for courses in Hegel's philosophy of religion.

3. *Establishing the Texts*

The only finally satisfactory way to appreciate the precision, thoroughness and dynamic of what has gone into the establishment of the newly available Hegel lecture materials on the philosophy of religion is to read through Hodgson's Editorial Introduction to Volume One of the English edition and especially through Jaeschke's more detailed Editorial Preface in the German edition. However, as part of our project in understanding Hegel's philosophy of religion we can, for present purposes, focus on lecture sources in general, on the editions' overall source-critical method, and on the sources for each lecture series. We have already touched on previous editions and, in the final section of the present chapter, will briefly refer to the philosophy of religion lectures in relation to Hegel's other Berlin lectures.

3.a. Lecture Sources in General

Jaeschke and Hodgson divide all sources known to have existed into three groups: Hegel's handwritten papers; auditors' transcripts, which serve not as sources of the lectures themselves but of the edition of the lectures; and, material transmitted in a secondary fashion either by brief literary references or through other editions of Hegel's philosophy of religion lectures.[21] Hegel's own known handwritten papers include the 1821 manuscript, a *Convolut* or gathering of more or less developed preparatory sketches and notes, and other loose sheets related to the philosophy of religion. Of these materials from Hegel himself only the manuscript and several of these last mentioned sheets remain today. Material from the *Convolut* must be recovered from the Friends Editions. Then the editors distinguish three types of auditors' transcripts: verbatim transcripts; fair copies written up later from notes; and, more freely edited transcripts. Twenty-three transcripts or parts of transcripts are known to have existed, of which twelve have been lost and eleven are still available for consultation.[22] Finally, material transmitted in a secondary fashion had to be identified from previous editions or other references in which the material is contained or cited.[23]

3.b. The Overall Source-critical Method

The limited number of extant sources, as well as their varying nature and quality, make for a less than satisfactory text situation. Given this situation, and in line with contemporary historical-critical interests and requirements, the present editions are necessarily constructed on the basis of an explicit, carefully worked out methodology.[24] Although the re-establishment of the German text of each lecture series calls for a somewhat different approach with regard to each lecture series, the editors follow a general process of subtraction (*Subtraktionsverfahren*).[25] This is an overall process of moving from more easily identified lecture materials to a, consequently possible, further sorting out of special materials from previous editions. This sorting out consisted in an eight-step procedure of subtraction[26] based on what has previously been identified as well as on information gleaned from Marheineke's two introductions to the Friends Editions and on information from other relevant secondary references. With more specific reference to the German texts, orthography has been modernized and, generally, variations in transcript readings have not been indicated. Special materials from previous editions have been footnoted at appropriate points.[27] The English translation, which will be discussed below, was made on the basis of these now established German texts. This process has produced a reliable text for each of the first three lecture series and some idea of the content and development of the 1831 lectures. Barring discoveries of new sources, the texts here established, with the addition of certain text-critical apparatus especially for the 1821 manuscript, will surely form the basis for the later *Gesammelte Werke* edition in which the various philosophy of religion lecture series will be inserted in their wider historical sequence.

Though these editions, and in particular the German edition, are more than study editions and somewhat less than the final historical-critical edition,[28] Jaeschke justifiably claims that the present edition contains the most clearly identified and systematically elaborated text presently possible.[29] The overall subtraction method appears at first terribly complex. But it slowly comes across as enlightened critical common sense and, finally, as the self-evident procedure to follow. This is perhaps the most convincing argument for the reliability of these texts and of the editorial work involved in reestablishing them.

3.c. The Four Lecture Series

Despite his ongoing interest in religion, Hegel lectured on the philosophy of religion for the first time only in 1821, and then from April 30 to August 25 with 49 auditors.[30] The sources for these lectures are Hegel's extant handwritten manuscript plus variant and supplemental materials extracted from the second Friends Edition. These variant or supplemental materials belong to, but are not presently specifically attributable to,[31] either Hegel's lost handwritten notes (*Convolut*) or Henning's lost transcript. They are footnoted in the German edition and keyed to the manuscript text by line reference.[32] As previously mentioned, in the English text these variant or supplemental materials are footnoted at the bottom of the page. Due to the complexity of the apparatus in the German text, the German arrangement of these sources for the 1821 lectures can be adequately appreciated only on the basis of a reading of editorial remarks made concerning the editing of the manuscript[33] and concerning the procedure for identifying material from the two Friends Editions.[34] In regard to the manuscript itself, in both the German and English editions, over and above producing a faithful reading, there was the difficult editorial and judicial task of establishing an apparatus appropriately relating Hegel's margin remarks and additional materials to the manuscript text itself. The decision was taken to integrate later expansions of the manuscript text into the text. Each integration of marginal notes or additional materials is noted in the footnotes. Other marginal notations, which are not so clearly considered expansions, are placed in the footnotes. The result is a text providing, as compared with that of Lasson,[35] reliable access to the differentiated original. When they are compared with the Ilting German text,[36] in which all marginal materials are footnoted, the present German and English texts produce a more fluent reading in line with Hegel's own intentions.

Hegel's second series of lectures, April 26 to August 26, 1824, was delivered to 63 auditors.[37] The editorial approach employed in establishing the text of these lectures[38] is quite different from the more straightforward utilization of Hegel's extant manuscript for the 1821 lectures. Of the five auditors' transcripts available today, the editors chose to make the still extant fair copy of Karl Gustav von Griesheim the basic text. In fact, Hegel himself had at least occasionally lectured from another copy of this transcript in 1827. Griesheim's transcript of the 1824 lectures is variously corroborated, replaced, or supplemented by three control texts: the verbatim transcript by Carl Pasternaci and the fair copies by P. F. (or F. P.) Deiters and F. C. H. von Kehler. Heinrich Gustav Hotho's more freely edited transcript serves as a supplementary text and is placed in the footnotes. So the new editions retain well-known phrases, not directly attributable to Hegel, such as "Without the world God is not God."[39] Additional similar and variant material from the two Friends Editions are footnoted as well. Some of these are identifiable as belonging to the *Convolut* or as possibly being notations on the Griesheim text used by Hegel and now lost. The result of this prolonged and impressive editorial work is a reliable, clear, easy-to-read and almost elegant rendering of the 1824 lectures, with a considerable amount of immediately available either supplemental or variant material.

Hegel's 1827 lectures, delivered from May 7 to August 10, attracted 119 auditors.[40] Since all the 1827 auditors' transcripts available for the use in the redation of earlier editions of Hegel's lectures have been lost, the critically identified 1827 text, as transmitted in Lasson's edition, takes on the character of a source for the present editions.[41] Therefore, the critically retrieved Lasson text serves as the basic text for the 1827 lectures. Additionally, three markedly inferior but still helpful auditors' transcripts of the 1827 lectures have recently been discovered. These three, namely, the verbatim transcript by Ignacy Boener and the two fair copies by Joseph Hube and an by anonymous auditor, function as control texts. Whereas for the 1824 lectures uncorroborated Griesheim texts were retained in the body of the lectures, here otherwise unsecured Lasson texts are placed in footnotes. The end result of this impressive editorial work is reliable access to the systematically organized 1827 lectures. Less secure Lasson and variant Friends Editions texts are footnoted at appropriate places in the text. Furthermore, Friends Editions texts identified as belonging to the *Convolut* or to the 1831 lectures are also conveniently footnoted. For the sake of completeness it is important as well to recall that texts identified as Hegel's notations to the Griesheim text have already been footnoted to the 1824 lecture texts.

We know neither exact dates nor numbers of auditors for Hegel's 1831 lectures.[42] Though the 1831 text situation is now better than in Lasson's day,[43] sources remain quite limited. Two secondary transmissions, placed at the end of the first volume in both the German and English editions, enable the editors to indicate the general structure of the 1831 lectures, which apparently followed quite closely that of 1827. The first of these two secondary transmissions, namely, several pages of 1831 texts identified from the Friends Editions,[44] develops what is for the philosophy of religion lectures a new point: the relationship between religion and state. The editors then add the second of these secondary transmissions, which is a series of excerpts from a transcript by David Friedrich Strauss. There are further secondary transmission materials for the 1831 lectures printed after the 1827 text in the second and third volumes of the German and English editions. Finally, it is important to remember that other 1831 materials from the Friends Editions are footnoted to earlier lecture series, and especially to the 1827 text.

Through these 11 years Hegel struggled to give adequate systematic expression to his philosophy of religion by changing the structure of these lectures and by enriching them with the regular addition of further content. These lectures were certainly influenced by other parallel Berlin lecture series.[45] Already now we can say that reading these volumes of Hegel's philosophy of religion lectures, in conjunction with the exhaustive endnotes or footnotes and against the background of Jaeschke's Editorial Preface and Hodgson's Editorial Introductions, leaves us with the distinct impression that these lectures constituted an ongoing, though variously directed, polemic with the then contemporary alternative philosophical, religious, and theological attitudes. These polemical lectures reveal the seriousness with which Hegel committed himself to the philosophical interpretation of religion.

4. The English Translation

In retrospect, Prof. Hodgson's earlier, student edition translation of Part Three of Hegel's lectures on the philosophy of religion, *The Christian Religion*, seems to have been quite a helpful proving grounds, or test case, for working out a basic approach to the translation of Hegel's works. It is not hard to recognize a certain continuity between the basic principles and guidelines of translation enunciated in the student edition and carried over into the present three-volume edition.[46] But, even more important, and striking, is the further elaboration, considerable development, and continuing refinement of these principles and guidelines in the new edition. The experience gained from working on the earlier study edition has served Hodgson and his translation associates well as they worked toward, and achieved, accuracy of translation, consistency of style, and a fluent, precise English while preserving something of the oral character of the original.[47]

Hodgson was responsible for the translation of Parts One and Three of the 1821 manuscript, J. M. Stewart for the 1824 transcripts (and Part Two of the 1821 manuscript), and Robert F. Brown for the 1827 transcripts. Joseph P. Fitzer shared in the translation of Part One of the 1824 lectures. H. S. Harris reviewed the translations, while Hodgson bore final responsibility for the volumes as a whole.[48] The translation team was able to achieve such a fine, consistent text by submitting their work to one another for review, by having the whole reviewed by Harris and Hodgson, by working out a set of common guidelines and principles,[49] and, finally, by progressively establishing a German-English Glossary.[50] This general approach to translating longer Hegel materials has broken new ground. It should facilitate further efforts at Hegel translations in the future. The establishment of a standardizing, yet flexible, glossary will both help solidify recent trends in Hegel translations and will give well thought out direction to those translating other Hegel lecture materials.

The principles which guided the translations and the procedures by which the work was carried out are easily available in the various Editorial Introductions to these volumes. Therefore we can be satisifed with giving, in more limited fashion, a taste of the difficulties encountered in translating Hegel from German into English. We will concentrate on the interpretation and translation of two key word clusters in Hegel's vocabulary: *sein* and *Aufhebung/aufheben*.

Hodgson draws attention to the many difficulties involved in translating the verb *sein*. "The most complex translation problem we have faced focuses on the simple verb *sein* ('to be') and related forms: the present participle *seiend* and the nouns *Sein, Seiende,* and *Dasein*."[51] If we turn to the *Science of Logic*,[52] we see that Hegel begins his presentation of the movement of pure thought with "being" (*Sein*) as first thought determination. "Being" is immediate, undifferentiated, and empty or without content. "Determinate being" (*Dasein*), as thought determination or moment in the movement of pure thought, is placed by Hegel fourth after "being," "nothing," and "becoming." Consequently for Hegel *Dasein* is more concrete and determinate than "being." To capture and maintain this distinction between "being" (*Sein*) and the more concrete and actual notion of "determinate being" or "existence" (*Dasein*) in the nominal, verbal, and participial forms, the translators have had to resort to such expressions as "actual being" for *Seiende* and "existence" or "determinate being" for *Dasein*. Often we would quite spontaneously tend to translate the verb *sein* by "exists" or "exist." But, as Hodgson points out, this might lead to the false implication (false at least from the perspective of Hegel's thought) that God exists in the way other objects exist. Furthermore, when speaking of God in Hegel's presentation of his systematic thought, we must adapt the way in which we refer to God in terms of "being" to the specific philosophical sphere or moment within which the reference is being made. Consequently, the translators variously express the verb form "is" (*ist*) either by underlining the word "*is*" or by adding a word or two. They add such words as "found," "known," or "present." For example, "God is [present] for me in devotion." While it might, at first sight, seem that the translator is simply discussing technical matters of translation and searching out suitable words and phrases equivalent to the German original, we quickly come to see that such questions force the translator of Hegel's texts up against very fundamental and quite disputed aspects of Hegel's philosophy.

Aufhebung/aufheben is the second example of a word cluster which is both difficult to translate and touches the very heart of Hegel's thought. Hegel sees in this ordinary German word a richness of connotation which allows him to express the complex nature of dialectical transition from one thought or moment to another. When he uses the term to express a movement or transition, he usually intends to speak of a threefold activity: negation; preservation; and, development, advance or raising to a higher level.[53] In this way Hegel can see the progression from one thought determination, or, again, from one philosophical moment or sphere, to another as a negation of what came before. But, equally, for Hegel nothing is left behind. What arises in consciousness or in thought takes up and contains, as negated, what went before. And this very taking up of the previous thought determination or moment, as negated, is as such an integrating progression or movement ahead toward further determination. To put this complex transition into fluent and consistent English is quite a challenge. Recently it has been suggested that the best way to render *Aufhebung/aufheben* into English is by repeatedly speaking in terms of negation, preservation, and advance.[54] Another alternative, and this is the one adopted by the Hodgson translation team, has been regularly, though not always, to translate *Aufhebung* and *aufheben* respectively by the increasingly accepted English words "sublation" and "sublate."[55] But even the choice of these specific forms of sublation as *terminus technicus* has itself been challenged. It has been said that the words "sublation" and "sublate" seem to stress (excessively?) the negative aspect of the transition to which Hegel is referring.[56] However, the *Oxford English Dictionary* (1933) gives "sublate" as the word translating Hegel's *aufheben* and the dictionary clearly indicates *aufheben*'s doubled sense of negate and preserve. A random check of another dictionary gives as a second meaning to "sublate": "to cancel but also preserve and elevate (an element in a dialectic process) as a partial element in a synthesis."[57] The above proposal to state all three aspects of *aufheben* each time has the advantage of assuring exact comprehension, but will surely prove cumbersome. It would seem that the option taken in these volumes often to use "sublation" and "sublate" will clarify and further formalize the technical English translation of *Aufhebung* and *aufheben* by forms of "sublate."

5. *The General Indices*

We should take special note of the four extensive general indices to Hegel's philosophy of religion as a whole. In the German edition these indices have been placed in the second half of Volume 4b. Two of them, a bibliography of sources for Hegel's philosophy of religion and an index of biblical references, are available in the English edition as well.[58] The other two sets of indices are a fourfold index of various contents and an index of historical persons named. These two indices are found only in the German edition. However, they can be used with the English edition since it gives the German edition's parallel pagination in its outer margins.

In both the German and English editions the bibliography of sources for Hegel's philosophy of religion lectures begins with a brief introduction by the editors.[59] The 253 main entries represent editions of sacred texts and studies of languages, as well as classical and modern secondary literature in German, French, English, Italian, Latin, and Greek. These are works which Hegel explicitly mentioned or which can, with a great deal of certainty, be ascertained on the basis of the formulations he used. Of the 253 main entries, 113 are marked in the German and English editions by an asterisk to indicate that they were cited in the auctioneer's catalogue of the contents of Hegel's library. Additionally, 52 entries are signed with a small triangle in the German edition, and by a dagger in the English edition, to point out that these are works to which Hegel alluded and for which we can identify the edition he used. The 88 remaining entries identify works which Hegel probably used, but to which there are no specific allusions. These various entries are the result of impressive sleuthing.

The German index of various contents is subdivided into *"Philosophica et Theologica," "Mythologica," "Realia,"* and *"Nomina propria."* The German Volume 4b containing these various general indices ends with a *"Personenverzeichnis"* or *"*Index of Persons.*"*[60] Though the first of these subsections of the index of various contents does not aim at completeness,[61] it does contain an enormous listing of technical and philosophical terms found in the lecture materials as well as in the endnotes. References to the endnotes are italicized. The indications of Hegel's usage of such terms as "incarnation" (*Inkarnation*) or "subjectivity" (*Subjektivität*) allow us to explore specific questions or concepts and the way, or ways, Hegel employs them throughout the three volumes. *"Mythologica"* gathers the names of gods and persons as well as certain terms commonly associated with mythology, understood in a wide sense of the term. *"Realia"* brings together in one list "actual features of the respective religions"[62] such as feasts and organizational structures. *"Nomina propria"* includes names of religions, peoples, texts, and places which, however, do not fall under the categories either of historical persons or mythical figures. This index allows us, for example, to seek out references to a certain religion outside of Hegel's specific treatments of that religion.[63] These who want to study Hegel's philosophy of religion will find a gold mine in these very reliable indices.

6. *Further Research Opportunities*

Jaeschke has carefully warned against an excessively optimistic hope of resolving, by editorial work, questions which can be handled only on the basis of philosophical reflection.[64] By way of example, we could recall that, after the second Friends Edition, there occurred even greater divergence in the philosophical interpretation of Hegel's thought than had existed before the editions' appearance. And this despite the fact that the second edition was initially supposed to overcome such divergence of interpretation.[65] Now, toward the end of the twentieth century, the present editions themselves constitute a contribution to the editorial history of Hegel texts. They provide that kind of easy access to Hegel's thought, in the richness of its flexibility and overall development,[66] which anyone who has struggled with the older editions cannot but appreciate. The separate editing of the four lecture series has also helped to resolve a myriad of merely apparent problems, such as sorting out many of the transitions and developments within each series.

However, the "editorial clarifications" achieved in these new editions of Hegel's philosophy of religion lectures go far beyond philological considerations. Indeed, these editions not only provide access to, but contribute directly to, the philosophical interpretation of Hegel's thought in its context. Consequently, they contribute to philosophy in general. They make this contribution, first of all, by taking seriously Hegel's claim that truth is the end result inclusive of the process.[67] To the extent that the present text situation permits, the serial presentation of Hegel's lectures makes the real Hegel available. This is the Hegel who developed his varying argumentations in an ongoing polemic with alternative positions.

Second, these editions make a philosophical contribution by opening the way to further serious research and creative philosophical reflection.[60] The separate printing of the lecture series, and the editors' positions taken in both the German edition's Editorial Preface and endnotes and in the English edition's Editorial Introductions and footnotes, open up many topics for further study, research, and doctoral dissertations. Among such topics: the polemical character of Hegel's philosophy of religion in general, and of specific lecture series; Hegel's overall intention to do philosophy of religion and his struggles to give it an adequate systematic expression; possible development from one lecture series to another and within specific series; the interrelationships among, and mutual influences of, Hegel's various Berlin lectures on one another; the possibility of a more accurate interpretation of Hegel on the determinate religions,[69] which in turn might provide help in present philosophical and theological efforts to reinterpret the relationship between Christianity and the other religions of the world.

Here we can touch on only a couple of these areas for future research. First, Jaeschke carefully points out that, if pushed to the extreme (*Zugespitzt*), the only structural element common to the four lecture series is the major triadic division into "Concept of Religion, Determinate Religion, Consummate Religion."[70] Though he further specifies this statement elsewhere in the Editorial Preface,[71] it would also seem important to complement the statement by underscoring as well a certain continuity in Hegel's thought. This continuity could be indicated, for example, by the consistent internal systematic presentation of, and apparently structurally important role of, "immanent" Trinity in the consummate religion.

Second, while admitting for Hegel the special importance of logic for philosophy of religion, Jaeschke suggests that Hegel's parallel lecturing on logic and philosophy of religion is due only to the appropriateness of handling both in the relatively shorter summer semesters.[72] Elsewhere, when he lists those courses which may have contributed to Hegel's philosophy of religion lectures, he fails to list the lectures on logic.[73] This failure may be due to the fact that the question Jaeschke is then discussing is the influence, in terms of content, of the other parallel Berlin lectures on the philosophy of religion lectures. Nevertheless, Jaeschke would here appear to be somewhat uncomfortable with stressing the role of logic in relation to philosophy of religion, or at least in relation to the interpretation of Hegel's philosophy of religion.[74] Recently, Hodgson seems to be emphasizing somewhat more the "substantive connection" between Hegel's philosophy of religion lectures and those on logic and "metaphysics."[75] There is surely a great deal of further work to be done on the possible relationships between philosophy of religion and logic in Hegel's thought.

The more general question concerning the relationship between Hegel's lectures on the philosophy of religion and those on logic opens up the further question of the possible relationship, for Hegel and/or for the reader, between particular logical thought determinations and various determinate religions. More specifically, Jaeschke has elsewhere warned against a merely formal interpretation of consummate religion as "immanent" and "economic" trinity in terms of specific syllogisms from Hegel's logic. He quite rightly points out the recent plethora of divergent syllogistic interpretations, the value of which might appear to remain rather vague.[76] Though these questions push beyond the scope of our present discussion, we can expect that the recent editions will open the way to further reflection on how, and to what extent, we might legitimately interpret Hegel's presentations of the consummate religion in syllogistic terms.[77]

These editions make a philosophical contribution by providing access to the real Hegel and by opening up topics for further research. Now toward the end of the twentieth century they mark a new beginning in the study of Hegel's philosophy of religion. But, from a philosophical perspective, perhaps what will be most exciting is the way in which these editions may encourage new, critical, and creative appropriations of Hegel's reconceptualization of God and religion. Perhaps these editions, with all their differences from the two Friends Editions, will still, like them, prove fecund beyond present expectations. Though in a sense the editorial history of Hegel's lectures on the philosophy of religion comes to an end with these editions, the historical impact of Hegel's lectures on the philosophy of religion surely will not. Along with the other new Hegel editions, these philosophy of religion texts should guarantee that the twentieth-century Hegel Renaissance continues well into the twenty-first century.

NOTES

[1] (Berlin: Reimer, 1905).

2 (Tübingen: Mohr, 1907)/partial English translation, G. W. F. Hegel, *Early Theological Writings*, trans. T. M. Knox (Chicago: University of Chicago Press, 1948).

3 *Ciò che è vivo e ciò che è morto della filosofia di Hegel* (Bari: Laterza, 1907)/English translation, *What Is Living and What Is Dead in the Philosophy of Hegel*, trans. Douglas Ainslie (London: Macmillan, 1915).

4 *Genèse et structure de la "Phénomenologie de l'Esprit" de Hegel* (Paris: Aubier, 1946)/English trans., *Genesis and Structure of Hegel's "Phenomenology of Spirit,"* trans. Samuel Cherniak and John Heckman (Evanston, IL: Northwestern University Press, 1974).

5 *Introduction à la lecture de Hegel* (Paris: Gallimard, 1947)/English translation, *Introduction to the Reading of Hegel*, trans. James H. Nichols (New York: Basic Books, 1969).

6 Georg [György] Lukács, *Der junge Hegel. Über die Beziehungen von Dialektik und Ökonomie* (Zürich: Europa-Verlag, 1948), 2nd ed.: *Der junge Hegel und das Problem der kapitalistichen Gesellschaft* (Berlin: Aufbau-Verlag, 1954)/Eng. translation, *The Young Hegel. Studies in the Relations between Dialectics and Economics*, trans. Rodney Livingston (Cambridge, MA: Massachussetts Institute of Technology Press, 1976).

7 (London: George Allen and Unwin, 1958).

8 *Hegel Bibliography. Background Material on the Internation Reception of Hegel within the Context of the History of Philosophy*, compiled by Kurt Steinhauer, Keyword Index by Gitta Hausen (Munich: K. G. Sauer, 1980).

9 V 3:iv/L 1:iv. Walter Jaeschke has recently indicated in private correspondence that French and Italian translations are in preparation. Note also that the historical-critical edition of Hegel's manuscript for the 1821 lectures on the philosophy of religion is now in print: G. W. F. Hegel, *Gesamelte Werke*, vol. 17: *Vorlesungsmanuskripte I (1816-1831)*, ed. Walter Jaeschke (Hamburg: Felix Meiner, 1987).

In this first chapter all references (except in footnote 31 below, where the author of the Hegel lecture transcript is clearly indicated) either to the German three-volume edition (V 1, 2, 3) or to the English three-volume (L 1, 2, 3) and one-volume (L 4) editions of Hegel's lectures on the philosophy of religion are to editorial materials by Jaeschke and Hodgson. From our Ch. 2 on through to the Conclusion of the present volume, references without further qualification to these German and English editions will indicate Hegel lecture materials. From Ch. 2 on editorial material will be cited by referencing Hodgson's or Jaeschke's name plus the preposition "in." E.g., Jaeschke, in V 3:xxi. Note the list of abbreviations of works by Hegel at the beginning of the present study.

[10] V 3:xxxix. G. W. F. Hegel, *Werke, Vollständige Ausgabe durch einen Verein von Freunden des Verewigten*, vols. 11-12: *Vorlesungen über die Philosophie der Religion. Nebst einer Schrift über die Beweise vom Daseyn Gottes*, ed. Philipp Marheineke (Berlin: Duncker und Humblot, 1832). Jaeschke (V 3:xliii n. 36) indicates early review literature on this edition. On this first Friends Edition and the history of the subsequent edition, see also the presentation by Hodgson, L 1:20-33. Where Jaeschke and Hodgson present parallel editorial information, we will often cite only from Jaeschke's somewhat more detailed presentation.

[11] V 3:xl-xliii.

[12] G. W. F. Hegel, *Werke, Vollständige Ausgabe durch einen Verein von Freunden des Verewigten*, 2nd ed., vols. 11-12: *Vorlesungen über die Philosophie der Religion. Nebst einer Schrift über die Beweise vom Daseyn Gottes*, ed. Philipp Marheineke [and Bruno Bauer] (Berlin: Duncker und Humblot, 1840). This edition is reviewed by Eduard Zeller, "Hegel's Vorlesungen über die Philosophie der Religion (Zweite Auflage, Berlin, 1840)," conveniently reprinted in *Die Flucht in den Begriff*, ed. Friedrich Wilhelm Graf and Falk Wagner (Stuttgart: Klett-Cotta, 1982) 114-139. See also Godwin Lämmermann, "Redaktion und Redaktionsprinzipien der Vorlesungen über Religionsphilosophie in ihrer zweiten Ausgabe," in *Die Flucht in den Begriff* 140-158.

[13] V 3:xlvi-xlvii.

[14] V 3:xliii-liv.

[15] V 3:xlviii.

[16] G. W. F. Hegel, *Vorlesungen über die Philosophie der Religion*, (Philosophische Bibliothek, vols. 59, 60, 61, 63 bound in two volumes), ed. Georg Lasson (Hamburg: Felix Meiner, 1925, reprinted 1974).

Reviewed by Emanuel Hirsch, *Theologische Literaturzeitung* (1925), cols. 421-423, (1928), cols. 376-379, (1930), cols. 425-427, cited by Henri Rondet, "Hégélianisme et Christianisme: Réflexions théologiques," *Recherches de Science Religieuse*, 26 (1936) 421 n. 1. Prof. J. Kevin Coyle kindly pointed out this early French language observation on the difficulty of working with the Lasson text.

[17] V 3:liv-lv.

[18] On the history of these editions, note in particular: Walter Jaeschke, "Der Aufbau und die bisherigen Editionen von Hegels Vorlesungen über Philosophie der Religion" (M.A. thesis, Die freie Universität Berlin, 1970- 1971); "Hegel's Philosophy of Religion: The Quest for a Critical Edition," *The Owl of Minerva* 11, 3 (1980) 4-8, and vol. 11, 4 (1980) 1-6; "Probleme der Edition der Nachschriften von Hegels Vorlesungen," *Allgemeine Zeitschrift für Philosophie* 3 (1980) 51-63; Peter C. Hodgson, "Plans for Completing the English Study Edition of Hegel's Lectures on the Philosophy of Religion," *The Owl of Minerva* 11, 4 (1980) 6-7; Robert F. Brown, "Hegel's Lectures on the Philosophy of Religion: A Progress Report on the New Edition," *The Owl of Minerva* 14, 3 (1983) 1-6. Note the background studies: Reinhard Heede, "Die göttliche Idee und ihre Erscheinung in der Religion. Untersuchungen zum Verhältnis von Logik und Religionsphilosophie bei Hegel" (Ph.D. dissertation, Philosophical Faculty of the Westfälischen Wilhelms-Universität zu Münster/Westfalen, 1972); "Hegel-Bilanz: Hegels Religionsphilosophie als Aufgabe und Problem der Forschung," in *Hegel-Bilanz. Zur Aktualität und Inaktualität der Philosophie Hegels*, ed. Reinhard Heede and Joachim Ritter (Frankfurt am Main: Klostermann, 1973) 41-89. Further remarks in: Karl-Heinz Ilting, "Zur Edition," in G. W. F. Hegel, *Religionsphilosophie*, vol. 1: *Die Vorlesung von 1821*, ed. Karl-Heinz Ilting (Naples: Bibliopolis, 1978) 737-765. Reviews of the Ilting edition: Peter C. Hodgson, in *The Owl of Minerva* 11, 2 (December 1979) 4-7; Herbert Huber, "Zum Vorlesungsmanuskript von 1821. Bemerkungen zur Edition von K.-H. Ilting," in *Die Flucht in den Begriff* 159-162. Also pertaining to the background literature for these editions, Peter C. Hodgson, "Editor's Introduction," in G. W. F. Hegel, *The Christian Religion: Lectures on the Philosophy of Religion*, Part Three: *The Revelatory, Consummate, Absolute Religion*, ed. and trans. Peter C. Hodgson (Missoula: Scholars Press, 1979) vii-xxix. For a review of this edition of

Hodgson's, and of the edition by Ilting, see Walter Jaeschke, "Die Flucht vor dem Begriff: Ein Jahrzehnt Literatur zur Religionsphilosophie (1971-1981)," in *Hegel-Studien* 18 (Bonn: Bouvier, 1983) 297-309. More specifically on the new and unabridged English edition, see Hodgson, L 1:xi-xvi.

19 L 4:ix.

20 L 4:11-15, 492.

21 V 3:xix, and on sources in general, see V 3:xix-xxxviii. See L 1:8-20 and, for a helpful, schematized overview, L 1:22-23

22 V 3:xxx-xxxviii.

23 V 3:xxxviii.

24 See esp. V 3:lvi-lxii, lxxvi-lxxxvi.

25 V 3:lxxvi.

26 E.g., V 3:lxxix.

27 V 3:lviii, lxxvi.

28 V 3:lvi.

29 V 3:lxxxiv. Those who might have relevant information concerning possible further sources are asked kindly to make this known (Jaeschke, V 3:lxxxvi).

30 V 3:xii.

31 V 3:lxxix.

32 In the three-volume German edition text lines in each of Hegel's divisions of the philosophy of religion are separately numbered consecutively from beginning to end.

33 V 3:lxii-lxvi.

34 V 3:lxxvi-lxxxiv, esp. lxxvi, lxxix.

35 See n. 8 above.

36 See n. 10 above.

37 V 3:xii.

38 See V 3:lxvi-lxx.

39 "Ohne Welt ist Gott nicht Gott" (my trans., Hotho 1824 lecture transcript). V 3:lxviii and 212-213 note. See L 1:308 n. 97 (Hotho 1824 lecture transcript).

[40] V 3:xii.

[41] See V 3:lxxi-lxxv.

[42] V 3:xii.

[43] V 3:lxxv.

[44] V 3:lxxvi-lxxvii.

[45] V 3:xvii-xviii.

[46] Concerning the translation of the study edition, see Hodgson, "Editor's Introduction," in *The Christian Religion* xxiii-xxvi. Concerning the new translation, see L 1:52-58; L 4:6-7 n. 4.

[47] These are indeed the edition's own goals. See L 1:52, 54. This judgment is based on random checks of various paragraphs and on a review of the translations of the first paragraph, in each of the four lecture series, of each of the three major subdivisions of Hegel's philosophy of religion. Various principles behind specific translations could always be further discussed. We might, for instance, wonder if it would not have been better to follow more closely the forms of italics or emphasis found in the German texts, especially with regard to the 1821 manuscript. And occasionally we might wonder whether the addition of a clarifying word, whether in brackets or not, really reflects the German original. Nevertheless, the reasons for translating various texts in specific ways have been thought through to the point where the translators can defend quite well the choices they have made. A final note. It is important to recall that the English translation is based on the newly established German texts and not on the German texts of previous editions. For further discussion in regard to this last point, see Errol E. Harris's review of *Lectures on the Philosophy of Religion*, vol. 3: *The Consummate Religion*, by G. W. F. Hegel, ed. Peter C. Hodgson, in *The Owl of Minerva* 20 (1988) 101-105, and Peter C. Hodgson, "A Reply to Professor Harris," *The Owl of Minerva* 20 (1989) 252-256.

[48] L 1:xiv-xv; L 2:2; L 3:5-6; L 4:ix.

[49] L 1:52.

[50] L 3:8. Note also Eric von der Luft's "Annotated Glossary of Hinrichs' Terminology," which is a very valuable guide to, and

discussion of, Hegelian terms, in *Hegel, Hinrichs, and Schleiermacher on Feeling and Reason in Religion* (Lewiston: Edwin Mellen, 1987) 173-213.

[51] L 1:57. On the translation of "being," see L 1:57-58 and L 3:8.

[52] On "being," GW 11:43.20-44.6/GL 83; on *Dasein*, GW 11:59.20ff/GL 108ff.

[53] Eric von der Luft draws attention to Hegel's remarks on *Aufheben* in GW 11:58.1-26/GL 106-108. *Hegel, Hinrichs, and Schleiermacher* 180.

[54] von der Luft, *Hegel, Hinrichs, and Schleiermacher* 181.

[55] L 3:400.

[56] Piere-Jean Labarrière, Review of *Hegel's Trinitarian Claim*, by Dale M. Schlitt, in *Archives de Philosophie* 50 (1987) 318.

[57] *Webster's Seventh New Intercollegiate Dictionary* (Springfield, MA: G. and C. Merriam, 1971) 875.

[58] The "Bibliography of Sources for Hegel's Philosophy of Religion," in V 4:835-858/L 2:783-806 and L 4:503-526. The index of "Biblical References," in V 4:860-865/L 2:807-808, L 3:409-411 and L 4:537-538.

[59] V 4:835-836/L 2:783-784 and L 4:503-504.

[60] *"Philosophica et Theologica,"* V 4:866-985; *"Mythologica,"* V 4:985-996; *"Realia,"* V 4:996-1003; *"Nomina propria,"* V 4:1003-1014; *"Personen-verzeichnis,"* V 4:1015-1024. The various volumes of the English editions provide very helpful but more limited indices for each volume.

[61] V 4:867.

[62] V 4:996.

[63] V 4:1003.

[64] E. g., "Probleme der Edition," 62-63 (see n. 10 above).

[65] V 3:xlii, l-liv.

[66] V 3:lxxxv.

[67] By way of shorthand reference note E § 14.

[68] In addition to these remarks, see Walter Jaeschke, *Die Religionsphilosophie Hegels* (Darmstadt: Wissenschaftliche Buchgesellschaft, 1983) 74-78.

[69] V 3:lix-lxi.

[70] V 3:xvii.

[71] E.g., V 3:lxx.

[72] V 3:xii.

[73] V 3:xvii-xviii.

[74] But see Jaeschke's longer discussions in: Friedrich Hogemann and Walter Jaeschke, "Die Wissenschaft der Logik," in *Hegel. Einführung in seine Philosophie*, ed. Otto Pöggeler (Munich: Karl Alber, 1977) 75-90; Walter Jaeschke, "Absolute Idee – absolute Subjektivität. Zum Problem der Persönlichkeit Gottes in der Logik und in der Religionsphilosophie," *Zeitschrift für philosophische Forschung* 35 (1981) 385-416; _____, *Die Religionsphilosophie Hegels* 110-147.

[75] L 4:3-4, 11-15, 492.

[76] Jaeschke, *Religionsphilosophie* 133-140.

[77] See also Ch. 6 below.

PART TWO

HEGEL'S TRIPARTITE PHILOSOPHY
OF RELIGION

CHAPTER TWO

THE CONCEPT OF RELIGION

As we mentioned in Chapter One, the twentieth-century Hegel Renaissance continues with the new editions of his Berlin lectures, and especially with the editions of his lectures on the philosophy of religion. These editions present, separately published in three volumes, the three parts of Hegel's philosophy of religion. Here in the second part of our study, in Chapters Two, Three, and Four, we will successively treat each of the three parts of Hegel's philosophy of religion. In the present chapter we will look at Hegel's concept of religion. In Chapter Three we will follow the dialectical progression of Hegel's presentation of determinate religion, namely, of the various religions of the world other than the consummate religion, which Hegel identifies historically with Christianity. In Chapter Four we will summarize the development of the consummate religion, which is for Hegel the religion of absolute subjectivity and of freedom.

We will examine each of these three parts of Hegel's philosophy of religion in three steps. First of all, we will introduce the specific German and English volumes in question. With this introduction we will, in fact, also be more indirectly introducing the particular part of Hegel's philosophy of religion presented in that volume. Second, we will analyze selected important aspects of Hegel's philosophical interpretations of religion as these interpretations are found in the various parts of his tripartite philosophy of religion. Third, as we did at the end of Chapter One, at the end of each of these three chapters we will propose further areas of research opened up by these new editions. In these three chapters the areas of research to be suggested will be more directly related to the particular part of Hegel's philosophy of religion under discussion.

Along with Chapter One, these three chapters allow us to appreciate the current text situation with regard to Hegel's philosophy of religion. They provide further indications of ways in which these newly established texts continue the twentieth-century Hegel Renaissance. Furthermore, they have the perduring value of introducing us to certain basic characteristics of Hegel's four series of Berlin lectures on the philosophy of religion. In these chapters we point out a number of questions still being discussed in the area of Hegelian philosophy of religion. These three chapters should help provide us with a good grasp of Hegel's approach to the philosophy of religion and give us a further familiarity with his terminology. Then, in the third section of our study, we can plunge into more focused analyses of specific questions and religious themes or representations in Hegel's philosophy of religion.

1. *An Overview of the First Volume*

Hegel consistently entitles Part One of his philosophy of religion The Concept of Religion. In each of the four philosophy of religion lecture series, Part One is preceded by an Introduction. The German volume containing this Part One (V 3) includes a preliminary remark and then the Editorial Preface to the three volumes as a whole. We have discussed this Preface at length in Chapter One above. The parallel English volume (L 1) opens with a Preface, which is followed by helpful editorial information and then the longer Editorial Introduction. We have already referred to parts of this Editorial Introduction in Chapter One above. The Editorial Introduction's Subsections Seven and Eight sketch out the structure and development of Hegel's various Introductions and presentations of The Concept of Religion.[1] Even with these helpful sketchings there is considerable room for further detailed analysis of these Introductions and of Hegel's various developments of The Concept of Religion. That there is such space for further analysis is witnessed to by the fact that the English editor has revised, and greatly lengthened, his own treatment of The Concept of Religion in his new Editorial Introduction to the more recent one-volume English edition of Hegel's philosophy of religion lectures.[2]

In each of the unabridged German and English editions, after the Editorial Preface or Editorial Introduction there follow the sequentially printed Introductions to Hegel's 1821, 1824, and 1827 lectures. Next come the similarly arranged and printed lecture materials on The Concept of Religion. After these there follow a secondary transmission on the relationship of religion to the state (1831) and a supplement containing pertinent excerpts from D. F. Strauss's reworked transcripts of the 1831 lectures. The editors close the volumes with further editorial information.

Since the nature and quality of the sources out of which the lecture series are reconstructed are so diverse, the technical apparatus used to indicate the sources and types of materials drawn upon must necessarily become quite involved. With regard to each of the three volumes of the German and English editions, it is essential early on in our study to become familiar with the editorial information contained in the section, "Signs, Symbols, Abbreviations." With regard to the German edition, it is equally important to become familiar with the ways in which further Hegel materials are footnoted and the valuable endnotes are keyed to the Hegel texts. With regard to the English editions, we need to be aware of the ways in which the very useful footnotes make available both editorial observations and further Hegel materials. These endnotes and footnotes give witness to an encyclopedic knowledge of both the Hegelian corpus and the thinkers to whom Hegel alludes.

2. *Hegel's Concept of Religion*

Hegel worked out his philosophy of religion at an early stage in the modern history of the philosophy of religion. Speaking in a very general and preliminary fashion, we can already now say that he saw religion as the relationship between God and finite human consciousness. Already now, while speaking in this very general way, we must point out that Hegel did not envision this relationship as being one between two fully independent and fully separately existing realities. He insisted that God and finite consciousness were moments of one another. In line with this understanding of the relationship between God and finite human consciousness, Hegel interpreted the various religions of the world philosophically in terms of, and as moments in, an overall movement of spirit as the self-development of absolute divine subjectivity.

Even if we refer again to the remarks we have already made in the Introduction to our study, to speak here of spirit and absolute or inclusive divine subjectivity might easily sound like a jargonistic stringing together of seemingly empty Hegelian terms. In order, therefore, to understand Hegel's philosophy of religion in general, and his concept of religion in particular, we need to recall that he lectured in a specific and, indeed, often polemical context. To understand something of this context, and to appreciate what Hegel is getting at with his specific philosophy of religion terminology, it will be helpful to proceed in three steps. First of all, we need to see what he means when he defines religion in terms of thought. Then we will take a look at how he sets up his starting point in each of the four philosophy of religion lecture series. And, finally, we will analyze in more detail two of his lecture presentations of Part One, The Concept of Religion.

2.a. Religion and Thought

Throughout the years of his mature systematic reflection, at least from his 1807 *Phenomenology of Spirit* on through to the third original edition of his *Encyclopedia* in 1830, Hegel consistently described the human being (*Mensch*) as the one characterized by thinking (*Denken*).[3] He therefore quite naturally would go on to propose and argue that those things which distinguish the human being from animals, namely, realities such as religion, law, and ethical living were also, in their human specificity, to be defined in terms of thinking.[4] When it came to philosophy in general, Hegel gave a first, and very wide, description of it as "the thinking study of things."[5] But much more lies implied in this seemingly quite innocent and generally acceptable description of philosophy. In fact, as we will shortly see, there is also much more than we might at first suspect involved in his definition of religion in terms of thought.

Before we come to the question of religion, we need to examine briefly what Hegel means by thought. Perhaps the most difficult initial hurdle to be overcome by the English-speaking reader in attempting to understand Hegel's philosophy in general, and especially his philosophy of religion, is the need to come to terms with his use of this word "thought."

Hegel is always doing philosophy. Therefore, for him all is thought, or at least to be considered in relation to thought. To try to think of anything outside of a relationship to thought, outside of this fact of its being thought, would for him be a mere abstraction. For those of us used to what we might call the English-speaking world-view and its ways of thinking, it might seem as if by thought Hegel meant what we often understand by experience. And, in an initial way, such a comparison can be helpful in trying to understand Hegel. In fact, to some extent the comparison is true. For there is a certain parallel between Hegel's use of thought and the English-speaking world's use of experience. This parallel exists at least in two senses. First, experience is as basic, and slippery, a notion in English as thought or *Denken* can be in German. To many an English speaker thought seems to be a highly mediated and complex reality. Likewise, and perhaps even more so, to many a German speaker experience seems to be equally highly mediated and complex. Yet, second, and more importantly, experience and thought both tend to function similarly as the fundamental category respectively in much English-language reflection and in much German-language reflection. For example, in the English-speaking world, to indicate an interest either in the process of experience or the result of what we have gone through, we often ask questions like, "What are you experiencing?" "Does that fit your experience?" or, "What kind of experience was it?" In the German-speaking thought world, even today the more basic philosophical question tends to be, "How can it be thought?" (*"Wie kann man es denken?"*)

There are, furthermore, some moments when Hegel himself seems to give the impression that an identification of experience and thought might be in order. He initially describes the movement of his

Phenomenology of Spirit as the "science of the *experience* which consciousness goes through."[6] And then, in the Introduction to the *Phenomenology*, he calls the dialectical movement of consciousness "experience" (*Erfahrung*).[7] He even defines consciousness (*Bewußtsein*) itself in terms of thought.[8] Evidently Hegel's understanding of thought is rich and complex. To this we must return in a moment.

In attempting to understand Hegel, it can, then, at first be helpful to call attention to the fact that thought functions in his philosophy in as basic and all-pervasive a way as experience does in much English language philosophical reflection, or even in everyday English speech. Nevertheless, it would be a mistake to continue this perhaps helpful analogy or comparison too far. Simply to equate our more common English-speaking notion of experience, or even our more philosophically refined notions of experience, with Hegel's understanding and use of thought would surely lead to a fundamental misunderstanding of what Hegel is up to and what he is trying to do. For one thing, Hegel himself explicitly objected to certain understandings of experience, or at least to certain understandings of the relationship between experience and thought. For example, he was adamantly against considering experience as some form of prior given. As an example of this understanding which Hegel rejected, we could cite the instance where religious feeling would be considered a form of prior experience with thought then seen as a sort of reflection (*Nachdenken*) following consequent to, and upon, that prior experience.[9] More generally speaking, he manifested a certain general reserve or hesitation concerning the notion of experience. His fundamental philosophical tissue, or the notion according to which, and in terms of which, he understood all else was not that of being, nor again that of love or history, and certainly not that of experience. Rather, he understood all else in terms of the notion of thought.

If we look at this question of experience and thought from the other side, namely, from the point of view of Hegel's interpretation of what we might, in the English-speaking world, more commonly refer to as experience, we could well say that for Hegel all human experience *is* thought. But, in this case, we must still, if we are to understand Hegel, look briefly at what he means by thought when he subsumes experience into, and under, the category or term "thought." And we need to see how thought functions in his philosophy and, more particularly, in his philosophy of religion.

Briefly, then, by thought Hegel means that movement of concepts or thought determinations which expresses itself in language but which is not reducible to language. He means conscious, reflexively available and examinable thoughts. In the process of elaborating his philosophy, he further distinguishes different ways in which thought occurs or functions. For example, in the *Science of Logic* or the *Logic* at the beginning of the *Encyclopedia* he writes of a movement of pure thought. There he sees thought as this formal, dynamic movement or immanent and consistent development of thought categories or determinations, "concepts," we would probably say today.[10] Here the movement of thought occurs, of course, in and through finite human thinking. Since, as we mentioned earlier, the human being is defined in terms of thought, it is easy for Hegel to write of this movement of logic or pure thought in terms of subject and subjectivity. He identifies the self as such with this movement of thought. And this movement of self-developing thought expresses for him the very structure of inclusive subjectivity. It does this in the sense that the subject is seen to be one with the object or other which, itself as other, is only "momentarily" present in pure thought. So Hegel's movement of pure thought, his logic, is a theory of subjectivity and, equally, a theory of truth. It is, for him, the logical structure of the movement of spirit.

When Hegel, then, uses the term "concept" (*Begriff*) he means that simple unity of thought and objectivity which constitutes the structure of truth. In the philosophy of religion, more specifically, he refers to that which holds together the disparate aspects of a religious representation such as Trinity or incarnation. He sees the concept, then, as a totality, as a unity of subjective and objective.[11] (And shortly we will see more exactly how Hegel uses this term "concept" as the first part of his philosophy of religion.) But, for Hegel, in the movement of logic or pure thought the concept is not the final form of the structure of truth in the movement of that pure thought or logic as truth and as subject. Nor is it the final form in the philosophy of religion.

Hegel goes on to speak of the "idea" (*Idee*) as the unity of concept and reality.[12] It is against this background understanding of "idea" that he will so often speak of the divine idea in his philosophy of religion. There he will speak of the divine idea as the unity of the concept of religion and the reality attained by that concept in and through the various finite or determinate religions. But here we are getting ahead of ourselves. We need to recall that, in the form of logic or pure thought which we are now discussing, Hegel presents the movement of thought as taking place in more abstract form. Here the movement of thought occurs without the ongoing and explicitly mentioned distinction between self and other constitutive of consciousness and, particularly, of religious consciousness.

Hegel further describes and qualifies various forms of thought as he discusses thought on various levels throughout the outline of his philosophy in the *Encyclopedia*. He regularly works with the distinction between "understanding" (*Verstand*) and "reason" (*Vernunft*). Understanding, for Hegel, is that form of thinking which distinguishes and maintains separation. Reason is that synthesizing form of thought, comprehending thought (*begreifendes Denken*) which sees the inner unity already present in contradictory affirmations. As he did with regard to logical thought, Hegel again calls this movement of reason, which includes but surpasses the form of thought which is understanding, spirit. This movement of reason is true, inclusive and, now, absolute subjectivity.

To do justice to Hegel we would really need to say much more concerning his understanding of thought. We will in fact return to the question of thought and its various forms here and there in the following chapters. Still, with these basic remarks on what Hegel means by thought in mind, we can better appreciate what was his intention in choosing to work with thought and why we cannot simply equate his usage of thought and our contemporary multiform English-language use of the notion of experience. It is true that Hegel would quite naturally have been oriented toward the notion or category of thought in view of the philosophical context within which he thought. It would seem quite natural for him, in critical dialogue with Kant and Fichte, and even the earlier Schelling, to work in terms of thought and the self-positing or movement of thought. We need only think of Fichte's attempts to work with the ego and the arising of the non-ego, or of other attempts to overcome the dualism inherent in Kant's philosophical position.

In the final analysis, what leads Hegel to choose to work with the notion of thought is his desire to work in what we would today call the public realm. He wanted to argue his case in discursive fashion, that is, in a way open to examination by others. To accomplish this he chose to work with reflexive thought as that human phenomenon to which he could point and with which he could argue beyond the realm of the merely subjective or the merely objective. It was a brilliant choice on his part. This intention of his to work in the public realm is the basic reason why we cannot simply identify a contemporary understanding of experience with Hegel's notion of thought. Hegel wanted to work with experience only in so far as it was critically available in the form of reflexive thought. Experience, in almost any developed understanding of the word, is not as such so easily available to direct reflexive examination and argument.

However, interesting and valuable as was Hegel's option, it was not one he could carry out free of all difficulties. From our later historical perspective, we might, for example, simply mention that many post-Hegelian thinkers have challenged both the notion of a movement of thought occurring without external conditioning and the hope that the fullness of the human phenomenon could be available to reflexive thought. With more specific reference to religion, Hegel is forced, by the inner logic of his position, to express even, and especially, the movement of divine life in terms of a reflexively available conceptual thought.[13]

In light of what we have said concerning Hegel on thought, we can now return more explicitly to the question of religion and thought in order, in preliminary fashion, to introduce several aspects of Hegel's concept of religion as a movement of thought. His basic understanding of religion indeed remained constant throughout the years of his mature systematic reflection, at least from his 1807 *Phenomenology of Spirit* on. He understood religion but, more exactly, the philosophy of religion, as the dynamic and dialectical relationship between God and finite spirit (human beings in their consciousness and thinking), a relationship occurring in thought as religious consciousness. Hegel's philosophy of religion was a thinking through of the movement of thought in so far as that thought is characterized by a distinction between the finite self and the divine other or God. This relationship was for Hegel a dynamic one in which, essentially, finite spirit was elevated, in its consciousness, to the infinite. So religion was a movement from finite to infinite. However, as the years went on and he continued his lectures on the philosophy of religion, Hegel saw more clearly how he could root this movement or transition from finite to infinite in a more inclusive movement of divine subjectivity. He worked out his more speculative understanding of religion as the consciousness of God, with God here as subjective genitive. For Hegel, it was the appearance of God in and through this movement of finite consciousness. As a movement which took the finite up into the infinite this appearance of God constituted his speculative understanding of religion. In other words, it was the movement from initial infinite, God, othering God self in the finite and, then, as enriched return taking up the finite into the infinite. This latter or true infinite grounded and made possible the movement of religion as an elevation of finite spirit to the absolute, namely, to God as absolute subjectivity.

2.b. Beginnings and Polemical Contexts

After having seen something of what Hegel meant by thought and by speaking of religion in terms of thought, we can now take a second step in our effort to understand Hegel's concept of religion. We are now in a position to look at how and in which contexts he, in his various lectures on the philosophy of religion, proposed to begin the overall speculative movement of divine subjectivity.

It was apparently no mere coincidence that Hegel rather abruptly decided to lecture on the philosophy of religion at the University of Berlin in 1821. It was in this same year that Friedrich Schleiermacher, Hegel's colleague at the University of Berlin, published the first volume of his now famous and still much discussed theology, *The Christian Faith*.[14] Schleiermacher presented Christianity as the result of the feeling of utter dependence. In moving so quickly in 1821 to lecture on the philosophy of religion, Hegel was able to disseminate his own position in the form of a philosophy of religion. However, it would seem that he was not merely attacking a rival colleague. Rather, he seems to have been working both out of a longer range development internal to his philosophical system and, more immediately, out of concern over the theological basis of the Evangelical Church of the Prussian Union.[15] In the context of this religious and political controversy with Schleiermacher over what would be the basis of that church union, Hegel provided a clear alternative to

Schleiermacher when he identified his own starting point in religion not in a sense of dependence but in a "totality." He saw the philosophy of religion as starting in and with an initial unity of object and religious consciousness of that object. "But the object of which we are treating is religion itself; in it however we at once come across two moments: a) the *object* in religion and b) the consciousness, *subject*, human being, which relates itself to it – religious feeling, intuition and so forth."[16] In starting here with such an initial unity, Hegel remains consistent with his overall mature speculative and systematic way of proceeding.[17]

After this initial and well-known argument with Schleiermacher (carried on as well by Hegel's Heidelberg student, H. F. W. Hinrichs), Hegel's polemical attitude toward Schleiermacher climaxes in the 1824 lectures.[18] Hegel's alternative to Schleiermacher's position remains, as in 1821, the original unity of object and religious consciousness. But now the inner dynamic relationship constituting this unity as the speculative concept of religion is made explicit: religion is "this idea, the idea of spirit, which relates itself to itself, the self-consciousness of absolute spirit."[19] This noticeable breakthrough to the explicitly stated speculative concept of religion is reflected in an intended structure which is, in general, systematically and logically more rigorous than that of 1821. Apparently, however, various external circumstances led Hegel, during the course of his lectures, to modify his outline as originally proposed in the Introduction.[20] Though the 1824 lectures are in fact more systematically structured than those of 1821, they still represent a transitional series leading to the 1827 lectures, whose fully achieved systematic structure corresponds to the speculative concept of religion.[21]

By 1827 Hegel was apparently less concerned with Schleiermacher and more directly addressing his more immediate competition from the mid-1820's on, namely, neo-pietism. At the same time he was on the defensive as he responded to attacks that his thought was atheistic or Spinozist, with these terms here understood to mean pantheistic.[22] Both on systematic grounds and in view of the polemical context it would appear to be no coincidence that Hegel now determinedly opened the first part of his philosophy of religion, The Concept of Religion, with a presentation on the concept of God. As early as 1824 Hegel had described religion as a dynamic inclusive totality, as spirit relating itself through finite spirit to itself, and thus as absolute spirit. Now religion itself is clearly defined as the self-positing concept of God.[23] Hegel claims that God cannot adequately be conceived in terms of Spinozistic substance. To be adequately conceived God must be seen to be a movement of the sublation of substance in spirit.[24] With this affirmation Hegel has integrated the criticized notion of God merely as substance into his wider philosophical interpretation of religion. In this way he was clearly making his opponents' objection of pantheism into a moment in his own argumentation.

The significantly more limited available 1831 material shows that, as was the case with the earlier lectures, Hegel continued to begin his systematic philosophy of religion with a unity.[25] The speculative concept of religion and the speculative concept of God remain, as in 1827, identified: "This is the concept of religion, that God knows God self in spirit and that spirit knows itself in God."[26] In varying polemical contexts, and whether in its pre-1824 formulation or from the 1824 speculative breakthrough, namely, the self-relational understanding of religion as God knowing God self in and through finite spirit, Hegel consistently begins his lectures on the philosophy of religion with the affirmation of an originary unity. Out of this unity he will elaborate a basic movement from implicit to explicit. This movement will be one of differentiation and subsequent enriched advance as return to unity. We will see this movement spelled out in his various elaborations of the concept of religion as Part One of his philosophy of religion.

2.c. The Concept of Religion

So far in our effort to understand Hegel's concept of religion we have, first of all, briefly discussed his understanding of thought and of religion as thought. We then remarked on the unity with which he begins each of his four lecture presentations of the philosophy of religion. We can now appreciate more exactly the fact that Hegel's overall understanding of religion remained consistent and, relatively speaking, constant throughout the years of the Berlin lectures.

In brief recapitulation we can again note that for Hegel religion was indeed characteristic of humans (*Mensch*) in so far as thinking (*Denken*) was constitutive of being human. Religion was itself the manifestation of absolute spirit in and through a movement of thought. Hegel continued to see religion as the vehicle of truth for all people. It gave expression to the true content of the reconciliation of divine and human, of infinite and finite, but still as yet in the inadequate form of representational thinking (*Vorstellung*). According to Hegel this reconciliation will achieve its own appropriate expression and true form as the self-mediation of philosophical thought. Religion itself remained the consciousness of God, namely, the unity of divine and human still characterized by that type of distinction constitutive of consciousness as such. Through the Berlin years Hegel would come, in a more explicitly speculative or integrating way, to express his interpretation of religion as the self-revelation of God in and through the finite. He would present religion as God's own coming to self-consciousness, and as the very self-development of God. Through the years Hegel came more clearly to express religion as a movement of self-positing divine inclusive subjectivity.

Hegel's general understanding of religion remained constant throughout the Berlin years. Nevertheless, Hegel changed his various presentations of the concept of religion considerably from one lecture series to another. We will examine certain aspects of what he actually says concerning the concept of religion in two quite diverse, but also quite representative, presentations of the concept of religion. This examination will help shed further light on what Hegel means when he speaks of religion, and, more precisely, the philosophy of religion, in terms of and as a movement of subjectivity. With this examination we see again the importance of these new editions of Hegel's lectures on the philosophy of religion.

The 1821 Lectures

Toward the end of the Introduction in the 1821 lecture manuscript Hegel says that the philosophy of religion offers, in line with his general understanding of philosophy, "a thinking, comprehending cognition of religion."[27] For the next page or so he alludes, more than directly refers, to the moments of the concept of religion. He interweaves these moments with a very brief outline of the whole of the philosophy of religion. By way of anticipation of our discussion in Chapter Four below, we might already now note that he ends the Introduction with a short reflection on the consummate religion in relation to the concept of religion and the determinate religions.[28] But we must return more directly to the question of the moments of the concept of religion. These moments of the concept, and here is meant not the de facto division of Part One, The Concept of Religion, but these moments in as they constitute the overall development of the concept, are listed very generally as follows: the concept of religion itself, the development and positing of the concept, and the consummation of the determinations of the concept as return of the concept to itself. Hegel describes this dialectical movement as the absolute method.[29] Surely this is a reference to his discussion of absolute method at the end of the *Logic*.[30] There, in looking back over the whole movement of logic as one of pure thought, Hegel had proposed that method was simply the development of pure thought from its beginning in being to its final form as absolute idea. He generalized that method was, then, a structured movement from beginning through progression to result.

At the end of the 1821 Introduction Hegel had interwoven these moments of the concept with a brief outline of the philosophy of religion. Now, in the first part of the philosophy of religion, namely, The Concept of Religion, he presents them as momentary totalities. In typical Hegelian fashion, each of the moments in the development of the concept are to be the whole of the concept at that point in its development. These moments are at least initially given a more dyadically expressed formulation. Yet they are here, as compared with the brief treatment in the Introduction, treated more with regard to the inner formal structure of the concept of religion itself.

Hegel treats these moments more in terms of this inner formal structure of the concept of religion particularly in certain parts of the first and second subsections of his 1821 manuscript discussion of the concept of religion. His presentation is complex and difficult to follow. Nevertheless, we can conclude, from what he has actually worked out, that he presented the moments of the concept of religion in two stages.

In the first subsection,[31] on the basis of what is available from religious representation, Hegel gives his overall description of religion as the unity of two moments, namely, the object or God and consciousness of that object or the finite subject.[32] He immediately labels these two moments the objective and subjective sides.[33] By means of a preliminary reflection first on the objective side, then on the subjective side, and then again by means of a sort of interplay of the two, he hints at a somewhat more speculative (self-positing or self-developing) interpretation of religion. With a reference to God as the object or content of religion, an object which is both known and is spirit or self-positing, he goes on to affirm "that the subjective aspect is an essential moment [of religion]."[34] By implication, then, the subjective aspect is an essential moment of God. It is with this move that Hegel can introduce cultus (*Kultus*) or the subjective side to religion as essential to the concept of religion.[35] He can then speak of two essential moments in the concept of religion, namely, first of all the form and content of the concept of God and, second, cultus as the subjective relationship to God.[36]

Hegel quickly rounds out his discussion of cultus, and again widens his focus, with a more triadic structuring of three moments to the concept. He sketches a triply subdivided movement. First, out of the affirmation of the *an sich* and original oneness of the existing unity of divine and human in human form as the incarnation of God, Hegel expands the discussion to affirm the determination of absolute unity.[37] Second, he indicates the moment of separation (*Trennung*) and of difference (*Verschiedenheit*), in which God is the absolute positive. Over against this absolute positive the world is seen as the negative of God and, thus, as evil or wickedness.[38] Third, he posits the subjective moment come to be moment of the object. That is, he affirms the infinity of self-consciousness, or a spiritual self-consciousness, as a having been taken up out of time.[39] Hegel has now arranged his initially more dyadic sketching of objective and subjective moments in a more philosophically expressed triadic form. Concerning this dyadic, and then triadic, form, Hegel affirms: "This is religion in general, and these are the more precise determinations of the concept, which directly constitute its content."[40]

In the second subsection of The Concept of Religion, on a sheet inserted into the manuscript,[41] Hegel sketches a sort of second stage or more speculative reflection on the concept of religion. We could even say he proposes a more systematic reflection on the concept of religion. Here, of course, by systematic we must understand the self-positing and self-development of the concept of religion according to the overall rhythm constitutive of Hegel's speculatively formulated "system." In this more speculative or "systematic" reflection he first recalls the constitutive characteristic of speculative philosophy, which is the grasping of everything as idea. Speculative philosophy is the grasping of truth as the discernment of the unity of opposed and, thus, abstract determinations.[42]

In a second paragraph[43] in this second subsection on The Concept of Religion, Hegel turns to religion, which he describes as the standpoint of truth. He insists that religion is not the standpoint of any merely one-sided or finite truth. Rather, religion is the standpoint of absolutely self-determining truth. He immediately speaks of God as this unity which contains within itself limit and difference, with difference present precisely as difference. Otherwise God would simply be that abstraction we call the highest being.

Hegel brings together, in the third paragraph[44] on this inserted sheet, what has been said so far in the previous two paragraphs. He does this by insisting that it is this speculative element of self-positing and resultant unity which comes to consciousness in religion. Then he goes on to observe that religion itself is this speculative movement, but in the concrete forms of representation, namely: "God and community, the cultus, absolute objectivity and absolute subjectivity."[45] He ends this inserted speculative summary analysis: "Here the concept of religion [is] initially more abstract. Its two moments, the moments making up the antithesis [to which we have referred,] are (a) absolute universality, pure thinking, and (b) absolute singularity, sensibility."[46] He develops the speculative relationship between these two moments in the rest of this subsection.

The new editions of Hegel's lectures have made possible a more certain reading of Hegel's two efforts, here in the 1821 manuscript, to lay out the inner structure and moments of the concept of religion. In his presentation Hegel comes across as one somewhat torn between a desire to be faithful to the phenomenologically observable more dyadic analysis of religion, which he works out at least partially as an alternative to Schleiermacher's approach,[47] and the thrust in his speculative approach toward a more triadic conceptualization. This is not to say that there is no speculative aspect present already from the beginning of Hegel's initial presentation at the beginning of The

Concept of Religion. We are only saying that these new editions allow us to sense a certain tension in these apparently more quickly sketched presentations.

Hegel prolongs these presentations of the moments of the concept of religion with a consideration of the inner necessity characteristic of the structure and dynamic of the concept of religion. He gives particular consideration to the elevating move from finite to infinite, which constitutes the essence of religion.[48] When we couple Hegel's concern for inner necessity both with his insistence that limit is to be found within God and with his speculative definition of truth, it is difficult for us not to think of Hegel's understanding of the dialectic of the true infinite.[49] It is difficult not to suspect that his understanding of the true infinite underlies his speculative interpretation of the concept of religion and of the development of God in the 1821 manuscript.[50]

The 1827 Lectures

Those who prefer to read Hegel from the general perspective of his *Science of Logic* will especially enjoy working with the transcription of Hegel's 1827 lectures on the philosophy of religion. This is particularly true with regard to the Introduction and Part One, The Concept of Religion, and with Part Three, The Consummate Religion. Here, as almost everywhere in his thought, points remain unclear and interpretations certainly disputed. Still, already from the Introduction on Hegel has arrived at a certain integration in his presentation. He has resolved a number of questions with which he struggled in the 1821 and 1824 philosophy of religion lectures.

In so many of his major presentations, such as the *Science of Logic*, the *Phenomenology of Spirit*, and the *Encyclopedia*, Hegel has proposed to lay out an immanent and consistent self-positing movement of thought. Here too, in and with the 1827 lectures, he has generally speaking been able to develop the philosophy of religion as an at least intended essentially immanent and consistent self-positing movement of thought. Already in the Introduction to the 1824 lectures he had set out the task of the philosophy of religion as one of grasping the teaching on God only as the teaching on religion.[51] But it is with the 1827 lectures that he fully works out an elaborated, truly speculative interpretation of religion. From beginning to end of these 1827 lectures the philosophy of religion is a movement of self-positing, inclusive divine subjectivity. It is the speculative development of the concept of God as spirit.[52]

This more integrated structure will facilitate our survey of highlights in the Introduction and The Concept of Religion in the 1827 lectures.[53] In the third part of the Introduction,[54] Hegel presents several first reflections on the moments of the concept of religion. This he does in preparation for his outline, by now succinctly summarized, of his triply divided philosophy of religion into the concept of religion, determinate religion, and the consummate religion. Most striking is the way in which he, at least as presented in the transcription, seems to have found his philosophical stride. He seems, with renewed courage and firmness, to assert what he had both remarked on in the Introduction to the 1821 manuscript[55] and so impressively presented at the end of the *Science of Logic*:[56] "There can be but *one method* in all science, in all knowledge. Method is just the self-explicating concept – nothing else – and the concept is one only."[57] Therefore any determination of the concept of religion in determinate religion is the determinateness of the concept itself.[58] Any return out of this its own determinateness is an enriched return of the concept to itself as true concept, the absolute idea or true religion.[59] The overall movement of the philosophy of religion is, therefore, the development (*Entwicklung*) of the concept of religion.[60] Hegel grounds these affirmations concerning the nature of the concept by identifying the concept with spirit, whose essential characteristic is to manifest itself and, then, through this self-manifestation to come in return to itself. This movement of spirit is a movement of freedom as presence to oneself.[61]

After these preliminary remarks, Hegel sketches the three moments of the concept of religion as the outline of Part One, The Concept of Religion. Here he follows the general presentation of the concept as thought determination which he had worked out in the *Science of Logic*. He works with his understanding of the self-deployment of the concept as an immanent and consistent internal movement from universality to particularity to individuality. For present purposes we can concentrate on the formal structure of this self-deployment of the concept. We can more loosely paraphrase what

Hegel means by these three terms. Universality is the concept as simple relationship to itself, unposited negation. Particularity is the concept as differentiation, that is, as relation to its other (universality) and equally as being inclusive of that other. It is posited or expressed negation of universality. Individuality is the concept as self-related determinateness. It is the negation of the previous negation. In the movement of logic or pure thought, the thinking of individuality is the establishment of further determination. It is a concretizing advance which is, for Hegel, equally an enriched return to the unity previously identified as universality.[62]

Hegel interprets the three major parts of the philosophy of religion in terms of these three moments of the concept. The basic overall determination of this Part One is that of universality, but a universality as yet without the presence of particularity as such. In this Part One, particularity is not yet either explicitly posited or given expression for itself. At least by implication, then, if the basic determination of Part One is universality, particularity will serve as basic determination of the second part of the philosophy of religion, namely, determinate religion. And individuality will be the basic determination of the third part of the philosophy of religion, which is the consummate religion. However, if we continue now to focus our attention on this Part One, we see that Hegel further identifies an initial unity within this overall determination of Part One as universality. He asserts the presence of this unity on the basis of the affirmation, first of all, that religion is a relation of the subject to God, who is spirit. He affirms this initial unity, secondly, on the basis of the fact that, more speculatively stated, religion is spirit conscious of itself. That these two affirmations are one is the first moment of the idea, namely, substantial unity.[63] We should of course recall that this substantial unity is itself the result of all that has come before it in the development of Hegel's encyclopedic system of thought.

The second sketched moment of the concept of religion,[64] the second to this first universal and, by implication at least, therefore now also the particular within the presentation of the concept of religion, is relationship or the going apart of this substantial unity. This is where religion really begins, for it is here that spirit realizes itself in the realm of distinction characteristic of subjective consciousness. Hegel foresees treating this relationship in terms of feeling, representation, and understanding (*verständiges Denken*). This second moment of the concept of religion is, therefore, the relationship of the feeling, representing, and thinking subject to God.

The third moment of the concept of religion is, again here according to the Introduction and, at least by implication, the moment of individuality. It is the moment of cultus[65] as the sublation of the separation of the subject from God. This sublation occurs both by means of the elevation of the subject to God and by means of the awareness that God is present in the heart of the subject.

Since here, with the 1827 lectures, Hegel for the first time achieves a truly speculative presentation of the self-positing concept of religion,[66] he needs only the briefest of introductory remarks before going on to elaborate the moments of the concept themselves. So much of what formerly seemed to be extraneous, or at least externally treated, material now finds its place within the presentation of the appropriate moment of the concept.

In the presentation of the first moment of the concept, namely, the concept of God,[67] Hegel shows a primary preoccupation with establishing the fact that what he referred to in the Introduction as a "substantial unity" is, indeed, a "spiritual unity" (*geistige Einheit*).[68] That with which the philosophy of religion begins is the concept of God, and of God as absolute substance. The philosophy of religion begins with the universal and immediate or first. It begins with that which is thought and which is available to more abstract thought (*Denken*). But this substance is equally *an sich* subject and spirit, that which is, so to speak, to develop otherness out of itself. It is this first spiritual unity or divine universality which others itself in judgment (*Urteil*). This self-othering, which Hegel appears comfortable describing both in terms of moments of the concept and in terms of the concept's self-othering in judgment, constitutes the second moment of the concept of religion.

This second moment is the knowing of God.[69] It is the moment of consciousness in which God is known variously through immediate knowing, feeling, representation, and thought. Here Hegel speaks first of immediate knowing or faith as the certainty that God is, that He is the object of consciousness. And this certainty is an initial or undivided unity.[70] He sees feeling as expressing the subjective side to, or the experience of, having God as object of consciousness.[71] Representation, in turn, concerns the objective side, the content of this certitude. In religion God is present to human beings in this representational form as object of consciousness.[72] Then Hegel speaks of the knowing (*Wissen*) of this object or representation as the movement of concrete thinking in so far as it is mediated knowing. "Mediated knowledge is knowledge of necessity regarding the content."[73] Knowledge of God always involves mediation, "Hence it is not only obvious but inherent in the matter itself that, whenever we speak of knowing God, our discourse at once takes the form of a *syllogism*."[74] In the 1827 lectures it is here that he then brings together the cosmological, teleological, and ontological proofs for the existence of God within his treatment of religious knowing as an elevation to God.[75]

Hegel proceeds to the third moment of the concept of religion, to cultus, by means of a reference back to the second moment, the knowing of God. He now describes this overall second moment as a theoretical relationship in which attention concentrates on the object known, on God, and not on the subject as the one knowing God. But the truth is that here there is question of a relationship between subject and object.[76] It is by means of this recall of such a relationship that Hegel moves into the presentation of cultus as the practical relationship between subject and God. He terms this relationship one of will. Cultus, then, can be seen as a form of self-consciousness,[77] since it is in the action of cultus that we know ourselves as enjoying God's presence, "joining myself as myself in God together with myself."[78]

After indicating that the presupposition of all cultus is that reconciliation has already been completed, and after indicating that the basis for cultus is the presupposition that God alone is truly actual,[79] Hegel sketches the forms of cultus itself.[80] First, there is the innerness of devotion. Then cultus in the doubled external forms of sacraments and sacrifice. The negation of self, which had in fact already occurred in theoretical knowledge, now occurs in devotion. This negation of self then takes place consciously in sacrifice, because there the subject is concerned primarily with itself. By sacrifice we come to the consciousness and enjoyment of being in unity with God. The third and highest of these forms of cultus is repentance and remorse, which together are the moment of negation of our specific subjectivity. For repentance and remorse are the renunciation of what is innermost. Hegel is recorded as speaking in terms of "heart" and "will." He immediately links these words with those of "the universal" and "the true" so that he can make a quick transition to ethical life (*Sittlichkeit*) as the most genuine cultus. His linkage to the word "true" allows him to indicate the final move to philosophy as a continual cultus. It is rather fascinating to see how, for Hegel, cultus is a movement, still in representational form, of spirit in and through finite subjects. Cultus is the movement from inner experience to external forms as the negation of that finite subjectivity on to the realization of the religious reconciliation of divine and human in ethical life. Cultus culminates in philosophical thought.

The moments of the concept of religion are: the metaphysical concept of God, the appearance of divinity in theoretical knowledge, and cultus or the practical knowledge of God. According to Hegel these moments have variously appeared in, and structured, each unity or finite religion in the realizing progression of determinate religion.[81] Hegel had begun the 1827 lectures with the concept of God as a spiritual unity. After the long route through determinate religion, he will return to these moments of the concept of religion. They will have become the object of religious consciousness in the consummate religion, and thus moments of the concept of the consummate religion.[82]

Hegel's concept of religion comes to be seen, both in the general sense of that phrase and in its use to designate Part One of his philosophy of religion, as a complex, dynamic, and developing movement of thought. We have already said that Hegel works with religion as thought. We need to recall that by thought here he means, most importantly, that movement of conceptual reflection which integrates disparate elements commonly distinguished and separated in everyday religious thinking. He begins each of his lecture presentations of the philosophy of religion, that is, he begins Part One or The Concept of Religion, with the affirmation of an initial unity. This unity is originary in the doubled sense of the word. It is the first moment in the laying out of the philosophy of religion. It is, likewise, that initial moment which, in being thought through, progressively gives rise to all further moments in the development of the philosophy of religion. For Hegel the philosophy of religion is, indeed, the movement of spirit from implicit to explicit, from unposited to posited, from more abstract to more concrete and determinate. The philosophy of religion is a movement of self-relationality patterned and established by the dynamic which the concept of religion or, equally, the concept of God, itself is. The dialectical movement of thought, which the philosophy of religion is, gains in an as yet self-contained concreteness and determination as it develops through the inner dialectic constitutive of the concept of religion. The concept of religion, or the concept of God, gains in real concreteness and determination as it dialectically progresses through the various finite religions and arrives at its fulfillment in the consummate religion.

3. *Further Research Opportunities*

As we have seen, in The Concept of Religion Hegel works directly and explicitly with fundamental philosophical and philosophy of religion themes such as faith, immediate and mediated knowledge of God, and the nature of religion. He is in fact concerned with what it means to be human, to be religious, to do philosophy and philosophy of religion. Hegel's more formal considerations of these basic questions here in The Concept of Religion render his interpretations more transparent. They make his unique overall approach to the philosophy of religion stand out more clearly. His direct and formal attention to such transcendent themes guarantees that his various workings out of this Part One can provide an excellent basis or, again, point of departure for further reflection either on his own philosophy or on fundamental questions of perduring value and importance. By making these varied efforts of Hegel's to articulate the structure, really the essence, of religion available to us in reliable form, the new editions have opened many opportunities for further research and reflection.

We can enumerate a few of these areas for further research and, by so doing, perhaps also further our understanding of Hegel's own concerns in elaborating his philosophy of religion. First of all, we will remark on questions more internal to the interpretation of Hegel's philosophy of religion. Then, we will point out several questions or themes which might be taken up, using Hegel's Part One as a point of departure and ongoing reference or dialogue partner.

We will start from more specific considerations and slowly widen the scope of our interest. We can, first, indicate the need to do further comparative study of the various ways in which Hegel presents the self-development of the concept of religion or, more exactly with regard to the 1827 lectures, the concept of God. The shifting ways in which he integrates the material treated in Part One could be traced along various trajectories. For example, there is the general movement from 1821 on to a more speculatively integrated, and clearly presented, self-deployment of the concept in three moments. There is, also, the trajectory of shifting polemical concerns weaving its way through the lecture presentations of The Concept of Religion from one lecture series to another. Furthermore, there is the simple fact that in successive years Hegel tended to lecture somewhat extemporaneously on the basis of his 1821 manuscript and of one or more auditors' transcripts. All of these trajectories would need to be considered in any adequate comparative study of his presentations of the concept of religion. Only in this way can we come to a formal, yet well-rounded, critical appreciation of Hegel's nuanced understanding of religion and of the philosophy of religion.

Such a nuanced understanding of Hegel's philosophy of religion will facilitate further comparative studies of the ways in which Hegel, in his various lecture series, sees the concept of religion achieving greater determination through its self-realization in the various finite religions and, finally, in the consummate religion. It would be of great interest to follow, in some detail, how, and to what extent, Hegel might have worked out possibly differing relationships, in the various lecture series, between the moments of the concept of religion and the moments in the various religions. This should provide greater insight into just how he variously structured his presentations of the philosophy of religion. Such a procedure would also help us see, in more exact and detailed fashion, how he conceived of the philosophy of religion as a philosophical presentation of divine subjectivity. It should enable us to discover how he worked with the notion of freedom as self-determination and "being at home in the other" (Beisichsein im Anderssein).[83] It may well be that, by means of this notion of freedom, he tried, in various ways, to relate religions in a certain dialectical progression.

If we widen the focus of our attention somewhat, we come to the question of the relationship between the dyadic and the triadic in

Hegel's philosophy of religion. Right away we need to recall that, when we speak of dyadic and triadic with regard to Hegel's thought, we are always referring to a movement of thought. For Hegel it is always a question of movement. Our reference to dyadic and triadic is simply a short-hand way of referring to the structured aspect of the determinate movement to which Hegel argues. With this important caveat in mind, we can say that, in a sense and somewhat analogously the relationship between the dyadic and the triadic in Hegel's philosophy of religion might also be called the relationship between the phenomenological and the speculative.[84]

Already with the 1821 manuscript, and from that time on, we see that Hegel has worked with the notion of religion as the elevation of consciousness from the finite to the infinite, a more dyadically formulated conception. He maintains this movement especially throughout his presentation of determinate religion. And yet he seems more and more to integrate this dyadically structured movement into a more inclusive triadic one. This triadic, or more speculative movement Hegel would say, is one in which the absolute others itself in a movement which is the making explicit of what was implicit within it. That is, distinction and otherness come to the fore and stand out in their own right. Then, this realm of distinction and explicit otherness, namely, the realm of consciousness, moves forward to the reintegration of the first and second moments. This realm of differentiation returns, now in enriched fashion, to the initial unity out of which it arose. In some sense this triadic movement is one from initial infinite to finite to inclusive infinite. It is the discovery that identity is the identity of difference, the wholeness or totality of difference.

Hegel has a tendency dialectically to interrelate such "alternative" movements. Any mere juxtaposition of the two movements, without a further internal ordering and relating of them, would seem somehow to force him into some form of antinomy. And he would want to avoid such an antimonial situation at all costs. As we have suggested in the Introduction to this volume, it would seem that the movement of thought, in its triadic formulation, constitutes a logical and, consequently, for Hegel an ontological presupposition for the dyadically structured movement from finite to infinite. It would seem that the triadic formulation makes explicit the grounding, which occurs more implicitly, in the functioning of the dyadic movement of thought as a transition from finite to infinite. Though both forms of thinking are surely essential to Hegel's project, the triadic formulation would seem better able to express the overall movement of inclusive subjectivity and, thus, of freedom.

Much work could be done on further clarifying just how Hegel has variously related these two formulations of the movement of thought in his various lecture series on the philosophy of religion. It would be of great interest to be able to ascertain more precisely to what extent, and how, each of the two presentations is dependent on the other. Furthermore, there is always the additional question of whether one of the two presentations of the movement of thought could make up or compensate for any possible weaknesses in the argumentation or presentation of the other movement.

These dyadically and triadically structured movements are, for Hegel, both movements of comprehending or integrating thought. In a way, they variously give expression to Hegel's formulation of what we might more easily today refer to as the structure and movement of the "experience of God." Hegel has raised, in a particularly direct and acute fashion, both the question of this notion of an "experience of God" and the broader question of the relationship between experience and thought. In his treatment of the relationship between experience and thought he has in fact raised the very question of what it means to be human. Consequently, it would be of great help, and great importance, to clarify further what Hegel seems variously to mean in the different lecture series when he speaks of experience, of thought, and even of faith and feeling. Often great thinkers have really only sketched out a position. They have left a great deal of room for further reflection and for the development of their positions in a number of possible directions. More specifically, with the new editions there is much that can be done to explore exactly what Hegel means and understands when he speaks of religion as thought and of the philosophy of religion as a movement of thought. He is always doing the philosophy of religion and he is always concerned with something in relation to thought. Any other concern would, for him, be an abstraction from the fact that we are actually thinking the reality in question when we refer to it. And yet, he seems also to want to speak of the overall phenomenon of religion itself, in as it is lived and practiced in various social groupings, as thought. Does he mean simply in relation to thought?

There are other areas of research which might, more generally, take Hegel's presentations of the concept of religion as point of departure, and even point of ongoing reference, for further constructive reflection. We can simply mention the areas of the study of religion, of philosophy, and of theology.

Hegel lived and worked before the era of great specialization in the study of religion. Consequently, his wide-ranging efforts to treat religion in the fullness of its varied expression certainly form at least a partial background for many of the modern disciplines in the study of religion. The new editions of Hegel's philosophy of religion will surely facilitate historical as well as more constructive studies by those who wish to refer back to Hegel from the perspective of their particular disciplines. This will be the case whether those who wish to refer to Hegel work in the history of religions, the comparative study of religion, the sociology of religion, the psychology of religion, the social and cultural anthropology of religion, in theology, or in a renewed and renewedly creative philosophy of religion.

Hegel claimed that philosophy and religion had in common the same content, namely, God as the truth.[85] Since for Hegel philosophy was "the thinking study of things" (*Gegenstände*),[86] he argued that philosophy was itself theology: "Thus philosophy *is* theology, and [one's] occupation with philosophy – or rather *in* philosophy – is of itself the service of God."[87] His more nuanced position in the various philosophy of religion lectures, now readily available, continues to present a challenge to those who would see in philosophy only the thinking treatment of language or of inference. His wide-ranging claims, and the rigor of his argumentation, continue to present opportunities for taking a fresh look at what philosophy is and might become.

But there is another sense in which Hegel's claim that philosophy is theology remains a challenge to contemporary thinking and, consequently, the occasion for further research and reflection. In the twentieth century both philosophy and theology have suffered a sort of identity crisis. Not only are both domains of study and reflection characterized by a seemingly ever increasing internal pluralism, but the very universalizing claims of both have been challenged. Theology of course is understood not only to be the study of God, but usually is taken to mean reflection on reality from the perspective of a specific religious tradition. In its general lines that tradition is generally accepted as normative ("faith seeking understanding"). At least with regard to this aspect of theology's self-understanding, the discovery of the perspectival and even conditioned character of thinking has, in principle, proven less of a problem for theology than it has for philosophy. But most philosophers have traditionally considered philosophical thinking and reflection to be universal in its significance and applicability. Now, especially in the twentieth century, philosophers have come more and more to admit that their thinking is itself socially and culturally conditioned. Philosophical thinking or reflection is also carried out from a particular perspective. To the extent that philosophers recognize the conditioned and perspectival character of their thinking, they and speculative or constructive theologians begin to look more alike. They tend to proceed in somewhat similar ways. As theology and philosophy both formerly did, Hegel himself worked with an understanding of thought as universal in its formulation and in its relevance. He carried the notion of thought as universal to new heights. It was for him, in a real sense, only internally self-conditioned. Thought was inclusive.

These new editions of Hegel's lectures on the philosophy of religion now make it possible for us to return anew to this claim of Hegel's concerning the universal character of thought. But we return to that claim from what we might call, historically speaking, a post-Hegelian point of view. These editions open new opportunities to confront Hegel's claims with post-Hegelian hesitations concerning the value and competence of reflexive thought. With regard to such hesitations we need only think, for example, of Freud and Nietzsche. It would indeed be fascinating to see a mutual interaction between Hegel's carefully worked out claims and subsequent thinkers' refusals to accept such claims. In this confrontation, Hegel's proposal to have established a logic of pure thought might need qualification. But he might just have focused on some of the strengths of reflexive or comprehending thought which could still be of extreme value in coming to terms with cultural and intellectual pluralism. It just might be that his emphasis on self-reflexive thought will prove the means to embrace an enriching pluralism without falling into a simplistic and, from the point of view of what it means to be human, reductionistic and debilitating relativism.

Perhaps with Hegel's guidance we can rediscover, both in philosophy and in theology, the value of the universalizing, or at least generalizing, tendency innate in, and constitutive of, the very reality of thought itself. Perhaps we can reaffirm ways in which both philosophy and theology are an elevation of the finite to the infinite. More concretely, critically self-reflexive thought is surely one of the means by which we, as human beings, change our ways and correct our errors. It is also one of the ways by which we can live in and between two or more different cultural contexts without going schizophrenic.

Especially when taken together with his other writings, Hegel's now differentiated sketchings of the concept of religion and its dialectical movement provide rich material for further reflection on Hegel's thought itself. In addition, they become the occasion, and point of departure, for further constructive interpretations of religion, philosophy, and theology. The dialectically progressing movement of the concept of religion will find its realization for Hegel in the philosophically interpreted actual history of various religions of the world. As he would say, the concept of religion posits itself in and as determinate religion.

NOTES

[1] See Hodgson, in L 1:1-81. On Hegel's various "Introductions" note also the comparisons by Robert F. Brown, "Hegel's *Lectures on the Philosophy of Religion*: A Progress Report on the New Edition," *The Owl of Minerva* 14, 3 (1983) 3-6.

[2] Hodgson, in L 4:26 n. 17.

[3] E.g., E 2.

[4] E § 2 and R.

[5] *"denkende Betrachtung* der Gegenstände." E § 2/SL § 2.

[6] "Wissenschaft der *Erfahrung,* die das Bewußtseyn macht." GW 9:29.18-19/PS 21.

[7] GW 9:60.15-18/PS 55.

8 E § 467 R.

9 E § 2 R.

10 On logic or pure thought, and for a brief resume on thought in its various forms, see E § 467 R. On logic, see further in Schlitt, *Hegel's Trinitarian Claim* 11-49.

11 On the concept in the *Science of Logic*, see GW 12:32.1-52.26/GL 600-622; and in the philosophy of religion, see V 3:327.825-328.861.

12 E § 213; GW 12:174.24-25/GL 757.

13 Note Hegel's use of religious language to describe logic as the presentation of God as God is in God's eternal essence before the creation of nature and finite spirit. GW 11:21.16-21/GL 50. For a more external, but still very helpful, indication that thought and experience cannot simply be equated in Hegel's philosophy, see the interesting proposal by so famous a Hegel interpreter as Hans-Georg Gadamer. He tried to rehabilitate Hegel's notion of the bad or false infinite, namely, infinite progression, by shifting from the notion of thought to that of experience. *Truth and Method* (New York: Continuum/Seabury, 1975) 310-325. On Hegel's notion of the infinite, see n. 49 below.

14 Jaeschke, in V 3:x-xii. Friedrich D. E. Schleiermacher, *Der christliche Glaube nach den Grundsätzen der evangelischen Kirche im Zusammenhange dargestellt*, vol. 1 (Berlin: G. Reimer, 1821). See von der Luft, *Hegel, Hinrichs, and Schleiermacher*, with excerpts from Schleiermacher on pp. 214-238. For a brief comparison of Schleiermacher and Hegel on the crucial question of the notion of feeling, see Hodgson, in L 4:31 n. 18.

15 Jaeschke, in V 3:xii.

16 V 3:95.12-15. "Aber der Gegenstand, den wir betrachten, ist die RELIGION selbst; in ihr aber treffen wir sogleich die zwei Momente an: a) den *Gegenstand* IN der Religion und b) das Bewußtsein, *Subjekt*, Mensch, der sich zu ihm verhält – die religiöse Empfindung, Anschauung, usf." (my trans.).

17 Note, for example, Hegel's starting with the unity which is sense certainty in the *Phenomenology*. See GW 9:63.4-8 and 64.1-11/PS 58-59. And the unity which is pure being in the *Science of Logic* and in the *Encyclopedia*. See GW 11:43.20-44.6/GL 82; E § 86 with R/SL.

[18] Jaeschke, in V 3:xi, xviii. See, for example, Jaeschke's references to Schleiermacher in the endnotes to V 3:43.308 (in V 3:382), V 3:43.315-316 (in V 3:382-383), V 3:51.486 (in V 3:385), V 3:184.587 (in V 3:397). On Hinrichs, see von der Luft, *Hegel, Hinrichs, and Schleiermacher.*

[19] "diese Idee, die Idee des Geistes, der sich zu sich selbst verhält, das Selbstbewußtsein des absoluten Geistes." V 3:22.667-668 (my trans.).

[20] See V 3:55-60.

[21] Jaeschke, in V 3:lxix-lxx.

[22] Jaeschke, in V 3:xviii.

[23] V 3:277.383-279.434, with 325.784-326.791.

[24] V 3:269.129-270.164; 323.691-694.

[25] V 3:353.96-98.

[26] "Dies ist der Begriff der Religion, daß Gott sich weiß im Geiste und der Geist sich in Gott." V 3:354.130-131 (my trans.).

[27] "Religionsphilosophie denkende, begreifende Erkenntnis der Religion." V 3:27.652-653/L 1:109. See also V 3:10.205-208. On Hegel's very general statement concerning philosophy, see n. 5 above. On Hegel's Introduction and The Concept of Religion in the 1821 lectures, see the fine, succinct overview by Hodgson, in L 1:60-61 with 66-67 and 68-70 with 78-79 along with the footnotes to the Introduction and The Concept of Religion; and the critically evaluative discussion in Jaeschke, *Die Vernunft in der Religion* 229-240.

[28] V 3:28.660-29.683, along with 27.655-659.

[29] V 3:28.671-672; see also V 3:106.200-204.

[30] GW 12:236.1-253.34/GL 824-845. On method, see also V 3:106.200.

[31] See especially V 3:95.8-105.197.

[32] V 3:95.12-15.

[33] V 3:95.24.

[34] "daß *die subjektive Seite wesentliches Moment* ist." V 3:97.62-63/ L 1:188.

[35] V 3:98.86-99.88. The Hodgson translation of Hegel's lectures on the philosophy of religion translates *Kultus* by "cultus" rather than by "cult."

[36] V 3:99.93-98.

[37] V 3:102.160-103.178. At this point Hegel's move from incarnation to the wider structure of the concept of religion is reminiscent of his move in the *Phenomenology* from the affirmation of the incarnation to the need to make explicit what was implicit in the incarnation, namely, to an "immanent" and "economic" trinitarian structure to religious consciousness in revelatory religion. See Schlitt, *Hegel's Trinitarian Claim* 146-158 esp. 148-149.

[38] V 3:104.179-186.

[39] V 3:104.187-105.195.

[40] "Dies ist die Religion im allgemeinen, und dies die näheren Bestimmungen dieses Begriffs, die dann unmittelbar ihren Inhalt ausmachen." V 3:105.196-197/L 1:196.

[41] V 3:113.399-115.447, but on religion itself esp. V 3:114. 419-115.447. See L 1:204 n. 57 and 207 n. 61.

[42] V 3:113.399-114.418.

[43] V 3:114.419-115.430.

[44] V 3:115.431-438. Concerning difference, which Hegel mentions in this paragraph, see further remarks in Ch. 5 and Ch. 7 below.

[45] "Gott und Gemeinde, Kultus; absolute Objektivität und absolute Subjektivität." V 3:115.441-443, and see lines 439-443/L 1:207.

[46] "Hier *Begriff* der Religion zunächst abstrakter – Die zwei Momente in ihrem Begriff – des Gegensatzes a) absolute Allgemeinheit – reines Denken b) absolute Einzelheit – Empfindung." V 3:115.444-447/L 1:207.

[47] See nn. 14-17 above.

[48] See especially V 3:130.768-142.974.

[49] That is, neither the merely abstract infinite posited over against finitude nor the bad or false infinite of infinite progression. Rather, for Hegel the true infinite is the one which goes over into, or

posits itself as, the otherness which is finitude. Then, in turn, this finitude is seen, as the other of the infinite, to be moment of the true infinite, namely the infinite inclusive of finitude. For a resume of Hegel's logical presentation of the true infinite, see Schlitt, *Hegel's Trinitarian Claim* 252-267.

[50] Note the remarks on God at the end of Hegel's observations on inner necessity, V 3:139.924-142.974. For questions as to whether or not Hegel has been able to work out a more systematic explication of the concept of religion in the 1821 manuscript, see Jaeschke, *Die Vernunft in der Religion* 236.

[51] V 3:33.83-88. See Jaeschke, *Die Vernunft in der Religion* 242.

[52] This is of course not at all to say that the other lecture series do not have their specific strengths, nor that some important points may not have been left behind. On The Concept of Religion in the 1827 lectures, see also the discussion, from the perspective of the question of "identity," in Ch. 5 Subsection 2a below.

[53] On the 1827 Introduction and The Concept of Religion see Jaeschke, *Die Vernunft in der Religion* 254-271; Hodgson, in L 1:63-65, 66-67, 74-79 and footnotes to the Introduction and The Concept of Religion; Hodgson, in L 4:26-39.

[54] V 5:83.506-92.758.

[55] V 3:28.671-672; see also V 3:106.200-204.

[56] GW 12:236.1-253.34/GL 824-845. On method, see also V 3:106.200.

[57] "Es kann nur *eine* Methode in aller Wissenschaft, in allem Wissen sein. Methode ist der sich explizierende Begriff, nichts anderes, und dieser ist nur einer." V 3:83.512-514/L 1:174.

[58] V 3:83.515.

[59] V 3:84.552-556.

[60] V 3:84.564.

[61] V 3:85.567-587.

[62] Hegel's sketching of the outline: V 3:86.591-89.672. On the concept as universality, particularity and individuality, see Schlitt,

Hegel's Trinitarian Claim 70 n. 110. Further helpful literature: André Léonard, *Commentaire littéral de la logique de Hegel* (Paris: J. Vrin, 1974) 326-334; John Burbidge, *On Hegel's Logic. Fragments of a Commentary* (Atlantic Highlands, NJ: Humanities, 1981) 112-124.

63 V 3:86.592-87.621.

64 V 3:87.622-88.662.

65 V 3:88.663-89.672.

66 Jaeschke, *Die Vernunft in der Religion* 254-255, 262; Hodgson, in L 1:366 n. 6.

67 V 3:266.36-277.381.

68 V 3:274.286. With regard to this unity note the important statement, "Die ganze Philosophie ist nichts anderes als ein Studium der Bestimmung der Einheit; ebenso ist die Religionsphilosophie nur eine Reihenfolge von Einheiten, wo immer die Einheit, aber diese Einheit immer weiter bestimmt wird." V 3:276.359-362/"The whole of philosophy is nothing else but a study of the definition of *unity*; and likewise the philosophy of religion is just a succession of unities, where the unity always [abides] but is continually becoming more determinate." L 1:379-380.

69 V 3:277.383-278.396. The long treatment of the second moment of the concept of religion is found in V 3:277.383-329.902. And see V 3:336.54-337.58.

70 V 3:282.460-465 with 283.500-502.

71 V 3:286.579-594 with 291.738-739.

72 V 3:291.739-292.743; see also V 3:298.907-913.

73 "Das vermittelte Wissen ist das der Notwendigkeit in Rücksicht auf den Inhalt." V 3:302.44-45/L 1:407-408.

74 "Damit liegt es nicht nur nahe, sondern in der Sache selbst, daß, insofern vom Wissen Gottes gesprochen wird, gleich von der Form eines Schlusses die Rede ist." V 3:309.260-310.262/L 1:416.

75 V 3:308.214-329.902. In the 1824 lectures Hegel had worked his treatment of the cosmological, teleological, and ontological proofs for the existence of God into his presentations of the various religions.

76 V 3:330.904-923.

77 Jaeschke, *Die Vernunft in der Religion* 271.

78 "mich als mich in Gott mit mir zusammenzuschließen." V 3:332.964/L 1:443.

79 V 3:332.965-979.

80 V 3:333.991-335.53.

81 See n. 68 above, and note Hegel's review of determinate religion. V 5:189.340-196.599. This subdivision of Hegel's introductory remarks is delineated by Hodgson, in L 3:262 with editorial n. 44.

82 V 5:177.3-21. Hegel's position here in 1827 is essentially the same as that of the 1821 manuscript. See the beginning of the manuscript on the consummate religion (V 5:1.1-13) and n. 37 above.

83 See Jaeschke, *Die Vernunft in der Religion* 228, where he cites V 3:85.585-587 (1827). Note also the succinct secondary transmission: "Diese Idealität ist die aufgehobene Vermittlung, aufgehobene Unterschiedenheit, vollkommene Klarheit, reine Helligkeit und Beisichselbstsein; die Freiheit des Begriffs ist selbst die absolute Beziehung auf sich, die Identität, die auch die Unmittelbarkeit ist, vermittlungslose Einheit." V 5:274.126-130/"This ideality is sublated mediation, sublated differentiatedness, perfect clarity, pure transparency and being-present-to-self. The freedom of the concept is itself absolute self-relatedness, the identity that is also immediacy, unity devoid of mediation." L 3:355 (1831).

84 Peter C. Hodgson discusses this question of phenomenological and speculative in Hegel's philosophy of religion in "Hegel's Approach to Religion." He makes a number of insightful observations which would prove most helpful in the pursuit of points raised in this discussion of the relationship between triadic and dyadic in Hegel's philosophy of religion. See also Ch. 6 n. 21 below and the Introduction n. 2 above.

85 E § 1. See Stephen Rocker, "Hegel's Rational Religion. The Identity of Content between Philosophy and Religion," Ph. D. dissertation, Department of Philosopy, The University of Ottawa, 1989.

86 See n. 5 above.

[87] "Die Philosophie ist daher Theologie, und die Beschäftigung mit ihr oder vielmehr in ihr ist für sich Gottesdienst." V 3:4.28-30/L 1:84.

CHAPTER THREE

DETERMINATE RELIGION

In Part Two of his philosophy of religion, Determinate Religion, Hegel interpreted the history of religions other than Christianity as, at least in principle, the realization of the structure of the concept of religion. For him this realization occurred as a dialectically progressing, sequential movement of finite religions. They progressed dialectically in a double sense. First, he saw these religions as standing over against one another. Hence they were finite. Yet, second, they were equally serially related in that one followed phenomenologically after the other. Each was a momentary totality in the movement of spirit. Hegel changed the order of presentation of some of the religions from one lecture series to the next. However, at least generally speaking, in each of these differently ordered lecture presentations the series of finite religions were to have revealed an ever more determinate content. For Hegel the historical development of these religions was the path by and through which spirit progressed toward the consummate religion.

Hegel's complex philosophical reading of the multiplicity of concrete religions stands out in marked contrast to Kant's more Enlightenment, and especially ethically oriented, approach. Kant himself does indeed, with his universal moral religion of reason, stake out a particularly significant position in the early modern history of the philosophy of religion. But now, after Kant, neither Hegel himself nor Schleiermacher, but especially the earlier Schleiermacher of the *Speeches*,[1] would be content with Kant's approach to the philosophy of religion. Both Hegel and Schleiermacher were able to work with the flood of new information on the quite different religions of the world.

Indeed, the two of them form a most important part of the early nineteenth century post-Kantian background to the twentieth-century comparative, historical, theological and philosophical study of the religions of the world. To some extent they both seem to have profited from the learned reports and sacred texts becoming increasingly available on the European scene. However, among the two it was particularly Hegel who plunged into a prolonged, critical reading and constructive, systematic presentation of the religions of the world.

The new editions of Part Two of Hegel's philosophy of religion lectures witness to the earnest and effort with which Hegel threw himself wholeheartedly into the study of the religions of the world. We will review these efforts of Hegel's to grasp the unity within the multiplicity of religions in order better to understand his philosophy of determinate religion. We will proceed in three steps. First, we will examine the volumes of the new editions making this Part Two, Determinate Religion, available. Second, and particularly important for an understanding of Hegel, we will look at his constructive interpretation of determinate religion in two steps. We will analyze his four efforts to present and interrelate these religions. Then we will remark on continuities that can be discerned in his view of determinate religion. Third, we will indicate further research opportunities opened by these volumes.

1. *An Overview of the Second Volume*

As with Part One of Hegel's philosophy of religion lectures, this Part Two is published in a separate volume. It appears in the German edition as the fourth (V 4) in a series of ten volumes of selected manuscripts and transcripts of Hegel's various Berlin lectures. Likewise, the English edition of this Part Two is published in a single volume (L 2) and forms part of an announced ten-volume series of translations of those same Berlin manuscripts and transcripts. General editorial procedures and sources for the lecture materials in these German and English editions remain the same as for the first volume and for the three philosophy of religion volumes as a whole.

1.a. The German and English Editions

The German edition of Part Two is published in two sections with continuous pagination. Section "a" contains Hegel's 1821 lecture manuscript, edited lecture transcripts for the 1824 and 1827 lectures, material from the 1831 lecture series, and several loose sheets of Hegel's preparatory sketchings for the 1821 manuscript. Section "b" gathers together, in two subsections, appendices to Part Two of Hegel's philosophy of religion and, then, as mentioned and discussed in Chapter One above, appendices to the three parts of Hegel's philosophy of religion as a whole.

The German Volume 4a contains a preliminary editorial remark, then the sequentially arranged and printed lecture materials on determinate religion and, finally, six pages reproducing loose sheets of Hegel's sketches for his treatment of determinate religion in the 1821 manuscript. The first subsection of Volume 4b, the subsection which is of present interest, includes four appendices to Volume 4a: signs, symbols and abbreviations; endnotes (to be discussed shortly); additions to the endnotes; and, an index indicating the original locations of further special materials included from the two Friends Editions.

As is the case with the English edition of Hegel's philosophy of religion lectures as a whole, the English volume containing Part Two of Hegel's lectures follows the general layout and order of the presentation of Hegel's manuscript and the lecture transcripts as they are found in the German Volume 4a. However, as with the other English volumes, helpful editorial information and identifications of Hegel's references, often taken from the endnotes to the German edition, are placed in footnotes to the English translations of the four series of lectures. Such materials are frequently complemented with references to English translations of works cited. Further variant or supplemental Hegel materials are likewise footnoted to the appropriate lecture texts. What is of particular importance and value in this English edition is the longer Editorial Introduction. It contains an original analysis of the structure and development of determinate religion in the 1821 manuscript and in the subsequent lectures of 1824, 1827, and 1831. The Editorial Introduction ends with a very helpful schematic "Comparative Analysis of the Structure of 'Determinate Religion.'"

1.b. The Endnotes to the German Edition

The endnotes to the German edition of this Part Two of Hegel's lectures[2] have only been partially reproduced in the footnoting to the English edition. The German endnotes provide such a wealth of information that they deserve to be commented on at greater length. They contain a series of precise and detailed, separately printed, and therefore easily enough consulted, references.[3] These references elaborate on Hegel's brief, or even only implicit, indications of sacred texts and secondary source materials.[4] The endnotes also include occasional references to parallels, to further discussions or, again, to background considerations to be found in Hegel's other works. The notes are keyed to lecture texts and to footnoted contents for Determinate Religion in Volume 4a by means of asterisks printed on the inside margins of the lecture materials. The notes follow the general format of the Felix Meiner Verlag's ongoing critical *Gesammelte Werke* edition. The main difference is that these endnotes often contain longer (at times up to four or five pages) citations from the works either mentioned by Hegel or perhaps only suggested by the phrasing of his lecture materials.[5] Texts which the editor quotes in classical languages are accompanied by German translations. This generous presentation of longer citations saves the reader immense amounts of library legwork. It likewise assures the continued value of this edition even after the publication of the pertinent *Gesammelte Werke* volumes.

But this does not tell the whole story. Although the intention with the endnotes is not to elaborate a commentary,[6] when they are taken as a whole and read with the leisure they require they do much more than simply point out references. They help supply the literary and intellectual contexts for Hegel's often, at first sight, seemingly strange religious typologizing. Within these contexts Hegel's typologizing becomes much more understandable and, perhaps, therefore more acceptable. In fact the editor has also place the various religions, and Hegel's interpretations of them, in their wider historical contexts. This he has done by discussing at length, here and there throughout the endnotes, what access Hegel had to various sources, which among them he chose to rely on, and why he chose to do so. Apparently Hegel often quoted both ancient and modern sources by memory.[7] Consequently, errors of reference or interpretation crept in. The enormous amount of information gathered, since Hegel's day, concerning the world's religions reveals Hegel's then unavoidable errors of historical fact. These various errors are regularly, clearly, and carefully corrected. These corrections, plus the citations, explanations and qualifications contained in the notes deal with everything from Egyptian mythology[8] to the interpretation of Chinese characters[9] on to the innumerable references to the likes of Kant and Schleiermacher as well as to Hegel's other works. The editor's considerations are encyclopedic in scope. They reflect his wide competence in Hegel studies and in world religions.

When read in conjunction with the lecture texts, these endnotes allow us to enter a bit more into Hegel's world, and even into Hegel's classroom. There, in his classroom, listeners would have caught many of his more polemical references. But they must have strained to capture a Schwabian pronunciation of strange African or Asian names. More specifically, these endnotes have the potential to reveal a great deal about Hegel's approach toward, and use of, the various sources available during his time.

A first reading of text and endnotes shows Hegel to be, as we mentioned at the beginning of the chapter, intensely involved with a wide variety of sources. We must presuppose that not all the sources of information which he has consulted have been identified.[10] However, what has been found permits us to see him critically digesting everything from explorers' and missionaries' reports to ancient and more contemporary scholarly or more popular presentations of various religions. We likewise see him at work with various philosophical, historical, linguistic, and cultural studies of one or more of the world's religions. Hegel paid particular attention to sacred and classical texts either in the original language or, as with the Hindu *Ramayana*, in translation. However, tellingly, he gives no evidence of having read the *Koran*.[11] Apparently he also garnered information and insight from newspapers.[12] As previously mentioned, he appears ordinarily to have quoted from memory with the expected result: errors, in various degrees, of fact and interpretation. For example, whether due to some form of memory lapse or to other causes, an interesting mix-up seems to have occurred. Strauss records that, in the 1831 lectures, Hegel apparently confused the origins of Rome and Egypt when he spoke of Egypt as having been founded by a band of robbers.[13] With reference to questions of interpretation, it is, again by way of example, fascinating to see Hegel insert the term "life" (*Lebendigkeit*) in his discussion of a passage from Kant.[14] On another occasion, with regard to a Schelling text, Hegel goes beyond what is explicitly stated to claim that Schelling spoke of God as "intuiting intelligence" (*anschauende Intelligenz*).[15] Still, at other times we can see Hegel following quoted texts quite closely.[16] His translations of English texts into German are sometimes more exact that the official German translations.[17] He enters sufficiently into the materials he consults to be able, at times, to join in the scholarly discussion of specific questions such as the interpretation of symbolism in the Greek world. He can be seen to evaluate, critically compare, and even side with, the position of one author over against that of another.[18]

Indeed, Hegel gives the impression that he relentlessly pursued information on the world's religions. He went to some lengths to obtain a recently published book, or to incorporate a study available in the same year as his lectures.[19] In the 1824 lectures we find evidence that he made a sort of quantum leap with regard to his incorporation of new materials. Yet as late as the 1831 lectures he was still integrating new information. He seems to have used materials possibly taken from an 1830 volume found in his library.[20]

A review of these endnotes has made it quite clear that Hegel took sacred texts and other information on the world's religions very seriously.[21] He was surely conditioned by the very sources with which he wrestled, and limited by the resources available in his day. At times he shows a clear awareness of the historical limitations, and relative value, of these resources. He comes through as critically receptive to information from any source. He appears basically faithful to his sources in lecture summaries and in actual presentations of the sources. Hegel clearly manifests the basic German characteristics of "thoroughness" (*Gründlichkeit*), "sincere earnestness" (*redlicher Ernst*),[22] and industriousness (*Fleißigkeit*). Most importantly, he comes across as impassioned at the possibility of surfacing the deeper significance of all this information.[23]

2. Hegel on Determinate Religion

The *Gesammelte Werke* edition of Hegel's 1821, 1824, 1827, and 1831 lecture series on the philosophy of religion will disperse the 1821 manuscript and various lecture transcriptions in historical-critical fashion over a number of volumes. This will more easily allow for the study of the possible mutual influence of Hegel's various lectures upon one another at a given point in Hegel's teaching career. However, the present editions, with their gathering and parallel presentation of the various philosophy of religion lecture series, have their own perduring advantage. They facilitate comparative studies of Hegel's thought on, and his various efforts at, structuring his philosophy of religion over the eleven-year span of these lectures.[24] We will first look at the four lecture series. Then we will distill from them certain continuities running through Hegel's various presentations of determinate religion.

2.a. The Four Lecture Series – Hegel's Efforts at Interpretation

The Editorial Introduction to the second volume of the English edition of these philosophy of religion lectures already provides helpful outlines. It also contains lengthy comparative summaries of Hegel's varying presentations of the levels and forms of determinate religion.[25] Here we will work toward an understanding of Hegel's philosophy of determinate religion by rather more narrowly concentrating on a summary of several characteristics of each of the lecture series. We will give special attention to Hegel's treatments of Roman religion. This is the religion which, as the last of the finite or ethnic religions, brings to a close the movement of determinate religion. It equally constitutes the transition to the consummate religion, to Christianity.[26] We will base our remarks, concerning these series in general and on Roman religion in particular, mainly on what Hegel actually says and does in Part Two of his lectures. We will proceed in this way since Hegel at times, as, for example, in the 1821 lectures, seems to adjust his actual presentations of determinate religion after having worked out the Introductions and discussions of

The Concept of Religion.[27] In fact, in the case of the 1824 lectures Hegel does not even seem to get around to carrying out the plan he initially proposes until the 1827 lectures.[28]

The 1821 Lectures

Hegel's 1821 lectures on determinate religion are available in the form of an annotated manuscript with footnoted associated materials,[29] and several loose sheets[30] containing Hegel's preliminary sketchings for the 1821 presentation of Roman religion. His writing in the manuscript tends initially to be more sketched in format. But then, while retaining a somewhat staccato style, it shifts to more fully developed paragraphs.

At the beginning of this Part Two, Hegel announces he will – and in fact he does – structure his successive treatments of immediate religion, of the religions of sublimity and of beauty, and of the religion of expediency according to the development of the rhythm of the 1821 concept of religion. He sketches the movement of these religions as a progression from being through essence to concept.[31] With reference to their historical realization, he identifies these religions successively as "Oriental," "Jewish and Greek," and "Roman."[32] Hegel proposes to treat each type or category of religion in terms of the abstract or metaphysical concept of God, in terms of concrete representation or the ways in which God is known, and then in terms of the practical relationship of cultus.[33]

In his presentation of immediate religion Hegel carefully follows the proposed order. He includes under "metaphysical concept" a treatment of the cosmological proof for the existence of God. But what is quite striking about this manuscript presentation of determinate religion is his apparent attempt to remain true to his general methodological notion of a doubled and, in some sense, self-contradictory, second moment. More specifically, here in 1821 he writes of this second moment in terms of essence. So, when he comes to the religion of sublimity (Judaism) and to the religion of beauty (Greek religion), Hegel first elaborates a metaphysical concept common to both of them. He includes a consideration of the proof for the oneness of God and the proof from contingency to necessity in the presentation of the common metaphysical concept. Then he treats each of the two religions separately under the rubrics of concrete representation and cultus. So the two religions are both identical, in that they share a common metaphysical concept, and yet very different in their concrete representation and cultus or worship.

After presenting the religion of immediacy and then the religions of sublimity and of beauty, Hegel analyses the religion of expediency in the third major subsection to determinate religion.[34] He identifies this religion historically with Roman religion. Even from the preparatory sketchings we can see that it is clearly his intention to elaborate Roman religion both in terms of expediency (*Zweckmäßigkeit*)[35] and of finite ends. He proposes to present the state as unifying, single end (*Zweck*),[36] and as the moment by means of which he will make the transition to the Christian religion.[37] Under the rubric of the metaphysical (or here, "abstract") concept appropriate to Roman religion Hegel affirms, "God is that being which acts expediently, namely, which has determinate objectives in the world."[38] It is here, too, that he considers the teleological proof for the existence of God.

Hegel relies heavily on Moritz's study in discussing the concrete representation of the divine and in presenting the consequent cultus appropriate to the religion of expediency. But he does this precisely in order to argue, against Moritz, that there is a fundamental difference between the Greek and Roman religions.[39] Hegel shows great sensitivity to, and feeling for, the two religions. He argues that, in the Greek religion of beauty, the people are free before the gods, whereas in the practical and prosaic Roman religion of expediency the people are finally not free.[40]

Hegel continues to create a morbid atmosphere around the religion of expediency when he speaks of the various Roman gods. Appropriately parallel to the conception of the divine as that which fulfills needs, he understands the people's relationship as one of dependence (*Abhängigkeit*). He comes back, time and again, to this question of dependence, even seeing in it the root of superstition.[41] This repeated reference to, and stress upon, dependence surely reflects his ongoing polemic, throughout the 1821 lectures, with Schleiermacher's conception of religion. Schleiermacher had written of religion in terms of the feeling of absolute dependence.[42] While analysing the inner structure and dynamic of the religion of expediency, Hegel is implicitly identifying Schleiermacher's view of religion with that Roman debasement which ends in worshipping the emperor, the devil and, finally, death.

As is the case with the manuscript as a whole, this presentation of the religion of expediency is heavy with what can easily be identified as various thought determinations of logic. In the 1821 lectures Hegel has in fact attempted to elaborate a philosophical presentation of determinate religion as a finite dialectical movement of the concept of religion. It is particularly fascinating to watch him at work in his discussion of the religion of expediency. There he tries to bring together aspects of Roman religion which stem either from his placing it as third moment within determinate religion or as the end point in the progression of finite religions. He tries both to integrate his presentation of Roman religion as a third moment, namely, one in which he almost instinctively tends toward integration and resolution, with his determination to underscore the unresolved contradiction[43] constituting the religion of expediency as the abyss of finitude. Furthermore, it is in line with his overall casting of the religion of expediency in terms of the concept that, especially toward the end of the presentation, this religion's unfolding is seen to be laden with the interpretative categories of the concept: universality, particularity, and a certain form of individuality.[44] Nevertheless, even with the use of such logical categories which suggest the structure of inclusive subjectivity, for Hegel Roman religion remains religion in the form of unending finitude.[45] Spirit is now self-consciousness and subjectivity,[46] but a self-consciousness and subjectivity of the worst kind: unending reflection without content.[47] This communitarian sinking to the lowest depths of finitude, this absolute misfortune and pain of spirit, constitutes the necessary point of transition to the consummate religion.[48]

The 1824 Lectures

The 1824 lectures[49] are available in the form of Griesheim's almost elegantly written fair copy with footnoted corroborating, alternate, and supplemental readings taken from other auditors' transcripts. In comparing these lectures with those of 1821, we immediately notice two points: the enormous increase in material contained in these lectures and the considerably different arrangement of that material. There is an augmentation of material, first of all, in that under "immediate religion" Hegel is no longer satisfied with general references to, among others, Eskimo and African religions. He does continue to discuss these primordial religions. But he also further subdivides immediate or nature religion into the religions of magic (including the Chinese religions and Buddhism), Hinduism, Persian, and Egyptian religions. He then treats them individually.[50] There is an augmentation of material, secondly, in the more quantitative sense. He generally includes a much greater amount of material on the various religions. This again is particularly noticeable with regard to immediate or nature religion, where the incorporation of so much new material remains as yet somewhat undigested. There are whole blocks of exposition followed by more systematic reflection and constructive analysis.[51]

It is more difficult to analyze Hegel's considerably different 1824 arrangement of determinate religion. In the overall Introduction to these 1824 lectures Hegel spoke of the succession (*Reihe*) of different determinate religions as being contained in the succession of proofs for the existence of God.[52] Yet now in the introductory remarks at the beginning of Part Two, Determinate Religion,[53] he sketches a tripartite subdivision into nature religion, the spiritual religion (*Die Religion des Geistigen*), and the religion of external expediency or purposiveness. It is as if he is vacillating between the 1821 structure, though on a new basis, and his present interest in structuring the movement of determinate religion according to the cosmological and teleological proofs for the existence of God.

It is as if, in the actual working out of determinate religion, Hegel's sense of the macrodialectical wins out. That is to say, he takes into consideration the placement of Part Two of his lectures in relation to Parts One and Three. From the macrodialectical perspective this Part Two would tend toward a doubled presentation. He works with the idea of a doubled second moment, however, in combination with his concern to link religions and proofs. He ends up with his famous division of determinate religion into immediate or nature religion, where he treats of the cosmological proof, and the religions of spiritual individuality, where he again handles forms of the cosmological proof in relation to the Jewish and Greek religions and the teleological proof in relation to the Roman religion. This linkage of proofs and groupings of religions results in the de facto presentation of determinate religion as a doubled second moment between the concept of religion and the consummate religion. It is a second moment in which each division opens with the affirmation of a certain identity of metaphysical concept and yet, moreso than in 1821, a metaphysical concept of God appropriate to each religion. Hegel elaborates as well, in each religion, moments of representation and of cultus.

Hegel's presentation of the religion of external purposiveness or expediency, Roman religion, is, in contrast to his procedure in much of the rest of the 1824 lectures, considerably more condensed than in the 1821 lectures. Still, Hegel continues the basic lines of his overall interpretation as he had developed them in the 1821 lectures.[54] Despite the shorter treatment in 1824, the Roman religion appears no less morbid and the indirect references to Schleiermacher[55] no less severe. However, this new presentation of the religion of expediency does, in many ways, reflect the shifted structure and emphases of the 1824 lectures. The teleological proof has already been treated under the general metaphysical concept of the sphere of spiritual individuality. This sphere is then subdivided into the Jewish, Greek, and Roman religions. In the presentation of these religions Hegel treats of end (*Zweck*) respectively as an abstract singular, as a multiplicity, and as the widening on to an inclusive single end.[56] When he speaks of God as the power (*Macht*) ruling over the world, he sees Roman religion as, in its own way, having returned to immediate or nature religion.

Here in the Roman religion he continues the theme originally raised in immediate or nature religion, namely, the slow distinguishing and elevating of spirit over nature. This distinguishing and elevating also comes across as the theme of the elevation of the finite to the infinite. This elevation is in fact the function of the cosmological and teleological proofs. Finally, as in the 1821 lectures, so too here and earlier in the presentation of determinate religion,[57] Hegel speaks of determinate religion as a movement of subjectivity. In a general reflection at the end of the presentation on Roman religion, he interrelates the concepts of power, end or purpose, and rule in such a way that, along with the assertion that the finite is an abstraction which must go over into the infinite, he can arrive at the concept of infinite subjectivity. He now understands personhood or subjectivity as including purpose within itself.[58] Against more subjectivist and historicist positions, Hegel, in this presentation of an objective movement of infinite subjectivity, effectively repeats[59] the speculative definition of religion which he had stated earlier in these 1824 lectures. Religion is "this idea, the idea of spirit that relates itself to itself, the self-consciousness of absolute spirit."[60] It is with this reaffirmation of the speculative definition of religion that he makes the transition to the consummate religion.[61]

The 1827 Lectures

One of those who transcribed Hegel's 1827 philosophy of religion lectures and who became one of Hegel's followers as well, Heinrich Gustav Hotho, claimed that the years 1823-1827 were probably Hegel's most successful and richest.[62] Given the many areas in which Hegel read and lectured during these years, in a particular sense this claim may be true. Certainly the vast amount of material incorporated into the 1824 and 1827 lectures on the philosophy of religion, and these two major efforts to systematize this material on determinate religion, attest to intense efforts on his part.

The 1827 lectures are themselves considerably shorter than those of 1824. Part Two[63] of the 1827 lectures is only slightly more than half as long as the 1824 presentation.[64] The text, a critically edited version of that found in the 1925 Georg Lasson edition, reads more smoothly and easily than the texts of the two previous lecture series. Hegel returns to a three-fold division of determinate religion, but now with only brief overview sections for each of the divisions. The major emphasis is clearly on the religions themselves as forms or levels in the movement of determinate religion, and on the transitions from one religion to the next. Under immediate or nature religion Hegel now treats the religion of magic. The Chinese religion is a developed form of this religion, though placed almost as a separate religion. He continues with a presentation of Buddhism, still in conjunction with Lamaism. Then he presents Hinduism and, finally, the Persian and Egyptian religions. These last two are treated as religions of transition. The second section now includes only the Greek and Jewish religions, in this reversed order. In the third section Hegel again handles the Roman religion as the religion of expediency.

For the sake of brevity, we refer here in our resume of the 1827 lectures to these religions by the names of their historical realizations. However, in fact it is the interpretative and systematic analyses of these religions to which Hegel gives prominence in these lectures. He makes reference to their historical realizations more as a consequence upon their philosophical interpretation. It is here, then, in the 1827 lectures, that Hegel tends to distinguish more clearly between the constructive descriptions of the levels of determinate religion and their historical realizations. Yet it is, nevertheless, likewise in this lecture series that he more forcefully than in the previous two series insists on the fact that these forms and their realizations constitute a dialectically progressing uniserial history of religions.[65]

As was the case with the previous lecture series, Hegel's 1827 presentation of the religion of expediency – despite its brevity[66] and when read in conjunction with Hegel's later, recapitulative over-view[67] – allows for an understanding and appreciation of the 1827 elaboration of determinate religion as a whole. Already in the Introduction to the 1827 lectures Hegel had spoken of the coming into being of determinate religion on the basis of the concept's judgment (*Urteil*) or self-determination through separation into the determinate forms of religion.[68] In turn, briefly stated, there occurs in nature religion the slowly emerging distinction between spirit and nature. This distinction takes place as an elevation of self or subject over nature. Nature religion goes over into the religions of beauty and of sublimity. These two are, then, the religions whose common determination is a free subjectivity in which the spiritual raises itself partially over nature and remains still partially within nature.[69] The religion of beauty is taken up into the monotheistic religion of sublimity[70] and these two are united in the religion of expediency.[71] The plurality of ends or purposes present in the Greek religion and the as yet limited single end of the Jewish religion, where God is the God of one particular people, are taken up into the universal end of the Roman religion.[72]

As Hegel has done from The Concept of Religion on through his presentation of the various finite religions, here he sketches Roman religion or the religion of finite purposiveness in three stages. These stages are the metaphysical concept of God, the appearance of divinity in theoretical knowledge, and cultus or the practical knowledge of God.[73] Hegel's generally morbid picture of Roman religion remains the same as in his earlier lectures. Though this is the religion which unites the religions of beauty and sublimity, it does so only in a finite way. The individual self-consciousness remains subordinated to fate and to the one goal of world rule. Thus abstract personhood or subjectivity retains, unresolved, the contradictory affirmations of individual needs and the subordination of the individual to a universal but still finite end.[74] For Hegel[75] abstract subjectivity gives expression to moments which will be integrated only in the next, and final, level of religion, namely, the religion of spirit.

When read in conjunction with Hegel's later review of the movement of determinate religion,[76] the 1827 lectures appear to follow Hegel's so far variously elaborated general concern to structure a movement from substance to subject. This is particularly striking in view of his polemical reaction in 1827 to accusations of pantheism and in light of his previously attained speculative definition of religion. Having begun the 1827 lectures with the notion of God, he continues to emphasize God throughout the lectures. He constantly insists God is not only substance but subject. This movement from substance to subject occurs in determinate religion as a gradual elevation (*Erhebung*) of spirit over nature.[77] Hegel is, then, in effect repeating here on the level of determinate religion the finite-to-infinite movement constituting the cosmological and the teleological proofs for the existence of God. In these 1827 lectures he had already gathered and treated these proofs in The Concept of Religion. It is this constant reference to the elevation of spirit over nature which, when seen in the light of his final identification of concept and spirit,[78] allows Hegel in the 1827 lectures to integrate so many elements into his conception of determinate religion as a necessary movement of divine and human subjectivity.

The 1831 Lectures

In both the German and English editions, the 1831 lectures on determinate religion are available only under limited form. We have available to us excerpts from a transcript by David Friedrich Strauss,[79] a secondary transmission of the 1831 treatment of the teleological proof for the existence of God,[80] and materials from the first and second Friends Editions. These materials from the two Friends Editions are footnoted to appropriate places in the 1824 and 1827, and occasionally in the 1821, lecture texts. Such an arrangement of materials seems at first sight a bit scattered and, at times, confusing, as on pp. 352-358 of the German text where three different excerpts are run in continuing, parallel footnotes. But the arrangement quickly comes to be seen as both manageable and practical.

These materials allow for a sense of the overall development and thrust of the 1831 lectures. But they do not allow for as sure or as detailed a reading and understanding of the presentations of the various religions. Nor do they make possible as secure an interpretation of the overall movement of determinate religion. What can be said is that Hegel returns to distributing the proofs for the existence of God among the treatments of the various religions. Furthermore, he reduces the scope and treatment of nature religion, and he quite revamps the outline of the rest of determinate religion. Nature religion now consists of a reflection on "rational religion," then on what Hegel had previously treated of as primitive religion, and on the religion of magic.

Next, as second moment in this still triply subdivided presentation of determinate religion, Hegel brings to the fore his often repeated principle that religion properly begins only where there is the distinction constitutive of consciousness.[81] Yet he balances this observation with the remark that spirit has, nevertheless, already been present from the beginning of immediate religion in an individual and immediate way.[82] This allows him, then, to treat of the cosmological proof and to present what are now called the three religions of substance: Chinese religion, Hinduism, Lamaism/Buddhism.[83] Not only has Hegel, so to speak, upgraded these Far Eastern religions. He continues this upgrading trend by including Near Eastern religions as transitional forms under the third division of determinate religion, "The Religion of Freedom." The religions constituting these transitional forms are the Persian religion and Judaism as religions of the good, then the religion of anguish or pain[84] identified variously as the Phoenician[85] and perhaps the Syrian[86] religions, and, finally, the Egyptian religion as the religion of ferment. The Greek religion now comes in, along with a discussion of the teleological proof, as the second subdivision under "religion of freedom" with the Roman religion making up the third subdivision.

Strauss's excerpts are valuable in that they give an overview of the religions treated, but they do not provide the same taste, as do the footnoted materials, of Hegel working out the movement of determinate religion in terms of the positing (*Setzen*)[87] and self-realizing (*das sich Realisieren*)[88] of the concept. Determinate religion arises in the rupture or separation (*Entzweiung*) of the concept. It continues as the consequent movement of elevation of spirit over nature, the transition from one religion to another.[89] This elevation takes on a particular character in the 1831 lectures as the coming into being of the freedom of spirit.[90] While in the previous three lecture series Hegel had spoken of freedom mostly in relation to the religion of beauty or Greek religion, here in 1831 he appears, especially as seen in the footnoted materials, to read the whole movement of determinate religion in terms of freedom[91] and subjectivity.[92] This is shown in a particularly clear way when he gathers and presents the three religions of substance as second moment of determinate religion and when he calls the third moment "the religion of freedom."

Strauss's summary of the third "subdivision" of the religion of freedom, the religion of expediency or Roman religion,[93] indicates that Hegel retains his reading of it as morbid and last-end finitude. The texts available simply give no indication of a continuing polemic against Schleiermacher. Strauss does hint twice at a dialectic involved in Roman religion. This he does when he calls the Roman world the fate of the Greek world[94] and when he records two sides to Roman religion: the fact that the gods are, on the one hand, limited external powers of nature and, on the other hand, the presence of an abstract interiority, namely, fate.[95] But it is the footnoted material to the 1824[96] and 1827[97] lectures on Roman religion that gives the impression of a more developed dialectical relationship between the religion of expediency and the previous determinate religions. In fact, it is the footnoted material in general which provides more of a glimpse at what must, in the 1831 lectures, have been a highly developed philosophical analysis of the various religions. Time and again the footnoted material recounts interpretations using the logical cate-

gories of universal and particular, "in itself" and "for itself," otherness and mediation, finite and infinite.

Hegel maintains his affirmation of a history of religions in this
lecture series.[98] But now this history of religions is explicitly a history
of freedom. The footnoted material shows him apparently referring
more explicitly and more precisely to the second moment in his
philosophical presentation of religions as the moment of historical
existence.[99] Finally, in his excerpts Strauss catches the irony of the
Roman religion as a religion which was to have fulfilled needs and,
instead, only fostered resignation to non-fulfillment. It is the pain
caused by the Roman religion which becomes the birth pains of the
true religion.[100]

2.b. Continuities in Hegel's Position

These German and English editions have marvelously achieved
their goal[101] of facilitating a comparative study of Hegel's Berlin
lectures on the philosophy of determinate religion. Hegel's four
attempts to work out a philosophical interpretation of the non-
Christian religions come through loud and clear. This is the case
whether it be the 1821 structuring according to the triad "being/
essence/concept," the 1824 twofold division in line with the appropriate proofs for the existence of God, the particularly clear 1827 concern
for the relative adequacy of the concept of religion and the various
religions, or the 1831 stress on the movement of diremption and return
as a dialectical history of freedom. Hegel's shifting schematizations
remind us that, in the final analysis, the major efforts of the world's
greatest thinkers often come, after prolonged study, to be seen as
sketches toward an integrating envisagement rather than the last
word on a particular or given subject.

Recent studies of these Berlin philosophy of religion lectures
have, without of course denying important continuities in Hegel's
thought, rightly at this point in the history of Hegel scholarship
stressed the fundamental importance of acknowledging, and working from, the real differences existing among Hegel's various attempts to formulate a philosophy of determinate religion, or, perhaps
better, a philosophical reading of the history of religion.[102] It is the
strength of these German and English editions that they can encourage this needed study of differences while, at the same time, thereby

making possible a more responsible affirmation of a certain continuity in Hegel's approach. Throughout these Berlin lectures Hegel really does present not just a series of different readings. Rather, through them he proposes a unique and identifiable philosophical interpretation of determinate religion.

We can at least indicate that Hegel does in fact develop one basic philosophy of determinate religion throughout these diverse schematizations. We need but refer to his ongoing attitude and approach toward the non-Christian religions. First of all, his attitude to these religions is, even given its historical conditioning and limitations, fundamentally open and, it could be argued, in a sense appreciative. Hegel showed a great deal of respect for the given historical reality and religious phenomena themselves.[103] This respectful attitude is indicated by his critical use of sources available to him. It is dictated by his general stance on philosophy as reflection on what is. It is as if Hegel wished, at least in principle, to find room in his constructive analyses for any aspect of a religion which proved important to that religion and to its adherents. He was at least critically appreciative enough of the various religions that, even with his often negative judgments on them, he consistently presented them as necessary instances without which the consummate or absolute or true religion could not have come into being. We could say Hegel critically received the various religions. It is a tribute to his genius that he could, so to speak, have his cake and eat it too. He affirmed both the necessity of the finite religions and the consummate character of the absolute religion.

Hegel's general attitude of a basic but critical openness is rooted in his overall conception of philosophy's relationship to "existent" reality. If this is so, then his approach, throughout the 11 years of lectures, toward determinate religion is conditioned by his understanding of religion in terms of thought. It is not only for polemical but also, and especially, for systematic reasons that Hegel understands religion in terms of consciousness. As was mentioned in Chapter Two above, he understands religious consciousness as thought inclusive of the religious object and of the finite subject which is conscious of that object. Against the background of this understanding of religious consciousness, we can say that Hegel variously, and rather brilliantly, foreshadows later studies in the philosophy and theology of religions. This he does, for example, when he insists on the correlation between a religious community's conception of God and its conception of the human.

With this structure of consciousness as a relationship between object and conscious subject, a relationship occurring for Hegel in thought, it would seem he really had only one option if he wished to surface the inner structure of determinate religions and to express the correlative conceptions of divine and human appropriate to each religion. And this option was, at least in principle, in some way to use his own previously elaborated logical categories to express the connections within, and comparisons among, the various religions. Given both this understanding of religion as located in consciousness[104] and the way in which he went about constructing his systematic analyses of the various religions, Hegel could then sketch the dialectical movement of determinate religion as a universally formulated progression of dialectical transitions from one philosophically interpreted religion to another. It was a progression seen as the step-by-step, or level-by-level, elevation of spirit over nature. This elevation was a dialectically progressing elevation of finite to infinite ending, ironically, in the depths of finitude. It was, at least according to Hegel's expressed intention, to be a progression occurring chronologically as a history of religions.

It is true that Hegel argues this elevation of spirit over nature very differently in the various lecture series. But what saves our present brief generalization of his approach from being a mere abstraction is the fact that, in each of the lecture series, the movement of determinate religion is clearly conceived of as a movement, in line with Hegel's overall philosophical method, from indeterminate to determinate, from substance to subject and subjectivity. We need, of course, constantly to remind ourselves of, and even stress the diversity of his schematizations. Still, Hegel's ongoing attitude and approach would seem to justify the affirmation that, in and through these diverse organizations of determinate religion, Hegel has carved out for himself a distinctive and identifiable position. He has elaborated a philosophical interpretation of the history of religions as a movement, in and through human subjectivity, of self-positing divine subjectivity.[105]

3. *Further Research Opportunities*

In his various lectures on determinate religion Hegel proposes to have presented a dialectically progressing uniserial movement of logically structured philosophical reconstructions of the world's non-Christian religions. It was to be a progression reflecting, and reflected in, what was for Hegel the more or less historically sequential appearances of these religions. All of these religions, taken with their philosophical interpretations, were to be, each in its own way, expressions of the concept of religion. But they were as well to be only inadequate expressions of that concept. Thus they were to stand over against one another. They were to be finite religions.

Several important recent authors[106] seem correctly to agree that Hegel has not been able to argue convincingly to a single history of religions. Despite his best efforts, reality seems to have gotten away from him at this point. However, this massive effort of his, carried out before the division of the study of religion into so many sectors,[107] continues to offer a number of historical, interpretational, systematic, and reconstructive research challenges. These German and English editions now make possible the only appropriate way, first of all, to come to understand exactly what Hegel is saying and, then, to respond to these challenges. They make it possible to begin with a specific study of the individual lecture series, and this from a developmental perspective.[108]

Other than more generally descriptive and expository studies or studies of one or more determinate religions, there have been few works consecrated directly and explicitly to Part Two of Hegel's philosophy of religion lectures.[109] In one of these studies which treats more specifically of Part Two, Hans-Joachim Schoeps[110] lists three tasks for those looking at Hegel's philosophy of religion from a more or less historical perspective: 1) to identify Hegel's sources; 2) to evaluate Hegel's interpretation of these sources; 3) to compare Hegel's results with contemporary scholarship. As Jaeschke mentions,[111] much progress has been made, especially with the studies by Reinhard Leuze and Ignatius Viyagappa.[112] But it is really with the publication of the present volumes that the first task is accomplished and the following two can be fully carried out.

Besides the more strictly historical studies, there are a number of interpretative and systematic challenges to be taken up anew. There are a number of questions still to be pursued. We could, for example, think of the question of the various means Hegel used to elaborate his philosophically reconstructive analyses of the non-Christian religions. More specifically, there are the possible senses and ways in which Hegel might have used logical categories to construct his forms or levels of determinate religion. Further questions would include those concerning the structure and dynamics of the transitions Hegel proposes in the various lecture series and concerning the relationship between the various forms of determinate religion and their historical realizations. A good way to focus on what Hegel is up to in his various attempts at a philosophical presentation of determinate religion would be to study the ways in which he relates interpretation and construction. With reference to his working with particular religions, we might ask to what extent he interprets, and to what extent he constructs. It would be particularly interesting, for example, to see in greater detail how Hegel proceeds to integrate the greatly increasing amount of material concerning the "primordial" religions of Africa and the Americas.

More widely conceived, such questions as those of the relationship between interpretation and construction can be restated in terms of the need to examine more closely how Hegel might be thinking of dialectical progression in a less hierarchically understood fashion. This question of the relationship between interpretation and construction can take on still another coloring when it is rephrased in terms of how Hegel combines metaphysics and history. He seems to integrate metaphysics and history into a history of truth and of freedom. He makes the bold claim that this history of freedom is a movement of divine inclusive subjectivity.

Our reflections in Section Two of this chapter have already indicated some of the complex questions involved in any further efforts at interpretative and systematic research on Hegel's various presentations of determinate religion. Among the many areas calling for further study we might point out the need to look more closely at Hegel's understandings of the relationships between religion and culture. We should recall that for Hegel religion carries with it a built-in interest in the political and the societal. There is as well the need to state more precisely what is meant by affirming Hegel's in some sense appreciative reading of various non-Christian religions. This clarification of Hegel's stance vis-à-vis determinate religion as such, and his attitude toward the particular religions, will surely have to be carried out in two steps. First, it will be important to take into consideration the various aspects to, and the triple structure of, his notion of sublation or *Aufhebung*: preserving, negating, and taking up or moving ahead. Second, one will have to examine quite closely how, through the successive presentations of determinate religion and particularly in the 1831 lectures, Hegel seems to recognize in, and accord to, the various non-Christian religions a greater role in the realization of freedom.

A particularly complex case in point is Hegel's analysis and appreciation of Hinduism. This question is especially complex because Hegel's recognition of certain philosophic strengths in Hinduism is coupled with an overall dissatisfaction with the romanticist infatuation, current in his day, with the Orient and things Eastern.[113]

There are almost innumerable areas of further inquiry opened by the themes surfaced and gathered in the indexes to Volume 4 of the German edition. Among these themes there is one which deserves to receive further attention through an ever more concrete and detailed study of the various lecture series. This theme or question is the point proposed in Section 2b above. There we spoke of a substantial, and not merely nominal, continuity in Hegel's conceptualization of determinate religion. We suggested that Hegel continually argued to a philosophical interpretation of determinate religion as a movement from substance to subject. It was a movement of subjectivity.

In a more reconstructive vein, a phenomenon not to be overlooked is the recent tendency to respond to Hegel's view of determinate religion with a more pluralist approach, while nevertheless remaining in dialogue with Hegel. Jaeschke[114] first asserts that there is no one history of spirit. He then picks up on Hegel's frequent geographical references, and, in quite seminal fashion, proposes that Hegel has in fact elaborated not a history but a geography of typologies of religions. Hodgson,[115] in turn, very briefly refers to the possibility of mutual transformations among religions on the basis of structural analogies and thematic similarities. The challenge is to be able to pick up on insightful suggestions such as these, but to do so on the basis of an adequately reformulated dynamic movement of spirit.

Indeed there may be much more to Hegel's attempts at a philosophical interpretation of determinate religion, and therefore much more to understand, than has so far met the eye, whether Hegel's or our own.

NOTES

¹ *Über die Religion. Reden an die Gibildeten unter ihren Verächtern* (Berlin: Bei Johann Friedrich Unger, 1799)/Eng. trans. of the third edition, *On Religion. Speeches to Its Cultured Despisers* (New York: Harper and Row, 1958) 210-253. For a brief reference to Hegel in the context of a discussion of the development of the various approaches to the study of religion, see Wolfhart Pannenberg, *Basic Questions in Theology. Collected Essays*, vol. 2 (Philadelphia: Fortress, 1971) 72.

² Jaeschke, in V 4:653-820.

³ Jaeschke, in V 4:ix. The English edition has its own particular advantage in making available selected materials directly at the bottom of the relevant page of Hegel's manuscript or of the lecture transcripts.

⁴ Jaeschke, in V 4:x, 653.

⁵ Jaeschke, in V 4:653.

⁶ Jaeschke, in V 4:x, 653.

⁷ Jaeschke, in V 4:x. See Hodgson, in L 2:4.

⁸ E.g., Jaeschke, in V 4:785-786, 805.

⁹ E.g., Jaeschke, in V 4:760.

¹⁰ Note, for instance, the editor's further research work necessary to locate additional sources of Hegel's information on Lamaism. Jaeschke, in V 4:765-767.

¹¹ Jaeschke, in V 5:350.

¹² Jaeschke, in V 4:778.

¹³ Jaeschke, in V 4:805.

¹⁴ Jaeschke, in V 4:660.

¹⁵ Jaeschke, in V 4:762.

16 E.g., Jaeschke, in V 4:715-716.

17 Jaeschke, in V 4:718.

18 Jaeschke, in V 4:789-790.

19 E.g., Jaeschke, in V 4:699-700.

20 Jaeschke, in V 4:791.

21 Note, for instance, Ignatius Viyagappa's evaluation of how carefully Hegel read a particular Upanishad and summarized its most essential point. G. W. F. *Hegel's Concept of Indian Philosophy* (Rome: Università Gregoriana Editrice, 1980) 28.

22 Already in an 1803 letter to Goethe, Schiller cites these two characteristics in commenting on Hegel's strengths and weaknesses. In Günther Nicolin, *Hegel in Berichten seiner Zeitgenossen* (Hamburg: Felix Meiner, 1970) number 78. Cited in English in G. W. F. Hegel, *Hegel: The Letters,* ed. Clark Butler (Bloomington: Indiana University Press, 1984) 682.

23 On Hegel's sources for his interpretations of determinate religion, see Hodgson, who, in L 2:3-12, very helpfully identifies "major sources relating to Hegel's treatment of each of the determinate religions." On Hegel's sources, see also Hans-Joachim Schoeps, "Die außerchristlichen Religionen bei Hegel," in *Studien zur unbekannten Religons- und Geistesgeschichte* (Göttingen: Musterschmidt, 1963) 255-284 and Reinhard Leuze, *Die außerchristlichen Religionen bei Hegel* (Göttingen: Vandenhoeck und Ruprecht, 1975). And specifically on the sources for Hegel's treatment of the Hindu religion and philosophy, see Viyagappa, *Hegel's Concept of Indian Philosophy* 11-60, 167, 245-247, and bibliography 266-275. Leuze and Viyagappa are singled out by Jaeschke, in V 4:653, as being particularly helpful.

Our more generous evaluation of Hegel's approach toward, and use of, sources available to him needs, of course, always to be tempered by an awareness of various weaknesses. For instance, Hegel apparently did not take into consideration the significance of the subordination of the Vedic god of heaven as a way of expressing the dissolution of the old Vedic religion through Brahmanism. See Jaeschke, in V 4:771. As Hodgson, in L 2:4, points out, Hegel treated more of the classical expressions of the religions other than Christianity and showed less awareness of their historical development.

Authors who have touched on the question of Hegel's approach toward available sources have made generally positive judgements concerning Hegel's obviously historically conditioned use of these sources. Note the following observations. Gustav Mensching writes, "Bei der Fragwürdigkeit und Lückenhaftigkeit seiner Quellen muß es vielmehr gerade wundernehmen, wie richtig Hegel trotzdem zumeist den Geist der Religionen erkannt und dargestellt hat." "Typologie außerchristlichen Religion bei Hegel," *Zeitschrift für Missionskunde und Religionswissenschaft* 46 (1931) 336. And more exuberantly, Emanuel Hirsch: "1831, als er [Hegel] die Vorlesung zum letzten Mal las, besaß er auf Grund des Studiums aller einschlagenden Literatur eine reiche und gegliederte Anschauung der Welt der geschichtlichen Religionen und war damals vermutlich der einzige Mann in Europa, der hier eine wirklich universale Bildung besaß." *Geschichte der neueren Theologie*, vol. 5 (Gütersloh: Gerd Mohn, 1953) 247, cited by Schoeps, 255 n. 1. Leuze, 237-238, concludes that at times Hegel lagged behind the research available to him and at other times corrected and went beyond that research. Leuze's position is conveniently summarized by Walter Jaeschke, *Die Religionsphilosophie Hegels* (Darmstadt: Wissenschaftliche Buchgesellschaft, 1983) 78. Viyagappa, 59-60, draws conclusions more specifically limited to Hegel's use of sources on Indian thought and religion. He asserts that Hegel used, and used well, the best of what was available to him at the time on India. The cumulative effect of these generally appreciative and positive evaluations is not without significance for the question of whether Hegel was truly concerned with the genuinely historical.

[24] Hodgson, in L 1:xiii-xiv.

[25] Hodgson, in L 2:12-86, 88-89, and on the 1827 lectures, in L 4:40-59.

[26] See Hodgson, in L 1:35-36.

[27] Hodgson, in L 2:14, remarks that Hegel in fact works out more clearly the distinction between representation and cultus only after the 1821 presentation of The Concept of Religion. On this see Walter Jaeschke, "Zur Logik der Bestimmten Religion," in *Hegels Logik der Philosophie. Religion und Philosophie in der Theorie des absoluten Geistes* (Stuttgart: Klett-Cotta, 1984) 184.

[28] For example, Jaeschke points out that Hegel's proposed structuring of Part One, The Concept of Religion, of the 1824 lectures

on determinate religion according to the model "concept/knowledge/cultus" (*Begriff-Wissen-Kultus*) is only realized in Part One of the 1827 lectures. "Zur Logik der Bestimmten Religion" 184. This then with implications for the interpretation as well of the respective treatments of determinate religion.

29 V 4:1-137.

30 V 4:643-648.

31 V 4:1.1-4.73.

32 V 4:4.71-73.

33 Hodgson, in L 2:14.

34 V 4:95.288-137.494 with loose sheets 643.1-648.197.

35 V 4:643.1.

36 E.g., V 4:648.191-192 with 646.118-119.

37 V 4:648.193.

38 "Gott ist das Wesen, das zweckmässig handelt, bestimmte Zwecke also in der Welt hat." V 4:100.458-459 (my trans.).

39 Jaeschke, in V 4:811, referring to Karl Philipp Moritz, *Anthousa oder Roms Alterthümer. Ein Buch für die Menschheit. Die heiligen Gebräuche der Römer* (Berlin: F. Mauer, 1791). See also Hodgson, in L 2:26.

40 E.g., V 4:114.870-116.924.

41 V 4:125.181-182.

42 See Jaeschke, in V 4:817 with cross-references. Earlier Hegel had linked this feeling of dependence, and consequently Schleiermacher, with Judaism. V 4:64.489-490. See Ch. 2 Subsection 2b with accompanying n. 14 above.

43 V 4:134.435-439.

44 E.g., V 4:132.380-133.390 with 131.343.

45 V 4:137.493-494.

46 Note Hegel's own summary of the overall development of determinate religion in terms of subjectivity. V 4:131.359-132.377.

47 V 4:133.391-407.

48 V 4:130.336-338.

49 V 4:139-410.

50 On the varying ways Hegel interprets the subdivision of immediate or nature religion, see Hodgson, in L 2:30-44.

51 E.g., V 4:178.29-181.145, followed by 181.146-151 and 182.174 on.

52 V 3:58.707-711.

53 V 4:139.6-142.73.

54 See Hodgson, in L 2:55.

55 V 4:406.196-407.224.

56 V 4:398.926-939.

57 E.g., V 4:260.316-323 with 283.974-975.

58 V 4:408.286-410.344.

59 V 4:410.335-344.

60 "diese Idee, die Idee des Geistes, der sich zu sich selbst verhält, das Selbstbewußtsein des absoluten Geistes." V 3:222.667-668. In the English translation, L 1:318, the last five words are italicized.

61 V 4:410.345-346.

62 Quoted by Viyagappa, *Hegel's Concept of Indian Philosophy* 258.

63 V 4:411-591.

64 Hodgson, in L 4:56-72, is particularly helpful in comparing these lectures with the earlier and later ones. In L 2:56-57 he discusses various reasons for the briefer lecture series, including the fact that in 1827 the semester itself was considerably shorter.

65 E.g., V 4:415.35-48.

66 V 4:579.609-591.925.

67 V 5:190.395-195.563.

68 V 3:89.674-90.679. It is of interest to note that, in his recapitulative overview, Hegel is recorded as again referring to the sphere of immediate or nature religion in terms of "being." Hegel had previously done this in 1821. See V 5:191.418-419 and 434.

69 V 4:533.588 with 532.572-575.

70 V 4:561.180-183.

71 V 4:579.610-613.

72 V 4:580.626-638.

73 E.g., V 3:297.383-387 with 330.904-914.

74 V 4:590.894-918.

75 V 4:591.919-925.

76 V 5:190.395-195.563, to be read in tandem with the various references to substance, subject, and subjectivity to be found in the index "*Philosophica et Theologica.*" See Jaeschke, in V 4:955-960.

77 V 4:533.589-599.

78 V 5:193.515-194.519.

79 V 4:611-642.

80 V 4:593-607.

81 V 4:612.40-42, 414 note.

82 V 4:433 note.

83 V 4:618.241-248, 430-432 note.

84 V 4:629.612-630.

85 V 4:629.613.

86 V 4:503 note.

87 V 4:139 note, 423 note.

88 V 4:411 note.

89 V 4:412 note.

90 E.g., V 4:357 note. In L 2:81, Hodgson alerts us to the *leitmotiv* of freedom running particularly clearly through the 1831 lectures in so far as we have access to them today. With regard to Hegel's concern for the relationship between religion, state, and free political institutions, Hodgson, in L 2:81 n. 41, cites Walter Jaeschke, "Hegel's Last Year in Berlin," in *Hegel's Philosophy of Action*, ed. Lawrence S. Stepelevich and David Lamb (Atlantic Highlands, N.J.: Humanities, 1983) 31-48.

[91] E.g., V 4:397 note.

[92] E.g., V 4 notes to pp. 413-414, 431-432, 529, plus V 4:625.497-498.

[93] V 4:640.32-642.79.

[94] V 4:640.31.

[95] V 4:641.52-56.

[96] V 4:396-397.

[97] V 4:591.

[98] V 4:611.31-34 with pp. 139-140 note.

[99] E.g., V 4:445 note.

[100] V 4:641.74-642.79.

[101] Hodgson, in L 2:12. This goal is expressed as well more concretely by Jaeschke in terms of wanting to get rid of the misconception that Hegel merely imposed an abstract grid on historical data. Jaeschke, in V 4:ix. Note, however, Jaeschke feels the accusation is possible against Hegel's fomulations in the 1821 lectures. "Zur Logik der bestimmten Religion" 181.

[102] Stressing differences among the lecture series: Jaeschke, "Zur Logik der bestimmten Religion" 172-188; Hodgson, in L 2:1-90.

[103] But see n. 101 above.

[104] Note the more developed but catchy phrase regarding end or purpose in the 1827 presentation of Roman religion, *Sitz im Selbstbewußtsein*. V 4:590.902.

[105] For further remarks on the characteristics of Hegel's attitude and approach toward the determinate religions, see Reinhard Heede, "Die göttliche Idee und ihre Erscheinung in der Religion. Untersuchungen zum Verhältnis von Logik und Religionsphilosophie bei Hegel" (Ph. D. dissertation, Philosophical Faculty of the Westfälischen Wilhelms-Universität zu Münster/Westfalen, 1972) esp. 148-151; Leuze, *Die außerchristlichen Religionen bei Hegel* 238-240.

[106] Heede, "Die göttliche Idee" 177, speaks of Hegel's unsuccessful attempts to establish a correspondence between the history of religion and the moments of logic; Jaeschke, "Zur Logik der

bestimmten Religion" 172-188, continues forcefully to argue this position with regard to Hegel's not having been able to establish a consistent correspondence between logic and determinate religion; ____, *Die Religionsphilosophie Hegels* 78; Hodgson, in L 2:86-87, 90 is in substantial agreement with the overall position that Hegel was not able to argue convincingly to a single history of religions.

[107] Pannenberg, "Toward a Theology of the History of Religions" 72.

[108] Jaeschke, "Zur Logik der bestimmten Religion" 180.

[109] Those more analytic and critical studies of Part Two, which have come to my attention, are: Mensching, "Typologie außerchristlicher Religion bei Hegel" 329-340; Schoeps, "Die außerchristlichen Religionen bei Hegel" 255-284; Heede, "Die göttliche Idee" 147-181; Leuze, *Die außerchristlichen Religionen bei Hegel*; Jaeschke, *Die Religionsphilosophie Hegels* 75-78; ____, "Zur Logik der bestimmten Religion" 172-188; ____, *Die Vernunft in der Religion* (Stuttgart-Bad Cannstatt: Frommann-holzboog, 1986) 274-295; ____, "Hegel's Interpretation of the Non-Christian Religions in Relation to the Concept of Christianity as the Absolute Religion," a paper presented to the annual conference of the Hegel Society of Great Britain, Oxford, September, 1987; several studies in "Papers of the Nineteenth Century Theology Working Group," American Academy of Religion 1987 Annual Meeting, ed. Walter H. Conser and James Yerkes, duplicated at the Graduate Theological Union, Berkeley, California, 1987; Walter Jaeschke, "Between Myth and History: On Hegel's Study of the History of Religion" 59-70, Frank E. Reynolds, "Hegel Revisited: A History of Religions/Buddhist Studies Perspective" 100-111, von der Luft, "Hegel vs. (?) Judaism: A Reassessment" 112-123; Hodgson, in L 2:1-90; ____, "Logic, History, and Alternative Paradigms in Hegel's Interpretation of the Religions," *The Journal of Religion* 68 (1988) 1-20; Merold Westphal, "Hegel, Hinduism, and Freedom," *The Owl of Minerva* 20 (1989) 193-204.

[110] "Die außerchristlichen Religionen bei Hegel" 255.

[111] *Die Religionsphilosophie Hegels* 77-78.

[112] See n. 23 above.

[113] Among recent studies on Hegel on Hinduism, Viyagappa, *Hegel's Concept of Indian Philosophy* (see n. 23 above), has read Hegel's

interpretation considerably more positively than has Merold West-phal, "Hegel, Hinduism, and Freedom" (see n. 109 above). A further point for study would be the influence of Hegel's interpretation of Hinduism on modern Indian self-consciousness. I am grateful to Prof. Joseph Prabhu for calling attention to the complexities of Hegel's attitude toward Hinduism and Hegel's possible influence on modern Hindu self-consciousness. See also Hodgson, in L 4:46-47.

A number of the areas of study and of points mentioned in this paragraph and in the paragraph immediately preceding it as possible topics of further research originally surfaced in one way or another during the Nineteenth Century Theology Group's discussions at the American Academy of Religion's 1987 Annual Meeting. See n. 109 above.

[114] "Zur Logik der bestimmten Religion" 172-188; see Jaeschke, *Die Vernunft in der Religion* 274-295

[115] Hodgson, in L 2:87 and 90.

CHAPTER FOUR

CONSUMMATE RELIGION

What immediately meets the eye as we read Part Three of Hegel's philosophy of religion is his insistence that the consummate religion is the full realization of the moments of the previously presented concept of religion. Hegel so relates the consummate religion to the concept of religion that it seems as if he is trying to bring the whole weight of his system to bear on his presentation of the philosophy of religion, and especially on his development of the consummate religion. It is as if, in these presentations, he wishes to reveal the whole dynamic of his thought.

In Part One of his philosophy of religion Hegel presented the development of the concept of religion in a more formal way. We could say "abstractly" presented if, with Hegel, we understand abstract to mean that which is not as yet made explicit. In Part Two the more abstract concept became determinate and more concrete as it, so to speak, ran the course of finite religions. It gained in reality through this course, or movement, of self-realization. At the end of this self-othering movement the concept regains its initial integrity with the painful transition, through Roman religion, to the consummate religion, which is for Hegel historically realized in and as Christianity.

But the abstract concept of religion regains its integrity in such a way that the moments of the concept have become real and concrete. For Hegel the concept itself was already the structure of truth, inclusive subjectivity. Now, on the level of religious consciousness which we identify as the consummate religion, the concept becomes properly the divine idea as the unity of divine and human. God is seen as a trinitarian movement of absolute or realized divine subjectivity.

Given our previously mentioned understanding of the general relationship between concept and idea in Hegel's thought, we can say that the consummate religion is consummate precisely in so far as it fulfills, or realizes, these moments of the concept in a concrete and determinate way. In fact, the consummate religion is these moments in their full concrete manifestation. For Hegel the consummate religion can be this true manifestation, or realization, of spirit because it recapitulates in itself the reality gained by the concept in and through its long progression as the movement of determinate religion. If we wish to understand Hegel we must of course keep in mind the consummate religion's doubled relationship to its "past," namely, with determinate religion and with the concept of religion. Indeed, for Hegel the consummate religion achieves its consummate status precisely because it sublates, in itself, that actuality which the concept of religion gained through the philosophical history of religions. Ultimately for Hegel there is one movement of absolute spirit.

Nevertheless, while keeping the relationship of the consummate religion to determinate religion in the back of our minds, we will, in the present chapter, concentrate more explicitly on the consummate religion in its relationship to the concept of religion. For the consummate religion is consummate precisely in relation to the moments of the concept of religion. We will look at Hegel's philosophy of the consummate religion in three steps: 1) a review of the third German and English volumes as a whole; 2) a resume of Hegel on the consummate religion; 3) reflections on further research opportunities opened by these volumes.

1. *An Overview of the Third Volume*

These German (V 5) and English (L 3) volumes complete the three volumes of Hegel's lectures on the philosophy of religion. They contain Hegel's four Berlin lecture presentations of Part Three of his philosophy of religion, namely, The Consummate Religion. The publication of these volumes on the consummate religion should go a long way toward dispelling any lingering doubts as to whether Hegel, the philosopher, took Christianity and certain of its basic doctrines seriously. But, whether one will ever finally convert those still burdened with such doubts or not, there can be no doubt about the import and influence of Hegel's philosophical interpretations of Christianity on subsequent Western thought – both religious and more secular. These major efforts by Hegel, while in Berlin, to develop a speculative, dialectical presentation of the consummate religion are now for the first time conveniently gathered, and appropriately arranged, so as to be readily accessible.[1]

These German and English volumes on the consummate religion follow the same format and editorial principles as did the previous volumes of Hegel's philosophy of religion. The German volume opens with a preliminary remark by the editor. It continues with the sequentially arranged and printed lecture materials on the consummate religion. These include Hegel's own 1821 lecture manuscript with his many insertions and expansions, edited lecture transcripts for the 1824 and 1827 lectures, material from the 1831 lecture series, a number of loose sheets of his preparatory sketchings for the 1821 manuscript, and a page of fragments from lecture transcripts by Michelet.[2] These lecture materials are followed by five helpful appendices: signs, symbols and abbreviations; endnotes; an index indicating the original locations of further special materials included from the two Friends Editions; an index of biblical citations; and, an index of persons. Particular attention should here, as with the previous two volumes, be drawn to the series of precise and detailed endnotes[3] which follow the admirable format of the previous volumes. In these notes the editor fills out Hegel's citations, identifies literary and philosophical allusions, makes cross references to other of Hegel's works and, most helpfully, searches out Hegel's at times vague, if not veiled, biblical references. It might also be good to recall that the four appendices to the three volumes of Hegel's philosophy of religion lectures as a whole are to be found in the German Volume Four b.

The English volume containing Part Three of Hegel's philosophy of religion lectures follows the general layout and order of the presentation of Hegel's manuscript and the lecture transcripts as they are found in the German volume. As with previous volumes in the English edition, editorial materials are again footnoted along with further Hegel materials. The Editorial Introduction contains an original analysis of the structure and development of the consummate religion in the various lecture series. It ends with a schematic "Comparative Analysis of the Structure of 'The Consummate Religion.'"

2. Hegel on the Consummate Religion

Comparative overviews of the additions and subtractions, shifts and developments in structure and "distribution of content" in Hegel's 1821, 1824, 1827, and 1831 Berlin lecture presentations of the consummate religion are now readily available.[4] These overviews confirm the impression we gain from a first reading of Hegel's own occasional outlines of his four presentations on the consummate religion. From these overviews we see that the presentation of the first sphere or element remains essentially the same but that there are important changes in the presentation of the second and third spheres or elements. Since these overviews are readily available, we can best work toward an understanding of Hegel's philosophy of the consummate religion if we simply follow our plan to concentrate more directly on Hegel's presentation of the consummate religion in relation to his presentation of the concept of religion. As we have already more generally stated, the consummate religion is meant by Hegel to be the fulfillment of the concept of religion. Indeed, the moments of the concept of religion form the object of Christian dogmatics.[5] Our approach is strongly suggested by Hegel's own overall structuring of the relationship between the consummate religion and the concept of religion. The new editions make it possible for us to follow that structuring. Again, we want to keep in mind what Hegel said concerning determinate religion.[6] Determinate religion is itself the dialectically structured progression of finite realizations of the moments of the concept of religion. It is the route through which, for Hegel, these moments come to be the object of religious consciousness in the Christian religion.

As end result or goal of the movement of spirit within the philosophy of religion, the consummate religion is for Hegel an advance in two ways. It is an advance, first of all, in relation to determinate religion, in that it includes, and takes up within itself, the actuality or the explicitation which has occurred in the movement of determinate religion. Second, it is an advance in the sense that its occurrence is equally an enriched return to the first moment of the philosophy of religion, namely, to the concept of religion.

At the beginning of our examination of Hegel's philosophy of the consummate religion it is important to recall that his overall understanding of religion remained consistent and, relatively speaking, constant throughout the years of the Berlin lectures.[7] He continued to see religion as the vehicle of truth for all people. Religion gave expression to the true content of the reconciliation of divine and human, of infinite and finite. But it expressed this true content still in the inadequate form of representational thinking (*Vorstellung*). Within this overall continuity in his understanding of religion, Hegel came, through the years, to express more clearly that religion was a movement of self-positing divine subjectivity. Though his general understanding of religion did indeed remain constant throughout the Berlin years, his various presentations of the concept of religion changed considerably from one lecture series to another. Furthermore, his presentation of the second and third spheres or elements of the tripartite consummate religion also went through some shifts in arrangement and distribution of theologoumena or theological content. Yet throughout the years, and throughout these changes, the consummate religion remained for Hegel the religion of absolute divine subjectivity and freedom. In view of such consistencies in overall understanding, and of such shifts in presentation of the concept of religion and of the consummate religion, it will be enlightening to examine what Hegel actually says about certain aspects of the relationship between the concept of religion and the consummate religion in two of his lecture series. We will look at his first development of the consummate religion, in 1821, in relation to the 1821 presentation of the concept of religion. Then we will turn to his later, 1827 version of the consummate religion in relation to the 1827 concept of religion. In this way we can arrive at a more nuanced understanding of what he intends when he speaks of religion and, more precisely, when he structures his philosophy of religion as a movement of inclusive divine subjectivity.

2.a. The 1821 Lectures

Since we have already, in Chapter Two above, followed at greater length Hegel's 1821 and 1827 presentations of the concept of religion, we can now proceed more quickly by rather briefly recalling the moments of the concept in the the 1821 lectures (and shortly below in the 1827 lectures).

In his various lecture series Hegel presents the moments or determinations of the concept of religion as momentary totalities. In the 1821 lectures he at least initially formulates the relationship among these moments more dyadically in terms of objectivity and subjectivity. In the first subsection of his manuscript discussion of the concept of religion,[8] he provides an overall description of religion as the unity of two moments. Religion is the unity of the object, or God, and the finite subject who is conscious of that object.[9] He immediately labels these two moments the objective and subjective sides of religion.[10] He insists "that the subjective aspect is an essential moment [of religion]"[11] and, by implication, of God. By means of this observation Hegel introduces cultus (*Kultus*), or the subjective side to religion, as essential to the concept of religion.[12] Then he quickly rounds out his discussion of cultus, and widens his focus, with a more triadic structuring of three moments to the concept. He sketches a triply subdivided movement: first, the determination of absolute unity;[13] second, the moment of separation and of difference, in which God is the absolute positive over against which the world is seen as the negative of God and thus as evil or wickedness;[14] third, the subjective moment come to be moment of the object, the infinity of self-consciousness. Hegel calls this third moment a spiritual self-consciousness as, we would say, the experience of having been taken up out of time.[15]

In the second subsection of The Concept of Religion[16] Hegel sketches a sort of second stage of, or a more speculative reflection on, the concept of religion. He first recalls the constitutive characteristic of speculative philosophy as the grasping of everything as idea. In speculative philosophy truth is the discernment of the unity of opposed and, thus, abstract determinations.[17] He then turns to religion,[18] which he describes as the standpoint of absolutely self-determining truth. He immediately speaks of God as this unity which contains within itself limit and difference, with difference contained precisely as difference. Hegel brings together[19] what he has said so far by insisting that it is this speculative element of self-positing resultant unity which comes to consciousness in religion. Then he further observes that religion itself is this speculative movement, but in the concrete forms of representation: "God and community, the cultus, absolute objectivity and absolute subjectivity."[20] He ends this speculative summary analysis with the words: "Here the concept of religion [is] initially more abstract. Its two moments, the moments making up the antithesis [to which we have referred, are] (a) absolute universality, pure thinking, and (b) absolute singularity, sensibility."[21] He goes on in the rest of the second subsection to develop the speculative relationship between these two moments.

Hegel prolongs these presentations of the moments of the concept of religion with a consideration of the inner necessity of the structure and dynamic of the concept of religion. He considers, more particularly, the elevating move which constitutes the essence of religion, namely, the move from finite to infinite.[22]

In turning now from our summary of the 1821 manuscript presentation of the concept of religion to the manuscript development of the consummate religion, we are immediately struck by the greater ease with which Hegel proceeds and with which the text on the consummate religion reads. This must surely be due to the fact that, whereas in 1821 he was for the first time working out in detail his philosophical concept of religion,[23] he had previously, and at some length, spelled out a philosophical reading of what he here calls the consummate religion. In the 1807 *Phenomenology*[24] he presented it as the revelatory religion, and in the 1817 *Encyclopedia*[25] as the revealed religion.

In the first paragraph[26] of his introductory remarks to the presentation of the consummate religion, Hegel makes reference back to the end of the general Introduction to the 1821 manuscript where he had spoken of the relationship between the moments of the concept of religion and those of the consummate religion.[27] He again insists that, in the consummate religion, the moments of the concept have themselves become the explicit object of religious consciousness in representational form. The concept of religion has become objective to itself. In a way itself revelatory of his own approach to the notion of time, Hegel alludes to the biblical idea of the fullness of time. He speaks of the appearance of Christianity as the fulfillment of religion,[28] the consummation of the concept of religion. The consummate religion is, then, for Hegel that newness to which we give expression when we speak of the idea as the unity of concept and reality. Here, on the level of religion, it is the movement of the absolute or divine idea (die absolute Idee, die göttliche Idee). So for Hegel it is in the Christian religion that God, who is known as absolute idea, is known as spirit. It is the idea of spirit to be the unity of divine and human, to be absolute spirit.[29]

Without intending artificially to impose the previously sketched moments of the concept upon Hegel's manuscript presentation of the consummate religion,[30] we can use the resumes, made here and earlier in Chapter Two above, of those moments as points of reference while we explore Hegel's presentation of the consummate religion. These resumes will help us see ways in which Hegel in fact elaborates the consummate religion as the religion of spirit.[31] They will help us understand how he works out the final formulation of the concept of God as the unity of divine and human, thus, as absolute spirit.[32]

This brief journey with Hegel, either here in the reading of the 1821 manuscript on the consummate religion or again in the following review of the 1827 lecture transcripts, is not meant to be an exhaustive survey of his thought on the consummate religion. In Part Three of this study we will follow at greater length his development of several themes in his presentation of the consummate religion. Presently we are more interested in illustrating just where he is going.

Here in Part Three of the 1821 lectures Hegel keeps to the same procedure he had followed in presenting the determinate religions. First he treats the consummate religion in terms of the abstract concept of God, then in concrete representation or the ways in which God is known, and, finally, in the practical relationship of cultus. Hegel introduces the ontological proof for the existence of God in his discussion of the abstract concept of God which he presents as appropriate to the consummate religion. Throughout the Berlin lectures on the philosophy of religion he will consistently link this proof, and the concern manifested in its elaboration for the relationship between the concept and the being of God, with the consummate religion and that religion's historical realization in Christianity. At the end of his introductory remarks to the three spheres of concrete representation,[33] Hegel gives a brief but handy overview of where he intends to go with these three spheres. He reads these as moments of the realization of the concept itself. Here he apparently means the concept of the consummate religion and, indirectly then, the concept of religion itself. In discussing these moments, it is as if Hegel, who had so clearly and so exhaustively presented the three moments of the concept in the *Science of Logic* as universality, particularity, and individuality,[34] cannot refrain from speaking of the determinations of the concept of the consummate religion without referring to them. Seemingly he cannot do less than at least to affirm a structural parallel between the three moments of the concept in the *Logic* and the three elements of "concrete representation" as moments of the concept of the consummate religion.[35]

Hegel labels the first of these spheres of concrete representation the concept in the element of universality.[36] This first sphere is the one in which God is present to religious consciousness in the form of the divine idea as self-thinking thought and Trinity.[37] The essentials of what Hegel has to say concerning this first sphere can be found in the first page and a half or so of his presentation.[38] Here he announces, with a flourish, that God is spirit, trinitarian, subjectivity, pure act, infinite differentiation which remains however within the eternal concept of absolute subjectivity, love.[39] "God is spirit, the One as infinite subjectivity."[40]

Hegel had long before made the methodological observation that the second moment in any dialectical movement was the hardest to think through.[41] In his preliminary overview[42] of the second sphere of concrete representation, he explicitly brings up the objective and subjective sides to the consummate religion: "To be the concept entails a determination of subjectivity by the absolute idea both from our point of view and equally within itself."[43] Here he proposes to treat of the religious representational understanding of God as creator and preserver, of the appearance of God in nature. In this brief section[44] he presents the world as other of God and yet as the presence of the divine idea in the immediacy of nature. The appearance of the world is interpreted as a moment of divine diremption expressed logically in terms of judgement of differentiation.[45]

In the preliminary overview[46] of the third sphere of concrete representation, Hegel writes simply and directly of the objectivity of finite spirit and the appearance of God to finite spirit. He speaks of the history of redemption and reconciliation. He makes the summary remark: "The subjective side of this history, as [it takes place] in finite spirit, in the individual, takes the form of the cultus."[47] But when he tries to work out this third sphere, he seems to loose control of the situation. In this long section,[48] which presents the incarnation of God as well as the questions of Christ's teaching, death, resurrection, and ascension, Hegel ends up with the observation that reconciliation has so far occurred only in the form of one individual. It has so far taken place only in the form of an exclusive individuality, which must also be individuality for others. The divine idea, so present, must become actual for the many others who comprise the community.[49] It is at this point that his elaboration of the consummate religion breaks the bounds or framework indicated in his earlier sketchings. It is as if he is unable to keep cultus, as integrating final moment, within the third sphere of concrete representation where reconciliation is to be made actual for the community.

Hegel goes on, then, in what he terms the sphere of infinite love and the kingdom of spirit, namely, the realm in which absolute freedom is to be known,[50] to present the triply staged development of the community from its origin, through its being, to its passing away.[51] Just before elaborating this triply staged development of the community he summarizes what he has done. First he had treated of the pure concept of God in the Christian religion (the abstract concept). Then he had laid out the concrete representation of this concept as three spheres, which he identified respectively as thought, representation, and actuality.[52] With this reference to the actuality of reconciliation Hegel would at first seem to be referring to the third of the spheres of concrete representation. In fact, however, he identifies this actuality, understood as the subjective realization of reconciliation, with the final major section on cultus. And so cultus follows as third section in the outer triad: the abstract concept, concrete representation as such, and cultus.[53] For it is here in cultus that the divine idea, the unity of divine and human, becomes actual for the individual members of the community. Already in regard to the first of the spheres under concrete representation Hegel had described God as spirit and infinite subjectivity.[54] Now he writes, "Spirit is the infinite return into itself, infinite subjectivity, not represented but actual divinity, the *presence* of God . . . The Spirit is . . . what is subjectively present and actual, . . . God dwelling in God's community."[55]

If we now look back over Hegel's 1821 manuscript presentation of the consummate religion in relation to the previously described moments of the concept of religion, we see clearly that Hegel has continued to work with the same overall view of religion. He saw religion as consisting of two sides, namely, the objective and the subjective. And he continued to stress the elevation of the subjective side to the objective side. This initially more dyadically structured formulation of religion, along with its more speculative interpretation in terms of unity, posited difference, and return, is made the object of religious consciousness. This becoming the object of religious consciousness takes place in terms of, and as, the objectivity of God. It occurs first as Trinity, then in the immediacy of nature and the divine-human unity of the Incarnation, and, finally, in the community which consists of those who actually enjoy the presence of God. As he did in the earliest presentation of the moments of the concept of religion, so too here, with regard to the consummate religion, he works back and forth with the notions of subjective and objective. The more speculatively expressed moments of the concept of religion are given a certain priority and prominence in so far as they structure the presentation of the consummate religion. These moments have become the object of religious consciousness. But, with his reference to the three forms of presence of God to religious consciousness, namely, to God present in thought, representation, and actuality, Hegel has equally, and perhaps more subtly, slowly shifted the emphasis from the objective side to the subjective side. He has made this shift in such a way that, by the moment of cultus, the objectivity of God becomes God subjectively present in the religious consciousness of the community. Thus God is present in self-consciousness.

Hegel's introductory remarks, made before the presentation of the abstract concept of the consummate religion,[56] can serve to summarize his 1821 view of the consummate religion. If we work backwards through these remarks we can see more clearly what Hegel is up to with his presentation of the consummate religion. He ends these remarks with the affirmation that the consummate religion is the religion of freedom[57] because it is the way to being in and for itself. Freedom is, for Hegel, expressible in the succinct phrase, "being at home with oneself in the other."[58] The consummate religion is the religion of freedom because it is the religion of reconciliation between divine and human.[59] Though the cleavage between divine and human has received its fullest expression in the Christian religion, the cleft has for Hegel equally been overcome. One is at home in the other. The consummate religion is this religion of reconciliation because it is the religion of truth.[60] God has truly appeared and is truly known as spirit, and this because the consummate religion is the religion of revelation. God reveals, and is revealed, as God really is.[61] Finally, what underlies all these affirmations concerning the consummate religion as religion of freedom, reconciliation, truth, and revelation is Hegel's vision of true subjectivity.[62] Hegel warns against any interpretation of religion as mere subjectivity, that is, as only the subjective side of the finite subject over against an equally abstract God conceived independently of, and as not including, the world. "God's consciousness and subjectivity – the genuine object – is the whole."[63] From the perspective of our reading of Hegel on the consummate religion in the 1821 manuscript, we can see him wrapping up his view on the consummate religion when he writes, "God *is* a process, [God is] self-consciousness, [God is] as an object, as truth."[64] According to the 1821 manuscript the philosophy of religion, and in particular the philosophy of the consummate religion, is a movement of infinite, namely, inclusive and, therefore, here absolute, divine self-positing subjectivity.

2.b. The 1827 Lectures

In view of our previous longer summary of Hegel's 1827 development of the concept of religion we can move forward by more briefly recalling the moments of the 1827 concept of religion. Then we will focus on how they become the explicit object of religious consciousness in the 1827 presentation of the consummate religion.

Moreso than in 1821, Hegel has managed to develop these 1827 philosophy of religion lectures much more in line with his preferred essentially immanent and consistent presentation of a self-positing movement of spirit. In these 1827 lectures he works out a truly speculative interpretation of religion. From beginning to end of these lectures the philosophy of religion is a movement of self-positing inclusive divine subjectivity. It is the speculative development of the concept of God as spirit.

We can recall the three moments of the concept of religion, as they are presented in the 1827 lectures, by means of a brief reference to Hegel's sketch of these three moments as the outline of Part One of the philosophy of religion, namely, The Concept of Religion.[65] The basic determination of this Part One is that of universality, with particularity still only implicitly present. Within, and as the initial moment of, the concept of religion Hegel further identifies an initial or substantial unity, namely, the first moment of the idea.[66] The second sketched moment of the concept of religion,[67] the second to this first universal and by implication at least therefore now the particular, is relationship or the going apart of this substantial unity. Here spirit realizes itself in the realm of distinction characteristic of subjective consciousness. Hegel foresees treating this relationship in terms of feeling, representation, and understanding (*verständiges Denken*). This second moment of the concept of religion is, therefore, the relationship of the feeling, representing, and thinking subject to God. Again here according to the Introduction, the third moment of the concept of religion is cultus. At least by implication, it is the moment of individuality.[68] It is the sublation of the separation of the subject from God by means of the elevation of the subject to God. It is the awareness that God is present in the heart of the subject.

In Hegel's 1827 elaboration of the moments of the concept, so much of what formerly seemed extraneous now finds its place within the presentation of the appropriate moment of the concept. In the presentation of the first moment, namely, the concept of God,[69] Hegel shows a primary preoccupation with establishing the fact that what he had referred to in the Introduction as a "substantial unity" is really a "spiritual unity."[70] That with which the philosophy of religion begins is indeed the concept of God. It is the concept of God as absolute substance, the universal and immediate, or first, which is thought and which is available to more abstract thought. But this substance is equally *an sich* subject and spirit. It is that which is to develop otherness out of itself. This first spiritual unity or divine universality others itself in judgement. This self-othering is, of course, a movement of progression and explicitation. It does not in any way presuppose a pre-existent and wholly developed initial self. This self-othering movement constitutes the second moment of the concept of religion, the knowing of God.[71]

This second moment is, then, that of consciousness in which God is known variously through immediate knowing, feeling, representation, and thought. Faith is an immediate knowing, the certainty that God is and that God is the object of consciousness. This certainty is an initial or undivided unity.[72] Feeling expresses the subjective side or the experience of having God as object of consciousness.[73] Representation, in turn, concerns the objective side, the content of this certitude. In religion, God is present to human beings in this representational form as object of consciousness.[74] Then Hegel speaks of the knowing (*Wissen*) of this object, or representation, as the movement of concrete thinking and mediated knowing.[75] Here he treats of the cosmological, teleological, and ontological proofs for the existence of God within his presentation of religious knowing as an elevation to God.[76]

Hegel proceeds to the third moment of the concept of religion, namely, to cultus, by means of a reference back to the second moment, the knowing of God. He now describes this overall second moment as a theoretical relationship in which attention concentrates on the object known, namely, on God, and not on the subject as the one knowing God. But the truth is the fact that there is here question of a relationship between subject and object.[77] By means of this recall of such a relationship Hegel moves into the presentation of cultus as the practical relationship between subject and God. He identifies this relationship as one of will. Cultus, then, can be seen as a form of self-consciousness,[78] since it is in the action of cultus that we know ourselves as enjoying God's presence, "joining myself as myself in God together with myself."[79] Hegel goes on to sketch the forms of cultus as such.[80] First, there is the innerness of devotion. Then cultus in external forms, such as sacraments and sacrifice. The negation of self, which had in fact already occurred in theoretical knowledge, now occurs in devotion and, consciously, in sacrifice because the subject is concerned primarily with itself. By sacrifice we come to the consciousness and enjoyment of being in unity with God. The third, highest form of cultus is that moment of the negation of our specific subjectivity in which there is a renunciation of our innermost in repentance and remorse. Hegel then makes a quick transition to ethical life as the most genuine cultus. And he indicates that the final move to philosophy is a continual cultus. So for Hegel cultus is a movement, still in representational form, of spirit in and through finite subjects. His presentation of cultus is rather fascinating. It is a movement from inner experience to external forms as the negation of that finite subjectivity, on to the realization of the religious reconciliation of divine and human in ethical life and, finally, in philosophical thought.

We can list the three moments of the concept of religion in the 1827 lectures as the metaphysical concept of God, the appearance of divinity in theoretical knowledge, and cultus or the practical knowledge of God. Hegel had begun the 1827 lectures with the concept of God as a spiritual unity. Then he followed these three moments as they appeared, and were realized differently, in each finite religion throughout the long route of determinate religion. Now in the consummate religion he returns explicitly to these moments of the concept of religion in so far as they have become the object of religious consciousness. They are now the moments of the concept of the consummate religion.[81] Though Hegel's position is more clearly stated here, it remains essentially the same as the one he had already taken in the 1821 manuscript.

The relationship between the moments of the concept of religion and their objectification as moments of the concept of the consummate religion is clear and consistent, even in formulation, in the 1827 lectures. The relationship is so evident that, for present purposes, we can presuppose, and profit from, much of what we have already said concerning the moments of the concept of religion. With regard to the moments of the consummate religion, it will be sufficient for us to draw more briefly, and primarily, upon Hegel's preliminary outline and overview of the three elements of the consummate religion.[82] We will make some additional reference to the actual presentation of these elements and to Hegel's introductory remarks, which, in the 1827 transcript, are to be found immediately preceding Hegel's preliminary outline. When we highlight Hegel's presentation of the consummation of the moments of the concept of religion in, and as, the object of religious consciousness in the consummate religion, it is of cardinal importance that we note his early introductory remark that the consummate religion is idea.[83] When he says this he is thinking of the absolute idea as the unity of concept and reality. So he means that the consummate religion is idea in so far as it is the unity of the concept of religion and of that reality which has been gained by the concept through the long route of determinate religion. The concept as idea is that which is true. It is absolute spirit.[84] The consummate religion, in turn, is true religion and is the religion of spirit.

Hegel uses this understanding of idea, and more specifically his understanding of God as absolute divine idea,[85] to ground his twice sketched outline or division of the three elements of the consummate religion.[86] In the first of these two sketchings,[87] he speaks of what he had, in the 1821 lectures, identified as the objective and subjective sides to the concept of religion. He had also indicated that these were the objective and subjective sides to the fulfillment of the concept of religion in the consummate religion. But now he is recorded as speaking, in more speculatively integrated fashion, of "the three ways by which the subject is related to God, the three modes of God's determinate being for subjective spirit."[88]

After this first outline, which is presented in more external fashion,[89] Hegel in a sense appeals to experience, or to a phenomenological reading of experience. He says that we as finite spirit know there is a first or thinking moment without cleavage, then a moment of division or cleavage and, third, the moment of feeling or subjectivity, namely, the moment of return to self.[90] He identifies these three moments, respectively, as those of universality, particularity, and individuality.[91] However, he asserts that, since these are not had in an external way, they are the differentiation made by the absolute, eternal idea itself in the three moments of the consummate religion. He then continues to present the three elements of the second, briefer and more speculatively integrated outline of the consummate religion.[92]

The first element in this more speculatively integrated outline is the eternal idea. This eternal idea is God before the creation of the world[93] and as present to thought.[94] What Hegel had in the overall Introduction to the 1827 lectures called a substantial unity,[95] and then in The Concept of Religion a spiritual unity[96] has now become the explicit object of religious consciousness as Trinity in the consummate religion. This unity is now the movement of divine self-othering and return. It is a movement which remains self-enclosed. The movement is one of spirit, a movement from the universal through judgement to the other as the particular or difference. It continues, as movement, then, to the realization that the two are the same. The movement of thought arrives at an affirmation of identity. Each of these three moments is, in its own way, the totality of the universal idea. Expressed in terms of sensibility, this movement is that of the Holy Spirit, a movement of eternal love.[97]

The second element, that of diremption and reconciliation, is the moment of separation come to be the explicit object of religious consciousness. Hegel had, in the Introduction, referred to the going apart of the initial substantial unity[98] and, in The Concept of Religion, to the real moment of religion, namely, to the theoretical relationship of the knowledge of God.[99] Here in The Consummate Religion this "going apart" and this theoretical relationship become, through judgement, the diremption of the trinitarian concept of God into a variety of religious representations. These representations, which give expression to the contradiction of being separated from God, are: a created world and natural humanity; the fall; evil. But as element of knowledge of God, and thus as elevation to God, this theoretical relationship equally finds religious representational expression in objective reconciliation between human and divine. This objective reconciliation is religiously represented as the idea of reconciliation immediately and sensibly present in the historical Christ. It finds expression in the unity of divine and human, in the death of Christ, and in the resurrection of Christ, with the resurrection seen as a transition from sensible to spiritual presence.[100]

So, in the second element of the consummate religion the focus was on the sensibly present eternal idea. In the third element of the consummate religion the focus is on the finite subject within the spiritual community. The third moment of the concept of religion, namely, cultus or the presence and enjoyment of God as self-consciousness, comes to be the object of religious consciousness in the consummate religion as the divine idea. It is the unity of divine and human now actualized in subjectivity.[101] This third moment of the consummate religion is equivalent to what Hegel had effectively called self-consciousness in The Concept of Religion.[102] His centering on the finite subject as locus of the actualization of reconciliation is all the more fitting in this 1827 presentation of the third element of the consummate religion. It is fitting since, from the beginning of this lecture series, Hegel has so clearly identified the concept of God and the concept of religion. Appropriately, then, for Hegel, "thus the community itself is the existing Spirit, the Spirit in its existence [*Existenz*], God existing as community."[103] After again recalling both that the first moment is the idea in its simple universality and that the second moment is the idea as particular,[104] Hegel is recorded as saying: "The third element, then, is this consciousness - God as the Spirit. This Spirit as existing and realizing itself is the community."[105]

This realization of God as spirit in and through the community of finite subjects occurs according to a triply developed movement of the origin of the community, the subsistence of the community, and the realization of the spirituality of the community. For present purposes it is not necessary to lay out in detail the steps Hegel elaborates in this tightly presented development of the spiritual community.[106] However, what is of particular interest and import is his reference, once again, to the notion of unity. To underscore the continuity in Hegel's 1827 lectures, we can perhaps be permitted to repeat that Hegel had, in the overall 1827 Introduction, described the initial unity as a substantial unity, and then, in The Concept of Religion, spoken of a spiritual unity. This spiritual unity came to be the explicit object of religious consciousness first as Trinity and, from the point of view of his system and of his speculative presentation, consequently as sensible presence of the identity of divine and human, namely, of the eternal idea in a finite human subject. This *an sich* unity or reconciliation of divine and human becomes itself the object of consciousness in the subjectivity of the spiritual community of finite subjects. It is their explicit and reflexive participation in, and enjoyment of, the divine, which they have discovered within their hearts. "The third aspect is the relationship of the subject to this truth, the fact that the subject, to the extent that it is related to this truth, arrives precisely at this conscious unity, deems itself worthy of this known unity, brings this unity forth within itself, and is fulfilled by the divine Spirit."[107] In the 1827 lectures Hegel has finally come to elaborate, in rigorous though very brief fashion, the further realization of this spiritual community in two directions. He speaks of this further realization, first, in rightly ordered ethical living.[108] Second, he notes this realization in and as the transition from religion to philosophy. He says that the still representationally realized reconciliation of divine and human in the community develops into the final moment of self-mediation as the identification of concept and self in philosophical thought.[109] For Hegel, the original spiritual unity that was the initial concept of God in The Concept of Religion has come to full explicitation. It has become the object of religious consciousness in three ways: in the spiritual community, in its real and ideal actualizations in ethical living, and in philosophy. The concept of religion has become objective to itself in a series of religious representations. Through these representations it goes beyond itself.

These unities, which Hegel has elaborated from the beginning of the concept of religion on through to the third moment of the consummate religion, are all, in their own ways, momentary totalities. Hegel intends each of these unities to be the realization, implicitly or explicitly, of the dialectical movement of self-positing and self-developing subjectivity. It is this same dialectical movement of subjectivity that he had so much earlier elaborated as self-relationality and the structure of freedom in the rarefied atmosphere of the *Science of Logic*. In the *Logic* he had spoken of what we would call inclusive subjectivity (*übergreifende Subjektivität*).[110] Here in the 1827 lectures on the philosophy of religion he appropriately speaks of absolute, infinite subjectivity (*die absolute unendliche Subjektivität*),[111] since the philosophy of religion is the self-positing movement of the concept of religion. In this self-positing movement, concept and reality are united in an inclusive moment of unity. This is the unity or identity to which we refer when we speak of the consummate religion as the variously manifest absolute, eternal, and divine idea. The consummate religion is movement of spirit as absolute spirit. Both in the *Logic* and in these 1827 lectures the structure of true subjectivity remains that of inclusive self-relationality. The difference lies for Hegel in what is included, and hence in the result.

3. Further Research Opportunities

The publication of these editions of Hegel's Berlin lectures on the philosophy of religion, and in particular the publication of Part

Three or The Consummate Religion, has made it possible for us to
study more closely, and more accurately, exactly what Hegel was up
to in his philosophical presentation of religion. We can appreciate
much more his immense efforts to elaborate his philosophy of religion, and especially his notion of the consummate religion, as a
movement of self-positing divine subjectivity. He has indeed carved
out a unique position among those attempting a philosophical reading of religion. But he has equally left posterity with enough questions, both philosophically fundamental and Hegel-specific, to
demand serious study and reflexion for generations to come. In fact
many of the questions he raises are so basic that the philosophical
mind must, in one way or another, ever return to them.

We can group some of the more Hegel-specific questions according to the three spheres, or elements, constituting the consummate
religion. First of all, there is the concrete representation of God
appropriate to Christianity interpreted as the consummate religion.
With regard to this representation it has often enough been asserted
that Hegel's God is not self-conscious until the moment of self-
consciousness in and as the spiritual community.[112] Now that the
various lecture series are available, it would be of great value to take
another look at this view. It may be that Hegel has given further
nuance to his own presentation, especially in the lectures from 1824
on. It might, with such a second look, become clearer that, with regard
to the question of divine self-consciousness, we need to continue to
qualify the view that Hegel allows for divine self-consciousness only
in the moment of the spiritual community. It may be necessary to take
more adequately into consideration the complexity involved in
Hegel's assertions concerning the first sphere of the consummate
religion. Hegel spoke of this sphere, namely, the one in which God is
presented in terms of Trinity, as object of thought. Though here God is
object of thought, the sphere as a whole is, in its presentation, equally
prior to the establishment of the distinction which is constitutive of
religious consciousness. It is prior to this distinction at least in the
sense that such distinction or difference is understood to be structured in the second sphere. This first sphere is not yet properly the
sphere of representation. Perhaps more concentrated reflection on the
fundamental notion of subjectivity as characteristic of this first divine
sphere will provide help in coming to scholarly agreement as to what

structural elements of self-consciousness it would, from a Hegelian perspective, make sense to affirm of the first sphere.

Closely related to this question of the way in which divine subjectivity is verified in the first sphere is the ongoing reflection on whether Hegel has in fact established a triunity (*Dreieinigkeit*) or a diunity (*Zweieinigkeit*). Hegel himself, of course, spoke unabashedly of Trinity as *Dreieinigkeit*, which seems to have been the term current in his day for Trinity. There are a number of factors involved in this discussion, such as, for example, the fear (perhaps unfounded) that use of the term *Zweieinigkeit* would fail to stress sufficiently the newness of the third moment arising in any Hegelian dialectical movement of self-positing subjectivity. Further reflection and discussion might, on the one hand and in one sense, reveal this to be more of a question of terminology than substance. But, on the other hand, the problematic concerning a triunity or a diunity in Hegel's presentation of God at least opens the door to serious discussion of the nature of Hegel's dialectic. What we can assert for sure concerning Hegel's interpretation of "immanent" Trinity is that each of the three moments is meant to be a momentary totality with the third as inclusive, enriched advance as return to the first moment.[113]

Reference to the second sphere or element of the consummate religion is made somewhat more complex by the way Hegel has structured his various lectures on the consummate religion. With regard to the 1821 manuscript we need, here for practical reasons, to refer both to the moment of diremption and to the third concrete sphere, namely, to that of initial reconciliation. In speaking of the later lectures we can refer more directly to the doubled second moment of diremption and initial reconciliation. This very need to speak in more complex fashion of the second moment of the consummate religion points out the importance of further reflection on why, and how, Hegel came to structure his presentations of Christology and initial reconciliation so differently. There must have been many factors influencing his different presentations. Are there perhaps underlying logical considerations which played a role in these shifts?

With regard to the second element of the consummate religion there are further research opportunities which come quickly to mind. First of all, it would be of interest to study Hegel's working with biblical texts.[114] Second, there remains his more general attempt to give a philosophical reading of Christology. Recently Walter Jaeschke has proposed a most ingenious solution to the Christological question, which had split the Hegelian school into right and left wings shortly after Hegel's death. We cannot do justice here to Jaeschke's carefully laid out and argued proposal.[115] However, we can at least indicate that he proposes to resolve the overall question of the relationship between philosophical thought and history with specific reference to the "isness" of reconciliation between divine and human in the historical person of Christ. He does this in two steps. In the first step, he asserts that it is philosophy's task to reflect on, but not as such to argue from, the existence of the individual pointed to by the believing community. In the second step, he uses an analogy between Hegel's particular "Lutheran" understanding of the Eucharistic bread and the spiritual community's relationship to the God-man. Jaeschke writes of the parallel between the divine's being present only in the Eucharistic bread's consumption and the spiritual community's philosophically interpreted assertion of reconciliation's having occurred in the God-man. In this way Jaeschke attempts to overcome the dichotomizing argumentation as to whether it is the historical fact of reconciliation in Christ which grounds the faith of the community or whether it is the faith of the community which grounds the assertion of reconciliation in Christ. This proposal, taken up for consideration in conjunction with the very helpful comparative Christological study by Peter C. Hodgson,[116] opens up a whole host of questions concerning Hegel's, and even the more general, philosophical interpretation of Christology. There remains much to be studied with regard to the ways in which Hegel presents Christ as other to the spiritual community.

If we turn to the sphere of cultus, the third element of the consummate religion from 1824 on, we find openings toward a number of research questions. Perhaps of particular interest is the varying relationship Hegel sees between reconciliation in the Christian religion and that reconciliation's realization in worldly reality. His reflections on the relationship between religion and ethical living provide not only food for historical study, but points of reference and comparison for contemporary reflection on the social character of being human. One more specific form this particular research question might take is the relationship, for Hegel, between the kingdom of God and the state. Again, from a more theological perspective, his interpretations of spiritual community, cultus, church, doctrine, grace, and the kingdom of God all form an interesting background to contemporary efforts to integrate previously more separately treated theological questions. Further research, particularly on the basis of these German and English volumes on the consummate religion, should help us understand various forms of twentieth-century philosophical and theological indebtedness to Hegel.

While remaining with more Hegel-specific questions, we can widen somewhat the scope of our concern to include reference to Hegel's more general interpretation of the Christian religion as the consummate religion. We could, first of all, underscore his apparent ease at using varied logical thought determinations to describe the development of the consummate religion. Hegel speaks quite freely of a movement from universality through particularity to individuality. He equally thinks in terms of concept, judgement, and syllogism. This, at least at first sight, rather loose usage of such logical thought determinations seems to cause some consternation. Perhaps light can be shed on this problem, and future research encouraged, by reference to Hegel's way of proceeding in the *Science of Logic*. There Hegel carefully presents and places each logical thought determination. Technically speaking, he is not to use it in argumentation until that thought determination has been presented within the overall self-positing movement of logical thought. But once the determination has been presented he can, on the basis of its continuing but sublated presence, use it in his argumentation toward the appearance of, logically speaking, later thought determinations. In fact, in Hegel's *Logic* presentation is argumentation. Perhaps we can expand this general understanding of Hegel's approach in the *Logic* to an interpretation of his procedure in the encyclopedic system as a whole. From the point of view of his overall encyclopedic system, in the philosophy of religion Hegel is elaborating the penultimate moment of absolute spirit. It is, then, as if he feels himself at least to some extent free to work with various combinations of previously presented logical and philosophical thought determinations as he develops his philosophy of religion.

Among these wider, yet still Hegel-specific, questions there remains the question of the relative value of Hegel's various presentations of the consummate religion. Among these we could list his overall outline and approach as intended, and then somewhat differently carried out, in the 1821 presentation of the consummate religion. Then there is the more straightforwardly trinitarian or triadic structure in the lectures from 1824 on. It would be interesting to explore further what are the strengths, weaknesses, and significance of each of these two "alternative" developments of the consummate religion. Do they each reflect aspects of Hegel's overall dialectical method? Is one form to be preferred to another, depending on the perspective from which the evaluation is made? And again, from a more historical point of view, it would be of interest to follow up on the suggestion that the appearance of Philipp Marheineke's theological studies in 1819 and 1827 might have influenced Hegel toward a more explicitly trinitarian structure for the consummate religion.[116]

These new editions of Hegel's Berlin lectures on the philosophy of religion, and these volumes on the consummate religion in particular, open out to such questions as those of Hegel's use, and even the more general employment of, temporal and spatial images to express mediation. Questions also arise concerning the relationship between reason and history, and concerning such more recently much discussed notions as those of totality, identity, difference and otherness. Such questions and concerns have reemerged in twentieth-century thought and can only profit from being taken up again, even if in much humbler ways, in relation to Hegel's towering contributions.

Finally, Hegel's pointing to Christianity as the historical realization of the consummate religion often seems suspect to the contemporary more pluralist mindset. Hegel has been variously accused of merely presupposing Christianity's, or at least his philosophically interpreted Christianity's, overall superior status vis-à-vis the other religions of the world. He has also been accused of merely presupposing its consummate significance in relation to the concept of religion. Especially in the 1827 lectures the parallel between the moments of the concept of religion and those of the consummate religion is so great that some will suggest he simply read Christianity back into the concept of religion. In his defense we must immediately underscore that he does consistently give reasons, anchored in his own philosophical system, for each of his remarks on Christianity. Furthermore, again at least partially in his philosophical defense, even with regard to Christianity Hegel reads its basic dogmas and themes in line with his own underlying philosophical understandings of subjectivity and freedom. Perhaps if Hegel should be accused of anything, it should be less that he presupposed Christianity's consummate position, and more that he worked with a fundamental philosophical understanding of reality which underlies all else he does, including his presentations of the concept of religion and of the consummate religion. If Hegel is to be accused of anything, perhaps he should be accused of having decided to work with an underlying, we might even say "western," approach to history and, more fundamentally, to the relationship between identity and difference.[118] It is to this question of identity that we now turn in the first of our explorations in the following Part Three of our ongoing effort to understand Hegel's philosophy of religion.

NOTES

[1] As was mentioned in Ch. 1 above, a study edition had previously made Hegel's lectures on the consummate religion available in English translation: G. W. F. Hegel, *The Christian Religion: Lectures on the Philosophy of Religion, Part III: The Revelatory, Consummate, Absolute Religion*, ed. and trans. by Peter C. Hodgson (Missoula, Mont.: Scholars Press, 1979).

[2] The 1821 lecture manuscript, V 5:1-97; 1824 transcripts, V 5:99-176; 1827 lectures, V 5:177-270; 1831 lectures, V 5:271-289; loose sheets, V 5:291-303; Michelet, V 5:305.

[3] V 5:311-365.

[4] See the excellent survey by Hodgson, in L 3:9-57, with the schematic overview on pp. 54-55 as well as in L 4:493, 500-501, and on the 1827 lectures, in L 4:59-71; also Jaeschke, *Die Religionsphilosophie Hegels* 93-97; and the discussion in Jaeschke, *Die Vernunft in der Religion* esp. 303-308.

[5] This wording follows that of Jaeschke, *Die Vernunft in der Religion* 297. Note also Hodgson, in L 1:110 editorial n. 71.

[6] See Ch. 3 above.

[7]Hodgson, in L 1:59.

[8] See esp. V 3:95.8-105.197.

[9] V 3:95.12-15.

[10] V 3:95.24.

[11] "daß *die subjektive Seite wesentliches Moment* ist" V 3:97.62-63/ L 1:188.

[12] V 3:98.86-99.88.

[13] V3:102.160-103.178.

[14] V 3:104.179-186.

[15] V 3:104.187-105.195.

[16] V 3:113.399-115.447, but on religion itself esp. 114.419-115.447. See L 1:204 n. 57 and 207 n. 61.

[17] V 3:113.399-114.418.

[18] V 3:114.419-115.430.

[19] V 3:115.431-438.

[20] "Gott und Gemeinde, Kultus; absolute Objektivität und absolute Subjektivität." V 3:115.441-443, and see lines 439-443/L 1:207.

[21] "Hier *Begriff* der Religion zunächst abstrakter – Die zwei Momente in ihrem Begriff – des Gegensatzes a) absolute Allgemeinheit – reines Denken b) absolute Einzelheit – Empfindung." V 3:115.444-447/L 1:207.

[22] See esp. V 3:130.768-142.974.

[23] Jaeschke, *Die Vernunft in der Religion* 230.

[24] GW 9:400.1-421.18/PS 453-478.

[25] G. W. F. Hegel, *Sämtliche Werke, Jubiläumsausgabe in zwanzig Bänden*, ed. Hermann Glockner, vol. 6: *Enzyklopädie der philosophischen Wissenschaften im Grundrisse und andere Schriften aus der Heidelberger Zeit*, first original edition 1817 (Stuttgart: Frommann, 1927) §§ 465-471.

[26] V 5:1.1-13.

[27] V 3:28.676-686.

[28] See V 5:315 note to V 5:1.9, citing Mark 1:15, Gal. 4:4, and Eph. 1:10.

[29] V 5:5.120-6.134.

[30] Note Jaeschke's warning in *Die Vernunft in der Religion* 303.

[31] E.g. V 5:76.104-106.

[32] E.g. V 5:6.131-134.

[33] V 5:15.383-16.413.

[34] GW 12:32.1-52.26/GL 600-622.

[35] V 5:15.387-390.

[36] V 5:15.391-392, 16.424-425.

[37] V 5:15.393-395.

[38] V 5:16.414-17.447.

[39] V 5:16.419-432.

[40] "Gott ist GEIST, Einer, als *unendliche Subjektivität*" (V 5:17.446/ L 3:78).

[41] GW 12:245.27-246.17.

[42] V 5:15.396-405.

[43] "Begriff zu sein ist eine Bestimmtheit der Subjektivität, für uns von der absoluten Idee aus, ebenso in ihm selbst." V 5:15.396-397/ L 3:77.

[44] V 5:24.648-28.778.

[45] V 5:24.653-665.

[46] V 5:16.406-410.

[47] "und dann diese Geschichte als an diesem, den *Einzelnen*, is Kultus, als die subjektive Seite." V 5:16.409-410/L 3:77.

[48] V 5:28.779-69.915.

[49] V 5:69.898-915.

[50] V 5:71.953-955.

[51] V 5:78.150-97.649.

[52] V 5:77.135-139.

[53] On these complex shifts, see further in Jaeschke, *Die Vernunft in der Religion* 303-308; Hodgson, in L 3:11-14, 20-21.

[54] V 5:17.446.

[55] "Der *Geist* ist die unendliche Rückkehr in sich – unendliche Subjektivität, nicht vorgestellte, sondern als die WIRKLICHE *Göttlichkeit, als die gegenwärtige,* . . . sondern *das subjektiv Gegenwärtige* und Wirkliche, . . . *Gott in seiner Gemeinde wohnend.*" V 5:76.88-98/L 3:140 (trans. slightly amended).

[56] V 5:1.14-5.110.

[57] V 5:5.107

[58] Hodgson, in L 3:11. For the German phrase, *"Beisichsein im Anderssein,"* see Jaeschke, *Die Vernunft in der Religion* 228, 243, and further remarks on p. 296. On Hegel's use of *Beisichsein,* see the references in V 4:874.

[59] V 5:4.95-103.

[60] V 5:4.79-94.

[61] V 5:2.38-4.78.

[62] V 5:1.14-2.37.

[63] "aber sein *Bewußtsein, Subjektivität – der wahrhafte Gegenstand* ist *dies Ganze.*" V 5:1.16-17/L 3:62.

[64] "er ist als ein Prozeß, Selbstbewußtsein, als *Gegenstand,* als Wahrheit." V 5:2.22-23/L 3:42, trans. slightly amended.

[65] V 3:86.591-89.672.

[66] V 3:86.592-87.621.

[67] V 3:87.622-88.662.

[68] V 3:88.663-89.672.

[69] V 3:266.36-277.381.

[70] V3:274.286.

[71] V 3:277.383-278.396. The long treatment of the second moment of the concept of religion is found on V 3:277.383-329.902. And see V 3:336.54-337.58.

[72] V 3:282.460-465 with 283.500-502.

[73] V 3:286.579-594 with 291.738-739.

74 V 3:291.739-292.743; see also 298.907-913.

75 V 3:302.44-45.

76 V 3:308.214-329.902.

77 V 3:330.904-923.

78 Jaeschke, *Die Vernunft in der Religion* 271.

79 "mich als mich in Gott mit mir zusammenzuschließen." V 3:332.964/L 1:443.

80 V 3:333.991-335.53.

81 V 5:177.3-21.

82 V 5:196.600-199.688.

83 V 5.179.54.

84 V 5:195.556-563.

85 V 5:197.607.

86 While calling attention to the difference in enrichment or inclusiveness of content between the use of "absolute idea" at the end of the *Logic* and with regard to the consummate religion, Jaeschke rightly emphasizes the importance of the absolute or eternal idea as the true metaphysical concept of the consummate religion. *Die Vernunft in der Religion* 311-312.

87 V 5:197.608-198.651.

88 "die dreierlei Verhältnisweisen des Subjekts zu Gott, drei Weisen des Daseins Gottes für den subjektiven Geist." V 5:198.652-653/L 3:273.

89 V 5:196.605-197.607.

90 V 5:198.656-660.

91 V 5:198.660-662.

92 V 5:198.666-199.688.

93 V 5:198.667-670.

94 V 5:197.608-617.

95 See n. 66 above.

[96] See n. 69 above.

[97] V 5:201.703-720.

[98] See n. 67 above.

[99] See nn. 71-76 above.

[100] See V 5:197.618-198.645 with 198.671-199.678 with the text itself 215.75-251.24.

[101] V 5:198.646-651.

[102] See n. 78 above.

[103] "So ist die Gemeinde selbst der existierende Geist, der Geist in seiner Existenz, Gott als Gemeinde existierend." V 5:254.80-81/L 3:331.

[104] V 5:254.82-88.

[105] "Das Dritte ist dann dies Bewußtsein, Gott als Geist. Dieser Geist als existierend und sich realisierend ist die Gemeinde." V 5:254.88-89/L 3:331.

[106] See Schlitt, *Hegel's Trinitarian Claim* 212-227.

[107] "Die dritte Seite ist das Verhältnis des Subjekts zu dieser Wahrheit, daß das Subjekt, sofern es im Verhältnis zu ihr ist, eben zu dieser bewußten Einheit kommt, sich dieser gewußten Einheit würdigt, sie in sich hervorbringt und vom göttlichen Geist erfüllt wird." V 5:254.101-105/L 3:331-332.

[108] V 5:264.374-265.389.

[109] V 5:268.494-269.509.

[110] On subjectivity in Hegel's *Logic*, see again Schlitt, *Hegel's Trinitarian Claim* 19-28. Note Jaeschke's pointing out that Hegel's philosophy as a whole is a philosophy of subjectivity which turns on the necessity of subjectivity's elaborating content out of itself, *Die Vernunft in der Religion* 357.

[111] V 5:193.496-195.555.

[112] This position has recently been espoused with regard to the 1821 manuscript in a very interesting study by Herbert Huber, *Idealismus und Trinität, Pantheon und Götterdämmerung. Grundlagen und*

Grundzüge der Lehre von Gott nach dem Manuscript Hegels zur Religionsphilosophie (Weinheim: Acta humaniora, 1984) e.g. 19-22. See the review of this study by J. Schmidt, S.J., in *Theologie und Philosophie* 61 (1986) 131-133.

[113] On this discussion see, with references, Jörg Splett's most thoughtful review of my study, *Hegel's Trinitarian Claim*, in *Theologie und Philosophie* 61 (1986) 133-135. Further on this question in Jaeschke, *Die Vernunft in der Religion* 318-320.

[114] See, e.g., Xavier Tillette, "Bible et philosophie. La bible des philosophes" (photoreproduced course notes, Paris: Institut Catholique de Paris, 1983) 103-106, 112-116. For further references, see Steinhauer, *Hegel Bibliography* 778.

[115] Jaeschke, *Die Vernunft in der Religion* 328-348.

[116] "Hegel's Christology: Shifting Nuances in the Berlin Lectures," *Journal of the American Academy of Religion* 53 (1985) 23-40.

[117] Observation by Jaeschke, *Die Vernunft in der Religion* 307 n. 24, citing Philipp Marheineke, *Die Grundlehren der christlichen Dogmatik* (Berlin: F. Dümmler, 1819); ____, *Die Grundlehren der christlichen Dogmatik als Wissenschaft* (Berlin: Duncker und Hümblot, 1827).

[118] Of course, in turn it may well be that Hegel's understanding of identity and difference itself has roots in Christianity.

HEGEL'S RELIGIOUS DIALECTIC OF IDENTITY AND DIFFERENCE

CHAPTER FIVE

IDENTITY AND RELIGION

In Part One of our effort to understand Hegel's philosophy of religion we reviewed the current text situation that we encounter toward the end of the twentieth century. In Part Two we took a longer look at each of the moments in Hegel's tripartite philosophy of religion. Now in Part Three we will examine some of the ways in which Hegel proposes to resolve the age-old philosophical question of the one and the many. He reflects constructively on this perennial question, which we want to consider here only in a very general way, in terms of the relationship between unity or, better, identity and difference. And since he carries out this reflection on the problem of the one and the many, of identity and difference, out of his own post-Cartesian and post-Kantian context, we should not be surprised if he frames his solution in the form of a movement of inclusive subjectivity. In fact, Hegel regularly works with the question of the relationship between the one and the many, between identity and difference. In one way or another he was concerned with this question from his early reflections on to his 1807 *Phenomenology of Spirit* and throughout the development of his encyclopedic system. Within this encyclopedic system, it is in his philosophy of religion, and especially his philosophy of the consummate religion, that he reveals his solution as a movement of absolute divine subjectivity.

Here in the first chapter of Part Three we will review the way in which Hegel responded to his general concern to establish a philosophically adequate understanding of the relationship between identity and difference. This review will help us both to situate Hegel's treatment of religion within his overall philosophy and to see how crucial religion was for Hegel in the attainment of true identity. Then in Chapters Six, Seven, and Eight we will examine three specific themes with which he works in his efforts to give expression to the realizations of unity or identity through which spirit moves in the consummate religion. These four chapters, which touch in different ways on Hegel's various formulations of the question of identity, will continue to help us see more clearly in what sense his overall philosophy is one of subjectivity. More specifically, they should aid us in our understanding of how his philosophy of religion is a movement of divine subjectivity.

As we turn now, more specifically, to our review of Hegel on identity and religion, we should immediately note the remark that German Idealism was the first western philosophical stream to articulate fully the notion of identity as inclusive of identity and nonidentity or difference.[1] This claim might need to be qualified in order further to acknowledge the ongoing insight of prior western intellectual and, more specifically, trinitarian traditions.[2] But be that as it may, the articulation of the inclusive character of identity surely reaches its apex in Hegel's philosophy and, in a particular way, in his philosophical interpretation of religion from the 1807 *Phenomenology of Spirit* on to the 1830 edition of his *Encyclopedia of the Philosophical Sciences in Outline* and the various lectures associated with it.

Looking directly to Hegel's systematic thought in its compass and rigor provides us with a unique opportunity to review his classic western understanding of the relationship between identity and difference. At the same time, our wider focus on Hegel's systematic thought provides the occasion to examine certain aspects of his powerful, but often critiqued, understanding of the relationship between identity and religion.[3] In order to structure this review of Hegel on identity and religion, and in order to give it a certain sense of direction, we can formulate a twofold aim, namely, one which is both historical and systematic. Our aim is historical in that we will review Hegel's conception first of identity and then of religion in relation to identity. It is systematic in that we will argue that religion is the in fact irreplaceable basis for the achievement of such identity in Hegel's systematic thought.

If, while trying to think along with Hegel, we attempt to review the relevant secondary literature, we quickly realize that the sheer quantity of such literature has become all but unmanageable. Even if, as is presently the case, we concentrate on the questions of identity, and of religion in relationship to identity, we run up against an immense accumulation of relevant secondary literature.[4] Fortunately, Hegel himself speaks quite explicitly of identity and of religion. Happily, too, the observation that great thinkers often express the essentials of their position in specific, delimited texts, is particularly true of Hegel. It is true above all for internal, systematic reasons. Hegel's philosophical system, in its speculative formulation, is a movement of the self-positing and self-development of absolute spirit. It is a teleological, and progressively more concrete, series of momentary totalities. This brilliant formulation[5] of Hegel's grounds and justifies focusing on specific texts. In the *Phenomenology* these momentary totalities are presented in specific, delineatable texts as taking the form of shapes or figures (*Gestalt*)[6] in the progression of Spirit from consciousness to self-consciousness on to absolute knowing. In the *Encyclopedia* these momentary totalities are presented as thought determinations (*Gedankenbestimmung*) in logic[7] and as various steps (*Stufe*) in the realphilosophical spheres of nature and finite spirit.[8] In this chapter we will, in somewhat Germanic fashion, concentrate more on Hegel's explicit discussions of identity and of religion in the encyclopedic and associated lecture formulations of his systematic thought.[9]

More specifically, now, in this chapter we will begin with a consideration of identity in the *Science of Logic*. This *Logic* itself presents and, as logical or pure thought, is for Hegel the first moment in the self-development of absolute spirit. We will then turn briefly to realizations of identity beyond the sphere of logic in the "real-philosophical" spheres of nature and spirit. It is within the real-philosophical sphere of spirit, and, more precisely, at the end in the sphere of absolute spirit, that Hegel places his philosophy of religion as second moment between art and philosophy. Following Hegel, then, we will discuss his understanding of the nature of the relationship between identity and religion in the light of religion's penultimate systematic position just before the final moment of philosophical thought.

1. Identity

Hegel reflects on the notion of "identity" (*Identität*) in his smaller *Logic*, which forms the first part of the *Encyclopedia*,[10] but especially in the *Science of Logic*.[11] When he spoke of "logic," he meant the immanent and consistent[12] self-positing and self-determining movement of pure thought, which, of course, is to occur in and through human thinking. The movement of logical thought determinations takes place, for Hegel, in the human thinking of them. But this thinking of them is to sublate the finite and limited character of human thinking. He meant, therefore, an objective or absolute logic, in which form and content were the same. Thought was its own content, hence logic was absolute form.[13] Hegel envisaged this pure thought as an internal dialectical development beginning in the thought determination, "pure being," as the initial moment of pure thought itself. This movement of pure thought continued, as a self-sublating series of transitions, from one thought determination to another until the final determination, the absolute idea. The absolute idea was itself an enriched return to the immediacy of pure being.[14] This logic or pure thought can be described as the non-temporal, speculative dialectical movement of thought determinations. These determinations progress immanently and consistently on the basis of self-contradiction. They progress according to a triadic rhythm which we can describe, on the widest level of the movement of logical thought, as a movement from being to essence to concept.

The transitions, which constitute this development, occur in the first part of the *Logic*, namely, in the logic of being, as one category's "having gone over into" (*übergegangensein*) the other. When these categories are thought through in their immediacy, the transition to the other has already occurred.[15] In the second part of the *Logic*, in the logic of essence, these determinations are in general called "determinations of reflection" (*Reflexionsbestimmung*). Since they are now, on this logically more determinate level, determinations of reflection, they are usually doubled determinations. Yet they equally stand freely on their own with their other already included within them. The transition from one determination of reflection to the other occurs as "appearance in the other" (*scheinen in dem Entgegengesetzten*).[16] As mentioned, they are generally presented in pairs or in a doubled relationship. In the *Logic*'s third part, namely, in the logic of the concept, these "determinations of the concept" (*Begriffsbestimmung*)[17] are explicitly the momentary totality of the concept in its self-development as pure thought.[18] Here the transition occurs as a development (*Entwicklung*) of one into the other.[19]

We will concentrate on the logic of essence. For it is here that Hegel, after discussing essence as "illusory being" or *Schein*, and then after a very dense study of "reflection," presents identity as the first of a dialectical triad of determinations of reflection: "identity, difference, contradiction" (*Identität, Unterschied, Widerspruch*). The last of these, namely, contradiction, settles into the thought determination "ground" (*Grund*). This triadically, and then in effect tetradically, structured movement of pure thought recalls and repeats, in a way appropriate to the logic of essence, Hegel's famous initial movement of logical thought. This initial movement was one from being through nothing to becoming, with the last of these determinations settling into the concreteness of *Dasein*. Hegel presupposes, and draws upon, these initial thought determinations in order to present the progression from identity through difference to contradiction and ground.[20] As was the case with the question of the way he placed being at the beginning of the movement of logical thought, so too his specific positioning of identity will have important ramifications. Position is significant for Hegel. It is important not only in the realphilosophical spheres such as history, the history of philosophy, and the philosophy of religion, but as well and especially in the *Logic*. His general intention toward comprehensiveness means that nothing is to be lost. Rather, all is to be acknowledged, placed, negated, and yet taken up and preserved (*aufheben, Aufhebung*). It is especially in the *Logic* that he is able to make a critique of a particular philosophical stance or individual thinker.[21] He can make this critique by his very presentation and positioning, contextualizing we could say, of this stance or attitude within the dialectical rhythm of his method as beginning, progression, and result.[22] Therefore our review of Hegel's presentation of identity, with some reference to difference, contradiction, and ground, will help us to clarify the terminology he uses and our understanding of the structure of identity with which he works. Our review will also allow us to refer to some of the understandings of identity which Hegel found important though, taken by themselves, inadequate.

Hegel's direct presentation of identity, namely, as the first in this dialectically appearing series of ever more determinate determinations of reflection, occupies only slightly more than a page of his massive *Science of Logic*.[23] In the encyclopedic *Logic* Hegel presents identity in a three-line paragraph with an accompanying one-page remark.[24] We will concentrate on the longer *Logic*. Our intention is not to reargue Hegel's position but, rather, to summarize particularly relevant aspects of his description of identity.[25]

1.a. The Logic of Identity, Difference, and Contradiction

In his introduction to the three specific determinations of reflection, namely, identity, difference, and contradiction, Hegel places identity first: "Essence is at first, simple self-relation, pure *identity*. This is its determination, but as such it is rather the absence of any determination."[26] He points out, secondly, that the proper determination of essence is difference, indeed difference as external and indifferent difference or diversity, and then as opposed diversity or opposition. Thirdly, for Hegel opposition reflects itself in itself as contradiction. In turn, by means of the dialectical explicitation of the unity implicit in it, this contradiction settles into ground as the truth of essence, the unity of identity and difference.[27]

More specifically, then, Hegel presents identity in two subsections. In the first of these he opens the presentation by recalling, in five lines,[28] that essence is simple immediacy, but equally sublated immediacy. It is immediacy as that absolute negativity in which otherbeing and the relationship to the other have disappeared into pure equality with self. "Essence is therefore simple identity-with-self."[29] This simple identity is the immediacy of reflection, but not simply the immediacy of the logically earlier being and nothing. Now this simple identity is "essential identity" (*die wesentliche Identität*). By this stage in the movement of pure thought or logic Hegel takes great pains incessantly to remind the reader that otherness here is neither something external nor that to which the thought determination in question can be related. Rather the relation is now always a self-relation. It is a relation of reflection in which the other is posited as a self-positing of any first moment. More particularly here, the other always appears within the totality which the thought determination is, thus making it a determination of reflection. The unity here in question is "not a restoration of itself from an other, but this pure origination from and within itself."[30] This unity is essential identity.

Hegel then claims that this essential identity is not an "abstract identity" (*abstracte Identität*). It is not an identity arising out of a negative reference to something different, when that something different is understood in the sense of being rigidly separated from, and existing independently of, itself.[31] Here Hegel is applying a remark he made earlier in the Introduction to the *Science of Logic*. There he warned that the greatest danger in treating of logical thought is to conceive of thought determinations as static entities rather than as more fluid momentary totalities which are constituted by their very transition into the other.[32]

By placing identity as first momentary totality in a series of dialectically progressing determinations of reflection Hegel has situated, and made a critique of, all those positions which conceive of identity as that which is simply posited over against difference. He is surely thinking, for example, of Fichte's philosophy and of Schelling's earlier philosophy of identity.[33] It is to this earlier philosophy of Schelling's which Hegel, according to the more generally accepted interpretation, had referred in the Preface to his *Phenomenology* when he wrote of the "night in which, . . . , all cows are black."[34] In his added remarks in the *Logic* he reacts against this conception of an abstract identity, an identity expressed in the sentence or principle of identity, "A is A." He labels this principle "the expression of an empty tautology."[35] It is only understanding (*Verstand*) which remains trapped in this simplistic view of identity.[36] Only such understanding does not realize that a moment of negation is already implied in the alternative formulation of this principle, "A cannot at the same time be A and not-A."[37] After this brief condemnation of abstract identity, Hegel returns to his own train of logic. He ends this first section on identity with the affirmation that the simple negativity, in the mode of being, is identity itself. As such, this simple negativity or identity is the same as essence.[38]

The second section or half of Hegel's presentation of identity[39] is a text particularly difficult to follow. In a sense it encapsulates the whole dynamic of Hegel's dialectical thinking. Here in this second section Hegel first thinks through the move from essential identity to absolute difference (*der absolute Unterschied*). He again recalls that identity is not a determination of essence, but is essence itself, the whole reflection and not merely a moment of reflection. Essential identity is absolute negativity, achieved negation of negation appearing in its renewed immediacy. Essential identity stands as *an sich* or "implicit" inclusion of otherness, an inclusion not yet made explicit. Nonbeing and difference have disappeared in the arising of the thought determination "identity." Hegel then appeals to the principle that differentiating is the positing of nonbeing (*Nichtsein*) as the nonbeing of the other. But then he moves quickly to assert that, if the nonbeing of the other is the sublation of the other, it is equally the sublating of differentiating. The result is that differentiating remains at hand (*vorhanden*) as the absolute negativity. Differentiating is self-relating negativity as a nonbeing which is the nonbeing of itself. Consequently, there arises a nonbeing which has its own nonbeing not in an other but in itself. Hegel concludes, "What is present, therefore, is self-related, reflected difference, or pure, *absolute difference*."[40]

Hegel goes on to try to clarify this, at first sight convoluted but not at all untypical, argumentation with a further reflection on essential identity as "reflection-into-self."[41] He presents it as an inner repulsion (*Abstossen*) which is immediately taken back. In his presentation and in his further explication already here on the level of *an sich* or first moment, Hegel tries to think through what essential identity is so that he may thereby come to assert the contradiction that identity, in its own self, is absolute non-identity.[42] With the dialectical assertion that identity is absolute negativity inclusive of sublated otherbeing, and thus equally non-identity, he can now assert as well that identity is not only totality but reflection. Identity posits its other. So identity likewise has, as determination, to be over against non-identity. For Hegel identity is both first inclusive momentary totality and, equally, a thought determination of simple equality with itself over against absolute difference.[43]

By means of this doubled presentation of identity as inclusive of sublated otherness, or difference, and as first determination over against absolute difference, Hegel has, in effect, elaborated his conception of identity as the unity of identity and difference. He will go on in the logic of essence to think through the appearance of difference as a series of several ever more explicitly internally contradictory momentary totalities in the movement of pure thought. Difference will come to be seen as momentary totality negating, but including, identity. It will be seen as having been posited by the very thinking through of an original identity. The original moment of essential identity, as itself inclusive of sublated difference and as first moment in this dialectical appearance of determinations of reflection, sets the pattern for what will become explicit in the doubled result: contradiction[44] and ground.[45]

Hegel will push this thinking through of the ever more explicit contradiction constitutive of difference, of diversity, opposition, and contradiction until the unity underlying their contradictions becomes fully explicit.[46] This explicitation of that unity is, finally, the settling of contradiction into ground.[47] As we have mentioned, it is a settling parallel to Hegel's earlier presentation of the collapse of becoming into *Dasein*.[48] The collapse of contradiction into ground occurs as the mutual cancelling out of the independence (*Selbständigkeit*) of contradiction's themselves self-contradictory moments, namely, the positive and the negative.[49] As renewed first moment, "*Ground* is the unity of identity and of difference."[50]

Though Hegel's dialectic continues on in the rest of the logic of essence and into the logic of the concept, we can stop at this point to summarize his understanding of identity as the unity of identity and non-identity. With contradiction, but especially ground, Hegel has returned, in a more determinate and enriched way, to the original moment of essential identity. What was only *an sich* or implicitly expressed there, namely, the presence of difference as otherness, becomes *für sich*, or is made explicit, in the thought determination "difference" as the otherness of, and yet being inclusive of, identity. By highlighting ever more explicitly the contradiction between identity and difference, a contradiction internal to the determinations of reflection in question, Hegel argued to a concept of identity inclusive of difference. He arrived at a unity of essential identity and absolute difference. He sought to establish a first moment of identity which posited or, we might equally say, when it was thought through, gave rise to, difference. Difference, in turn, when thought through, gave rise to a more explicit concept of identity inclusive of difference, namely, of contradiction settling into ground. In fact, this dialectical pattern illustrates, in the manner of appearance in the other as appropriate to the logic of essence, the entire movement of Hegel's thought.

The utter importance of this dialectic of identity, difference, and renewed inclusive identity can be underscored by recalling Hegel's presentation of the "true infinite" (das wahrhaft Unendliche, die wahrhafte Unendlichkeit) in the logic of being.[51] There Hegel elaborates his logical reformulation of what is religiously expressed as the relationship between God and world. He conceives of the true infinite as infinity inclusive of finitude. The true infinite is resultant infinity inclusive of an initial or abstract infinite[52] and of finitude. Both this initial infinite and finitude are, at first thought, considered to be independent and opposed to one another. But, then they are thought dialectically to have gone over into one another in such a way that they finally become resultant inclusive infinite. This dialectical pattern of enriched rhythmic return pulsates through the logic and within the realphilosophical spheres of nature and spirit. It is a dialectical movement given generalized formulation at the end of the Science of Logic[53] as the method (Methode) or self-positing and self-determining of the concept as inclusive subjectivity and even subject. The self-determination of the concept is a movement from beginning (Anfang) as immediate and universal, through doubly structured dialectical progression (Fortgang, Fortgehen) as negation of the beginning, on to result (Resultät) as negation of the first negation. Result is thus enriched return to the beginning. From the perspective of his overall systematic and speculatively formulated presentation, for Hegel, each beginning is, in its own way, identity. Each doubled moment of progression is difference constituted and characterized by contradiction. Each result, whether considered in its singular fullness or its at times indicated doubled "becoming" and "settling down into," is inclusive totality as identity inclusive of identity and non-identity. Each result is an explicitation of the unity already implicit in the contradiction constituting progression. Each result is the expressed unity of, and underlying, the previous contradiction. It is the identity of difference. As this identity of difference each result is an advance as enriched return to the originary identity.

1.b. Identity and Existent Reality

For Hegel the sphere of logic presents the archetype[54] of his concept of identity. From the logic we can already intimate how his logical structuring of identity proposes to respond to the questions of individual, societal, religious, and philosophical alienation.[55] In itself the movement of logic or pure thought is, in its return through absolute idea to the originary unity of pure being, identity inclusive of identity and non-identity in two senses. As the self-determination of the concept, logic is itself an inclusive totality. It is identity inclusive of posited and sublated difference. But the sphere of logic is equally only a first moment, with all that such a positioning entails in Hegel's speculative systematic thought. The sphere of logic as a whole can be characterized as essential identity. It is but the first moment in his triadically structured encyclopedic presentation of the self-development of absolute spirit It is but the first moment in the movement from logic through nature and finite spirit to the enriched return of spirit to itself in the final, integrating unity of philosophical thought. And philosophical thought is itself enriched return to the immediacy of logic.[56] In asking Hegel about the nature of identity, we find ourselves swept up into Hegel's own speculative systematic thought, into the overall movement of spirit and true subjectivity. He answers the question about the nature of identity by plopping his whole philosophy in our laps, or, more accurately, in our minds.

With our present move from logic on to Hegel's "realphilosophy," we intend only to recall in a quick, but respectful, manner several representative instantiations of Hegel's view of "identity in and inclusive of difference." Given the relative brevity of our following observations, it is important to remember that for Hegel we are not merely to impose the structure of logically formulated identity on the various realizations of spirit. Rather, our task is to discover progressively more internally satisfactory realphilosophical realizations of unity or enriched identity. These realizations are to be seen as arising immanently and consistently as a series of totalizing self-manifestations of spirit in nature and through finite spirit to absolute spirit. Here we will follow the appearance of these realizations in a more general way and, in the following three chapters, we will analyze three major formulations of the interrelationship between identity and difference in Hegel's philosophy of the consummate religion.

The Realphilosophical Sphere of Nature

Hegel conceives of nature as the opposite both of the "prior" sphere of logic as a whole and of the absolute idea which arises at the end of the movement of logical thought. In his philosophy of nature, nature is pure externality as opposed to the pure internality of logical thought.[57] As is to be expected, Hegel begins his philosophy of nature with a movement of philosophical notions in the realm of immediacy. Broadly stated, these notions are those of space, time, place and motion, and matter. In view of the importance given to spatially and temporally grounded philosophical visions during the 20th century, on another occasion it would be important to pursue, in more detail, the way in which Hegel relates these supposedly indifferent[58] philosophical notions in terms of the initial logical dialectic of being/nothing/becoming/*Dasein*. For present purposes it will be sufficient to indicate that space (*Raum*), as pure externalization, is, nevertheless, for Hegel itself characterized by a dialectic of negation and negation of negation. Space can be seen as an essential identity already inclusive of difference even in the abstract universality of its self-externality.[59] Time (*Zeit*) is the same as space, but only in a negative formulation. Time is intuited becoming.[60] By a series of dialectically related mutual transitions of space into time and time into space, Hegel argues that place (*Ort*) is "the *posited* identity of space and time [and] is also the posited *contradiction* set up by the mutual exclusiveness of space and time."[61] This mutual transition as place, which is now posited in a temporal manner, constitutes motion (*Bewegung*). As Hegel revealingly concludes, "To an equal extent however, this becoming is itself the internal collapse of its contradiction, it is therefore the immediately *identical* and *existent* unity of place and motion, i.e., matter."[62] Place, motion and matter, arising as moments of becoming collapsing into *Dasein*, reproduce in the sphere of nature the logical movement from contradiction to ground. They are the realization of inclusive identity arising out of, and as, the identity of mutually contradictory moments of identity and non-identity.

The Realphilosophical Sphere of Spirit

If we move on to the philosophy of spirit, the third part of the *Encyclopedia*, we find there a triadically structured presentation of subjective spirit, objective spirit, and absolute spirit. Though Hegel is always working in terms of reality as thought and thus as formally structured, we can say that in the sphere of subjective spirit he focuses on spirit in its more individual realizations. This sphere of subjective spirit presents the self-development of spirit in three major stages. The first of these, "Anthropology,"[63] treats of spirit in its immediacy as soul (*Seele*) in finite spirit. The third of these stages, "Psychology",[64] treats of spirit thematically as spirit (*Geist*). In the second stage, "The Phenomenology of Spirit,"[65] on which we will now focus our attention, Hegel presents spirit in its self-development as the soul having become "I" (*das Ich*), often translated in English by "ego."

In developing the "I" as the result of the movement of spirit as soul, Hegel immediately indicates that the phenomenological "I" is anything but presuppositionless.[66] By means of a series of introductory remarks[67] he presents consciousness (*Bewußtsein*) as the initial and, consequently, immediate identity of the natural soul which has now come to be the pure ideal identity of the "I." For Hegel the "I" is absolute negativity. It is, implicitly, identity in otherness. The "I" and consciousness as such are identified. In this consciousness which the "I" is, the "I" includes the object as implicitly sublated.[68] As only Hegel can say, the "I" is "*one* side of the relationship and the *whole* relationship."[69] Already in this expression we can see that he is going to conceive of the "I" as the totality of the initial moment of phenomenological consciousness. He is going to present the "I" as selfhood both in one way or another over against an object and as the resultant unity of "I" and object. The "I" is initial identity, namely, identity over against non-identity or difference, and identity of identity and non-identity.

Hegel works out this conception of the "I" in terms of a series of successive totalizations.[70] These totalizations are quite reminiscent of what he had described in the *Phenomenology* as inclusive forms or shapes of consciousness. These totalizations are inclusive in that they include both consciousness or self and the object of consciousness. They have come to be seen as forms or shapes of spirit.[71] There in the *Phenomenology* Hegel had described the arising of these forms or shapes rather ingeniously as experience (*Erfahrung*).[72] Here in the encyclopedic phenomenology, these successive totalizations occur as ever more adequate interrelatings of "I" and object (*Gegenstand*). To phenomenological consciousness, the development (*Fortbildung*) occurs as change in the given object in question in each totalization. But in fact a change in object brings about a change in the "I" as well.[73]

So, initially the "I" and object are identified in consciousness. Then, through a series of successive totalizations, the "I" and object are distinguished in consciousness.[74] They are reidentified in the sense that "I" and object are seen to be one and the same in self-consciousness (*Selbstbewußtsein*).[75] Given his speculative systematic approach, Hegel can, in this phenomenological development, speak literally of self-integration.[76] Consciousness develops as the movement from the certainty of self-relating to that self-relating's truth in self-consciousness. This occurs in the sense that self-consciousness is the explicitation of the originary self-certainty.[77] Throughout this phenomenological development from self-relating to self-consciousness, Hegel typically works in terms of ever internally doubled totalizations of "I" and other.

In self-consciousness, this doubled structuring of consciousness gives rise, as a movement of self-determining negation of negation, to the acknowledgement of the other itself as "I" over against oneself. Here Hegel discusses the process of being a free self for the other, a process of recognition (*Anerkennen*)[78] as a struggle (*Kampf*).[79] At this point he introduces his famous relationship between lordship (*Herrschaft*) and bondage (*Knechtschaft*).[80] Though we need not enter into the detail of this struggle in its various forms, we should note that the series of contradictions arising within recognizing self-consciousness[81] has given rise to a number of one-sided relationships.[82] These result in the transition to universal self-consciousness, to "the affirmative knowing of one's self in the other self,"[83] in which each self has absolute independence. Hegel asserts that these single beings are held in the unity of consciousness and self-consciousness as appearing in one another. "In this identity however, their difference is a wholly indeterminate variety, or rather a difference which is not a difference. Their truth is therefore the being in and for self of the universality and objectivity of self-consciousness, – *reason*."[84]

In the third and final subsection of the encyclopedic phenomenology, Hegel, in two articles or paragraphs, describes reason (*Vernunft*) as "the simple *identity* of the *subjectivity* of the concept with its *objectivity* and universality."[85] This universality of reason now signifies the object, which is merely given in consciousness, but is itself inclusive of the "I." This universality or reason "also signifies the pure *I*, the pure form which includes and encompasses the object within itself."[86] For Hegel the "I" as original self-certainty, as self-relation, has come to its own truth. It has come to the certainty that its own determinations are equally determinations of the essence of things. The "I," as this identity, is truth as knowledge, "the self-certainty which is Spirit."[87]

As throughout his philosophy, here Hegel has identified the "I" with thought. Within the context of his encyclopedic presentation, the "I" has been given the characteristics earlier ascribed to the thought determination "identity." What Hegel had referred to as "form" (*Form*) and "content" (*Inhalt*) in his Preface to the *Phenomenology of Spirit* can be applied, respectively, to "I" and "object" here in the encyclopedic phenomenology.[88] That is, Hegel describes the phenomenological "I" as the initial identity or unity of consciousness. Then in each succeeding totalization "I" refers to the initial, dialectical moment of immediacy, the "in itself" which is an essential identity. This is the "I" as the immediacy or certainty of selfhood in its experience of opposition, which latter is the negativity characteristic and constitutive of otherness. But more importantly for Hegel, "I" refers as well to the resultant identity appearing out of each successive dialectical interrelationship of "I" and object. This resultant identity is, therefore, identity of identity and non-identity. In reason as movement of spirit, this identity of identity and non-identity is seen to be self-determining differentiation and sublation of difference in renewed identity.

Hegel goes on, in the sphere of objective spirit,[89] to present spirit's self-realization in the notions of right (*Recht*), of morality

(*Moralität*), and of social ethics (*Sittlichkeit*). The individual identity already posited in the sphere of subjective spirit, and in particular in phenomenology, finds its own fulfillment for Hegel in the societal notions of family (*Familie*), civil society (*die bürgerliche Gesellschaft*), and the state (*Staat*).[90] Far from being any simplistic subordination of individual to society, of one to the many, for Hegel this further self-development of spirit is the individual finding his or her own freedom and truth in the sphere of social ethics. He goes on, in the third section of the philosophy of spirit, namely, in absolute spirit, to integrate the spheres of subjective and objective spirit.[91] This integration of subjective and objective spirit in absolute spirit is the establishment of a renewed identity of what can be termed the more individual and more societal realizations of spirit. He elaborates this identity in monosubjectival terms, though absolute spirit is for Hegel beyond any ordinary distinctions of one and many.[92] Hegel integrates the one and the many in an inclusive totality, identity of identity and non-identity, what he calls concrete universality (*konkrete Allgemeinheit*).[93] He integrates the one and the many, identity and difference, in a movement of inclusive subjectivity.

1.c. Further Remarks on Identity

Hegel variously speaks of identity in the rarified atmosphere of logic as pure thought or in the realms of nature and of finite and absolute spirit. In whatever realm, whenever it is a question of his speculatively formulated presentations he continually relates the one and the many in his own characteristic way by reaffirming identity as inclusive of difference. The one is the one of the many and the many are the many of the one. Essential identity, or the first moment in any speculatively formulated dialectical movement, is always identity implicitly inclusive of difference. Difference, or the second moment in any such dialectical movement, is always meant to be doubled and to express contradiction. Identity, as the unity of the two (or more), is only implicit in contradiction. Resultant identity, or the third moment in any such dialectical movement, is always meant to be identity now explicitly inclusive of difference. It is the identity *of* difference. This dialectical movement, and consequently the identity Hegel variously affirms, is always an identity in and as thought. In fact, it is finally seen to be self-positing and self-determining thought. It is reason or spirit. In the self-development of spirit resultant identity is the grounding return to essential identity.[94]

It has taken some time for us to arrive at these affirmations. And, strangely enough, so far we have not needed to refer to religion during our discussion of the question of identity. In his more systematic thought, as found in the *Phenomenology* and in the *Encyclopedia* with associated lectures, Hegel locates religion as penultimate self-realization of absolute spirit. He places it immediately before philosophy. Philosophical thought is, in its renewed immediacy (or here we could equally well say identity), enriched and grounding return to pure being. It is enriched return to the initial moment of logic as pure thought. In a very real sense, then, prior to his treatment of religion Hegel has, on the one hand, elaborated a secularized systematic notion of identity. But, on the other hand, in choosing to situate religion as penultimate moment in the self-development of absolute or inclusive spirit, he is saying that the final identity of concept and reality, of subjective and objective, was not attainable, on any level, without religion. For, in the *Phenomenology* and in the encyclopedic system, we can already now say that without the philosophy of religion there could be no attaining the identity of spirit as unity of concept and reality.[95]

2. *Religion and Identity*

This initial affirmation concerning the relationship between religion and identity leads us now to a review of certain aspects of Hegel's philosophy of religion from the perspective of our concern for the question of identity. We want to state, in more precise fashion, Hegel's understanding of the specific and necessary role of religion in the attainment of identity inclusive of difference.

Already at the end of the introductory pages to the penultimate Chapter Seven of the *Phenomenology* there is discernible a certain outlook which will develop into the triadic structure of Hegel's later philosophy of religion lectures. As we have seen in Part Two above, the Berlin lectures are consistently developed in three steps: The Concept of Religion; Determinate Religion; and The Consummate Religion. Without as yet distinguishing clearly between the concept of religion and the first of the series of determinate religions, in the *Phenomenology* Hegel does speak first of the concept of religion or immediate and natural religion. Then he refers to the religion of art, wherein spirit knows itself in the form of the self. Third, he mentions the revelatory religion, in which the self-consciousness of spirit has appeared in the form or shape of the unity of consciousness and self-consciousness.[96]

In the *Encyclopedia* he treats of religion in very condensed fashion, as would be appropriate to his intended "outline of the philosophical sciences."[97] He in fact identifies the whole third, and final, subsection of the philosophy of spirit, namely, "absolute spirit," as religion.[98] Absolute spirit, the unity of subjective and objective spirit,[99] of the previous individual and societal realizations of spirit, is "self-centred *identity*, [and] is always also identity returning and ever returned into itself."[100]

To unravel these almost cryptic remarks in the *Encyclopedia* on the nature of religion, we must turn to Hegel's Berlin lectures on the philosophy of religion. Recent studies,[101] as well as our analyses in Parts One and Two above, will now allow us to make the briefest of references to development in Hegel's speculative conception of religion, propose several generalizations concerning his philosophical reading of religion, and then take a more focused look at the 1827 lectures from the perspective of our present preoccupation with the question of the role of religion in relation to identity.

In his four series of Berlin lectures on the philosophy of religion Hegel has generally structured his philosophy of religion in the well-known, previously mentioned threefold format.[102] He characteristically begins each of his four series of philosophical interpretations of the communitarian experience of God[103] by positing an originary unity or totality, an initial identity. Already from the 1821 lectures on, Hegel, in a position initially intended to contrast with Schleiermacher's,[104] conceives of religion as an originary totality inclusive of two moments or sides. These are, as we mentioned in Chapter Two above, on the one hand, God as the object of religious consciousness and, on the other hand, religious consciousness itself.[105] By the 1824 lecture series Hegel gives clear expression to the speculative concept of religion as "the idea of spirit that relates itself to itself, *the self-consciousness of absolute spirit*."[106] But it is from the 1827 lectures on that, throughout the lectures, he consistently identifies the concept of religion, in its development, with the self-development of God as absolute spirit.[107] He elaborates the three moments of the concept of religion on the basis of the logical moments of the concept: universality, where Hegel treats of the problem of beginning with God;[108] particularity, where he examines various forms of religious consciousness;[109] individuality, where he very briefly discusses cultus.[110] As moments of the concept of religion these present the very development of God. They structure Hegel's presentation of the realization of the concept of religion in the series of determinate religions.[111] These moments of the concept are realized as well in successively more explicit ways in each of the serially related determinate religions. For Hegel they find their full explicitation in the consummate religion, Christianity, as the enriched return to the concept of religion and, then, that concept's sublation in philosophical thought.

We should briefly recall that Hegel's philosophy of religion was typically meant to be an immanent and consistent philosophically informed communo-historical and dialectically progressing uniserial movement of determinate religions. It culminated in the appearance of the consummate religion. These determinate religions and the consummate religion were presented as successively more explicit realizations of the self-consciousness of God. God is represented as a movement from substance to subject. God is finally adequately philosophically reconceptualized as absolute spirit. In its representational form "religion is the truth *for all people.*"[112] In, through, and for finite consciousness or spirit[113] religion is a movement of reconciliation through divine self-othering and return. Hegel's phenomenological presentation of a "history of religions" is carried out as a speculative philosophy of religion in which Hegel intends to expose the conceptual necessity with which the determinate religions, and especially the consummate religion, develop. Hegel's philosophy of religion presents, in its treatment of the determinate religions and the consummate religion, a *Phänomeno-theo-logik.*[114]

2.a. Hegel's 1827 Lectures on the Philosophy of Religion

In Chapter Two above we reviewed Hegel's 1827 presentation of the concept of religion. This we did in a more general way and in comparison with his presentation in the 1821 lectures.

Then in Chapter Four we more briefly considered the moments of the 1827 concept of religion in relation to the elements of the consummate religion as they were presented in the same lecture series. Now we will take another look at the three moments of the concept of religion in the 1827 lectures,[115] but this time from the perspective of our present concern to understand the relationship between identity and religion in Hegel's philosophy. In our present examination we will underscore the identification Hegel makes between religion and the self-development of absolute spirit in order that we may surface implications of this identification for an understanding of the relationship between religion and identity.

During his presentation of the first moment of the concept of religion, "The Concept of God,"[116] Hegel is quite concerned to refute the charge of pantheism or Spinozism.[117] He notes that "here [in pantheism] everything is identity, or unity with self."[118] But he distinguishes between an abstract identity, which is mere unity without reference to plurality or further determination, and that identity which constitutes a spiritual unity. This latter is simply not as yet further determined. Here Hegel is referring to a totality whose determination it is to determine itself as particularity or difference.[119] He insists that it is God, understood as this spiritual unity, namely, universality or the universal, with which religion and, more precisely, the concept of religion begins.[120] He justifies his understanding of God here as an as yet unexplicitated totality by affirming that God is the result of all that has proceeded so far in the encyclopedic philosophical system.[121] For Hegel a beginning which is a result[122] is a momentary inclusive totality as yet indeterminate and undifferentiated within. In this sense, then, God is substance, absolute substance.[123] But, as Hegel had written so many years earlier in the Preface to the *Phenomenology*, "everything turns on grasping and expressing the True, not only as *substance* but equally as *subject*."[124] To assert that God is absolute substance is for Hegel not at all to exclude from God either subjectivity or that internal self-differentiation which is constitutive of spirit. Hegel simply wants to insist that this differentiation will not occur either independently of God or outside of God as one moment over against another.[125] Here we are still only at the beginning.[126] At first the concept of religion presents itself only as one, as that absolute available to thought, which as absolute still absorbs thought in itself. Properly speaking, this is not yet for Hegel the realm of religion, which requires consciousness and distinction.

What Hegel is doing here is responding cleverly, and with supreme self-confidence, to his critics by incorporating their objection (that God is substance) as the first, but only the first, moment in his own argumentation. He has described this first moment of the concept of religion as an undifferentiated identity. And yet, as result it is inclusive identity. In the *Logic* Hegel had referred to such a conception as essential identity.[127]

Hegel begins the second moment of the concept of religion, "The Knowledge of God,"[128] with a small section[129] from which we can draw sufficient information for present purposes. At the very beginning of this small section he reaffirms that the divine universality, which he has discussed so far, is spirit in its indeterminate universality. Now the second moment is that of difference or distinction as such, where religion, properly speaking, begins.[130] The distinction here in question is a "spiritual distinction" (*geistiger Unterschied*). It is consciousness in which there is distinguished, in phenomenological fashion, the object or God and the subject or the thinking religious consciousness.[131] True to his method, Hegel here elaborates the second moment as doubled moment. It is the moment in which God is spirit existing for spirit, the infinite as object of finite consciousness.[132] He goes on to offer "a speculative phenomenology of the forms of religious consciousness (immediate knowledge or faith, feeling, representation, thought)."[133] In this first elaboration of religious consciousness inclusive of its object, Hegel has set up the framework for his differentiation of the various determinate religions. These religions varyingly emphasize the diverse ways of knowing God.[134] He posits non-identity or difference as difference of the originary identity, namely, of the concept of God. Yet it is equally difference inclusive of identity.

The third moment of the concept of religion is cultus.[135] Hegel first sketches his interpretation of cultus in comparison with the previous moment, "The Knowledge of God."[136] He recalls the development so far from the beginning in substantiality and then progression or the bringing into reality of a humanity which has its own actuality only in God. It is this characteristic of humanity, namely, having its own actuality only in God, which Hegel sees as the basis for cultus.[137] He goes on to list the three progressively more humanly and consciously involving forms of cultus: devotion; external forms such as sacraments through which feelings are evoked; and the inner sacrifice of one's heart to God, ethical life (*Sittlichkeit*) combined with the consciousness of God.[138] Hegel closes the 1827 presentation of the concept of religion with two points which help elucidate his conception of cultus. First, he refers to the essential moment of negation in cultus and asserts that philosophy, which arises out of religion, is "continual cultus" (*beständiger Kultus*).[139] Second, he closes the whole section on the concept of religion with a concise resume which we can paraphrase: religion is the relation we have to God in thinking. God is for thought because God is the universal in and for itself. This universal's self-particularization is judgement, the differentiation of particular spirit over against absolute spirit. Hegel summarizes the knowledge of God as a theoretical relationship or elevation to God, and cultus as a practical relationship, namely, the knowledge of this elevation to God. So cultus or the third moment is knowledge of this knowledge, true religion.[140] Hegel's presentation of the concept of religion exhibits the logical rhythm of the development of the concept as such, universality/particularity/individuality.[141]

In order to identify more exactly the structure of cultus as the moment of individuality in the self-determination of the concept of religion, it will be helpful for us to return again to Hegel's sketch of his interpretation of cultus[142] as compared with the prior moment, "The Knowledge of God." Hegel observes that in this prior moment we or, as he says, I have, in knowing God, raised myself into the spiritual sphere which is God. In so doing I have entered into a theoretical relationship,[143] a relationship in which I have lost myself in my object.[144] But such an absorption in the object known does not exhaust the reality of what is at hand. Not only am I filled by the object known, I stand reflexively over against it. The situation is one of "I" and object, namely, of two which are different.[145] Then in a longer paragraph Hegel is recorded as sketching an application of his notion of the practical relationship as the one in which I know the object, I know this relationship of myself filled with and yet over against the object, and I know that I am to bring about my unity with the object. For Hegel the role of cultus is to bring about this unity of myself with this object. This unity is truth. So, in this way I know myself in the truth.[146] Here Hegel has set up the doubled relationship of the object in me and myself in the object in such a way that the task of cultus is to bring to expression the unity, or identity, already implicit in the doubled relationship. Cultus brings to expression, and is, the identity of this doubled relationship or difference.

Hegel carries out his dense, compact sketching of what cultus is by introducing the practical relationship as a movement of will (*Wille*). Will is for him a movement of thought which distinguishes, and yet works toward overcoming the distinction.[147] In a sort of mini-dialectic, he asserts that it is in will that one is free, or, for oneself, as subject in the first instance over against the object.[148] Other objects are over against myself as my limit (*Schranke*). Yet in will I am at the same time goal oriented. So will is the activity of sublating this finitude and contradiction, namely, that an object remains a limit for me. In this practical determination or orientation (*Bestimmung*) I need to assimilate the object, and yet in this very need I am limited.[149] The other, which in religion is God, is had as object.[150] "Insofar as human beings look back upon themselves, this object is an other for them, something lying beyond them."[151] In the practical relationship which cultus is, God is on one side and I on the other. "The determination is *the including, within my own self, of myself with God*, the knowing of myself within God and of God within me."[152] For Hegel, in this concrete unity which cultus is,[153] I, with my subjective personality, take part in the absolute enjoyment of having myself included in and with God. I take part in the enjoyment of finding my truth in God, of "joining myself as myself in God together with myself."[154]

Recalling again that Hegel sees this practical activity of cultus as resulting, finally, in the transition to the renewed immediacy of philosophical thought[155] will allow us to recognize in cultus the structure of identity inclusive of difference. This doubled, originally contradictory relationship of self and God as united, and yet as over against one another, comes to be seen as the doubled presence of God in oneself and oneself in God. The identity of this doubled presence is the explicitation of the unity underlying the doubled becoming settling into the renewed immediacy or identity of philosophy. Cultus settling into philosophy is the identity of God and the knowing of God. It is the identity of identity and difference or non-identity.

2.b. The Necessary Relationship between Religion and Identity

We see from this review of Hegel's concept of religion that, in the overall movement of self-determining absolute spirit, the relationship between religion and identity can in no way be conceived of as an extrinsic relationship. Rather, religion itself forms the penultimate self-realization of absolute spirit. It is, as Hegel never tires of insisting, the true content of reconciliation achieved as yet in the inadequate form of representational thought. Finite spirit remains conscious of itself as over against infinite spirit.[156] Only in philosophical thought, which is the final sphere of absolute spirit's self-realization and which occurs or arises out of the sphere of religion, will content and form be adequate in the self-mediation of the concept as self.[157] This mediation of concept and reality, of identity and non-identity, and, we could say, of the one and the many, is renewed identity as enriched return to the initial sphere which is logic, and to the absolute idea.[158]

In situating religion as penultimate sphere Hegel has irrevocably wedded his speculative systematic formulation of the achievement of the self-mediation of absolute spirit, namely, of identity inclusive of identity and non-identity, to religion. He has bound identity and religion together in both the phenomenological and the encyclopedic formulations of his system. In Hegel's doubly formulated systematic position religion plays a triple role in relation to the establishment of identity. First, religion is itself the penultimate realization of that identity. Second, it is necessary condition for the final achievement of identity as mediation in philosophical thought and, through philosophy, teleological condition for the possibility of any mediation. Third, religion, as the various determinate religions and the consummate religion, corresponds to, and grounds, the various, as previously mentioned, in a sense secularly developed realizations of subjective, but especially objective, spirit.

At the end of his presentation of objective spirit, Hegel proposes that there arise in world history various national spirits (*Volksgeist*). The thinking spirit of world history transcends the limitedness of these national spirits in the knowledge of absolute spirit.[159] For Hegel, however, states themselves, as expressions of the various national spirits, are the organization and actualization of ethical life. Since varied determinate religions correspond to these various states, Hegel can set up an interpretation allowing for, and affirming, a particular role for religion and now, specifically, for a determinate religion in regard to each of these actualizations of ethical life. Just as in his systematic thought as a whole religion plays a particular role in the achievement of identity, so too this role is repeated in the various historical realizations of objective spirit. Though religion does arise out of ethical life and out of that life's organization into a state, religion remains the absolute *prius* of both.[160] By attributing to religion a teleologically grounding role vis-à-vis objective spirit, and thereby of subjective spirit as well, Hegel is able to elaborate a "secularized," and initially independent, presentation of the development of personal and societal identity. Yet, at the same time he can affirm the impossibility of separating religion and these other realizations of identity from one another. All these realizations of identity are, in various ways, mutually dependent on one another. In the end, however, personal and societal identity are rooted in religion as their reconciling truth.[161]

We can close our remarks concerning Hegel's own conception of the relation between religion and identity with the question, "Is religion indispensable in the achievement of 'identity'?" In regard to Hegel's systematic position as he elaborated it, the response must be an unqualified "yes." Without the movement of spirit through the sphere of religion there would be no grounding return in philosophical thought to the originary identity of logical thought. But it is possible, from a somewhat more external perspective, to ask if mediating identity could not be attained through some other realization of spirit than religion? The answer to this question can only be a "yes" and a "no," with the "yes" being a rather hollow one. Someone could attempt, so to speak, to replace religion by another sphere of absolute spirit. However, this could never be done in any simplistic shuffling of historical forms, given the way in which Hegel relates logic and the various spheres of nature and spirit. These latter spheres contain logic as their "inner formative principle" (*innern Bildner*).[162] For Hegel the dialectical advance toward philosophical mediation must occur as the self-realization of absolute spirit according to the logic of the concept. It is a logic which arises out of the historical forms themselves and is not in any way imposed like a mere grid. Second, given Hegel's analyses of intuition (*Anschauung*), representation (*Vorstellung*) and thought (*Denken*),[163] the penultimate realization of identity must occur in the form of representational thinking where the reconciliation takes place objectively and is then realized for each individual.[164] Third, if Hegel's dialectical method were to be retained, the suggested substitution for religion would still have to be the reconciliation of subjective and objective spirit. It would have to constitute a moment in the sphere of absolute spirit. It would have to be a movement of absolute subjectivity. Hegel would himself hardily hesitate to identify such a proposed replacement realization as religion.[165] Any historical realization of spirit chosen to replace religion would have to meet such conditions that it would itself fit Hegel's philosophically informed description of religion. Given Hegel's systematic dialectic, religion is indispensable in the achievement of identity.

NOTES

[1] Rüdiger Bubner, *Zur Sache der Dialektik* (Stuttgart: Reclam, 1980) 136. Cited by Katharina Comoth, "Hegels *Logik* und die spekulative Mystik," in *Hegel Studien*, vol. 19 (Bonn: Bouvier, 1984) 84 n. 59.

[2] See further remarks by Comoth, "Hegels *Logik* und die spekulative Mystik" 84. See also the short but seminal article by J. Patrick Atherton, "The Neoplatonic 'One' and the Trinitarian 'APXH,'" in *The Significance of Neoplatonism*, ed. R. Baine Harris (Norfolk, VA: International Society for Neoplatonic Studies, Old Dominion University, 1976) 173-185. Prof. Bernard McGinn kindly drew my attention to this study by Atherton.

[3] See, for example, the more widely formulated critique in Schlitt, *Hegel's Trinitarian Claim*. Among the many challenges to Hegel's relating of religion to identity, i.e., here to philosophical thought, see, for example, Paul Ricoeur, "The Status of *Vorstellung* in Hegel's Philosophy of Religion," in *Meaning, Truth, and God*, ed. Leroy S. Rouner (Notre Dame: University of Notre Dame Press, 1982) 70-88.

[4] In addition to the items on Hegel on identity or on religion and identity listed in Steinhauer, *Hegel Bibliography*, and regularly in the bibliography provided by the *Hegel-Archiv* in *Hegel-Studien* (Bonn: Bouvier, 1976 on), see in particular the articles in Wilhelm Raimund Beyer, ed., *Hegel Jahrbuch 1979* (Cologne: Pahl-Rugenstein, 1980); ___, *Hegel Jahrbuch 1980* (Cologne: Pahl-Rugenstein, 1981). More generally on the notion of "identity," see the articles in Odo Marquard and Karlheinz Stierle, eds., *Identität* (Munich: Fink, 1979), and among

these articles in particular on the concept of "identity," Dieter Henrich, "'Identität' – Begriffe, Probleme, Grenzen" 133-186.

5 Note Ricoeur's positive evaluation of this characteristic of Hegel's thought, "The Status of *Vorstellung*" 74.

6 E.g., GW 9:61.31-37/PS 56.

7 Note, for instance, the usage in E §§ 79, 82 R, 85.

8 E § 249, 386.

9 Without intending in any way to give the impression that Hegel is uninterested in the question of identity and religion in the *Phenomenology*, it might be pointed out that in the *Phenomenology* he uses the specific word "identity" (*Identität*) as such only six times, two in Chapter Seven on religion, and four in the more speculative and formal "Preface" written after the *Phenomenology* text itself. In these instances Hegel is generally speaking of identity in one specific way, namely, as a pejorative descriptor for that metaphysical stance which, according to him, remains frozen on the level of distinguishing understanding (*Verstand*) as opposed to his own more dynamic view of mediating reason (*Vernunft*). References to the *Phenomenology* cited by Joseph Gauvin, *Wortindex zu Hegels "Phänomenologie des Geistes."* *Hegel-Studien*, Beiheft 14 (Bonn: Bouvier, 1977) form-number 4968. See also n. 34 below.

10 E § 84-244.

11 In this chapter preference will be given to the larger *Science of Logic*. Hegel's encyclopedic or smaller treatment of logic will be referred to only in a secondary way. *Logic* so italicized will refer to Hegel's published *Science of Logic* and "logic" without italics will refer to Hegel's movement of pure thought.

12 Walter Jaeschke, "Äusserliche Reflexion und immanente Reflexion. Eine Skizze der systematischen Geschichte des Reflexionsbegriffs in Hegels Logik-Entwürfen," in *Hegel-Studien*, vol. 13 (Bonn: Bouvier, 1978) 86.

13 E.g., GW 12:25.34/GL 592.

14 See further in Schlitt, *Hegel's Trinitarian Claim* 14-28.

15 GW 11:44.24/GL 83; E § 161, 240.

16 E §§ 161, 240.

17 GW 12:32.21/GL 600.

18 GW 12:16.16-18, 31.1-7/GL 582, 599; E § 160.

19 GW 12:59.9-12/GL 630; E § 161.

20 On identity, difference, contradiction, and ground, see GW 11:258.1-293.34/GL 409-447; E §§ 112-121; on being, nothing, becoming and *Dasein*, see GW 11:43.17-44.29, 56.21-57.37/GL 82-83, 105-106; E §§ 86-89.

21 On critique see the helpful remarks in L. Bruno Puntel, *Darstellung, Methode und Struktur. Untersuchungen zur Einheit der systematischen Philosophie G. W. F. Hegels. Hegel-Studien*, Beiheft 10 (Bonn: Bouvier, 1973) 66-67, 73-74, 78-79.

22 On method see GW 12:236.1-253.34/GL 824-845; E §§ 238-243.

23 GW 11:260.19-36, 261.25-262.15/GL 411-413, to which can be added the introductory remark, GW 11:258.12-13/GL 409. Note also related remarks, GW 11:258.20-260.18, 261.1-24, 262.16-265.27/GL 409-411, 412, 413-416.

24 E § 112 with R.

25 For a more precise reargumentation of Hegel's moves, see Hinrich Fink-Eitel, *Dialektik und Socialethik. Kommentierende Untersuchungen zu Hegels "Logik"* (Meisenheim am Glan: Hain, 1978) 94-101; also the very clear and helpful commentary by John Burbidge, *On Hegel's Logic. Fragments of a Commentary* (Atlantic Highlands, NJ: Humanities Press, 1981) 73-84; and on the encyclopedic *Logic*, André Leonard, *Commentaire littéral de la logique de Hegel* (Paris: J. Vrin, 1974) 149-180.

26 "Das Wesen ist *zuerst* einfache Beziehung auf sich selbst; reine *Identität*. Diß ist seine Bestimmung, nach der es vielmehr Bestimmungslosigkeit ist." GW 11:258.12-13/GL 409.

27 GW 11:258.14-19 with 280.33-283.4/GL 409 with 433-435.

28 GW 11:260.21-25/GL 411.

29 "Das Wesen ist also einfache *Identität* mit sich." GW 11:260.24-25/GL 411.

[30] "nicht ein Wiederherstellen aus einem Andern, sondern diß reine Herstellen aus und in sich selbst." GW 11:260.28-30/GL 411.

[31] GW 11:260.30-33/GL 411-412. See also the further remarks on abstract identity, GW 11:261.1-24/GL 412-413.

[32] GW 11:19.24-37/GL 48.

[33] Recall Hegel's earlier studies on, or referring to, Fichte and Schelling, *Differenz des Fichte'schen und Schelling'schen Systems der Philosophie*, in GW 4:1-92/*The Difference between Fichte's and Schelling's System of Philosophy*, trans. H. S. Harris and Walter Cerf (Albany: State University of New York Press, 1977); *Glauben und Wissen*, in GW 4:313-414/*Faith and Knowledge*, trans. Walter Cerf and H. S. Harris (Albany: State University of New York, 1977). Interestingly, Atherton, in "The Neoplatonic 'One' and the Trinitarian 'APXH'" 173-185, effectively though not so explicitly sees Hegel's reaction to the notion of identity espoused by Schelling as parallel to the reaction of classical trinitarian thought to the internally undifferentiated notion of identity insisted upon by neoplatonism. For Atherton both Hegel and the classical trinitarian traditions have rejected an internally undifferentiated notion of identity in favor of one whose very nature includes a moment of differentiation.

[34] "die Nacht . . . worin, . . . , alle Kühe schwarz sind." GW 9:17.28-29/PS 9.

[35] "der Ausdruck der leeren *Tautologie*." GW 11:262.20/GL 413. See GW 11:262.16-265.27/GL 413-416.

[36] See GW 11:262.16-265.27/GL 413-416 in conjunction with, e.g., E § 80.

[37] "A kann nicht zugleich A und nicht A seyn." GW 11:258.28-29/GL 409. See GW 11:265.4-5/GL 416 in its wider context, GW 11:265.4-15/GL 416.

[38] GW 11:260.33-36/GL 412.

[39] GW 11:261.25-262.2/GL 412-413.

[40] "Es ist also der sich auf sich beziehende, der reflectirte Unterschied vorhanden, oder reine, *absolute Unterschied*." GW 11:262.1-2/GL 413.

41 "die Reflexion in sich selbst." GW 11:262.3/GL 413.

42 GW 11:262.10/GL 413.

43 GW 11:262.13-15/GL 413.

44 On contradiction, GW 11:279.1-283.4/GL 431-435. See Peter Rohs, *Form und Grund*. *Hegel-Studien*, Beiheft 6 (Bonn: Bouvier, 1969) 73-76; Fink-Eitel, *Dialektik und Sozialethik* 124-144.

45 Hegel's direct presentation of ground begins at GW 11:291.1/ GL 444; E §§ 121-122. See Rohs, *Form und Grund* esp. 122FF.; Fink-Eitel, *Dialektik und Sozialethik* 145-148.

46 Note, for example, that opposition is already *an sich* or implicitly contradiction, since opposition is the unity of those which are only in so far as they are not one, and the separation of those which are only as separated in the same relationship. GW 11:279.24-26/GL 431. See GW 11:282.37-38/GL 435.

47 GW 11:280.33-283.4/GL 433-435. Ground is "something that has become" (*ein gewordenes*), GW 11:282.16-17/GL 434.

48 GW 21:93.18-94.10/GL 106.

49 E.g., GW 11:280.34-281.6/GL 433. See Rohs, *Form und Grund* 74-75.

50 "Der *Grund* ist die Einheit der Identität und des Unterschieds." E § 121. See GW 11:282.33-37/GL 435.

51 Hegel presents the moments "finitude – infinite – true infinite" in the second edition of the *Logic*, GW 21:104.19-120.22, 123.20-137.15/GL 116-133, 136-150. For a summary, see Schlitt, *Hegel's Trinitarian Claim* 254-262.

52 But note Hegel's description even of this first infinite: "Diese *Identität* mit sich, die Negation der Negation, ist affirmatives Seyn, so das Andere des Endlichen, als welches die erste Negation zu seiner Bestimmtheit haben soll; – jenes Andere ist *das Unendliche*." GW 21:124.2-5/"This *identity with itself*, the negation of negation, is affirmative being and thus the other of the finite, of the finite which is supposed to have the first negation for its determinateness; this other is *the infinite*." GL 137.

53 GW 12:237.24-253.34/GL 825-844, but note especially GW 12:245.27-249.7/GL 834-838; E §§ 237-243.

54 We can recall that Hegel speaks of the mutual relationship between logic and the realphilosophical spheres, namely, all but the logical sphere. Logic both is and contains the spheres of nature and spirit in as it is their "archetype" (*Vorbildner*). The realphilosophical spheres in turn contain logic as their "inner formative principle" (*innern Bildner*). GW 12:25.29-33/GL 592. On this relationship see further in Heinz Kimmerle, "Hegels 'Wissenschaft der Logik' als Grundlegung seines Systems der Philosophie. Über das Verhältnis von 'Logik' und 'Realphilosophie,'" in *Die Logik des Wissens und das Problem der Erziehung*, Nurnberger Hegel-Tage 1981, ed. Wilhelm Raimund Beyer (Hamburg: Meiner, 1982) 52-60.

55 See Günther Rohrmoser, *Subjektivität und Verdinglichung. Theologie und Gesellschaft im Denken des jungen Hegels* (Gutersloh: Mohn, 1961); William V. Doniela, "Identity and Difference: Social Source of Hegel's Logic," in *Hegel-Jahrbuch 1980* (Cologne: Pahl-Rugenstein, 1981) 39-43.

56 Summarized in E § 574.

57 E § 247.

58 E § 248.

59 E §§ 254-256 with Remark to § 256.

60 E § 257 but esp. § 258.

61 "die *gesetzte* Identität des Raumes und der Zeit, ist zunächst ebenso der gesetzte *Widerspruch*, welcher der Raum und die Zeit, jedes an ihm selbst, ist." E § 261/PN § 261. See also E § 260.

62 "Dies Werden ist aber selbst ebensosehr das in sich Zusammenfallen seines Widerspruchs, die *unmittelbar identische daseiende* Einheit beider, die *Materie*." E § 261/PN § 261.

63 E §§ 388-412.

64 E §§ 440-482.

65 E §§ 413-439. For an introduction to this encyclopedic phenomenology, see M. J. Petry, in PN 3:359ff.

66 Petry, in PN 3:361.

67 E §§ 413-417.

68 E § 413.

69 *"Eine* Seite des Verhältnisses und das ganze Verhältnis." E § 413/PN § 413.

70 "Successive totalizations" (*totalisations successives*) is a phrase borrowed from Pierre-Jean Labarrière, *Structures et mouvement dialectique dans la "Phénoménologie de l'Esprit" de Hegel* (Paris: Aubier-Montaigne, 1968) 65 but also 43.

71 E.g., GW 9:61.31-37/PS 56.

72 GW 9:60.15-18/PS 55.

73 E § 415.

74 E §§ 418-423.

75 E §§ 423 and 424.

76 E § 428.

77 E § 416 with 424.

78 E § 430.

79 E § 431-432.

80 E § 433.

81 E §§ 432-433.

82 E §§ 434-435.

83 "das affirmative Wissen seiner selbst im andern Selbst." E §436/PSS § 436.

84 "Aber ihr Unterschied ist in dieser Identität die ganz unbestimmte Verschiedenheit oder vielmehr ein Unterschied, der keiner ist. Ihre Wahrheit ist daher die an und für sich seiende Allgemeinheit und Objektivität des Selbstbewußtseins, – die *Vernunft.*" E § 437/PSS §437.

85 "die einfache *Identität* der *Subjektivität* des Begriffs und seiner *Objektivität* und Allgemeinheit." E § 438/PSS § 438 (trans. slightly amended). The two articles in question are E §§ 438-439.

86 "Als des reinen *Ich*, der über das Objekt übergreifenden und es in sich befassenden reinen Form." E § 438/PSS § 438.

87 E § 439.

88 See Schlitt, *Hegel's Trinitarian Claim* 136-139.

89 E §§ 483-552.

90 E §§ 518-552.

91 Note E § 553.

92 E § 554.

93 E § 552.

94 Recall again Hegel's remarks on method at the end of the *Science of Logic* and the encyclopedic *Logic* (see n. 53 above) and the grounding moment of philosophy at the end of E §§ 572-577.

95 It is interesting to note already now that Hegel describes as religion the overall, uniserially and dialectically developed movement of absolute spirit as art, religion and philosophy. E § 554.

96 GW 9:368.19-37/PS 416.

97 As indicated by the title, *Enzyklopädie der philosophischen Wissenschaften im Grundrisse*.

98 E § 554.

99 E § 553-554.

100 "ewig in sich seiende als in sich zurückkerhende und zurückgekehrte *Identität*." E § 554/PM § 554.

101 See on Hegel's earlier development, Raymond Keith Williams, *Introduction to Hegel's Philosophy of Religion* (Albany: State University of New York Press, 1984). On the Berlin *Lectures*, Hodgson, in L 1:58-81.

102 Among the differences, however, we should note that, unlike for the later lecture series, at the end of the 1821 lectures Hegel speaks of the disappearance of the religious community.

103 On Hegel's philosophy of religion as a philosophy of community, see Trutz Rendtorff, *Kirche und Theologie. Die systematische Funktion des Kirchenbegriffs in der neueren Theologie* (Gutersloh: Mohn, 1966) 63-113.

104 See Ch. 2 Subsection 2b above.

105 V 3:95.12-15/L 1:186. For this and the following two notes see Ch. 2 Subsection 2c above.

106 "die Idee des Geistes, der sich zu sich selbst verhält, das Selbstbewußtsein des absoluten Geistes." V 3.222.667-668/L 1:318. See briefly in Hodgson, "Hegel's Approach to Religion" 168.

107 The question of the relationship between "God" and "absolute spirit" in Hegel's thought remains complex and highly disputed. But, in any case, whenever Hegel speaks of God he is always already working with his own logically reformulated, philosophically informed, and fully reconceptualized concept of God. See further in Ch. 6 below.

108 V 3:86.595-597 with 87.622 and 266.36-277.381/L 1:178 with 366-380. For this and the following two notes see Hodgson, in L 1:74-77.

109 V 3:277.382-329.902/L 1:380-441.

110 V 3:330.903-338.62/L 1:441-449.

111 Hodgson, "Hegel's Approach to Religion" 170.

112 "die Religion ist die Wahrheit *für alle Menschen.*" E § 573 R/PM §573 R, trans. amended.

113 V 3:221.661-670/L 1:318.

114 Heede, "Die göttliche Idee" 56-57.

115 V 3:266.36-338.62/L 1:366-449. On the concept of religion in the 1827 lectures, see also Ch. 2 Subsection 2c above.

116 "Der Begriff Gottes," V 3:266.36-277.381/L 1:366-380.

117 For a listing of the attacks on Hegel as a pantheist, see Jaeschke, in V 3:404, note to V 3:273.244-245. See also Hodgson, in L 1:375 n. 20.

118 "Identität nun ist alles, Einheit mit sich." V 3:272.234-235/L 1:374.

119 V 3:276.352-359/L 1:379. And as applied to the unity of God, V 3:277.376-379/L 1:380.

120 Unlike the order followed here, Hegel first presents his own direct affirmation concerning the beginning of the concept of religion, V 3:266.37- 272.229/L 1:366-374, before his polemic against those who accuse him of pantheism (see n. 117 above).

121 V 3:266.48-267.59/L 1:367.

122 V 3:267.60-71/L 1:367-368.

123 V 3:269.123-126/L 1:369.

124 "Es kommt . . . alles darauf an, das Wahre nicht als *Substanz*, sondern eben so sehr als *Subjekt* aufzufassen und auszudrücken." GW 9:18.3-5/PS 10.

125 V 3:269.129-149/L 1:370-371.

126 V 3:269.147-149/L 1:371.

127 GW 11:260.30/GL 411.

128 "B. Das Wissen von Gott." V 3:277.382-329.902/L 1:380-441.

12 V 3:277.382-281.443/L 1:380-385.

130 "Das erste in dem Begriff der Religion ist diese göttliche Allgemeinheit, der Geist ganz in seiner unbestimmten Allgemeinheit, für den durchaus kein Unterschied ist. Das zweite nach dieser absoluten Grundlage ist der Unterschied überhaupt, und erst mit dem Unterschied fängt Religion als solche an." V 3:277.383-387/"The first [moment] in the concept of religion is this divine universality, spirit wholly in its indeterminate universality for which there is positively no distinction. The second [moment] after this absolute foundation is distinction in general, and only with distinction does religion as such begin." L 1:380-381.

131 V 3:278.388, 397-401/L 1:381.

132 See, e.g., V 3:279.429-433/L 1:383.

133 Hodgson, "Hegel's Approach to Religion" 169. See V 3:281.444-329.902/L 1:385-441, but more restrictedly V 3:281.444-308.213/L 1:385-413.

134 Note Hegel's discussion of development "out of" the concept, V 3:83.512-84.551/L 1:174-175.

135 V 3:330.903-338.62/L 1:441-449.

136 V 3:330.903-332.972/L 1:441-444.

137 V 3:332.973-979/L 1:444.

138 V 3:332.980-334.43/L 1:444-446.

[139] V 3:334.44-335.53/L 1:446-447.

[140] V 3:336.54-338.62/L 1:448-449.

[141] Hodgson, "Hegel's Approach to Religion" 168-170.

[142] Note again, and particularly, V 3:330.903-332.964/L 1:441-443.

[143] V 3:330.903-913/L 1:441.

[144] V 3:330.913-914/L 1:442.

[145] V 3:330.914-920/L 1:442.

[146] Paraphrasing V 3:330.924-930/L 1:442.

[147] On will, see, e.g., E §§ 469-482.

[148] V 3:331.933-935/L 1:442.

[149] V 3:331.937-948/L 1:442-443.

[150] V 3:331.949-950/L 1:443.

[151] "Indem der Mensch auf sich zurücksieht, ist dieser Gegenstand ihm ein Anderes, ein Jenseits." V 3:331.950-952/L 1:443.

[152] "die Bestimmung ist diese, mich mit Gott in mir selbst zusammenzuschließen, mich in Gott zu wissen und Gott in mir." V 3:331.957-959/L 1:443.

[153] Note that the Lasson text had added to the end of the quote in n. 152 immediately above, "diese konkrete Einheit." See V 3:331, note to text line 959/"this concrete unity." L 1:443 n. 173.

[154] "mich als mich in Gott mit mir zusammenzuschließen." V 3:332.964/L 1:443.

[155] See n. 139 above.

[156] On the difficult question of the identity of content between religion and philosophy, see further in Schlitt, *Hegel's Trinitarian Claim* 35 n. 127, and the recent, longer systematic study by Rocker, "Hegel's Rational Religion."

[157] E § 573.

[158] E § 577.

[159] E § 552.

[160] E § 552 R.

[161] E § 552 R, with § 554.

[162] GW 12:25.29-33/GL 592.

[163] More particularly in relation to art, religion and philosophy, see, e.g., E §§ 556ff.

[164] Note Hegel's insistence in the 1827 *Lectures* that reconciliation first occurred objectively before it can be made available to others in and as cultus. V 3:332.965-972/L 1:443-444.

[165] Hegel's subtle, even cryptic reference in E § 554 to the whole sphere of absolute spirit as religion recalls again both the intrinsic relationship he sees between religion and identity and gives evidence of his intention to name "religion" that which, from the perspective of his encyclopedic system, immediately precedes the moment of renewed identity.

CHAPTER SIX

THE WHOLE TRUTH: TRINITY

According to Hegel religion is indispensable in the achievement of identity. But religion is not merely a means to the achievement of this identity. Rather, religion is itself the realization of inclusive identity for humankind as a whole. Those who occupy themselves with philosophical thought will be able to come to the true formulation of identity inclusive of difference. They will think this inclusive identity as a conceptually necessary dialectical movement of thought. But for the vast majority of people this realization of inclusive identity occurs in the realm of religion. For it is there that people realize the appropriate relationship between identity and difference, the one and the many or, from another perspective, self and other.

In Chapter Four we saw that for Hegel this realization occurs, on the religious level, most explicitly in the consummate religion. When presenting this religion, he develops, as he would say, "lively" (*lebendig*) formulations of the true content of identity inclusive of difference. In his philosophy of the consummate religion Hegel develops his own unique post-Kantian form of this unity or totality, namely, of identity inclusive of difference. He thinks this unity through as an overall movement of inclusive and absolute divine

171

subjectivity. He presents this movement of divine subjectivity in a particularly fascinating series of philosophical readings of the various spheres or elements of the consummate religion. In the present chapter, and in the next two chapters, we will follow Hegel's own development of the consummate religion. We will think along with Hegel in a general way and without trying to exhaust the riches of his thought. Here in Chapter Six we will think through certain aspects of his dialectical interpretation of Trinity. In Chapter Seven we will look at one of the ways in which he works with the idea of difference or otherness to interpret the movement of incarnation. Then, in Chapter Eight, we will enter into his philosophical reading of the religious representation, "kingdom of God." It is with this metaphor that Hegel reintegrates what he has worked through in his philosophical reading of Trinity and of incarnation.

Now, in the present chapter, we will think over Hegel's philosophical interpretation of Trinity as his response, on the religious level, to the overall problematic of the one and the many, of identity and difference, self and other. Indeed, his philosophy as a whole was a philosophy of subjectivity and can be seen as his general response to the eternal question of the one and the many. His philosophy of religion and, more specifically, his dialectical reconceptualization of the trinitarian God in terms of, and as, a movement of divine subjectivity, constitute particularly revealing forms of that response. Hegel's response, whether in its more general formulation or in its more specific forms as a philosophy of religion and as Trinity, has had quite a pervasive impact on modern culture and thought. His overall dialectic, and of course its expression as a dialectical movement of trinitarian divine life, has seemingly been so impressive, even persuasive, that we would be hard pressed to try to delimit its at least indirect influence on nineteenth and twentieth-century western thought. Hegel's dialectic and its religious expression have likewise had significant impact on certain currents of eastern thought.

This influence and impact should come as little surprise in view of the insight, industry, and intention toward inclusiveness with which Hegel, in developing his dialectic, and particularly its trinitarian form, handled so many universal themes. Among such themes we could list alienation, personhood and subjectivity, spirit, freedom, history, universality and particularity, community, infinity, revelation and knowledge of God. In the present chapter we will touch upon some of these themes while we lay out an overview of what Hegel said about Trinity, and then how and why he argued so forcefully concerning the importance of Trinity. This summary presentation should contribute to our understanding of Hegel's thought itself. It should also provide background for, and further facilitate access to, subsequent post-Hegelian reconceptualizations of God and Trinity. Hegel surely has much to contribute to the contemporary constructive philosophical and theological discussion.

As we consider Hegel on Trinity, we will need to leave aside any lengthy discussion of relevant secondary literature. References to the Hegelian corpus itself will serve more to exemplify and indicate general source areas. We will not try either to provide a final documentation for the statements made or to follow, in any detail, shifts and developments possibly occurring during Hegel's "mature" period from about 1807 on.[1] We will, rather, in a more synthesizing way consider his mature systematic reinterpretation of Trinity. We will consider Hegel's understanding of Trinity in three steps. That is, we will respond to the three questions of "what," "how," and "why" Hegel made such great efforts to give a philosophical interpretation to the doctrine of Trinity.

In our first step we will survey what was the shape and final result of his efforts. In a sense our remarks here will already form a response to the question of how Hegel reconceptualized Trinity as movement of divine subjectivity. Here we will also, in a sense, anticipate certain aspects of the question of why Hegel bothered with Trinity in responding, effectively, to such concerns as the relationship between the one and the many, between identity and difference, and between finite and infinite. In the second step of our synthesizing look at Hegel's thought on Trinity we will examine more particularly how he argued his position by grounding it in logic. And in the third step we will explore why Hegel elaborated Trinity as he did.

1. The Shape and End Result of Hegel's Efforts

We can conveniently summarize what the immediate results of Hegel's philosophical efforts to reconceptualize Trinity were, namely, his efforts to develop a trinitarian philosophy of inclusive and, here in the philosophy of religion, absolute subjectivity, by briefly sketching several aspects of his more significant explicit treatments of Trinity.

Already now at the beginning of our consideration of Hegel on Trinity we need to make a certain clarification. It will be helpful to indicate that he elaborates what we can, in a sort of shorthand form and with certain qualifications, refer to by using terminology current in contemporary trinitarian theology. In current theological usage "immanent" Trinity refers to distinction or difference within the divine itself. "Economic" Trinity refers to the externalization of this distinction in human history. Throughout his writing and teaching Hegel had regularly enough discussed what has thus come to be identified as "immanent" and "economic" Trinity.[2]

We can best obtain an initial grasp of his explicit trinitarian thought by selectively reviewing the ways in which he positions and structures Trinity in three of the texts where he deals with the "realphilosophical"[3] spheres: the *Phenomenology of Spirit*; the 1830 *Encyclopedia*; and his four series of Berlin lectures on the philosophy of religion.

Hegel's *Phenomenology of Spirit* was published in 1807. Within the context of his mature systematic position it can be seen as a "first work" – perhaps overly ambitious and surely the most debated but, in some ways, also the most fertile of his works. It was a sort of "first love" to which he returned time and again, at least for examples. The *Phenomenology* presents the long journey from consciousness to self-consciousness as a series of shapes or figures of consciousness. These shapes or figures of consciousness have come to be seen as the self-manifestation of absolute spirit. The point of view from which the author writes is that of the final chapter, "Absolute Knowledge," where concept and self are identical. As Hegel has so often said, the human being is essentially thought and thinking. He sees revelatory religion, and in fact the triune God, as the penultimate figure or shape of consciousness in this journey.[4] In, and as, this penultimate shape of consciousness, Trinity is presented as the explication of the prior incarnational immediacy of a sensuously perceived divine-human self. Trinity is, then, the shape or figure of revelatory religion developed by Hegel as the progressively more explicit presentation of trinitarian divine subjectivity. Trinitarian divine subjectivity is presented first as the immediacy of thought as such, then as the otherness of representation, and, third, as the inclusive element of self-consciousness itself, spirit in and as community. Each of these three moments of revelation is distinct in that it has its own internal structural configuration and dynamic. Each is, in its own way, the momentary totality of revelation as reconciliation. Each is momentary totality of the overall movement of spirit. It was apparently in the *Phenomenology* that Hegel first clearly elaborated the basic syllogistic structure of these momentary totalities.[5] Among these totalities, community represents an enriched return to the immediacy of "immanent" Trinity. But community, as well as the previous two momentary totalities, remains, on the level of religion, the true content representationally expressed as other than the self. According to Hegel the very inadequacy of this reconciliation, realized in and through full divine self-revelation, brings about the inner dynamic transition to the final shape of self-consciousness. This final shape is that of absolute knowledge, where form and content are adequate in the identification of self and concept. Inclusive or absolute subjectivity, realized representationally in the form of divine subjectivity over against religious consciousness, comes to appropriate philosophical expression in, and as, the overcoming of this otherness in self-determining absolute knowledge.

We should recall that Hegel's 1830 *Encyclopedia of the Philosophical Sciences in Outline* begins with the movement of logic, understood as pure thought, and logic's initial moment. This initial moment is the thought category of pure being, the being of pure thought. The *Encyclopedia* ends in an enriching advance, which, in the philosophy of absolute spirit, is equally enriched resultant return to what was the initial movement of logic. But now, at the end of this encyclopedic, self-developing movement of spirit, the logical concept has become the philosophical concept where form and content are truly and fully adequate. Hegel would say that concept and reality are united in the absolute idea. As its title indicates, the *Encyclopedia* constitutes an outline of Hegel's overall mature philosophical system. It does this, as we have intimated, not as a mere juxtaposition of philosophical sciences. Rather, it presents absolute spirit as idea developing from the immediacy of logic to the logical idea's self-othering in nature and finite spirit. This development of spirit continues as enriching, advancing return through finite spirit in philosophic thought to the renewed and enriched immediacy, or identity, of the idea. This overall movement from logic to philosophy is a process of self-determination by absolute spirit. The movement of spirit occurs in logic as inclusive subjectivity, in nature as self-othering of the idea, and then as absolute subjectivity in and through art, religion, and philosophy. Within this overall process Hegel again places revealed religion as the penultimate sphere. He presents revealed religion schematically in the form of a syllogistically structured "immanent" and "economic" self-revelation as self-development of trinitarian divine subjectivity.[6] He employs an explicitly religious or representational, but nevertheless always philosophically informed, language to lay out "immanent" and "economic" Trinity as three syllogistically structured moments of universality, particularity, and individuality. He again develops the last of these, individuality, as a movement of three self-mediating syllogisms.[7] In the *Encyclopedia* this moment of individuality climaxes as the effective self-revelation of absolute spirit in and through finite spirit in community, the final moment of syllogistically structured divine trinitarian reconciliation. In the sphere of religious representation this reconciliation remains the movement of self-determining divine subjectivity. It has not yet been explicitly established as mediation of the absolute self or concept in the form of philosophical thought.

Hegel lectured throughout his Berlin years on various sections of the material outlined in the *Encyclopedia* (first edition 1817, second and third original editions 1827 and 1830). As we have already indicated in Part One of our present study, the new editions of Hegel's *Lectures on the Philosophy of Religion* contain his 1821 manuscript as well as transcripts of his 1824 and 1827 lecture series along with fragments from his 1831 lectures. In the 1821 lectures Hegel had treated the absolute or consummate religion as the last of the determinate religions. From 1824 on he placed it more independently and prominently as the third, unifying moment bringing to fruition the initial unity of the concept of religion and the reality already achieved in the second moment, namely, that of the determinate multiplicity of world religions. In 1824 he simplified his 1821 doubly triadic structure of the absolute religion into a single triad of three elements in the development of the idea of God. This resulted in a return to the overall structure of the revelatory religion as found in the 1807 *Phenomenology*, a structure discernible as well in the *Encyclopedia*.[8] Hegel followed the same organization in the 1827 lectures, where religion, the consciousness of the all-encompassing object or God, has become the fully inclusive self-consciousness of absolute spirit. This inclusive self-consciousness is trinitarian divine self-positing subjectivity. It is a movement from universality to particularity to individuality.[9]

Hegel apportioned theological content somewhat differently in various presentations of the second and third moments in the movement of self-positing trinitarian divine subjectivity. Still the basic progression of this movement from first to second to third sphere or element is consistently describable in terms of moments of the concept as respectively universality, particularity, and individuality.[10] Indeed, it would seem that the richness of Hegel's thought allowed him to speak of these three moments or elements in many ways and on many levels. For present purposes it will be sufficient to summarize, in the briefest of fashions, the way in which Hegel in the 1827 lectures internally structured these elements of "immanent" and "economic" Trinity themselves according to a varied interrelationship of universality, particularity, and individuality.

We are here proposing that Hegel sets up the dialectical movement in each element in such a way that it develops according to, and therefore manifests, a specific syllogistic structure. When we speak of syllogism here, we should mention that we mean Hegel's particular interpretation of the syllogism and not merely the traditional understanding of syllogism as a form of three-termed movement of inference. Hegel gave to this traditional notion of syllogism a specific dialectical spin when he placed it as a thought determination or moment in the movement of pure thought. For him it was a movement of inclusive subjectivity. It was a self-mediating development of thought, progressing on the basis of a middle term, which mediated between the two extremes, or between the syllogism's major and minor premises. When allowance is made for the further elaboration in the *Encyclopedia*, it would seem that these syllogistic structures have remained constant and consistent in the various presentations from 1807 on.

In the 1827 lectures the first element is describable as the overall appearance of the divine idea in the realm of thought as universality, the immediacy of the "in itself."[11] This self-enclosed movement of "immanent" Trinity is for Hegel the concrete universal containing otherness within itself. It is, in its own way, the moment of initial identity. It contains this otherness within itself as a moment of judgment or separation as negation, but it does this only as a sort of play. The distinguishing is itself, as difference, nevertheless the entire idea. In line with Hegelian dialectic, the universal and its negation, i.e., its other, have become an identity. This inner dynamic of otherness, or particularity, functioning as mediating totality inclusive of the extremes of universality and of the resultant identity as individuality, presents the triadic structure of inclusive and, here, absolute subjectivity. When thought through, this movement of subjectivity takes on the form of the logical thought determination that Hegel calls the categorical syllogism (U-P-I).[12]

The second element is the appearance of the divine idea in the doubled movement of diremption and reconciliation.[13] It is the sphere of particularity, difference, and objectivity. It appears as the movement of judgment in which the divine idea comes into existence "for itself." In this element, characterized by contradiction, the divine idea others itself as an independent world out of which there arises finite spirit. Within this world finite spirit, in turn, distinguishes itself from nature and from its own nature. This distinguishing, which goes on within finite spirit, gives rise to the contradictory reality of finite spirit as both good and evil. The establishment of this contradictory character of finite spirit is itself the indication of an exigency for reconciliation. Such a reconciliation has to occur in an exclusive individuality, namely, in an individual divine-human self, in the mediating death of Christ. Hegel goes on to present reconciliation in the particularity of the community's consciousness of an immediate existence spiritually interpreted as the risen Christ. This historical appearance of the divine idea has taken place as a triadically structured movement. The movement occurs from God, as presupposed universality, to the particularity of the community's spiritual consciousness of the risen Christ by means of mediating individuality (the doubled individuality of nature and finite spirit). Mediating individuality culminates or reaches its climactic depths in the death of Christ. For the philosophically informed religious consciousness, this triadic structure of the absolute subject reveals the form of what Hegel identifies as the hypothetical syllogism (U-I/I-P).[14]

The objective reconciliation achieved in Christ has, in the third element, namely, in spiritual community,[15] become for Hegel the subjective relationship of the individual subject to this objective reconciliation with the truth. The previous two elements, and now this third element, are for Hegel the very progression of the idea of God.[16] They are the absolute eternal idea in itself, for itself and now "in and for itself." These elements are the very life and activity of God now consummated in the third element as the community or unity of the individual empirical subjects who are filled by the Spirit of God. These subjects are individuals who live in the Spirit of God and with whom the Spirit of God is dialectically identified. God existing in and as the community of finite subjects is the very realization of God as spirit, the Holy Spirit or reconciling return of the divine idea out of the self-othering of judgment, a movement of absolute divine subjectivity.

This third element develops as the reconciliation of the individual believer with the life, death and resurrection of Christ in three stages: the origin of the community in the outpouring of the Holy Spirit; the realization or actualization of the community through faith, doctrine, church, and eucharist; and, the realization of the spirituality of the community in universal actuality as philosophy. In the first stage, the community originates in the particularity of a shared religious consciousness. In the second stage, Hegel sees the various theologoumena there discussed as the reconciling active presence of the spirit, of the objectively presented universality of truth mediating the objective reconciliation, obtained in Christ, to the individual subjects. In the third stage, Hegel presents the movement from the shared conscious inner enjoyment of the presence of God, achieved in the second stage, to an adequate mediation in self-knowledge, in philosophical thought. The knowledge of being at peace with God has become a knowledge of being at peace with oneself. Here in philosophical thought, knowledge or subjectivity is recognized as developing out of itself and as reconciling itself with itself. This rationality is true freedom. Philosophy is the comprehending thought which, as essentially concrete, determines itself to its totality, the idea. It is absolute spirit, the very peace of God, true individuality. This mediation of particularity with inclusive individuality by means of objective universality (P-U-I) is, as religious reconciliation in community, the realization of what Hegel calls the disjunctive syllogism.[17] It results both in a grounding return to the immediacy or identity of "immanent" Trinity and in the advance to philosophical thinking.

Reconciliation, or divine self-revelation, as the realization of trinitarian self-determining absolute subjectivity, is, in the real-philosophical spheres of the *Phenomenology*, the *Encyclopedia* and the lectures on the philosophy of religion, always positioned as the penultimate but indispensable systematic sphere. It is here that alienation is really overcome. However, for Hegel it still occurs in the form of religious representation where form is inadequate to the true content, namely, to achieved reconciliation. Reconciliation indeed takes place in God, but still in God as Other. In comparison with his more hesitant position concerning the value of religious representation in the *Phenomenology*, by the time of the *Encyclopedia* and the Berlin lectures Hegel values this representational form, as we have mentioned, as the truth for all humanity.[18] Nevertheless, from the *Phenomenology* on he had consistently retained the view that this true content must, on the basis of the inner dynamic tension between content and form, sublate itself into the true form of philosophical thought. It must sublate itself into the form of the self-thinking idea as absolute spirit. In absolute spirit form and content, self and concept, coincide. As Hegel would say, concept and reality are united in the idea. In fact he has always interpreted the religious name or term, "God," from the perspective of the concept (*Begriff*). But, from a speculative systematic perspective or from the point of view of his system as a whole, it is in the sublation of trinitarian divine subjectivity in philosophical or self-identical thought that Hegel formally and explicitly reconceptualizes Trinity. Furthermore, it is with this move to philosophy that he retroactively grounds his interpretation of Trinity which he had previously developed in the philosophy of religion.

In his encyclopedic system as a whole, this final moment, namely, philosophical thought, is for Hegel the truth or perfect correspondence of subject and object, or better, of self and concept. It is this perfect correspondence or absolute spirit, this infinite or inclusive totality, only in so far as it is the end result inclusive of the whole process: the logical idea's self-differentiation into nature and finite spirit, and that idea's enriching return to itself in and through, while then sublating, finite spirit.[19] As the final moment, philosophy is for Hegel the grounding return to the immediacy of logical thought. Though many other reasons could be cited, it is this enriched and grounding return which finally justifies seeing Hegel's real-philosophical spheres themselves, and in particular his philosophical thought or concept, as his reconceptualization of Trinity. Moreover, it is this grounding return which justifies recognizing his logic as the appropriate systematic logical reformulation of "immanent" Trinity, with "immanent" carefully nuanced so as not to insinuate an independently *existent* reality. This grounding return on the part of philosophical thought explains why Hegel can use philosophically reinterpreted representational language to describe logic as the presentation of God as God is in the eternal divine essence before the creation of nature and finite spirit.[20]

When we look at his encyclopedic system as a whole, we see that, from the perspective of his system in its speculative formulation Hegel appropriately treats of "immanent" Trinity twice. First, as movement of self-determining inclusive subjectivity in the form of pure thought or logic; and, as moment of universality in the real-philosophical sphere of the philosophy of religion. He likewise treats of "economic" Trinity twice. He does this, first, in the realphilosophical sphere of the philosophy of religion as including "immanent" Trinity. He again treats of "economic" Trinity in philosophical thought as the grounding return both to the immediacy of "immanent" Trinity on the level of philosophy of religion and to the immediacy of logic on the level of spirit as a whole. The encyclopedic system is, in its totality, Hegel's philosophically reinterpreted presentation of "economic" Trinity inclusive of "immanent" Trinity. This latter, "immanent" Trinity, is the initial moment structuring the overall dynamic of divine self-revelation. From the perspective of his system in its speculative presentation, this overall dynamic of divine self-revelation is a movement from initial identity to difference to grounding return as renewed, inclusive identity. It is a movement from initial infinite, to finitude, to inclusive or true infinite.[21] In this way, logically reformulated as inclusive subject, religiously represented as absolute divine subjectivity, and philosophically reconceptualized as absolute spirit, Trinity is for Hegel the whole truth.

2. How Hegel Argued His Trinitarian Position

Since Hegel is always doing philosophy ultimately from the perspective of the concept, the above presentation of his realphilosophical trinitarian thought is, in a very real sense, itself already a response to the question of how he argued his trinitarian position. For Hegel correct presentation is argumentation. Nevertheless, it is important to turn more directly to the 1812-1816 *Science of Logic*[22] for two reasons. First, because for Hegel logic represents the appropriate reformulation of "immanent" Trinity as self-determining inclusive subjectivity. Second, because of his conception of the systematic relationship between the realphilosophical spheres and the sphere of logic, namely, the movement of pure thought as a series of self-positing thought determinations. For Hegel logic is discovered and "contained" in the spheres of nature and spirit since it is their "inner formative principle" (*innern Bildner*). Specific logical thought determinations are not merely structures externally or formalistically applied to moments in the spheres of nature and spirit. Rather, these thought determinations themselves arise out of, and are thereby revealed as, such inner formative principles. These principles can then be examined in the clarity of their archetypal expression as moments in the dialectical movement of pure thought. So logic itself likewise is and "contains" the spheres of nature and spirit in so far as it is their "archetype" (*Vorbildner*).[23] This movement of pure thought is its own content and, therefore, absolute form. Hegel's construction of a dynamic logic, a post-Kantian replacement for traditional metaphysics, forms his strongest and most prolonged argumentation for his philosophical interpretation of Trinity. He reconceptualized Trinity by means of an onto-logical reinterpretation of "immanent" Trinity.

Before turning directly to the *Logic* it will be helpful to recall that Hegel's reconceptualization of the triune God is a process of sublation (*Aufhebung*) in which there has occurred a triply structured transition of negation, preservation, and development. The Trinity of religious representation retains for Hegel the characteristics of three independently represented subjects in an inadequately purified parental and filial relationship. This is true particularly for popular piety, but also for dogmatic theology.[24] Hegel's reconceptualization negates such a representation. It negates as well the continuing projection of reconciliation in so far as it is achieved in a divine subject over against the self. The true content of this religious reconciliation is preserved, according to Hegel,[25] in the move to philosophical thought as the full mediation of subject and object, self and concept, in self-determining conceptual thought. As purification this transition not only negates but preserves in a truer form, and therefore develops, the true content expressed as Trinity. Nowhere can this sublation be more clearly seen than in Hegel's proposal to translate what appears on the level of religious representation as the divine freedom, namely, to create or not to create, into a logically necessary self-othering of the absolute idea in, and as, nature. This self-othering as logically necessitarian self-determination is called by Hegel "free self-release."[26]

Hegel understood logic to be an immanent and consistent internally self-justifying progression of thought determinations in three successive spheres. There is, first, the logic of being, then the logic of essence, and, third, the logic of the concept. He chose to work with reflexively available conceptual thought so as to argue not on the basis of opinion but in the public realm. Already in the philosophy of religion Hegel had, in principle, elaborated creation and crucifixion within "immanent" Trinity by means of his understanding of difference as negation. Now in the dialectical movement of self-positing and self-determining logical thought he has integrated positivity by defining it as otherness characterized as negation. It is, then, the overcoming of this negation in the realization that the other is the other *of* the initial identity which constitutes the fundamental dynamic of self-determining pure thought. Logic presents the structure of inclusive subjectivity as self-relationality.

The speculative dialectic of self-relationality is what underlies all of Hegel's mature systematic thought, including his reconceptualization of trinitarian divine subjectivity. The dialectic can be summarized by referring to the movement of Hegel's first logical thought determinations, being/nothing/becoming,[27] and by exegeting them in the light of his final remarks on method.[28]

In the first logical triad, being becomes determinate through nothing, and it does this in and through the fact that resultant becoming, namely, the explicit, positive thought that nothing is, settles in determinate being, *Dasein*. This Hegelian dialectic is a movement from the positive to a negation to the negation of this negation and, thus, to a renewed positive. It is a movement from beginning through progression to result. In this totally immanent, consistent, and self-grounding movement of pure thought, the initial positive, in this instance being, is an immediacy with a content and a determination as yet *an sich*. The initial positive is a unity unposited, still only implicit and, therefore, not yet available to itself. In this sense the initial, positive beginning (being) is characterized by a lack, the thinking of which gives rise to the negation of that beginning, that is, to nothing and to the contradiction that nothing is. Negation's arising remains immanent; this thinking is the movement of thought itself. The motivating force behind this progression lies, for Hegel, in the inability of immediacy to rest in its lacking. Immediacy cannot be thought through adequately without there occurring a transition to the negation of the initial immediacy. This negation, then, is the other of initial immediacy and inclusive of that immediacy; it is *für sich*. This other, established on the basis of the internal inadequacy constitutive of immediacy, is difference, the other of initial identity and identity's determinate negation through which indeterminate identity is to become determinate.

This immediate dialectic of being and nothing, and Hegel's dialectical thought as a whole, are so constructed that immediacy requires a mediated and mediating difference arising out of itself in order to come to itself, to be *an und für sich* what it was originally only implicitly. Thinking through the contradiction constitutive of difference (exemplified in the first logical triadic by "nothing is") overcomes that contradiction by bringing to expression, in thought, the unity (becoming settling in *Dasein*) already contained in the contradiction itself. The result is self-mediation in which immediacy and difference, the positive and its negation, *an sich* and *für sich*, implicit and explicit arrive at a higher unity containing them as its moments.

This logic of Hegel's can be described as the speculative dialectical method in and through which the concept determines itself as a non-temporal movement of ever more determinate thought categories. Whereas Hegel's earlier discussed philosophy of religion, and especially his philosophy of the consummate or absolute religion, could well be termed a *phänomeno-theo-logik*, logic was constructed as an *onto-theo-logik*.[29] The logical transition from one thought determination to another has taken place in the logic of being as one thought category after another's "having gone over into" the other. In the logic of essence the transition constituting determinations of reflection occurs as "appearing in" the other. And, in the logic of the concept, each determination of the concept develops into its other. The thought determinations or categories are themselves, in the logic of being and in the logic of essence, implicitly, or in the logic of the concept, explicitly, non-temporal "momentary" totalities of the concept. There is no underlying subject or thinker. Each thought determination arises as a "momentary" totality within Hegel's dialectically developing method (beginning/progression/result). Each is, in its own way, a form of becoming (*werdend*).[30] To the extent, then, that the structure of "going over into" or self-donation is constitutive of all logical moments, Hegel's speculative presentation of the movement of pure thought is, from the initial moment of pure being to the resultant return as absolute idea, as a whole the systematic reformulation of "immanent" Trinity. It is equally the archetypal structure of "economic" Trinity. Furthermore, to the extent that such "self-donation" is the dynamic structure of personhood, or better, with reference to logic, of subjectivity, Hegel has managed to elaborate, in a logical formulation, what was for him represented in the consummate religion as a "tri-personal" God.[31] Though he carries out this elaboration in the singular and speaks simply of "person" or "subject,"[32] Hegel is, in regard to logic, not referring to an existent. He thinks, in a post-nominalist framework, of the concrete universal as the structure of subjectivity. In so thinking Hegel can be seen as attempting to move beyond the dichotomy between what would today be termed mono-subjectival and societal formulations of Trinity.

3. Systematic Concerns Motivating Hegel's Reconceptualization

In order to get at some of the systematic religious and philosophical concerns motivating his endeavor, we can reformulate the question of why Hegel reconceptualized Trinity as follows: What did Hegel see was at stake in his attempt to reconceptualize the trinitarian God from the perspective of the concept? So phrased, this question subsumes into one the questions of why he reformulated Trinity and why he did so in specific ways. We may now briefly answer this question from within the framework and perspective of Hegel's mature systematic and speculative position.[33] We can indicate what is at stake for Hegel by reviewing religious-representational formulations of his claim that God can be conceived adequately as person, subject, and spirit only if God is conceived as Trinity. We can then infer the underlying philosophical concerns which pushed him to reinterpret Trinity, and to do this in specific ways, from his resultant philosophical position as a whole.

In his manuscript for the 1821 philosophy of religion lectures on the consummate religion Hegel wrote, "God is *spirit* – that which we call the *triune* God."[34] God is spirit because God becomes the other and sublates this other.[35] Hegel claims that God remains but an empty word if God is not grasped as triune.[36] He is concerned to establish a concept of God which does not leave personhood behind.[37] There is, then, a particular earnest with which he allows his concerns to surface as he makes this claim that only if God is known as what would today be termed "immanent" and "economic" Trinity can God be known as spirit. Only as Trinity can God be inclusive subjectivity becoming absolute spirit finally as philosophical concept. We can further spell out these concerns of Hegel's by citing the consequences he draws from the successful, or unsuccessful, establishment of the trinitarian structure for which he so ardently argues. In the trinitarian divine self-othering and sublation of that otherness (not, of course a simple movement of othering and return but one of progression which is both development and enriched return), he recognizes the principle and axis upon which history turns.[38] World history is, for Hegel, a history of God.[39] This trinitarian dialectic is equally the principle of freedom,[40] the source of community,[41] the reason why God can be known,[42] and the justifying content of Christianity's distinctive truth claims[43] as the religion of absolute subjectivity[44] and freedom.[45] Trinity, the content of the true religion, is divine self-revelation.[46] According to Hegel, without a trinitarian structure to the divine there could be no true reconciliation in Christ.[47] God would, as mentioned, be an empty name, one-sided and finite rather than inclusive and infinite.[48] There could be no truth as mediation for there would be no possibility of a transition from religion, with its true content but representational form, to philosophy, where form and content would be identical.

In religion the overcoming of alienation in reconciliation is realized representationally in the trinitarian God as a movement of divine self-revelation and absolute subjectivity. That same content was to have received its adequate form in philosophical thought. It was to have been expressed in its necessary movement, namely, as a self-mediation which was to have been the identity of thought and reality, identity and difference or, from another perspective, self and concept.[49] In this sense Hegel's famous claim in the Preface to the *Phenomenology* that the true must be grasped not only as substance but also as subject[50] becomes an appropriate philosophical reformulation of his trinitarian claim. It reiterates his concern not to conceive of God as less than inclusive subject.

Hegel surmised that the orthodoxy of his day, with its supernaturalistic theology, tended to reduce God to an object and that its otherworldliness could lead to a this-worldly atheism. He realized, as well, that the developing bourgeois society might easily set itself over against the unified state and fragment it. This double estrangement in religion and society was, for Hegel, expressed paradigmatically in Kant's philosophical dualism. This religious and societal estrangement, along with its expression in Kantian dualism, formed an alienation which was grounded in Enlightenment thought. Hegel proposed to overcome this alienation by adopting, but more so adapting, Fichte's notion of the absolute, and then the positing, ego. If the self was, in some way, for Kant the source of all but the thing-in-itself, it only took one more step to propose that thought was the source of both phenomena and noumena, appearance and essence.[51]

Hegel's particular formulation of the concept of inclusive subjectivity meant he had to insist that truth could be mediated only by a content which was seen to be the other of itself and, indeed, was ultimately not other than itself.[52] Or again, religiously expressed, in the God-world relationship God must be seen as inclusive of the world. Hegel gave logical expression to this inclusive relationship in his elaboration of the true infinite as the mediation of infinite and finite, and thus as inclusive totality.[53] What he had termed the "bad infinite," or merely an infinite progression, had to go over into the concept of the true infinite, in which the thinking of finitude would result in the transition to the infinite, and vice versa. For Hegel the true infinite is finally, in its speculative formulation, the process of mediation in which the infinite, having become finite, sublates itself as its own difference or finitude into its own self-affirmation. The true infinite is the posited negation of negation.[54] It is identity inclusive of difference, the one inclusive of the many. To be anything less than inclusive would be to remain one-sided and finite.

In the context of the present discussion it is this concept of the true infinite as concrete universal, inclusive totality, or absolute spirit which provides the best access to the systematic religious and philosophical concerns lying behind Hegel's reconceptualization of Trinity. The true infinite, as a movement from the positive to its negation to the negation of this negation, recalls again how Hegel integrated the positivity of religion, or positivity in general, into a widened notion of reason. To the Enlightenment mind, positivity had designated a form of particularity which could not be deduced from universal reason. Hegel's definition of difference or otherness as negation allowed him to integrate particularity, as the other of universality, into the overall movement of reason itself.

To recapitulate, Hegel's dialectical and speculative reconceptualization of Trinity was his post-Kantian response to the problem of the one and the many or of the relationship between identity and difference. By means of this reconceptualization Hegel was able to give content to the term "God." In his philosophy of religion he understood God as absolute subjectivity and subject. Consequently, history became the history of God, and community the locus of spirit's self-realization. Freedom was understood ultimately as logically necessary but truly *self*-determination. Knowledge of God, Christianity's truth claim, and truth itself, were likewise grounded immediately in Hegel's reconceptualization of Trinity as movement of self-determining divine subjectivity. In eliminating the need for a distinction in "immanent" Trinity between divine essence and divine person, Hegel continued the modern turn to the subject. He was able to avoid a Cartesian appeal to God to guarantee truth and certainty in knowledge by making of the trinitarian God the very structure of truth itself. Hegel claimed to recognize in Trinity in general, and in the "inner" or "immanent" Trinity in particular, a congruity with his fundamental speculatively formulated dialectic of positive/negation/negation of negation. In the Christian doctrine of Trinity he discovered the means to give religious expression to mediation in the self as concept. This was his philosophical response to alienation. Perhaps in the post-Hegelian world it is still that philosophical response, in the form of the true infinite as inclusive totality which, when appropriately adapted, will prove most fecund for the contemporary reconceptualization of Trinity as the whole truth.

NOTES

¹ For an internal critique of Hegel's reconceptualization of Trinity, fuller reference to the Hegelian corpus and secondary literature, as well as for some initial remarks on the possible shifts and development during Hegel's work from the *Phenomenology of Spirit* (1807) on, see Schlitt, *Hegel's Trinitarian Claim*, and particularly concerning literature on Hegel's trinitarian thought, see p. 7. For a historical review of important literature see Jaeschke, *Die Religionsphilosophie Hegels* 83-86. And note the following more recent studies on Hegel on Trinity: Erik Schmidt, "Hegel und die kirchliche Trinitätslehre," *Neue Zeitschrift für systematische Theologie und Religionsphilosophie* 24 (1982) 241-260; Herbert Huber, *Idealismus und Trinität*; Katharina Comoth, *Die Idee als Ideal. Trias und Triplizität bei Hegel* (Heidelberg: Carl Winter Universitätsverlag, 1986); Jaeschke, *Die Vernunft in der Religion* 314-323. For further references to studies often more generally or more indirectly treating of Hegel on Trinity see Erwin Schadel, ed., with the co-operation of Dieter Brünn and Peter Müller, *Bibliotheca Trinitariorum. International Bibliography of Trinitarian Literature*, vol. 1: *Author Index*, vol. 2: *Indices and Supplementary List* (Munich: K. G. Saur, 1984, 1988) 2:233-234.

² Unless otherwise indicated, "Trinity" is to be taken in an inclusive sense to indicate both "immanent" and "economic" Trinity. For a most helpful overview of Hegel's discussions on Trinity see Jörg Splett, *Die Trinitätslehre G.W.F. Hegels* (Munich: Alber, 1965) esp. 78 on "immanent" and "economic" Trinity. Note that "immanent" Trinity will be used at the end of Section 1 of this present chapter to refer as well to Hegel's logic. For an example of the use of "immanent" and "economic" Trinity in contemporary theology, see Karl Rahner, *The Trinity* (London: Burns and Oates, 1970) esp. 21-24, 99-103.

³ As intimated in Ch. 5 above, "realphilosophical" is a term used technically to indicate all the Hegelian spheres of philosophy (here including his presentation "prior" to absolute knowledge in the *Phenomenology*) other than that of logic.

4 GW 9:409.3-421 end/PS 464.37-478 end.

5 See the background study by Hermann Schmitz, *Hegel als Denker der Individualität* (Meisenhan/Glan: Hain, 1957) 118-146. Note Hegel's own description of his trinitarian thought as a "syllogism of absolute self-mediation itself made up of three syllogisms" ("Schluß der absoluten Vermittlung mit sich, den drei Schlüsse ausmachen"). See Hegel's own review of 1. "Über die Hegelsche Lehre oder: absolutes Wissen und moderner Pantheismus," 2. "Über Philosophie überhaupt und Hegels *Enzyklopädie* der philosophischen Wissenschaften insbesondere. Ein Beitrag zur Beurteilung der letzteren. Von Dr. K. E. Schubarth und Dr. L. Cargonico," in *Berliner Schriften 1818-1831*, Philosophische Bibliothek, vol. 240, ed. Johannes Hoffmeister (Hamburg: Felix Meiner, 1956) 352. With regard to my interpretation of Hegel's trinitarian thought in syllogistic terms, I think it important to note that, in various discussions and in several written statements since the appearance of my study, *Hegel's Trinitarian Claim*, several Hegel scholars have argued either simply that Hegel's trinitarian thought is not syllogistically structured or, more nuancedly, that it is only the last of the three moments that is syllogistically structured (see, e.g., in n. 7 below, Emilio Brito's remark apparently more directly concerning "immanent" Trinity). Most do seem to agree that the overall third or last moment of of the consummate religion, that of individuality, is explicitly syllogistically structured by Hegel. At least Hegel says it is in E §§ 569-571. I myself would, however, want to continue to argue for a recognizable syllogistic structure consistently present at least in the first and third moments of Hegel's overall trinitarian thought. Despite shifts in his presentation throughout the Berlin years, it would seem to me that a fundamentally consistent syllogistic structure underlies even Hegel's shifting organization of the second moment, namely, that of creation and incarnation. The implications one might, then, want to draw concerning the type of relationship between this syllogistic structure and the shifting distribution of contents would be a question requiring further reflection and study. On Hegel's shifting distribution of content in the second moment or element see further in Ch. 4 Section 2 above and in Ch. 6 below.

6 E §§ 564-571, explicitly on syllogisms §§ 567-571. For a convenient parallel presentation of the English translations of Hegel's pre-

sentation of the revealed religion in the three original editions of the *Encyclopedia*, see John Burbidge, "The Syllogisms of Revealed Religion, or the Reasonableness of Christianity," *The Owl of Minerva* 18 (1986) 29-42.

7 The first sentence in E § 571 referring to three syllogisms constituting one syllogism is varyingly interpreted to indicate either all three moments of the concept or merely the three syllogisms constituting the moment of individuality. On the basis of a consideration of the overall structural dynamic of Hegel's thought, of the immediate context, and of other descriptions of Trinity by Hegel as syllogism, I am interpreting the disputed phrase to mean directly the three syllogisms making up the moment of individuality and, through them, as well all three moments of the concept. See Hegel's remark on Trinity and syllogism, cited in n. 5 above. Prof. Emilio Brito finds this syllogistic interpretation of Hegel's presentation of Trinity (and here I take it he means especially the moment of "immanent" Trinity) unconvincing since, according to him, the trinitarian concept is only virtually syllogistic. Brito writes, "Cette solution [with reference to Schlitt's interpretation of E §§ 569-570] . . . nous semble difficile à admettre : Hegel n'emploie jamais le terme de syllogisme à propos de la Trinité; et pour cause : le concept trinitaire n'est que virtuellement syllogisme; l'explicitation en syllogisme de la vie trinitaire déborde, à ses yeux, l'abstraction idéale de l'Éternel." Review of *Hegel's Trinitarian Claim*, by Dale M. Schlitt, in *Revue théologique de Louvain* 17 (1986) 369. I would suggest that perhaps the development toward further explicitness from Hegel's logically speaking earlier forms of the syllogisms to the later forms would take sufficiently into account both the movement, in the consummate religion, from more implicit to more explicit and the realization that, from the beginning of the presentation of the consummate religion, Hegel is already working with God as absolute subjectivity.

8 Allowing, of course, for the elaboration of the *Encyclopedia* moment of individuality itself in terms of three syllogisms. See E §§569-570.

9 E.g., V 5:254.80-89. See also the text following, V 5:254.90-105 and 255.136-256.141. Note that in view of V 5:198.660-662 the third element or community is to be identified as individuality or the individual. These three texts are from the 1827 lectures.

¹⁰ On the differences among the various Berlin lecture series see Ch. 4 Section 2 above. On the question of the development of Trinity in the *Phenomenology* in terms of self-consciousness and then, in the later writings, in terms of moments of the concept see Jaeschke, *Die ReligionsphilosophieHegels* 90. It might be helpful to recall that some Hegel interpreters have suggested this continuity of description is a rather more superficial or even artificial move on Hegel's part. See the important discussion of serious questions in Jaeschke, 94-97.

¹¹ V 5:199.690-215.73 with the overviews in 197.608-617 and 198.669-670.

¹² On the categorical syllogism, see GW 12:119.13-121.15/GL 696-698. In this syllogism the major or first extreme is in the mode of universality (U) (*Allgemeinheit*), the mediating or unifying middle term in the mode of particularity (P) (*Besonderheit*), and the minor or second extreme in the mode of individuality (I) (*Einzelheit*). On syllogism in Hegel's thought in general, see Schlitt, *Hegel's Trinitarian Claim* 101-106. Note that for Hegel it is possible to exchange the order of the extremes, as identified in terms of the moments of the concept, in a syllogism.

¹³ V 5:215.74-251.24 with the overviews in 197.618-198.645 and 198.671-199.678.

¹⁴ On the hypothetical syllogism, see GW 12:121.16-123.31/GL 698-701. In this syllogism the major or first extreme is in the mode of universality, the doubled mediating or unifying middle term in the mode of individuality, and the minor or second extreme in the mode of particularity.

¹⁵ V 5:251.25-270.520 with the overviews in 198.646-651 and 199.679-681.

¹⁶ V 5:196.601-197.607.

¹⁷ On the disjunctive syllogism, see GW 12:123.32-126.11/GL 701-704. With regard to further forms of the realization of this communitarian religious consciousness see Ch. 8 Subsection 1c below.

¹⁸ E.g., E § 573 R; E § 1. And already in the *Logic*, GW 12:236.27-29/GL 824-825.

¹⁹ On philosophy, see E §§ 572-577.

[20] GW 11:21.16-21/GL 50.

[21] In the Introduction to my study, *Hegel's Trinitarian Claim*, p. 6, I had written, "Systematically speaking, Hegel argues this [his] trinitarian claim as a movement from infinite to finite to inclusive or affirmative infinite with infinite understood as inclusive totality." I am grateful to Prof. Pierre-Jean Labarrière for having drawn attention to the ambiguous character of the phrase, "Systematically speaking." See his review of *Hegel's Trinitarian Claim*, by Dale M. Schlitt, in *Archives de Philosophie* 50 (1987) 281. In translating "systematically speaking" as "to say it in a systematic way" (*"Pour le dire de façon systématique"*), Prof. Labarrière would seem in effect to be indicating that the phrase could be taken simply to mean, "to say it in a summary or orderly, systematic fashion." In fact my general intention in using this phrase, "systematically speaking," was to say "from the point of view of Hegel's system." I would point out that the word "system" appears three times in the paragraph prior to my opening phrase in the next paragraph, "Systematically speaking." It would seem to me that a careful reading of the *Oxford English Dictionary* (1932) under "system," "systematic," and "systematically" would allow for an interpretation of "systematically speaking" as "speaking from the perspective of the system." What has become clearer to me is that I need to stress the word "speculative" so as to indicate clearly I am referring to the speculative formulation of Hegel's dialectic as a movement from an initial moment of immediacy. In light of Prof. Labarrière's observations, and after rereading Prof. Hodgson's article, "Hegel's Approach to Religion," I would now want to say more exactly, "speaking from the perspective of the speculative formulation of Hegel's thought." It should be noted that, though I have taken inspiration from Prof. Hodgson's article, I do not mean to imply necessarily he said what I am saying. Responsibility for my remarks here remain, of course, my own. On the notion of the speculative, see further brief observations in the Concluion at the end of the present volume.

Prof. Labarrière argues that my view of Hegel's thought as a movement from initial infinite to finite to true or inclusive infinite is reductionist, since with Hegel reflection takes off as much from the exterior as from the interior. He writes: "La 'these de base' de cette étude [*Hegel's Trinitarian Claim*] est que le mouvement de l'Esprit, chez Hegel, va toujours, primairement, de l'infini au fini : 'Pour le dire de façon systématique, Hegel asseoit sa requête trinaire sur le fait qu'il s'agirait d'un mouvement d'infini à fini allant jusqu'à un infini inclusif ou affirmatif, avec un infini compris comme totalité inclusive'. C'est negliger le fait, capital, que la 'réflexion' par autant de l'extérieur que de l'intérieur" (p. 281). Prof. Labarrière further recalls, and this I much appreciate, that there are binary, ternary, and even quaternary "schemas" of thought in Hegel's presentation of the movement of spirit. Therefore, to say that Hegel's thought, presented simply as one of a movement from infinite to finite to inclusive infinite, is an adequate "systematic" or organized summary of Hegel's thought is of course not true. However, I would want to remain with the fundamental affirmation that, from the point of view of Hegel's systematic or "mature" thought in its speculative formulation, for Hegel it is the movement from being to nothing to becoming/*Dasein* which, in its forward moving and retroactively grounding dialectic, underlies and makes possible the other structural movements. It is this speculative movement, as movement, which is very important here, and which comes to the fore particularly in the philosophy of religion. Hegel himself is not concerned with counting three or four or whatever. But he is concerned to establish the speculative dialectic of "in itself," "for itself," and "in and for itself," a dialectic which, I would want to argue, is the grounding movement making possible the often more phenomenologically expressed move from finite to infinite. The speculative dialectic of "in itself," "for itself," and "in and for itself" expresses the grounding movement of identity and difference, of subjectivity, freedom, and spirit. I would suggest that, from the point of the view of his speculative presentation, for Hegel the movement of spirit does not begin equally from finite and from infinite. The speculatively presented movement of spirit (and for Hegel presentation is argumentation) begins in and with pure being. Any other more multiple beginning to his speculative system would no longer allow Hegel to escape from what would then be an antinomical situation. It would ultimately be a denial of the idealist solution to the overcoming of alienation. Furthermore, Hegel has to be able coherently, consistently, and convincingly to argue this speculative movement of thought in its own movement. Indeed, he has to be able to argue each of his various formulations of the movement of thought in their very movement, while, of course acknowledging their appropriately understood interrelationships. The presentation of one form of the movement of spirit as thought cannot compensate for a weakness in the presentation, and consequently in the argumentation, of another form of that movement.

A final note. In my study of Hegel's philosophy of religion I have chosen to emphasize somewhat more the speculative formulation of Hegel's movement of spirit as a generally triadically structured movement of thought. This approach seems to me to reflect what Hegel actually did in his philosophy of religion, and especially his philosophy of the revelatory or consummate religion. Prof. Labarrière writes that, in my study of Hegel on Trinity, I have been "carried away" by my enthusiasm for the triadic to the point where I have uncritically "triadicized" Hegel's thought (p. 318). Prof. Labarrière's observation is very important in that it helps remind us of the danger inherent in any concentration of attention on the more speculative formulation of Hegel's thought. Certainly Hegel's thought is not that of a simple or mechanical exit and return. It is, of course, in its overall fundamental speculative formulation one of ordered advance through posited otherness to enriched resultant and grounding return. For a brief and clear statement by Hegel, see his remarks on religion, on determinate religion, on the consummate religion, and concerning his generalization of this dynamic to the whole of scientific knowing (*Wissenschaft*), V 5:177.3-21 (1827 Lasson text). See further remarks in the Introduction to the present study, n. 2 above.

[22] *Logic* so underlined refers to the published text of the *Science of Logic*. "Logic" not underlined refers to the dialectical movement of thought determinations as Hegel proposes them in the *Logic*. At times the *Logic* will be cited according to Hegel's 1832 revision of the first part of the *Science of Logic*, the logic of being (GW 21). Unless otherwise noted, the translation in GL will be cited for both the original and revised editions of the logic of being.

[23] GW 12:25.29-33/GL 592.

[24] See Jaeschke, *Die Religionsphilosophie Hegels* 89-90.

[25] Here we will not discuss the question whether Hegel's reconceptualization of Trinity is more or less compatible either with

the general Christian trinitarian dogma or with one or more specific Christian trinitarian theologies.

26 See especially at the end of the *Logic*, GW 12:252.25-253.34/GL 842-844. Unless this change from free creation to logically necessary self-othering is designated only as a change of form, it would seem necessary to speak of a "dialectical" identity of content between religion and philosophy in Hegel's system. The sublation in question is not simply a move interpretable as identical to the classical *bonum est diffusivum sui*, overflowing goodness or fullness. One could speak of the absolute idea's fullness in relation to its logically prior development and as the enriched return to the immediacy of the first moment of logical thought. However, the motor force in the self-othering here in question is the characteristic of the absolute idea as renewed *immediacy*, a "lacking" (*mangelhaft*) vis-à-vis the realphilosophical spheres.

27 GW 11:43.17-44.29 and 56.21-57.37/GL 82-83 and 105-106.

28 GW 12:236.1-253.34/GL 824-825.

29 Heede, "Die Göttliche Idee" 52-73 esp. 55-57, with literature on the term *onto-theo-logik* on p. 55. Note Martin Heidegger's particular reference to Hegel's logic as *onto-theo-logik* in *Identität und Differenz* (Pfullingen: Neske, 1957) 35-73/*Identity and Difference* (New York: Harper, 1969) 42-74.

30 Karl Heinz Haag, "Die Seinsdialektik bei Hegel und in der scholastischen Philosophie" (Ph.D. dissertation, Johann Wolfgang Goethe Universität, Frankfurt am Main, 1951) 20-22.

31 On the questions of "tri-personal" and dyadic versus triadic interpretations of Hegel's trinitarian thought see the helpful review and reflections with further references in Jaeschke, *Die Religionsphilosophie Hegels* 87-91. See also Jörg Splett, *Die Trinitätslehre G. W. F. Hegels* (Freiburg: Karl Alber, 1965) 145-148.

32 E.g., GW 12:236.3-20, 246.23-27, 248.14-16, 251.8-13/GL 824, 835-836, 837, 841.

33 To approach this question from a more historical-developmental perspective one could begin by consulting Schmitz, *Hegel als Denker der Individualität* 118-146, and Splett, *Trinitätslehre* 13-73, in

conjunction with, and in the light of, the two studies by H. S. Harris, *Hegel's Development*. *Toward the Sunlight, 1770-1801* (Oxford: Clarendon, 1972), and *Hegel's Development*. *Night Dreams, Jena 1801-1806* (Oxford: Clarendon, 1983).

[34] "Gott ist *Geist*, d.i. das, was wir *dreieinigen* Gott heißen." V 5:16.419/L 3:78.

[35] V 5:150.667-669 (1824 lecture transcript). Hereafter in this chapter the lecture series will be identified by date.

[36] V 3:43.292-310 (1824).

[37] See *Grundlinien der Philosophie des Rechts*, Philosophische Bibliothek, vol. 124a, ed. Johannes Hoffmeister (Hamburg: Felix Meiner, 1967) 324 35. The phrase in question is not found in the English translation.

[38] *Vorlesungen über die Philosophie der Weltgeschichte. Auf Grund der Handschriften herausgegeben*, Philosophische Bibliothek, vol. 171b-d, ed. Georg Lasson (Hamburg: Felix Meiner, 1976) 722.

[39] *Vorlesungen über die Philosophie der Weltgeschichte. Auf Grund der Handschriften herausgegeben*, Philosophische Bibliothek, vol. 171a, ed. Johannes Hoffmeister (Hamburg: Felix Meiner, 1970) 74.

[40] E.g., V 5:265.390-266.424 (1827). On the relationship Hegel sees between Trinity and the emergence of the spirit of freedom in modern social and political structures, see the remarks by Rolf Ahlers in his review of *Die Idee als Ideal: Trias und Triplizität bei Hegel*, by Katharina Comoth, in *The Owl of Minerva* 19 (1988) 199-200.

[41] Note the variously stated dialectical interrelationship between spirit and community, E § 554 with R; and, e.g., V 5:78.142-148 (1821).

[42] V 5:265.406-266.424 (1827).

[43] E.g., V 5:79.178-187 (1821).

[44] V 5:193.496-513 (1827).

[45] E.g., V 5:5.106-110 (1821); V 5:106.228-107.266 (1824).

[46] GW 9:405.16-25/PS 459; E § 564.

[47] V 5:250.995-251.9 (1827).

48 God as totality is spirit, V 5:281.97-282.109 (1831?). More philosophically formulated, E §§ 8, 74.

49 GW 9:427.28-31/PS 485; E § 571 with R.

50 GW 9:18.3-5/PS 10.

51 See, in general, Günter Rohrmoser, *Subjektivität und Verdinglichung. Theologie und Gesellschaft im Denken des jungen Hegel* (Gütersloh: Mohn, 1961).

52 E § 74.

53 On finite and infinite as thought determinations in the movement of pure thought, see GW 21:104.19-137.15/GL 116-150.

54 GW 21:135.35-136.2/GL 148.

CHAPTER SEVEN

INCARNATION AND OTHERNESS

1. *The Problematic*

Within Hegel's philosophy of religion it is his philosophical reinterpretation of Trinity which, as divine self-positing subjectivity and the whole truth, constitutes his full response to individual and societal alienation. But it is his philosophical reinterpretation of incarnation which constitutes the more immediate form of his response to that alienation. For Hegel the incarnation is the immediate reconciliation of infinite and finite in a divine-human unity. He interprets this movement of immediate reconciliation, namely, the appearance of the divine-human self or Christ,[1] as the paradigmatic religious presentation of his idealist understanding of the transition from identity to difference.

In Hegel's philosophy of religion this transition from identity to difference is often presented and discussed in terms of the appearance of otherness. This is quite appropriate for what can be called a *phänomeno-theo-logik*. Already now we can, in a very general way, say that in his philosophy of religion, or *phänomeno-theo-logik*, Hegel interprets incarnation in terms of otherness from three different perspectives. That is, he sees the divine-human self as other in a threefold relationship. From the speculative perspective, the most fundamental sense in which the divine-human self or unity is other is in relation to the initial moment of "immanent" Trinity. But this self is likewise, from a more phenomenological perspective, other in its immediate appearance to sensible religious consciousness. And it is other in its mediated relationship to the spiritual community, which has faith in its founder. For Hegel the movement of incarnation is the appearance of otherness. Christ, or the divine-human self, is momentary mediating and mediated otherness or other-being (Anderssein).

We can gain a better initial understanding of the problematic involved in Hegel's structuring of his interpretation of incarnation as appearance of otherness if we turn briefly to one of his somewhat earlier efforts to work out this structure. In fact Hegel returns several times to the theme of incarnation in what can be called his more "mature" period. At the beginning of this period, in his treatment of revelatory religion in the 1807 *Phenomenology of Spirit*, he rather intriguingly gives to the immediate appearance of Christ a first phenomenological priority over Trinity. He sees this appearance as the coming together, and consequently the reconciliation, of the previously elaborated doubled movement of spirit into an immediate concrete existence (*Dasein*). In the *Phenomenology* Hegel first argues to the appearance of this divine-human unity, which is sensuously intuited on the level of religious consciousness. After this first presentation of incarnation, he reflects on the overall threefold form of consciousness in order to lead into, and justify, the three ways in which he will unfold what is already implicit in this first presentation of incarnation. As first step in this unfolding he presents what would today be called "immanent" Trinity, or God "before" the creation of the world. Then he goes on to present the appearance of Christ a second time.[2]

In both of these *Phenomenology* presentations of incarnation Hegel quite openly and clearly qualifies the whole moment of incarnation, in its various senses, as one of otherness. For example, with respect to the initial phenomenological occurrence of incarnation he writes: "For Spirit is the knowledge of oneself in the externalization of oneself; the being that is the movement of retaining its self-identity in its otherness."[3] And further on in the same paragraph he speaks of the divine-human unity, which this individual human being is, as "being-for-an-other" (*Sein-für-Anderes*).[4] So, already with this first reference to incarnation Hegel has indicated a doubled sense of otherness. He writes of otherness both in relation to that which precedes the appearance here in question and in relation to the religious consciousness to which the appearance occurs. Slightly further on in the *Phenomenology*, where he develops the three modes of consciousness or thought with which he will elaborate the three developed moments of the revelatory religion, he writes briefly of the second moment of consciousness. He points out that this moment is one of representation (*Vorstellung*). This moment is itself, as such, the moment of otherness. He also speaks of the third form of consciousness, namely, that of self-consciousness. This third form of consciousness is the moment of return out of otherness. The fact that Hegel writes this way of the third moment is an indication that he is thinking of some form of relation of Christ (the other of and to God) also as other in relation to what is yet to follow in the dialectical development of spirit.[5]

Then, in the subsequent subsection of the *Phenomenology* presentation of the revelatory religion, namely, that of the three developed moments of revelatory religion, Hegel speaks of the second moment in the "immanent" Trinity in terms of momentary other-being.[6] When he then works out the second presentation of incarnation, he describes the overall movement of creation, along with the questions of good and evil, of redemption and reconciliation, as a whole in terms of the appearance of otherness. He likewise presents the dialectical interrelationship of the elements in this overall movement or progression in terms of a movement of otherness. In fact, for Hegel this movement of otherness, namely, the progression from creation to the death of the mediator, is itself characterized by a series of antitheses or contradictions internal to it. In fact these contradictions themselves constitute this moment.[7]

It is, then, in this earlier *Phenomenology* presentation of incarnation and otherness that we find a basis for an initial formulation of our overall thesis. Our brief review of Hegel on incarnation in the revelatory religion in the *Phenomenology* allows us to suggest the following position. We can now propose that, from the perspective of his speculatively formulated system, Hegel, in his "mature" period from the *Phenomenology* on, thinks of incarnation fundamentally in terms of a movement from identity to difference. He thinks of incarnation as a movement of divine self-othering. Later on in this same "mature" or more systematic period he does not abandon the idea that the incarnation constitutes an immediate moment of which the consummate religion, in its overall trinitarian formulation, is an explicitation. Nevertheless, in his treatment of the consummate religion he does, briefly in his *Encyclopedia*[8] and at considerable length in his Berlin philosophy of religion lectures,[9] present the incarnation only once, and more straightforwardly, after that of "immanent" Trinity. Furthermore, in the *Encyclopedia* and in the philosophy of religion lectures he seems to use terms such as "other-being" and "the other" less frequently than he does in the *Phenomenology*. There the dialectical development from self-consciousness to absolute knowledge, by way of religion, would naturally enough lend itself to a more explicit usage of the notion of otherness. So, in a sense the *Encyclopedia* and the lectures provide both a challenge, and a further opportunity, to examine whether or not, and how, Hegel continues in these later writings and lectures to think incarnation in terms of otherness.

Hegel's earlier efforts in the *Phenomenology* to think through a coherent philosophical Christology will, it would seem, always maintain a place of particular importance in studies of his thought. His two *Phenomenology* presentations of incarnation represent marvelously dense argumentations for his philosophical interpretation of incarnation in terms of otherness. But it is his constructive efforts in his Berlin lectures on the philosophy of religion which provide access to the longer developments of his later positions on incarnation. There do remain in these later lecture presentations of incarnation, along with that in the *Encyclopedia*, vestigial remarks indicating that it is the incarnation, and not the, speculatively speaking, prior appearance to thought of "immanent" Trinity, which gives rise to the consummate religion. Yet now, in the *Encyclopedia* and in the lectures, Hegel does more clearly present "immanent" Trinity as logical and systematic presupposition to incarnation.

We will concentrate primarily on Hegel's later philosophical reinterpretations of incarnation as movement of otherness. This will be done in line with our present interests to profit from the recent editions of Hegel's Berlin lectures. We want especially to understand whether, to what extent, and how Hegel continues, in these lectures, to think of incarnation in terms of otherness. We will focus on representative selections of his four treatments of the consummate religion. Furthermore, it will not be necessary to treat directly, or at length, of the *Encyclopedia* presentation of incarnation. We can touch upon the differences in interpretation between Hegel's presentation in the *Encyclopedia* and his presentations in the Berlin lectures from 1824 on during our analysis of the 1821 manuscript. We will, at least briefly, look again at these differences, with regard to the presentation of incarnation, during the course of our consideration of the structural differences between that manuscript and the later lectures.

There are several advantages to concentrating primarily on Hegel's presentations of incarnation as they are found within his overall philosophical reinterpretation of Christianity as the consummate religion. First of all, from a more extrinsic perspective, we can better appreciate the rich results of his having worked so intensely for a decade from 1821 to 1831 with the philosophy of religion and with the notion of incarnation. His ongoing efforts to give appropriate logical structure to his reading of the consummate religion, and his shifting polemic with various dialogue partners, provided Hegel with several opportunities to underscore various aspects of incarnation as movement of differentiation and as the appearance of otherness. Second, Hegel presents Christ's death as both the extreme of alienation and the definitive moment in objectively presented divine-human reconciliation. Therefore, from a perspective more internal to his thought, our decision to concentrate especially on presentations of incarnation in the lectures on the consummate religion will provide a privileged and focused concrete point of entry into the ways in which he conceives of, and works with, the notion of otherness.

We initially indicated three senses in which Hegel speaks of incarnation in terms of otherness. He refers to incarnation as moment of otherness in relation to "immanent" Trinity, in immediate relation to religious consciousness, and in relation to the consciousness of the spiritual community. We found these three senses discernible already in the *Phenomenology* presentations of incarnation. In the rest of this chapter we will focus primarily on the first of these ways in which we can see incarnation in terms of otherness. We will concentrate on the speculatively formulated and presented origin of Christ as other in relation to "immanent" Trinity.

We will here pursue our understanding of Hegel on incarnation and otherness by exploring two basic hypotheses which take their inspiration from the *Phenomenology* presentations of incarnation. More specifically, these two hypotheses are based in reflection on Hegel's *Phenomenology* interpretation of incarnation as a movement from initial identity to difference, the movement of divine self-othering. The first, and most obvious of our hypotheses, is that the content of the overall notion and logical movement of the arising of otherness, in its various Hegelian formulations, remains, from the perspective of his speculative formulation of the movement of thought, the fundamental interpretative logical category and movement Hegel uses to construct his philosophical Christology. Our particularly important task with regard to this hypothesis will be to discern in what senses we can say this movement of the arising of otherness is fundamental constructive category. More specifically, we will need to indicate what this movement is and of what it consists.

The second hypothesis follows upon the first. It is that there is in fact more to Hegel's understanding of otherness than would seem to be indicated by his often repeated reference to otherness in terms of negation. We will explore these two basic hypotheses by means of an examination of several ways in which Hegel, with regard to incarnation and Christ, makes appeal to, and uses, the notion and movement of otherness as self-othering or self-diremption of the divine idea. We will leave to another day, and another study, the more explicit discussion of Christ as the "result" of incarnation, namely, as considered explicitly in immediate relation to religious consciousness and in mediated relationship to the consciousness of the spiritual community.

It will be helpful to restate more generally our two hypotheses: the logical structure of otherness is the movement of thought underlying Hegel's interpretation of incarnation as movement and as result, and there is more to the notion of otherness in Hegel than first meets the eye. We will explore these hypotheses by means of an examination of representative selections from Hegel's relevant philosophy of religion texts and by means of brief interpretative reference to selected presentations of otherness in Hegel's *Science of Logic*.

Now, after our initial discussion of the problematic surrounding the question of incarnation and otherness we will, in the following section, review ways in which Hegel envisions incarnation as appearance of otherness and as moment of reconciling divine self-othering. We will carry out this review primarily in relation to Hegel's philosophical reading of the consummate religion. It might be well to recall again, as was mentioned in Chapter Four above, that it is especially in the later Berlin lectures where Hegel develops more explicitly the consummate religion as the systematic, speculative, and dialectical development of God or the divine idea as absolute subject and absolute spirit.

After this review of Hegel's envisagement of incarnation in terms of otherness, we will, in the third section of the present chapter, provide a general summary of what Hegel has in fact said concerning the self-othering of the divine idea. Then we will briefly mention some of the varied logical structures of otherness he laid out in the *Science of Logic*. This turn to the *Logic* will help us to understand better what is going on when Hegel speaks of incarnation in terms of otherness. It will also enable us see more clearly what Hegel means, most fundamentally, by his speculative understanding of otherness. Finally, we will conclude this third section with some further reflections on Hegel's interpretation of incarnation as the self-othering of the divine idea. We will look as well at some of the implications of this interpretation for an understanding of his speculative or idealist presentation of otherness.

2. *Incarnation as Self-Othering of the Divine Idea*

While still drawing inspiration from our previous reference to incarnation in the *Phenomenology*, we can speak of wider and more general, interrelated senses in which Hegel speaks of incarnation and of Christ in terms of otherness. First of all, already in his earlier Jena period he had described his system as a whole as "presentation of the incarnation of God in the sense of the self-construction of the absolute to totality."[10] It is equally true that for Hegel his later formulation of his system in the *Encyclopedia* is a presentation of the incarnation of God as self-positing development of the divine idea in, and as, nature and finite spirit, and then as absolute spirit.[11] The "self-othering" movements, which constitute the dialectical development of logical or pure thought, can themselves be considered, in their own ways and within the realm of logic, logical reformulations of the notion of divine incarnation. More specifically within the sphere of religion we can, in a very general way, consider the moment of representation or concretization within the overall presentation of the concept of religion an expression of the structure or form of incarnation. This moment of representation, or, as it is at least in principle more speculatively developed from the 1824 lectures on, this diremptive self-othering movement of the divine idea, is realized as a series of types of divine incarnation within the various forms of determinate religion.[12] For Hegel this moment finds its consummate expression in the specifically Christian religious representation of divine incarnation. According to Hegel's own affirmations, we must also include in this consummate expression that moment of real incarnation's prior structural parallel in the second moment of the "immanent" Trinity.[13]

As we have previously mentioned, the four lecture series have in common the affirmation that the whole movement of the consummate religion as trinitarian and incarnational reconciliation occurs in variously realized relation to religious consciousness. It will be helpful to recall the various instances in the realization of reconciliation. Reconciliation is a movement from "immanent" Trinity through creation and immediate reconciliation in the divine-human unity of a particular individual to the subjective realization of reconciliation in the spiritual community. Each of these instances is always to be seen as taking place within the overall understanding of religion as the relationship between God and the subjective religious consciousness.[14] In the later lecture series Hegel makes it clearer that this very divine self-othering is equally the source and cause of the dialectically progressing reconciliation of religious consciousness and God. It is the reconciliation of finite and infinite.

We need to underscore again that one of the elements common to all of the four lecture series is the fact that Hegel's presentation of incarnation, namely, the appearance of the divine idea, now occurs after the presentation of "immanent" Trinity. There remain, of course, occasional indications here and there of a continuing phenomenological and historical priority to the appearance of Christ vis-à-vis "immanent" Trinity. But what nevertheless makes difficult further generalization concerning Hegel's thought on incarnation as the self-othering of the divine idea is, first of all, the fact that Hegel distributes the Christological theologoumena, at least at first sight, structurally quite differently in the 1821 philosophy of religion lectures from the way in which he distributes them in the 1824, 1827, and 1831 lectures. A second difficulty, and one raised by this very difference in the distribution of Christological theologoumena, is the question of exactly what Hegel might then mean, or can even mean, by "otherness" when he speaks of the various ways of distributing the Christological theologoumena as movement of the appearance of otherness.

The immediately observable differences in distribution of Christological theologoumena make it necessary for us to review two specific lecture series representative of Hegel's two basic and, at least at first sight, alternative presentations of the Christological theologoumena. These two series are the 1821 and the 1827 Christological interpretations. Hegel's 1827 lecture interpretation can be considered representative of his general distribution of the Christological theologoumena in the 1824 and 1831 lectures. With regard to the 1821 and 1827 lectures, we will examine specific relevant texts in order to see what Hegel really says concerning incarnation and divine self-othering. We will be concerned to discern what type of structured movement is manifest in the progression of his thought. Here, as in Chapter Four above, we will find it helpful to understand what Hegel is saying by referring back to his prior presentation of the concept of religion. This reference back to the concept of religion will shed further light on what Hegel has written in 1821, or reliably reported to have said in 1827. This time we will refer to Hegel's presentations of the concept of religion from the perspective of our concern with incarnation. As was the case in Chapter Four, again here our longer reference farther back to Hegel's presentations of the concept of religion is justified, and even called for, by the fact that the moments of the consummate religion are themselves for Hegel, at least in principle, the consummation of the moments of the concept of religion.[15] After this review of the 1821 and the 1827 lectures we will, in section three below, turn to Hegel's *Logic* for further clarification of certain aspects of the Hegelian notion of otherness. We will do this in order to take a second look at Hegel's two, at least at first sight, quite different distributions of the Christological theologoumena. More particularly, we want to see how he could speak of incarnation in terms of differentiation and otherness.

2.a. The 1821 Lectures

Incarnation in the Consummate Religion

In 1821 Hegel structured his interpretation of the various forms of determinate religion in terms of the abstract concept of God, concrete representation or the ways in which God is known, and the practical relationship of cultus. He likewise structures his presentation of the development of the consummate religion along these same lines. Within this outer, triadically structured presentation of the consummate religion, he develops the second moment, that of concrete representation (with its overflow into the third moment or the practical relationship of cultus), as the development of the concept of the consummate religion. Thus this second moment is the realization of the concept of religion itself in three concrete spheres. The first of these spheres is the divine idea in the element of universality, "immanent" Trinity. The second is the movement of diremption and differentiation, or the divine idea in the immediacy of nature with the world seen as the other of God. The third is the objectivity of finite spirit and the divine idea as the appearance of God to finite spirit in the history of redemption and reconciliation.[16]

We are, specifically regarding the 1821 lectures, interested in what Hegel actually wrote regarding incarnation and otherness. We are here, for the moment, again taking incarnation in a very wide sense of the word. We will be interested as well in the particular way in which, more at length in this lecture series and more briefly in the *Encyclopedia*,[17] Hegel presents the Christological theologoumena in the third of the three inner spheres of concrete representation.[18]

The First Concrete Sphere

First of all, and very briefly, it is in the first of the concrete spheres of religious representation that Hegel sketches a sort of preliminary vision of the characteristics of the moment of incarnation. This he does when he writes of the second moment within "immanent" Trinity.[19] We should recall that this first concrete sphere, or "immanent" Trinity, is for Hegel the first concrete realization of the consummate religion. It is this realization in so far as the consummate religion is the very development of the divine idea in that idea's own self-determination. We need to recall, as well, that the divine idea is now the unity of concept and being or reality,[20] and it is this unity always of course in relation to religious consciousness. With this brief contextualization in mind, we can more easily see that this first of the concrete spheres is the movement of God as internal differentiation of love in the element of thought.[21] Furthermore, we should note that this first concrete sphere's presentation is quite clearly paralleled, both in terms of content and of structure, in the *Encyclopedia*.[22] The movement of differentiation here in question is not, of course, one of real incarnation. Rather, for Hegel it remains in the realm of thought. It is, immediately, love or the intuition of oneself in the other.[23] Though we are not dealing here with real incarnation, the words and phrases he uses to describe this movement will help focus our reading of later movements of othering.

With reference to this transitory moment of otherness within "immanent" Trinity, Hegel speaks particularly of difference (*Differenz, Unterschied, Verschiedenheit*), of being-for-itself (*Fürsichsein*), and of diremption, with the latter, particularly, taken as the determining and distinguishing of contradictions. However, as has been mentioned, all of this occurs in such a way that the appearance of finitude, or the reality of real emptying, has not yet taken place.[24] Interestingly, by means of a marginal note he makes brief reference to the notion of incarnation already here in the treatment of diremption in the "immanent" Trinity.[25]

Hegel writes, in summary fashion, "When we say, 'God in God self according to God's concept is the infinite, self-dirempting (and self-returning) power,' God is this only as infinitely self-relating negativity, i.e., as absolute reflection into self – which is already the definition of *spirit*."[26] The question we now want to pursue in a more direct examination of the second and third spheres of concrete representation is to what extent Hegel can, given his own dialectic, speak of the incarnation as movement or appearance of otherness. Movements of immediate diremption seem quite clearly to be movements of self-othering. But the question is, finally, twofold: whether he does bring together the notions of diremption and return in a possibly more inclusive notion of otherness, and whether he can logically justify such a linkage.

The Second Concrete Sphere

With these questions in mind, it is now necessary to make the transition to the second of the three concrete spheres. We need to do this in order to review Hegel's discussion of the world, with "world" here understood as nature unequivocally and explicitly presented as other to God. Hegel writes of the immediate appearance of the divine idea in nature.[27] In his presentation of the world and of nature as other-being (*Anderssein*), we can see Hegel sketching a number of points important to any consideration of the notion of otherness in his philosophy of religion and, especially, to any consideration of that notion in relation to incarnation in the consummate religion. He gives a rather straightforward and, at first reading, less dialectical 1821 presentation of the divine idea appearing in nature. That is, he writes of God as creator and preserver of the world. Here he rather straightforwardly describes other-being: "since other-being [is] defined as the totality of an appearance, it expresses in itself the idea, and this is in general what is meant by the *wisdom* of God in nature."[28] Among some of the specific characteristics of this other-being Hegel indicates both its being immediate, and therefore abstract, and its being considered on its own, and therefore momentary. He means momentary not in any merely temporal sense, but from the perspective of other-being's implicit identity with the initial idea, of which it is the appearance. Creation and preservation are to be seen as the moment of other-being and, thus, themselves moment of the idea. Other-being is simply what is "created." It is finitude and difference as the result of an act of judgment or separation. Of particular interest, finally, are Hegel's references to other-being as negation (*das Negative*) or negative moment (*das negative Moment*).[29]

In this initial text concerning the second of the three spheres of concrete representation Hegel has given a particular characterization to the movement of the divine idea. He presents the divine idea, in its self-diremption as the givenness of the world and of nature, as other-being. He uses language reminiscent of his efforts to present "nothing" (*das reine Nichts*) in the *Logic*[30] and nature in the initial moment of the philosophy of nature.[31] Both in the philosophy of nature and here he understands nature, as other-being, in terms of immediacy and negation. Here Hegel has in fact indicated many of the basic characteristics of his understanding of otherness, and he has done this in the immediacy of an initial presentation, But, whereas from the beginning of his *Phenomenology* presentation of creation and diremption he characterized it in terms of opposition and contradiction,[32] here in the original presentation in the 1821 manuscript he does not explicitly consider opposition until the very end of the presentation of the second concrete sphere. We might have expected an early reference to such opposition in that second concrete sphere taken as a whole. For Hegel is now speaking not merely on the level of nature, but of nature considered within the realm of spirit and, indeed, on the level of religion. Yet, in the major portion of this presentation of world and nature, the notion of contradiction, or at least of opposition, seemed at first to have escaped Hegel's notice. This is particularly surprising since the notion and structure of opposition are so important to any Hegelian presentation of differentiation and otherness within the realm of spirit. Interestingly, Hegel does add a marginal note toward the very beginning of this section on the second of the concrete spheres. Though we cannot be absolutely sure when he added this note, it was apparently subsequent to the first writing of the 1821 manuscript text. Hegel jotted in the margin, "Objectivity – development of the same – i.e., holding fast of the determinate distinctions [next line:] Son – abstract determination of other-being – antithesis of nature and finite spirit."[33]

It is as if Hegel had temporarily forgotten that he was now no longer working merely on the level of the initial moment in the philosophy of nature but on the level of absolute spirit. So he wanted, with this marginal note at the beginning of his remarks, to recall and mention the more dialectical consideration he had seen the need to introduce at the end of his presentation of this second sphere. Here, at the end he makes a brief reference to life and speaks of self-sacrifice. It is, he writes, the way in which nature goes over into spirit, in which spirit, in opposition to nature, arises as the explicitation (*für sich*) of what nature was *an sich*, "i.e., posited in immediate form or in other-being."[34]

The most immediate reading of this reference to other-being is, of course, with reference to nature in its character as being *an sich* in relation to the *für sich* of finite spirit. But unless we would want to predetermine that the characteristic movement of other-being is limited only to the *an sich* formulation of initial diremption, it would seem that Hegel is also saying that finite spirit can be considered a form of other-being. But now finite spirit would be so considered in its *für sich* condition as conscious finite spirit. Therefore, on the basis of this dialectical link between finite spirit and nature, and because of the fact that finite spirit is equally and primordially included in the reality expressed by the initial notions of world and nature, we can already now say that for Hegel the characteristics of the divine idea, in diremption, are also the characteristics, *mutatis mutandis*, of any further appearance of this divine idea in and through finite spirit. For Hegel, then, his reflection on finite spirit will be the making explicit of that other-being which nature was in the form of an immediate realization.

The Third Concrete Sphere

At the beginning of the third of the three spheres of concrete representation[35] Hegel characterizes this third sphere as "objectivity in the form of *finite spirit*, the appearance of the idea in and to the latter, *redemption* and *reconciliation* as the divine history itself."[36] He at least intends to bind together, and even identify, the self-othering of the divine idea (to the farthest extreme in and as finite spirit) with the divine idea's return to itself out of this self-emptying:

> This [is] the moment of divine, developed objectivity, wherein divinity arrives at its most extreme [mode of] being-outside-itself no less than it finds its *turning point* there; and this moment of return itself consists in both the most extreme estrangement [*Entfremdung*] and the pinnacle of divestment [*Entäußerung*].[37]

Hegel presents this self-othering to the extreme of finitude, which latter is itself for Hegel the turning point or moment of return, as a series of three themes distributed in two subsections. These two subsections make up the third concrete sphere. In the first of these two subsections[38] he interprets finite spirit and the story of the fall of Adam and Eve as moment of estrangement. In the second[39] he presents the themes of redemption and reconciliation. Already here in the 1821 lectures Hegel has set up for himself the challenge to hold together, in one sphere, the move to the extreme of finitude and the movement of return out of that finitude. And he has set this up so that it is to be accomplished within one concrete sphere, albeit here already clearly in the realm of finite spirit.

It will be helpful to make reference to the *Encyclopedia* before turning directly to the 1821 manuscript on the first of these two subsections of the last of the three concrete spheres of representation. What Hegel, in 1821, discusses in the first of these two subsections, namely, the moment of cleavage or estrangement, he handles as second half of the second sphere, namely, the sphere of particularity, in the various editions of the *Encyclopedia*.[40] Thus, by means of his reference, in the *Encyclopedia*, to nature and to finite spirit in one sphere, he there maintains the notion of opposition as characteristic constitutive of that second sphere more clearly than he does so far here in the 1821 manuscript. At the end of the *Encyclopedia* treatment of the second sphere, Hegel makes brief mention of the fact that finite spirit "is, when it thinks, directed towards the eternal."[41] When this reminder concerning finite spirit as thinking is taken together with the earlier *Encyclopedia* announcement of the entrance of true content into the world of appearance,[42] Hegel can be seen, with his explicit reference to thought, to be introducing the overcoming of the opposition of spirit to nature in principle and implicitly already here in the second moment. So for Hegel, again in principle, the movement of redemptive incarnation can be seen as occurring in the *Encyclopedia* already in and with absolute spirit's return to itself in the appearance of finite spirit as thought.

Unlike what Hegel did in the *Encyclopedia* when he located the opposition between finite spirit and nature in a second sphere, in 1821 he specifically develops the moment of contradiction in the first subsection of the third concrete sphere of the consummate religion. There he sketches out the finitude of finite spirit as a series of philosophical reflections more directly on the phenomenon of self-alienation. He carries these reflections out as well in the form of interpretations of myths of an original innocence and fall into culpability. Somewhat reminiscent of the *Phenomenology* presentation, with its multiple reference to otherness, Hegel twice speaks of this fall as a "becoming other" (*Anderswerden*).[43] Without following Hegel's reflections in detail we can simply say that he presents finite spirit as having its beginning in what he calls "natural humanity" or "natural spirit," which is itself an unresolved internal contradiction. This original state of so-called innocence is one in which finite spirit is, in its immediacy and individuality, "essentially what spirit ought not to be or to remain."[44] Hegel analyses finite spirit as a movement which begins in this original and unreflected unity with nature, namely, with its own individual nature. If we again sketch in large strokes, we can say that he interprets the adamic fall, and the consequent notion of culpability, as the necessary alienation arising out of willing as self-seeking. For Hegel this willing is equally a knowing (*Erkennen*). This willing is the willed resting of finite spirit with its nature as individuality against what it should be, over against universality. As such it is the cause of evil, and is evil.[45] Evil, or spirit's willing of its immediate nature, is a necessary step in the movement of finite subjectivity. So, in this interesting reinterpretation of evil as self-love, whereas the adamic state of innocence represents the condition of finite spirit as yet in undistinguished unity with its nature, a knowing willing introduces the necessary condition of finite spirit's being opposed to its true calling. Finite spirit opposes its true calling by remaining attached to its nature as to what it should not be, namely, as remaining over against the universality it should become. It is this condition of opposition or contradiction which Hegel develops as a series of ever-increasingly internally opposed dialectical interrelations of finite spirit and nature.[46]

With this first of the two subsections to the third concrete sphere of consummate religion, Hegel has work through the moment of opposition previously announced at the end of the second concrete sphere. He has done this by beginning anew in the immediacy of the primordial unity of finite spirit with its nature. He continues by pushing the opposition between finite spirit and its true determination to the point of internal contradiction within finite spirit. Thus he arrives at the point where finitude, as contradictory, cries out for, and creates the context in which, Hegel can turn to the themes of redemption and reconciliation. Rather than speaking of "turning toward," technically it would be more correct to say that the thinking through of the movement of absolute spirit as divine idea gives rise, in thought, to the religious themes of redemption and reconciliation.

Hegel has now set the stage for his philosophical interpretation of the incarnation specifically as the appearance of Christ. This is a stage on which knowing is both the occurrence of alienation or estrangement and the medium in and through which finite spirit arrives at religious reconciliation and philosophical mediation. We have previously mentioned Hegel's particular presentation of finite spirit as knowing being in the *Encyclopedia*. Now, likewise, in the 1821 lectures Hegel describes finite spirit, precisely in so far as it is knowing being, equally as the source of the explicitation of its own finitude and the turning point in the reconciling return to itself as spirit.[47] As is so typical of Hegel, he ends this first subsection to the third concrete sphere of the consummate religion by forging ahead to the next consideration. For Hegel presentation necessarily ends in transition. Here he writes, "[It] belongs to the divine life, which is divine spirit, to objectify itself in free and initially finite spirit, which [is] God *implicitly*" [*an sich*].[48] This reference to *an sich* immediately prepares us for the following explicitation of what has already taken place implicitly.

A first reading of the second subsection of the third concrete sphere of the consummate religion immediately reveals Hegel at work elaborating a philosophical interpretation of the Christian Christological theologoumena as a building upon and, more precisely, a making explicit of what he has so far laid out concerning finitude as nature and finite spirit. In the light of, and in line with, what Hegel has written so far, certain continuing references in this second subsection strike us immediately. He continues to refer to such notions as immediacy, possibility, the overcoming of the opposition between universality and individuality. We do indeed get the impression he is building on what he has already sketched out concerning finite spirit as such. Our immediate impression is further confirmed when we recall that earlier on, when he introduced the third concrete sphere of the consummate religion, Hegel had pointed out two sides to the history of the divine idea in finite spirit. He had referred to the history of finite spirit in its immediacy, and to this history in as it has become object to finite consciousness.[49] When the two sides mentioned by Hegel are taken to refer, respectively, to the first and second subsections of the third concrete sphere of the consummate religion, this introductory text confirms our first impression. Hegel's presentation of the Christological theologoumena is the making explicit, and rendering concretely individual, of what occurs in finite spirit as such.

Hegel indicates five steps or stages in the presentation of objective redemption and reconciliation within this second subdivision.[50] He had already laid out his philosophical reading of the finitude of finite spirit as its discovering, and willingly remaining attached to, its individuality over against universality – with universality expressed as finite spirit's own possibility.[51] Now he begins the first of the five steps in the presentation of objective redemption[52] by announcing that this second subsection of the third concrete sphere "is the elevation of spirit out of its natural will, out of evil, out of the willing of singular selfishness."[53] We are presently concerned primarily with the structure and movement of Hegel's thought in this presentation of redemption and reconciliation. Therefore, we should immediately note that this reference to "elevation" (*Erhebung*), and the consequent description of this overall second subsection as a movement out of finite spirit's alienation, should not too easily be identified simply with the moment of return, to which Hegel very generally refers. We need to remind ourselves that he describes the whole third concrete sphere both as a movement toward the greatest externalization and as a return out of that externalization.[54] Both of these movements, namely, of externalization and of return, are in fact continued in this elevation out of "natural will."

According to Hegel's presentation in the first stage or step in the presentation of the second subsection to his third concrete moment of representation, "This elevation consists generally in the fact that humanity comes to consciousness of the universal in and for itself, and indeed is conscious of it as *its* essence."[55] This statement would seem to be expanding on the conclusion, which Hegel had drawn a few lines earlier, that free finite spirit is implicitly God.[56] Still, the word "generally" (*überhaupt*) would seem to cover a bit too quickly, and perhaps too easily, the transition to a statement so fundamentally important for the further development of Hegel's philosophical interpretation of the Christological theologoumena. Nevertheless, in two paragraphs, with their accompanying marginal annotations and their differing perspectives,[57] Hegel, in a more strictly philosophical language, insists that finite spirit comes to the consciousness that both it itself, as infinite subjectivity, and universality, taken in and for itself as absolute objectivity (God as spirit), are equally essential. In view of its belonging to itself without self-seeking (*Selbstsucht*), finite spirit recognizes that it is the infinite form of consciousness. Finite spirit has its end (*Zweck*) internal to itself in this infinite form of consciousness, in its infinite freedom. So finite spirit realizes that it is precisely the universality from which it had earlier felt itself estranged.

Hegel repeats essentially this same thought in his second paragraph, but with several more explicitly religious terms. He will work with these religious terms in the following four stages of the presentation of redemption and reconciliation. Here he picks up more explicitly on the earlier assertion that the human being is implicitly God when he says that "by consciousness of the unity of divine and human nature we mean that humanity implicitly bears within itself the *divine idea* . . . as its own substantial nature, as its own vocation or the unique possibility of such a vocation: this infinite possibility is its subjectivity."[58] Previously, in his analysis of the finitude of finite spirit, Hegel had distinguished between what finite spirit in fact wills and what its possibility is.[59] Here he asserts that finite spirit recognizes that it is, itself, that very possibility. As in the previous paragraph, here Hegel again affirms that individuality and universality are reconciled in an inclusive universality. Finally, he recalls that this unity of divine and human nature has a meaning not only for the determination of human nature, but for the determination of the divine nature as well. For the unity of divine and human nature is a moment in the process of the divine nature and in the knowledge of God as spirit.[60]

With this brief, but very important, doubly presented first stage Hegel has asserted that incarnation takes place implicitly in all humanity, namely, in finite spirit as that which is conscious and knows. We see, in the complexity of his thought, the appearance of the divine idea in, as, and to finite spirit. It is an appearance as a certain converging of finite and infinite spirit in the unity of divine and human nature in the form of a self-positing movement of thought.

The second stage in the presentation of redemption and reconciliation,[61] to which we will return in the next chapter when we look at Hegel's philosophical interpretation of the religious theme or representation "kingdom of God," can now be treated more summarily. Here Hegel variously argues to the need for the divine idea, as unity of divine and human nature, to appear to finite religious consciousness as one unique individual. Interestingly, in the context of his discussion of incarnation, Hegel has found another way, perhaps we could say from a more horizontal perspective, of relating the many and the one, namely, the many in terms of finite spirit as such and the one in terms of this one unique individual. What is generally common to humanity as such (the general formulation of the many) must come to finite spirit as religious consciousness and be recognized or intuited as an immediate human being (the one). With regard to this "one" Hegel would say the one must be intuited as an actual empirical universal. It is this series of characteristics of the unity of divine and human nature, namely, immediacy, universality present as individuality, the divine idea appearing only once as this individual who is the Son of God, which indicate that, in this second stage of the movement of redemption and reconciliation Hegel is continuing the elevation out of mere natural willing. He is continuing this elevation as a doubled movement concretizing, in this one individual, both the direction toward further externalization and the direction toward integration or return. According to Hegel, universality and individuality are presented to intuiting religious consciousness as reconciled in the immediacy of one, and only one, concrete individual, namely, in exclusive individuality. Hegel has moved from the generalized many to the immediacy of one concrete individual.

In the third stage within the presentation of redemption and reconciliation[62] Hegel is concerned to explore how Christ, this individual, attests to being the divine idea, to being "the appearance of spirit in immediate existence and for immediate intuition."[63] He zeroes in, almost instinctively, on Christ's teaching as that which integrates Christ's life and destiny insofar as these two are taken as manifestations of the divine idea.[64] Hegel will come back more explicitly to the question of Christ's life and destiny or death in the next stage of redemption and reconciliation. Here he concentrates on teaching and, in a tightly knit paragraph,[65] describes it as that which can only be in inwardness and in thought. Consequently, Christ's teaching contains the universal. Teaching is itself the universal soil (*der allgemeine Boden*) in which spirit must know itself to be at home. For Hegel, then, Christ's teaching is the universal made objectively present to religious consciousness through Christ the concrete individual. Hegel continues to bring together universal and individual as he spells out various characteristics of that teaching.

For our purposes it will be sufficient to highlight Hegel's identification of love and of the kingdom of God as the content of Christ's teaching. Hegel echoes New Testament texts when he introduces the theme of love as the expression of the moral imperative.[66] He writes that Christ teaches love of neighbor, of the community, and of one's enemy. Then he introduces the notion of negation and negativity into his understanding of love.[67] He does this especially against the background of his reference to love of the community and to love as one's only purpose (*Zweck*). He also does this by means of reference to the element of renunciation in Christ's teaching when love is considered a breaking away from any particularity. In effect, here Hegel is interpreting the general notion of love as concern for the other.[68] But now he is interpreting it, in his own speculative fashion, as abstract personality and as that personality's identity. Hegel presents Christ's teaching on love as the direct opposite of his own earlier interpretation of evil, which he saw as the natural willing of one's own separate individuality and as a form of self-seeking. Hegel's response to evil, understood as self-seeking, is Christ's teaching understood in terms of self-giving love. Hegel gives this notion of a self-giving a speculative interpretation as the self-emptying and return of spirit.

In addition to his identification of the content of Christ's teaching as love, Hegel equally speaks of that content as the kingdom of God. It is this notion of the kingdom of God as content which, for Hegel, facilitates the transition from his interpretation of Christ's teaching to an elaboration of the importance of Christ's life and death. Already here in the third stage of the presentation of redemption and reconciliation he points out that the kingdom of God is defined in terms of Christ's relationship to God, and of humanity's relationship to God and to Christ.[69] Thus Hegel recalls that, in the philosophy of religion, he is always dealing with the object of religious consciousness in its relationship to finite spirit as religious consciousness and, conversely, with the relationship of finite spirit to that object. At the same time he leads in to the fourth, and longest, of the stages in his presentation of redemption and reconciliation, namely, that of "The Life and Death [of Christ]."[70] On the basis of the nature of the content of Christ's teaching and, more specifically, on the basis of his understanding of that content as the kingdom of God and, later, again as love, Hegel immediately affirms an internal and intrinsic relationship between that teaching and Christ's life and death. The transition from kingdom, or from teaching, to life and death is one "from the universal to determinacy, [namely,] to pass over into actuality. This movement, the process of determining, takes place in the life of Jesus."[71]

Though Hegel here mentions life, he is really interested in Christ's death. We can say this because he continues to pursue the presentation of the externalization of the divine idea in and through the life of this concrete individual, as the unity of divine and human nature, to the ultimate extreme of that externalization. He pushes the externalization of the divine idea through to the unity of divine with human in the highest, or should we say, lowest moment of finitude – death.

To underscore this externalization to death, it will be helpful to stop at several stations along the way of Hegel's speculative philosophical interpretation of Christ's death as essential moment in the history of the appearance of the divine idea. First of all, Hegel gives an overall speculative reading of the portrayal (*Darstellung*) of the kingdom of God in the concrete life and death of Christ:

> This portrayal – this objectivity of the intuition of the history of spirit – shows that spirit in itself, which is other than itself [as] the natural will and existence [of humanity], sublates this its other-being, and that it now is for itself in all its glory – namely issuing forth to be spirit through this history.[72]

Then, in the light of this overall philosophical contextualization, he goes on, in the rest of this fourth stage in the presentation of redemption and reconciliation, to give a closer reading of Christ's death. To use his own words added in the margin of the manuscript, Hegel speaks of Christ's death as the "becoming-other of the divine."[73]

It is important to quote the entire paragraph in which Hegel sketches out the more concrete negative side to what he has just described in an initial, more speculative and more inclusive general fashion. Here he writes of death as such and ends the paragraph with a reference to Christ's death:

> However, the pinnacle of finitude is not actual life in its temporal course, but rather death, the anguish of death; death is the pinnacle of negation, the most abstract and indeed natural negation, the limit, finitude in its highest extreme. The temporal and complete existence of the divine idea in the present is envisaged only in [Christ's] death.[74]

This death is, first of all, the highest self-externalization or divestment, we might even say self-emptying, of the divine idea.[75] But death is, secondly, the highest love. For love is the consciousness of the identity of divine and human, an identity carried to the extreme finitization of death. Hegel, in various ways, extols love as the giving of oneself to another. He writes of it as the giving up of one's personality, as "the supreme surrender [of oneself] in the other, even in this most extrinsic other-being of death . . . The death of Christ [is] the vision of this love itself – not [love merely] for or on behalf of others, but precisely *divinity* in this universal identity with other-being, death."[76] Here, then, for Hegel love is the speculatively "intuited" unifying of these extremes of divine and human.

It is as if this reference, in the manuscript, to the speculative triggers in Hegel's mind the fact that, in retrospect, death is a moment in the movement of spirit itself and for finite spirit, namely, for religious consciousness.[77] It is with this thought *of* spirit *for* spirit that Hegel can bring in the traditional sacrificial aspect of Christ's death. He presents it as the way to introduce, and affirm, the second or positive aspect of that death. He picks up, more concretely, on what he had earlier referred to speculatively as the sublation of other-being.[78] Hegel writes, in a phrase that is absolutely critical to any understanding of his presentation of the consummate religion, "In general, death is both the extreme limit of finitude and at the same time the sublation of natural finitude, of immediate existence, the overcoming of divestment, the dissolution of limitation. [Death is] the moment of spirit in which it grasps itself inwardly, the moment of perishing to the natural."[79] With this sentence Hegel has said essentially all he has to say regarding the death of Christ. He has pushed the reading of Christ's death to the point where it becomes his direct response to evil and culpability. It becomes his response to his earlier philosophical interpretation of evil and culpability as the natural willing of what should not be, namely, the willing of individuality abstractly opposed to universality. Throughout the rest of this fourth stage in the presentation of redemption and reconciliation, Hegel continues to stress that this death, as response to such natural will, had to be a fully natural death.[80] This death was, in fact, a death which pushed finitude to the farthest limit. Christ's death was that of a criminal on the cross.[81]

The fifth of the stages of Hegel's presentation of redemption and reconciliation is a brief and more transitional consideration of resurrection and ascension. Hegel gives these two religious representations a speculative interpretation. He sees them as the return of spirit to itself out of its self-externalization in death. It is within the context of this briefer, final reflection in the third concrete sphere of the consummate religion that Hegel gives a concise summary of the self-othering and return of spirit. This is the self-othering and return given religious representation in the life, death, and resurrection of Christ:

> In its development this [process is] the going forth of
> the divine idea into the uttermost cleavage, even to
> the opposite pole of the anguish of death, which is
> itself the absolute reversal, the highest love, contain-
> ing the negation of the negative within itself [and
> being in this way] the absolute reconciliation, the
> sublation of the prior antithesis between humanity
> and God.[82]

Hegel ends this third concrete sphere of the consummate religion with a brief, retrospective summary of the complex, and by no means merely mechanically to be understood, dynamic of self-othering and return of the divine in its movement thus far.[83] He realizes that so far he has only presented reconciliation in its objective appearance in Christ as concrete and exclusive individuality. He must go on to the presentation of the community. What strikes us here, in light of our concern to understand the incarnation as self-othering of the divine idea, is again Hegel's stress on the movement of spirit. Though he sketches his brief review of the three concrete spheres precisely in terms of what he has worked out in these three spheres, it is really the underlying movement of spirit as such which is of more fundamental concern to him. Among the several points he makes, we should specifically mention his insistence that God, as divine idea, is the universal realizing itself immediately in nature (second sphere), in the external which is equally internal in finite spirit (third sphere). The extreme of internalization is, at the same time, the extreme of external-ization. Finite spirit "is at the same time the consummation of externality in deepest cleavage, in conscious negation, and thereby the return of the eternal idea."[84]

It is this insistence of Hegel's on the fact that, for spirit, return occurs at the deepest moment of negation and finitude which brings together, and integrates, all that we have so far summarized, or excerpted and quoted, from Hegel's 1821 manuscript concerning incarnation. Hegel has worked with the notions of intuition, immediacy, of identity and difference, negation, diremption or exter-nalization, contradiction and finitude, and, more indirectly, of the one and the many, throughout his presentation of the consummate re-ligion from the second concrete sphere on. We could also make this same statement, to a certain extent, with regard to his presentation of the second moment in the first concrete sphere or "immanent" Trinity.

Throughout the second and third concrete spheres of the consummate religion, Hegel has pushed the movement of the self-diremption of the divine idea forward in very complex dialectical fashion to an inevitable climax and turning point in the death of Christ. Already with the appearance of the divine idea in and as finite spirit there was, in knowing, a first reference to, and occurrence of, elevation out of natural self-seeking willing. It is a tribute to the extreme richness and complexity of his thought that Hegel can perform what might appear to be a dialectical juggling act. He can affirm this initial *an sich* elevation while at the same time insisting on an irresistible, philosophically we could say necessary, progression to the very limits of finitude in death. In the second concrete sphere he wrote of the appearance of the divine idea in nature almost ex-clusively in terms of other-being. As he moved along in the third concrete sphere, where he treated of finite spirit, that cruder notion of immediate other-being took on the form appropriate to finite spirit. In this third sphere he spoke more of alienation and externalization, of negation and contradiction. Yet toward the end of this third sphere, especially with regard to the death of Christ, he returns to the language of other-being. It is as if he wants to renew awareness of the depths of contradiction and immediate difference between the representation of the divine idea as "immanent" Trinity in the form of love or initial inclusive universality and the representation of the divine idea in its total self-externalization in the death of one concrete individual, in the extreme of finitude. From what Hegel has written in the second and third spheres of concrete representation it would seem that, in the 1821 manuscript, it was at least his intention to maintain a certain dialectical tension between externalization and return within the notion of otherness. He seems to have wanted to maintain a sufficient dialectical tension within his understanding of otherness so as to be able to present incarnation as a movement from identity to difference in the form of the self-othering movement of the divine idea.

The Conceptual Structure of Incarnation

In Part One of the 1821 manuscript, The Concept of Religion, Hegel stresses that incarnation, or a "becoming human of God" (*Menschwerdung Gottes*), is an essential moment in religion as such and in any religion, determinate or consummate.[85] He is not, in any simplistic fashion, presupposing or imposing a notion of incarnation on all religions. Rather, he at least would claim that he is working out of his systematic conception of spirit as he elaborates his own philosophical interpretation of incarnation. In fact, he moves from this initial affirmation concerning incarnation to give a more speculative interpretation of the moments of the concept of religion in two different places in the manuscript treatment of the concept of religion.[86]

We cannot of course simply impose Hegel's first, and apparently quickly written, thoughts concerning the concept of religion, in grid-like fashion, onto the presentation of the consummate religion. This is true whether we refer to those thoughts as we find them, in general, in the first part of the manuscript as a whole, or, more particularly in the two more speculative interpretations to which we are presently referring. It is only later on in the same manuscript, after the first sketching of the the concept of religion, that Hegel works out the lecture presentation of the consummate religion. His thought is quite surely evolving as he works out the manuscript text. We cannot even as clearly distinguish here, with regard to the concept of religion, what Hegel will clearly distinguish in the presentation of the consummate religion. That is, here we cannot yet very clearly recognize a parallel to the distinction Hegel will make between the second and third concrete spheres of the consummate religion. Nor can we find here any indication of the transition he posits, in the consummate religion, from the third sphere to the moment of cultus.

Nevertheless, these two more speculative, perhaps we could also say more preliminary but still enlightening, sketchings of second and third overall moments of the concept of religion should help us to identify the underlying structure of the second and third concrete spheres of the consummate religion. For, as we discussed in Chapter Four above, these second and third concrete spheres, along with the first of them, are in principle for Hegel, as spheres of the consummate religion, to manifest a structured movement congruent with, and parallel to, the moments of the concept of religion. They are to be the moments of that concept become, in their necessary unfolding, objects of religious consciousness.[87]

Several of Hegel's remarks, in the first[88] of these two somewhat more conceptually expressed presentations of the moments of the concept of religion, confirm, in a general way, the fact that the second and third concrete spheres of the consummate religion overlap in their respective presentations of the divine idea. These remarks also give initial expression to the characteristics of the moments of the concept of religion which follow that of initial unity. These characteristics have in fact already come to light in our examination, above, of the manuscript presentation of the second and third concrete spheres of the consummate religion.

In surveying this first, more speculative, presentation of the moments of the concept of religion, we should note that Hegel's remarks in the paragraph[89] immediately following the reference to initial unity cannot, at least according to Hegel's expression here, refer only to the second of the concrete spheres of the consummate religion. This is so because, in this paragraph, Hegel writes not only of the world but of human beings and of evil. And these are themes he first treats at any length in the first subsection of the third concrete sphere of the consummate religion. Here, then, already in this paragraph concerning the second of the moments or determinations of the concept of religion itself, Hegel sketches out a number of conceptually expressed characteristics. These characteristics determine the fundamental direction of the movement that is this second determination of the concept of religion. They thus foreshadow his later manuscript presentations in both the second and third spheres of the consummate religion. This second determination of the concept of religion, the determination following that of initial unity, is, for example, described as that of separation and difference. Furthermore, Hegel writes, "God [is] the absolutely positive; therefore what differs from God [is] the negative. This negative appears on the side of worldly essence, of human being."[90] It is as if he wishes to underscore the fundamental and constitutive nature of the second determination as differentiation. He wants to stress that this differentiation, as negation, continues into and through the appearance of finite spirit.[91] Thus it continues into and through what will become the third of the concrete spheres of the consummate religion.

In what could be referred to as the third of the determinations of the concept of religion,[92] Hegel, again in very general fashion, indicates the subjective moment when he notes that the "absoluteness and infinitude of self-consciousness is represented in the doctrine of the immortality of the soul."[93] With this first conceptual presentation he tries, first of all, to push the presentation of differentiation into, and through, the appearance of finite spirit. He tries, second, to see that appearance as moment of return. It is this structure of differentiation and externalization, which is at the same time elevation from finite to infinite, that comes to expression in his efforts to reflect philosophically on the appearance of the divine idea in and as nature, finite spirit and incarnation. Here incarnation is to be taken in the more traditional sense of that word, namely, as appearance of God in and as one finite individual. At the end of a long reflection on the elevation from finite to infinite,[94] Hegel identifies this differentiation and elevation with the othering of the idea when he writes that "the finite world, nature and finite consciousness, are the antithesis, the other of the

idea." He goes on to stress the parallel he sees between the "immanent" trinitarian and "economic" trinitarian movements: "As religion
represents it, there is in God the other of God, God's *Son*, i.e., God as
other, the other that remains within love and within divinity; and the
Son is the truth of this finite world."[95]

Among the various remarks Hegel makes in the second[96] of
these two preliminary, and more speculative, sketchings of the determinations of the concept of religion, it is those at the very end of this
second sketching which are particularly relevant. They sum up, and
confirm, the general structure underlying Hegel's presentation of
incarnation as self-othering of the divine idea. Hegel, in effect,
announces the overall opposition constitutive of religion as such,
an opposition between universality and individuality: "Its [religion's]
two moments, the moments making up the antithesis [are]
(a) absolute universality, pure thinking, and (b) absolute singularity,
sensibility."[97] This opposition, pushed to its climax in the consummate religion with the incarnation as movement to the extreme
of death, itself comes in the consummate religion to be seen as
the means of an immediate reconciliation of such opposition. The
divine idea, or God as universality, and nature and finite spirit as
doubled individuality, are reconciled through the death of a concrete
individual human being in the exclusive individuality of a particular
individual who is representationally presented as risen from the
dead. Already in the 1821 manuscript presentation of the determinations of the concept of religion Hegel had sketched the overall logical
structure, and the overlapping externalization and return, of what
would be expressed in the consummate religion as its second and
third concrete spheres.

2.b. The 1827 Lectures

From 1824 on Hegel restructures the spheres of the consummate
religion. He shifts from the 1821 presentation of a series of three outer
determinations and three inner concrete spheres to one series of three
elements.[98] In the process he moves the Christological theologoumena of redemption and reconciliation from the third inner or
concrete sphere of the consummate religion. In the 1821 lectures he
had worked hard to try to keep the Christological theologoumena
together with the realization of reconciliation in cultus or communi-

ty.[99] Now, from 1824 on, he moves these theologoumena to the second half of the consummate religion's newly constituted second element. He now clearly conceives this second element as a movement of diremption and immediate reconciliation.

Of the various lecture series from 1824 on, it is those of 1827 which best represent these shifts in structure and distribution of thematic content. These 1827 lectures are particularly representative, first of all, because, with them, Hegel not only clearly proposes, but also definitely works out, his speculative concept of religion. His proposed dynamic structural parallel between the development of the divine idea in, as, and through the three elements of the consummate religion, and the self-positing movement of the moments of the speculative concept of religion, should, then, allow for a more succinct and direct examination of both the three elements of the consummate religion and the movement of the speculative concept of religion.[100] Secondly, it is with the 1827 lectures as well that he makes a more explicit effort to give a logical structure and underpinning to his observations and constructive philosophical interpretations.

This effort at logical structuring can already be seen in his initial, twice presented division[101] of the consummate religion where he more closely integrates religious consciousness and the object of that religious consciousness. The three elements of the consummate religion are described as three different ways in which God is in relationship with the finite subject and the finite subject with God. They are effectively three ways in which God and finite subject are other to one another. These three ways are the appearance of the divine idea, first of all, to thought in the realm of universality and, then, to sensible intuition and representation in the realm of particularity and, finally, to sensibility and subjectivity in the realm of singularity.

We turn now to a consideration especially of certain aspects of the first two elements of the consummate religion in the 1827 lectures. It will be important to keep in mind the nagging question why Hegel, on the one hand, continued to locate the Christological theologoumena in the third element or sphere of the revealed religion in his later 1827 and 1830 editions of the *Encyclopedia*. He did this, even while, on the other hand, clearly placing them in, and as, the second half of the second element of the consummate religion in the lectures from 1824 on.[102]

Incarnation in the Consummate Religion
The First Element

Hegel's fundamental, consistent, and perduring presentation of the first sphere or element of the consummate religion throughout the four lecture series on the philosophy of religion will, in the light of what has already been said concerning the 1821 lectures and in light of our discussion "in Chapter Six" above of Trinity in the 1827 lectures, now permit more direct reference to certain points concerning incarnation and otherness either more characteristic of, or made more clearly here in, the 1827 lectures.

Hegel sketches the dialectical structure and movement of God as spirit at least twice in the first element of the consummate religion. Within the context of a discussion of a finite way of understanding he, in a more general and for him valid formulation, writes: "God in God's eternal universality is the one who distinguishes God self, determines God self, posits an other to God self and likewise sublates the distinction, thereby remaining present to self, and is spirit only through this process of being brought forth."[103] Hegel underscores that it is precisely through the sinking into the other and, subtly noted, the having been immersed or sunk into the other, that this process occurs.[104] The second of these sketches of the structured movement of God as spirit is made in more explicitly logical language. He writes of life (*Leben*) as the movement of judgment or separation (*Urteil*) of the idea out of itself as universality. He notes the consequent arising of the particular (*das Besondere*) as other (*das Andere*). Thus, universal and particular stand over against one another. They are two distinguished moments (*zwei Unterschiedene*). These two differentiated moments are, of course, not really distinguished in the realm of universality which is being discussed here. The other which arises is only an ideal other. It is immediately sublated.[105]

These two more general sketchings of the structure and movement of God as divine idea in the realm of universality allow Hegel to speak of God here not only in terms of life, but of love. He essentially repeats, though now in clearer fashion, his 1821 position that love is both the discovery of oneself in the other and the overcoming of the difference inherent in the notion of otherness.[106] It is with these conceptions of life and of love that Hegel explicitly introduces the notion of contradiction into his presentation of the dialectic of God as the eternal idea. He insists, in various ways, that contradiction is found within the eternal idea itself to the extent that the difference between universal and particular, namely, between universal and its other as mutually opposed difference, is initially and momentarily not yet overcome. The mutual opposition is then overcome with difference's being thought within the wider dialectical context of a speculatively interpreted movement of life and of love. "The idea itself is the resolution of the contradictions posited by it."[107] In this first element, then, we can, in summary fashion, say Hegel has stressed that the second moment is one of particularity, of judgment and separation, of difference, of immediate appearance and even of sublation, namely, of being other to its other. This second moment thus constitutes a moment of contradiction. It is a contradiction which is immediately resolved when the second moment itself is seen as the very moment in and through which its own contradiction is overcome. The contradiction is resolved precisely when the second moment is seen as momentary totality in the movement of the divine idea, that is, when Hegel presents the divine idea as spirit by means of his speculative interpretation of life and love.

The Second Element

The characteristics of the second moment in the first element of the consummate religion equally characterize the consummate religion in its second element.[108] However, with regard to these characteristics, we need to make two points at the very beginning of this consideration of the second element of the consummate religion in the 1827 lectures. One is that, in 1827, Hegel distinguishes more clearly between the second moment in the first element and the overall second element than he does in the 1821 lectures. Generally speaking, in both lecture series he refers to the second moment in the first element as "the other" (*das Andere*). And in 1821 he usually refers to the second concrete sphere of the consummate religion or, in 1827, to the second element of the consummate religion as "other-being"

(*Anderssein*). But he seems to hold more clearly and consistently to this distinction in 1827 with the result that, in these 1827 lectures, he more forcefully stresses the initial independent being of the world and nature as other to, and then of, God.[109] Perhaps Hegel is continuing to defend himself against the charge of pantheism.

The second point to which we should draw attention is that, on the one hand, the term itself "negation" seems to play a very minor, if any, role in the elaboration either of the second moment of the first concrete sphere of the consummate religion (1821) or the first element of the consummate religion (1827). Perhaps Hegel's less well organized presentations of the first concrete sphere (1821) and the first element (1827) are simply not meant to be comprehensive. On the other hand, in 1821 the notion of negation clearly characterizes the second concrete sphere as well as aspects of the third concrete sphere of the consummate religion, including especially Christ's death.[110] And, by way of anticipation regarding the 1827 lectures, we can say that this notion of negation also qualifies the second element of the consummate religion to the extent that the second element is the overall presentation of the appearance of the divine idea. It is that appearance all the way to its final realization in the death of a particular, concrete individual.

As we have already mentioned, what is strikingly different here in the 1827 transcript in comparison with the 1821 manuscript is the fact that, with the 1824 lectures, and now in these 1827 lectures, Hegel brings together into one sphere the movements of diremption or estrangement and immediate reconciliation. He develops them as the second element of the consummate religion. Hegel himself must have been aware of the changes he had made already in the 1824 lecture presentation of the second element of the consummate religion. In fact, it would seem that in 1827 he regularly lectured from the Griesheim transcription of the 1824 lectures and had his own earlier 1821 manuscript available.[111] He followed, and further revised, the 1824 structuring and distribution of content rather than working strictly with that of 1821. Toward the beginning of the 1827 presentation of the appearance of the divine idea in the second element Hegel is recorded as stating quite directly, "The second element is, therefore, the process of the world in love by which it passes over from fall and separation into reconciliation."[112] It is as if, with this reference to love, and surely speculatively interpreted in view of the parallel reference to spirit,[113] he is giving the listener a clue as to the way in which he wishes to present diremption and immediate reconciliation in this second element. It is as if he is hinting at the way in which he intends to have diremption and reconciliation constitute one sphere.

Our present interests in Hegel's interpretation of incarnation in terms of otherness do not require that we make a detailed comparative analysis of the 1821 and 1827 presentations of the appearance of the divine idea in religious representational form (*Vorstellung*). Rather, it will be of greater direct value, while keeping in mind what we have already said regarding the 1821 presentation, for us to concentrate on critical moments in the 1827 presentation where Hegel may give some insight into how he tries to bring diremption and immediate reconciliation together in one sphere.[114] It is ultimately the structure and movement of the appearance of the divine idea in nature, finite spirit, and a concrete individual which, as movement of speculatively interpreted love, is in question when we see incarnation as self-othering of the divine idea. Within this structure and movement, the critical moments of particular interest will be those of the way in which Hegel first presents finite spirit, the need he posits for reconciliation, and death as the moment in which that reconciliation immediately occurs.

After a brief, general presentation of the second element and of the world as other-being,[115] Hegel immediately, by means of the assertion that the world is on the side of difference vis-à-vis the unity which is God, announces the division of the world into the natural world and into the world of finite spirit. Though he affirms this immediate division into nature and finite spirit, he quickly asserts that nature enters in relationship only to finite spirit. This is so because nature itself is not knowing and, consequently, does not know God.[116] Already in the first appearance of finite spirit, with this reference to knowing, Hegel alludes to the way in which, and the level on which, separation, alienation, and reconciliation will occur in this second element. Here in 1827 Hegel manages to characterize the second element, immediately from its beginning, by internal division. Perhaps his doing this is, in some way, tied in with the marginal note, concerning the appearance of finite spirit, which he had added to the beginning of the 1821 text on the world and nature as other-being.[117]

It is this division within, and characteristic of, the second element which Hegel then presents in a tight dialectical progression[118] through an analysis of finite spirit, or the human person, as initially good by nature, and yet equally initially bad or evil by nature. To top things off, he proposes the latter determination as the higher of the two. Hegel does not simply juxtapose, in antinomical fashion, two opposing determinations of finite spirit. Rather, he indicates dialectical advance or movement "forward" when he qualifies finite spirit's being evil by nature as the higher determination.

In view of the previously made longer resume and analysis of Hegel's 1821 presentation of finite spirit as both good and evil, it will now suffice to underscore again that it is by means of an analysis of what finite spirit is "in itself" (*an sich*), and should be in actuality or "for itself" (*für sich*), that Hegel can make the appropriate transition from external to internal contradiction. He very impressively moves from finite spirit's knowing that, in relation to God, finite spirit itself is both good and evil on to the knowledge that this contradiction exists within finite spirit itself. He continues the move as one to the knowledge that contradiction, as such, is indeed finite spirit's very determination or basic characteristic.[119]

With this well-structured analysis of the dialectical progression toward ever more interiorized contradiction or self-alienation as that which is constitutive of finite spirit, Hegel has in fact been arguing the need (*Bedürfnis*) for reconciliation. He has allowed the original division of the world into nature and finite spirit to be played out within finite spirit. Finite spirit, in knowing God and in knowing that it is separated ever more from that unity and good which God is, experiences the pain (*Schmerz*) of its own self-enclosed self-seeking existence. In its alienation from the world, where it does not find happiness, finite spirit equally knows and experiences its own unhappiness (*Unglück*).[120] Hegel pushes this doubled alienation, this doubled form of unhappiness, to its extreme by recalling that each side is one-sided, and therefore abstract. There is an unresolved total mutual opposition between the two forms of this doubled alienation. He gives this unresolved mutual opposition an interesting typological expression. He recognizes doubled alienation and mutual opposition in the pain characteristic of the Jewish religious consciousness, with its sense of separation from the universal, and in the profound sense of unhappiness weighing down the Roman religious consciousness, with its characterization as a paradoxical alienation from the world. It is, then, this immense sense of alienation, pushed to its extreme within finite spirit and expressed in the mutually one-sided antithesis between Jewish and Roman religions, which constitutes the deepest actually existing individual and religious need for reconciliation both with God and with the world.[121]

Earlier on, and in preliminary fashion, Hegel had interpreted the movement of diremption and immediate reconciliation in terms of love.[122] Here, in a way parallel to this earlier interpretation of reconciliation, Hegel had opened his reflection on the division, which is at first external to, and then internalized within, finite spirit, with the announcement that what is to be treated is first "the *need* for truth; the second is the *mode* and *manner* of its appearance."[123] This need for truth and reconciliation is found in the very antithesis or opposition constituting finite spirit as contradiction, because for Hegel "truth is the attainment of unity through the negation of the antithesis."[124] It is by means of this intimate linkage, and even dialectical identification, of need and response or appearance by way of the notion of an internal negation that Hegel proposes to bind together diremption and immediate reconciliation in this second element of the consummate religion. He proposes to work with a movement of negation of negation.

Hegel goes on, essentially as he did in 1821, to assert that finite spirit's being conceived as knowing is the condition of the possibility for reconciliation and, thus, for finite spirit itself's being implicitly this reconciliation.[125] Reconciliation of divine and human is already implicitly present in finite spirit as consciousness. He continues to argue to the necessary condition for finite spirit's coming to attain the certainty of the reconciliation of divine and human. If finite spirit is to come to reconciliation in actuality, then the immediate reconciliation of divine and human must come to finite spirit in the form of one particular individual.[126]

Hegel's 1827 presentation of the death of Christ is considerably shorter than his presentation in 1821. Still, he does here treat of Christ's death in a more explicitly speculative fashion. He does this in the sense that he considers it primarily from the perspective of the dynamic movement of spirit. He considers Christ's death within the complex movement, which spirit is, of self-positing and return. He lays the groundwork for his briefer presentation on the death of Christ with a discussion of other-being and its sublation.[127] As he once again points to the generalized division and antithesis, or opposition, constitutive of finite spirit and to the opposition existing between finite spirit and God, Hegel recalls as well that "This incongruity is the point of departure that constitutes the need [for reconciliation]."[128] He insists that this incongruity is real and resides in spirit, or spirit would not be spirit. Yet, from the perspective of divine unity, the incongruity between human and divine cannot attack or harm that unity which provides a context within which finite spirit and finitude are to be thought. In several sentences, which need to be cited at greater length, he is recorded as arguing this speculative contextualization by recalling the nature of the divine idea which others itself and sublates this its self-othering:

> The other-being, the finitude, the weakness, the frailty of human nature is not to do any harm to that divine unity which forms the substance of reconciliation. That no harm is done has been seen in the divine idea. For the Son is other than the Father, and this otherness is difference – otherwise it would not be spirit. But the other is [also] God and has the entire fullness of the divine nature within itself. The character of otherness in no way detracts from the fact that this other is the Son of God and therefore God. This otherness is what eternally posits and eternally sublates itself; the self-positing and sublating of otherness is love or spirit.[129]

In this text Hegel seems not to have hesitated to speak of otherness as differentiation and as the sublation of that differentiation. The 1827 transcript texts present Hegel as working with this same characteristic of otherness as, in some way, both diremption and reconciliation when he, from a more speculative standpoint, speaks of Christ's death as "the most abstract form of humanity, the greatest dependence, the ultimate weakness, the utmost fragility."[130] In what is effectively an application of the more general reference to otherness as self-positing and sublating movement of love, Hegel speaks of death, the negative, as otherness and the furthest extreme of humanity in which God is involved. Finitude and death are within God self.[131] Again with reference to the divine idea, and here in a summary recapitulation at the end of the presentation of the second element, Hegel is recorded as speaking of humanity and of finitude as other-being which itself is a moment, but equally disappearing moment, in God.[132] This is the return of love, of spirit.[133] Hegel had begun his philosophical interpretation of humanity's innocence, alienation within and over against God, and contradictory nature all in terms of truth. Here he maintains that initial concern for truth by means of his reference to spirit. However, he expresses immediate reconciliation most appropriately, on the level of the second element of the consummate religion, in terms of love.

The Conceptual Structure of Religion

It will come as no surprise that, in the more speculatively developed 1827 lectures, Hegel opens his overview of the subject matter, namely, his philosophy of religion, with a clearer and more integrated reference to method than we find in the 1821 lectures.[134] After all, he is speaking of the concept and of the absolute, here on the level of religion, as the divine idea. It would be hard to imagine him carrying out any reflection on the concept of religion as such self-relational inclusive or absolute subjectivity without thinking immediately of method as the self-explication and self-explicitation of the philosophical, or more precisely, logical concept. A longer quote from the 1827 transcript will give a good idea of what he is up to, here in the 1827 lectures, with regard to the philosophy of religion as a whole and, more specifically, with regard to the concept of religion, determinate religion, and the consummate religion:

> There can be but *one method* in all science, in all knowledge. Method is just the self-explicating concept – nothing else – and the concept is one only. Here too, therefore, the *first moment* is, as always, the *concept*. The *second moment* is the *determinateness of the concept*, the concept in its determinate forms. . . . . Therefore the *first moment* is the *concept of religion* or

religion in general, and the *second* is our consideration of *determinate religion*. And we do not derive the
determinateness from outside, but rather it is the free
concept that impels itself to its own determinateness.
.... For that reason we consider in the *third place* the
concept as it comes forth to itself out of its determinateness, out of its finitude, as it reestablishes
itself out of its own finitude, its own confinement.
This *reestablished concept* is the infinite, true concept,
the *absolute idea* or the *true religion*.[135]

After this preliminary, but all-important, speculative overview of the
structure and movement of the 1827 presentation of the philosophy of
religion, Hegel develops the concept of religion as a movement in and
through three moments: the concept of God; the knowledge of God;
and, cultus.[136] These three moments of the concept of religion reflect
the stringently coordinated methodological development he had
indicated in the Introduction to these lectures. These three moments
themselves pre-present, on their own level, what Hegel intends to be
the further progression of the philosophy of religion lectures and the
consummating presentation of the true religion.

Hegel presents each of the three moments of the concept of
religion as momentary totality. Each moment includes, in its own way,
a moment of negation and otherness. He begins with the concept of
God, which he insists is not only a substantial unity but, given the
level on which he is working, also a spiritual unity.[137] Hegel insists
that substance is equally *an sich* subject and spirit. For him the
fundamental determination of God, even as substance, is that God is
that out of which all comes and to which all returns and is immediately retained.[138] It is not hard to see how Hegel will propose that
this spiritual unity becomes object of religious consciousness as
"immanent" Trinity in the first element of the consummate religion.

Hegel provides easy access to his overall conception of the
second moment of the concept of religion in a brief, initial summary.[139] Here he sketches the second moment in terms by now quite
familiar. It is one of diremption, of separation, of judgment resulting
in particular over against universal, of a movement of the concept as
otherness out of itself. Hegel himself makes direct reference to the

logical notion of judgment, which he had worked out in the *Logic* and which he here presupposes.[140] But not only is the second moment the result of judgment, it is in fact difference itself, spiritual difference. And God, as spirit, is this judgment.[141] The second moment is considered, as moment, to include God and consciousness as well as nature and finite spirit. So, from the perspective of representation, one can begin either from God or from finite spirit in this consideration of the second moment of the concept.[142] It is, then, in the second of his two initial considerations beginning, respectively, with God and with finite consciousness, namely, from the perspective of finite spirit or consciousness, that Hegel affirms God is or exists for, and appears to, the human subject in so far as the subject is thinking being. And it is already here from the beginning of the concept of religion's second moment, in the light of this description of the finite subject as thinking being, that reconciliation is therewith implicitly accomplished.[143]

Then Hegel treats of the various proofs for the existence of God as a major part of this second moment of the concept of religion. They are, when considered from the perspective of unifying reason (*Vernunft*), seen as the elevation of the finite consciousness to God, an elevation of finite to infinite.[144] It is this second moment, as the judgement of self-othering and the movement of elevation, which Hegel sees made object of religious consciousness in the second element of the consummate religion, namely, in the divine idea's complex movement of diremption and immediate reconciliation.

We could go on to consider cultus as third moment of the concept of religion and then as third element of the consummate religion. In each of these two cases, within each of these two unities, there is affirmed a moment of negation in the form of self-sacrifice on the part of the members of the community. However, for present purposes we can remain with the first and second moments of the overall concept of religion. Here we see that, from the very beginning, Hegel makes every effort to establish the moments as momentary totalities inclusive of some form of differentiation. Ultimately, in each case he is working with the relationship between identity and difference.[145] In the first of the two moments of the concept of religion, it is the immediately disappearing differentiation which allows for the affirmation of spiritual unity. We must not content ourselves with any merely substantial unity. In the second moment it is the movement of differentiation which sets the stage for, and remains basic condition of, the possibility and actuality of a return out of differentiation. This differentiation is the necessary condition for an elevation of finite spirit to God. God, as spirit, returns to God self in and through finite spirit.

3. The Inner Dialectical Structure of Divine Self-Othering

3.a. Hegel's Presentations of Incarnation

A look back over what Hegel has either written or been recorded as saying concerning incarnation in its various senses quickly reveals his continual working with, and on the basis of, a conception of spirit. He works with an understanding of spirit essentially as movement of thought. Spirit is a movement of thought in the form of a self-othering and return,[146] indeed, here in the philosophy of religion, a movement of thought as inclusive divine subjectivity. From the *Phenomenology* on[147] Hegel had envisioned spirit as the reality of retaining one's self-identity in that which is other to, and of, oneself. He worked unabashedly with basically this same notion throughout his various presentations of the philosophy of religion in general and, more particularly, of the consummate religion itself and of incarnation in the consummate religion.

At first sight, it would seem as if Hegel maintained this reference to, and working with, the notion of spirit as complex movement of self-othering and return in what would seem to be structurally very different presentations of the revelatory, revealed, and consummate religion.

For example, on the one hand, he continually placed the return of spirit to itself, religiously expressed as redemption and reconciliation, in the third moment of the *Encyclopedia* presentation. This he also had done in the 1821 manuscript when he sketched redemption and immediate reconciliation in the consummate religion's third concrete sphere. Of course even here we must admit that, along with this similarity of presentation in the *Encyclopedia* and in the 1821 manuscript, there is a difference between these two presentations. Whereas in the *Encyclopedia* presentation reconciliation occurs both in its immediacy and in its realization in self-consciousness within the third moment of the revealed religion, in the 1821 manuscript Hegel separates the two, respectively, into the third concrete sphere and into the third moment of the outer triadically developed presentation of the consummate religion.

On the other hand, from 1824 on he presented redemption and immediate reconciliation as more or less second half of the second of the three elements of the consummate religion. Consequently, we might easily think that, from 1824 on, in Part One of the lectures on the philosophy of religion Hegel affirmed a movement of the concept of religion as one of self-othering and then of "subsequent" return. Such a structuring would result in a movement which, in its sequenced ordering, was no longer clearly reflected and realized in the way Hegel distributed Christological theologoumena in the second half of the second element of the consummate religion. Rather, from 1824 on, Hegel no longer followed his 1821 approach. He tried to integrate othering and initial return, namely, immediate reconciliation, in the second element. It would, then, at first glance appear that he had blurred his initial vision. Initially this vision would seem to have been expressed in the 1821 manuscript as a second concrete sphere, which is simply, and straightforwardly, self-othering as externalization and diremption, and a third sphere, which is simply, and straightforwardly, return.

To recapitulate, there seem initially to be quite striking differences in, and even seemingly fundamentally different structurings of, the presentation of incarnation between, on the one hand, the presentation in the 1821 manuscript and the *Encyclopedia* and, on the other hand, more or less that of the lectures from 1824 on. However, upon further reflection, the differing presentations appear less radically distinct, or even opposed. First of all, it is hard to see where Hegel ever really presents the moment of initial diremption as simple exteriorization without immediate reference to at least implicit (*an sich*) return. Even in the presentations of the moments of the concept of religion as movement of spirit, he tends to underscore the second determination as that of separation and differentiation while including reference to finite spirit which, as spirit, is itself the occasion both for further differentiation and for return.[148] The only possible candidate for a thoroughly straightforward presentation of the second determination or moment as pure externalization would be the second concrete sphere in the 1821 manuscript. But, even there Hegel ended the presentation with a moment of implicit return. And, indeed, he had added an initial marginal note in which he made reference to finite spirit.[149] Furthermore, in the *Encyclopedia* the second moment of the revealed religion is itself, in its presentation both of nature and finite spirit in one sphere, a movement both of diremption and initial return.[150] The third concrete sphere of the 1821 presentation of the consummate religion is also itself a sphere which includes within it, first of all, a further moment of cleavage in and as finite spirit and, then, a moment of reconciliation and return. In fact, Hegel has almost always maintained some form of explicitly doubled presentation of both diremption and return in the sphere or element in which he places the overall moment of diremption and, more specifically, in which he situates the Christian Christological the-ologoumena. What he has done from 1824 on, in the lectures on the philosophy of religion, would then seem to be to make explicit what was at least in a general way already affirmed in the 1821 lectures and in the various editions of the *Encyclopedia*.

A further glance particularly at his 1827 presentation of the second moment of the concept of religion and, then, in the consum-mate religion, at his speculative reading of life, love, and Christ's death, each as movement of spirit (a reading essentially common to the 1821 and 1827 presentations of the consummate religion) will shed more light on the way in which Hegel at least indicates that he intends to present incarnation as self-othering of the divine idea.

In the luminescent clarity of immediate conceptual formulation Hegel, in 1827, stresses that the concept of religion, in its moment of otherness, is a movement to the farthest extreme of finitude. It is an ongoing diremption appropriately carried out in and through finite spirit. But here his understanding of the self-determination of the concept of religion is not that of a merely self-externalizing, dare we say, merely neoplatonic movement. It is, at the same time and in the same movement, as occurring in and through finite spirit, both a moment of externalization and, equally, a movement of elevation from finite to infinite. It is this doubled movement which indeed constitutes, and consequently characterizes, the second moment of the concept of religion. If Hegel wishes to work with his overall notion of spirit as diremption and return, and if he wishes to do this in and through finite spirit, he has no choice, on the level of religion, but to present this doubled movement as simultaneously diremption and return in the form of a dialectically developed progression from implicit to explicit.

Given the fact that Hegel defines both absolute spirit and finite spirit in terms of thought, he must, as he did with absolute spirit, now also, with regard to finite spirit, see in it a doubled movement of thought as diremption and return. It is true that he can and must first stress diremption and then return. But he cannot entirely separate, or even clearly distinguish in any simple fashion, the two movements of spirit into different spheres. There cannot be pure diremption in one sphere or element, and pure return in the next. Once finite spirit, as movement of thought, enters on the scene, as it necessarily must in any Hegelian presentation of the philosophy of religion, there occurs, in parallel and not merely sequenced fashion, both redemption and return in and through that finite spirit as thought. This reflects, and even expresses, the necessarily self-contradictory character of finite spirit.

It would seem, then, that what Hegel is trying to do in describing incarnation as self-othering of the divine idea is to give expression to a very complex movement. It would seem he is trying to say that the movement of diremption is, at least from the perspective of the movement of the divine idea, so fundamental that it characterizes and gives an overall qualification to the entire second element of the consummate religion in the 1827 transcript. It seems he is trying to assert this overall qualification of the entire second element even while insisting that this overall movement of diremption is necessarily accompanied by a parallel, but in a sense subordinated, movement of return. The movement of diremption even gives this overall qualification to the second and third concrete spheres of the consummate religion in the 1821 manuscript and to the second and even a major part of the third moments of the revealed religion in the *Encyclopedia*. It is as if, from the 1824 lectures on, Hegel is so overwhelmed by, and consequently wishes so to underscore, the diremptive nature of death that he abandons his earlier attempt, in 1821, to maintain, in one sphere, the initial reconciliation attained in the appearance of Christ and the subjective realization of that reconciliation in cultus and community. He reallocates the Christological content of the consummate religion in order, we might then say more appropriately, to maintain death as the extreme of self-othering within consummate religion's second element.

In each case, whether in the 1821 distribution of the Christological theologoumena and in the similar placement in the *Encyclopedia* or in the distribution common to the later lectures from 1824 on, it is Hegel's vision of the death of Christ as final moment of the self-othering of the divine idea which immediately reconciles universal and individual, God and finite spirit. Hegel sees the death of Christ as moment of negation moving into negation of negation. Life and love, speculatively interpreted as movement of spirit in diremption and return, find their fullest expression in the death of Christ. For death is the uttermost moment of otherness in, and out of which, spirit arises. For Hegel, initial return or reconciliation occurs in and through the fullness of the realization of divine self-diremption in the death of Christ. Immediate reconciliation is the realization that diremption and return are identified in the death of Christ.

This review and, then, summary of what Hegel has actually said about incarnation as self-othering of the divine idea in his presentations of the consummate religion, along with the control reference to his sketchings on the concept of religion, reveal a complex interrelating of diremption and return or, religiously expressed, alienation and reconciliation. Particularly in the moments, spheres, or elements of realization where it was, from the perspective of his overall speculatively formulated system, most appropriate to speak of the relationship between the appearance of the divine idea and the finite religious consciousness to which the appearance occurs, Hegel effectively interweaves diremption and return. He does this while moving along the trajectory to the final realization of negation, to the moment of death.

Hegel tended, however, in the presentations of the concept of religion, and especially in his reference to method, as well as in the presentations of "immanent" Trinity, to present the moments of diremption and return in somewhat more sequentially unilinear fashion. This more sequential schematization of the essence of spirit as self-positing movement of thought would not be inappropriate to the rarefied atmosphere of the discussion of the concept of religion, or to the presentation of "immanent" Trinity. To some extent in both cases, but especially in the exposition of the first determination of the concept of religion, there is as yet, in principle, no explicit reference to finite spirit over against the religiously represented movement of divine subjectivity. Yet, even in these instances, Hegel did not in actual fact maintain so strict a sequentially laid out presentation of the moments of the movement of spirit as diremption and return.

3.b. The Logical Structure of Otherness

Now, after a review of what Hegel has actually said on incarnation as the self-othering of the divine idea, and after a clarifying reference to remarks concerning the determinations of the concept of religion, all still within the ambit of the lectures on the philosophy of religion, we will better understand what Hegel is up to if, in a sort of wider "system-control," we take a brief look at certain more directly relevant aspects of the presentation of otherness in the rarefied atmosphere of his *Science of Logic*. With regard to the *Logic* there is even less reference to any notion of finite consciousness representationally placed "over against" the self-positing and self-development of pure thought than in the development of the concept of religion or in the presentation of "immanent" Trinity within the philosophy of religion.

It is in the *Logic* that the "mature" Hegel inevitably bares his philosophical soul. There he lays out the structural movements of thought arising out of, and realized in, his various post-logic or realphilosophical spheres, namely, in the philosophy of nature and the philosophy of spirit. In our turn to this "inner" Hegel, for present purposes the important thing is not so much to attempt to summarize his complex presentation of the logic of otherness. Rather, in more limited fashion, we want to recall what he sees as the inner, speculative structure of the appearance of otherness. This will enable us, in the final remarks at the end of this chapter, to make several further observations concerning what he intended, and may have accomplished, by interpretating incarnation in terms of otherness.

Our having first reviewed Hegel's remarks, in his philosophy of religion, on incarnation and otherness should now help us hone in on certain aspects of his treatment of otherness in the *Logic*. Our prior review of Hegel's philosophy of religion should aid us in avoiding any merely external imposition of logical categories on what Hegel said in his philosophy of religion.

In his philosophical readings of the incarnation Hegel repeatedly refers to various forms of otherness such as, for example, "otherbeing" (*Anderssein*) or "the other" (*das Andere*), to the thought determination of judgment (*Urteil*), and to method (*Methode*). So it is these references, in his own interpretations and in his own remarks, which push toward, and guide the selection of, logical thought determinations on which to concentrate in order further to clarify the inner structure of incarnation. It is these interpretations and remarks of Hegel's themselves which suggest proceeding in four steps: first, a brief reference to what Hegel very generally means by otherness; second, a listing of the basic ways in which the presence of the other comes to explicit expression in the movement of logical thought; third, a remark on what he understands by judgment; and, fourth, a brief examination of certain aspects of the second moment in his overall presentation of method as movement from beginning through progression to result. Hegel locates his first thematic consideration of otherness toward the beginning of the first book of the *Logic*, namely, in the logic of being. In this first book's first edition (1812), he presents "otherbeing" or *Anderssein* as *Dasein* or determinate being in so far as it is nothing: "Determinate being as the negation [*das Nichts*] of itself, so that this negation of itself is equally determinate being. – Or determinate being is essentially otherbeing."[151] With his typical appeal to the thought determinations of being and nothing, which have preceded the presentation of otherbeing, Hegel goes on to affirm that this otherbeing itself is determinate being, but now as relation. "The *other* is *not this*."[152] By the second edition of this first book of the *Logic*, published in 1832, Hegel has considerably rearranged this initial presentation of otherness. Perhaps these changes reflect his years of work in the realphilosophical spheres and even his interpretations of incarnation in terms of otherness.

In a way parallel to the firmer stress on "the other" (*das Andere*) in the 1827 lectures on the philosophy of religion rather than the term "otherbeing" (*Anderssein*), more commonly used in the 1821 manuscript, Hegel now, in the 1832 edition of the logic of being, works more straightforwardly with the thought determination "an other" (*ein Anderes*). He treats of otherbeing in more subordinate fashion.[153] In this 1832 edition of the logic of being Hegel introduces *Etwas* or "something" earlier than in the first edition and identifies it with "a determinate being" (*Daseiendes*).[154] Then in a tightly knit paragraph,[155] in which he uses the previously presented thought determinations of being, nothing, and becoming, he argues that the first moment of something is itself something in so far as it is being. Furthermore, "The second is equally a *determinate* being, but determined as a negative of the something – an *other*."[156]

With these initial logical presentations of otherness as the negation of a determinate being, or of something, Hegel has clearly captured and expressed an element essential to any understanding of otherness. He has, so to speak, taken this essential element or aspect of otherness and run with it. With this initial logical presentation of otherness as negation he clearly announces the fundamental determination by means of which he then characterizes, and interprets, the notion of otherness throughout his entire encyclopedic system. It would seem that he always attempts to express otherness in terms of negation and, more particularly, as negation of that out of which it arises.

To return more directly again to the *Logic*, when one thinks through the various thought categories or determinations constituting the movement of pure or logical thought there are, for Hegel, three basic ways in which thought determinations arise one out of another. The presentation of otherness, or an other, as arising out of and due to the thinking through of the thought determination of a determinate being or of something already exemplifies how Hegel structures the transitions from one thought determination to another in the first book of the *Logic*, namely, the logic of being.

In the logic of being the transition, which gives rise to otherness, occurs as "transition into another"[157] or, better, "having gone over into another."[158] In the second book of the *Logic*, the logic of essence with its relative determinations of reflection, the dialectical progression takes place as "appearance in the other."[159] In the third book of the *Logic*, the logic of the concept, the resultant third moment of logic as a whole, Hegel characterizes the dialectical movement as development (*Entwicklung*)[160] in which each category is explicitly the totality of the concept.[161]

It was important for us to recall again these three ways in which transitions occur in the movement of logic or pure thought. For these are three ways in which otherness is seen to arise in the *Logic,* namely, as a "having gone over into," as "appearance in," and as "development into." These forms of transition reveal some of the richness of understanding Hegel has packed into his presentations of the appearance of the other and, from the point of view of his systematic exposition of the speculative movement of thought, the most fundamental meaning he gives to the notion of otherness. These three senses in which otherness arises in logical thought spell out aspects of the dynamic going on in Hegel's presentation of the incarnation as the appearance of Christ (including in this notion of appearance the life, teaching, death and resurrection of Christ), the reconciling other.

But, to return again to the *Logic.* The first two types of transition are taken up into and included, at least as previously occurring, in the movement or transition of judgment. It is this movement of judgment which is their truth in the form of the development of the concept as self-determining progression in the movement of pure thought.[162] Furthermore, Hegel himself explicitly identifies judgement and other-being when he states that judgment is the *Dasein* or other-being of the concept.[163] He gives ontological density to judgment as thought determination when, in taking advantage of the rootage of the German word for judgment, *Urteil,*[164] he brings together into one logical thought determination the notions of primordial or originary separation, of division, and of partition with the classical logical notion of judgment and with the idea of the self-othering of the concept.

It is, then, hardly surprising that Hegel spontaneously appeals to the thought category of judgment to spell out the speculative content he reads in various religious representations. When we take his overall philosophical system, and particularly his understanding of logic into consideration, we can appreciate how he would quite naturally speak in terms of judgment to express what he sees when he looks at either the appearance of nature and finite spirit in the religious representation of creation or, especially, the appearance of the redeemer and reconciler in the religious representation of incarnation.

We have made a brief sketch of Hegel's presentation of otherness as negation of that which was logically prior and made several remarks on judgment as the basic logical transition to which Hegel appeals in order to express the true or speculative content of creation and incarnation. After this sketch and these remarks it is now important to focus, from the perspective of our present concern for incarnation and otherness, briefly on his presentation of method as self-development of the absolute idea. Our focusing on Hegel's understanding of method, which he develops at the end of the *Logic*,[165] will enable us to see how he centers his treatment of otherness within the context of the rhythmic development of method.

Hegel's speculative dialectical method is structured movement of the concept from beginning, as immediate and universal, through dialectical progression, as negation of the beginning, on to result as negation of the first negation. The beginning is for Hegel likewise the beginning of the concept's progression and development. The moment of progression, as the moment of mediation through differentiation, is both the most difficult to describe and the one which most directly interests us. In absolute knowing the appearance of difference is the moment of judgment or determination. It is the moment in which the simple universal is able to show itself as the other. As Hegel writes, "This . . . moment of *judgment*, by which the universal of the beginning out of its very self determines itself as the *other of itself*, is to be named the *dialectical* moment."[166]

In this dialectical progression from beginning, as immediacy, to the second[167] moment as mediated, that is, as referred or related to an other, Hegel speaks of the universal becoming a particular in such a way that the second is the negation of the first. This negation is the other for itself, but equally the other of an other. Therefore the other includes its own other within itself. As this contradiction, the second moment is *"the posited dialectic of itself."*[168] The difference, which is only *an sich* or implicit in immediacy or initial identity, is made explicit in this moment which, as the determined, is difference, relationship and inclusive, mediated and mediating other.

Then the "third" moment of method, namely, result, arises out of what is for Hegel the essential moment of the concept, namely, the thinking of contradiction. Thinking the dialectical moment of difference or progression results in the explicitation or positing of the unity already contained in the concept's self-contradictory second moment or determination.[169] Hegel describes this depth of contradiction, which is being thought through, as the source of all activity. This moment of thought contradiction is that through which the opposition between concept and reality is overcome.[170] This turning point in the movement of the concept, namely, the thinking of contradiction, results in a second negation. This second negation is the overcoming of contradiction, a negation of negation. The negation of negation is absolute negativity, the moment of absolute mediation, the unity which is inclusive subjectivity. It is identity inclusive of difference. Hegel writes, "the *third* . . . is the positive resulting from sublation of the negative, the concept that has realized itself by means of its other-being and by the sublation of this reality has become united with itself."[171]

On the level of an absolute logic Hegel has, from the point of view of his speculative dialectical method, constructed a structured understanding of the movement of true or inclusive subjectivity: immediacy of beginning; progression through mediation; and enriched return as advancing, resultant unity of the two. In order to do this he has redefined the notion of positivity as negation, that is, the negativity of difference or otherness in relation to a beginning which, by definition, is simple identity and immediacy. His conception of positivity as related, inclusive negation allows him to conclude to a unity of identity and difference, immediacy and otherness and, we could even say, one and many. He concludes to a unity as total self-mediation. In this way objectivity, reestablished as the negation or otherness of initial subjectivity, is integrated as logically momentary totality in the self-development of inclusive subjectivity. It is this structured dialectical movement which constitutes the soul or inner dynamic of Hegel's presentation of the philosophy of religion as the speculative movement of spirit in the form of inclusive divine subjectivity.

3.c. Concluding Observations

Hegel referred to this methodic movement of the absolute idea toward the beginning of his 1827 presentation of the concept of religion. He made this reference to method in order to explain, and ground, his philosophical presentation of the concept of religion as well as his interpretation of determinate religion and of the consummate religion. In his presentation of method Hegel has recalled both his, from the point of view of his speculative systematic presentation, prior initial presentation of the other as the negation of something and his development of judgment as primordial or originary separation. In the *Logic* he has set out the structure of the movement of spirit as one of logically sequenced diremption as determination, and return as renewed and enriched resultant unity or immediacy.

If we again recall Hegel's moves in the 1827 lectures on the philosophy of religion, we see that he repeated this logically sequenced presentation of the constitutive moments of spirit in his presentation of the first element of the consummate religion, namely, "immanent" Trinity. However, in his prior development of the moments of the concept of religion he had sketched the movement of spirit as diremption and initial return in a logically sequenced presentation constituting the second moment of that concept. Then, in the second element of the consummate religion, he progresses from an initial self-othering of the divine idea into nature and finite spirit in a more parallel presentation of diremption and progressive return. He carries out this more parallel presentation by means of a dialectical analysis of contradiction. He pursues this dialectical analysis of the self-othering of the divine idea, within the overall movement of divine subjectivity, in and as one and the same element of the consummate religion.

So we find ourselves before seemingly differently structured presentations of the speculatively formulated movement of spirit. As was indicated toward the beginning of this chapter, we have concentrated more directly on Hegel's presentation of incarnation as the speculatively expressed dialectical movement of the self-othering of the divine. We have only more indirectly considered Hegel's notion of Christ as immediately available to religious consciousness. When we did consider Christ from the angle of his immediate presence to religious consciousness, it was still more from the perspective of the speculative self-othering of the divine idea. Furthermore, we have left to another study the question of how the risen Christ might be present, in more mediated fashion, to the communal religious consciousness.

While acknowledging these limitations to our reflection on Hegel's philosophical reading of the incarnation in terms of otherness, we can still say that we have chosen to remain with the grounding speculative movement of incarnation as appearance of otherness. We have concentrated on Hegel's paradigmatic idealist presentation of the speculatively expressed arising of otherness. Even with this more restricted posing of the question of incarnation and otherness, we find ourselves before two possible interpretations of Hegel's speculative presentation of otherness. That is, we seem to have two options: either see the arising of otherness as sheer movement of negation and diremption to the extreme in and out of which the movement of return occurs, or see the notion of otherness and the arising of otherness as in some way themselves referring both to diremption and to some form of return.

Faced with these at first sight seemingly alternative and mutually exclusive possible readings of Hegel on the speculative arising of otherness, and, consequently, finding ourselves before alternative readings of Hegel on incarnation, we can indicate three possible attitudes we could take concerning this situation. Sketching out these possible attitudes or stances should help us draw together a number of points previously developed during the course of our review of Hegel on the speculative interpretation of incarnation. It should also allow us to acknowledge, at least indirectly, the discomfort, and disagreement, a number of post-Hegelian thinkers have expressed with regard to Hegel's situating of difference within identity and of otherness as momentary totality in the speculative dynamic of inclusive subjectivity.

In the first of these possible stances, namely, in a more sympathetic reading of Hegel on this question of apparently irreconcilable alternative presentations of incarnation in terms of difference or otherness, we would want to make several points. We would want to stress the richness of his complex speculative presentation of the arising of otherness. From the perspective of this first stance vis-à-vis the self-othering of the divine idea, it would be important to insist on the arising of difference out of initial identity as an important idealist response to the question of the relationship between identity and difference, self and other, even the one and the many.

Furthermore, it would be necessary to underscore that, in order to understand Hegel, we must not misinterpret the reflexive structure of his thought. He is always thinking in terms of the movement of spirit. Speculatively formulated, this movement of spirit is a dialectical movement of diremption and retroactively grounding, enriched return. The overall effect is one of greater concretion and advance. Within the context of this speculative movement of spirit, he regularly speaks of self-determination (*sich bestimmen*), self-positing (*sich setzen*), and self-developing (*sich entwickeln*). It is not easy for us in English to capture the dynamic either of this overall self-reflexive movement of thought or of that movement's "momentary" externalization. Be that as it may, for present purposes what would be important would be to recall that Hegel is working with an overall speculatively developed movement of thought from implicit to explicit. His is an intended immanent and consistent movement of thought from less determinate to more determinate or concrete. Consequently, when we speak of the self-othering of the divine idea, or when we use phrases similar to this one, we are not in any way presupposing a prior, and fully existent, self. Rather, the reflexive element indicated by the particle "self" in the expression "self-othering" is simply an attempt to express Hegel's notion of that overall immanent and consistent progression from "in itself" to "for itself," from identity to difference, on the way to the unity of the two.

With these points in mind, in this first or more sympathetic stance vis-à-vis the two possible readings of Hegel on incarnation as the arising of otherness, we would conclude that he is justified in his various either sequenced or more parallel presentations of spirit as diremption and return. Therefore, he would be correct in his complex interpretation of incarnation as movement of divine self-othering as diremption and initial return. The differences in his presentations of the structured movement constitutive of spirit would be justified by appealing to the fact that, on the one hand, in the *Logic* he is merely laying out the logically sequenced movement of diremption and return in the form of pure thought without explicit reference to finite spirit. And this explanation would basically cover his presentation of "immanent" Trinity as well. On the other hand, his working with, and in the realphilosophical sphere of the philosophy of religion, requires that he take into explicit consideration finite spirit as thinking religious consciousness. Here Hegel is obliged by the fact that finite spirit is thought, and therefore already at least implicit reconciliation and return, to work out a different structuring in terms of a more paralleled presentation of diremption and return. Here Hegel works with a structuring that reproduces the movement of spirit in ways variously appropriate to the levels of the concept of religion and to the second element of the consummate religion. Hegel would claim that he can maintain differentiation and immediate return in one and the same element since the element thematizes the contradiction constitutive of, and therefore characteristic of, the second moment of method. He would point out that this second element is, most fundamentally, a movement of ongoing self-othering of the divine idea to the moment of death on a cross. Consequently, the second element is appropriately to be described in terms of otherness understood as negation and yet presented as a speculative movement of love which would include both diremption and initial return.

The second of these three possible attitudes or stances toward Hegel's presentation of incarnation in terms of otherness would consist in a more directly critical and negative reading of Hegel's efforts. From such a stance one would hesitate to accept the possibility that Hegel can, given his understanding of otherness in terms of negation, integrate spirit as movement of diremption and return into one sphere or element of the consummate religion. The essential aspect to, or argument in, this position would be the insistence that, for Hegel, otherness is to be seen in terms of negation. And so much of what Hegel says and writes seems to lend credence to the view that his interpretation of otherness, whether phenomenologically or speculatively expressed, leads to the conclusion that he effectively identified otherness and negation. One who took Hegel, so to speak, at his word concerning the relationship between otherness and negation would then tend to argue that Hegel's insistence on otherness as diremption and immediate return in a speculative movement of love is more bluster than argument. And, since incarnation, taken in the more restricted meaning of the appearance of a divine-human unity, would inevitably involve a movement of return and not merely one of diremption, one who would be proposing a more negatively critical reading of Hegel would then of course hesitate to accept as successful Hegel's efforts to interpret incarnation as a movement of self-othering of the divine idea.

There is a third possible attitude or stance with regard to Hegel's efforts to interpret incarnation in terms of the speculatively expressed appearance of otherness. This attitude would involve a reading which is both sympathetic and critical. It would, so to speak, incorporate elements from both of the previously indicated more sympathetic or affirmative and more negative evaluations of Hegel's efforts. Those taking this attitude would admit, along with those who are more directly and simply sympathetic to Hegel, that he has accomplished something significant in his presentation of incarnation as divine self-othering. They would insist that he has creatively interpreted Christ as enriching other. Yet with those who regret that they cannot accept, from within Hegel's system, a doubled presentation of otherness as moment of negation and as doubled movement of diremption and immediate return, they would suggest that he has not been successful in his effort to understand otherness both as negation and equally as parallel movement of immediate return.

Those opting for this third reading of Hegel would, instead, propose that his presentation of the consummate religion has forced him, perhaps not fully advertently, to face up to the fact that otherness is neither constituted, nor explained, solely by the notion of negation. They would say that he has indeed, in so speaking of the other in terms of negation, highlighted an essential and constitutive phenomenological characteristic of otherness or of the other. But they would insist that, in his realphilosophical presentations, he has run up against and could not avoid, at least indirectly, coming to terms with that stubborn facticity and positivity which seems somehow to burst the bounds of his dialectical method and which post-hegelian thinkers tended more and more to stress. Those who would tend to think more or less along the lines of this third attitude would acknowledge that Hegel had tried to make room for this stubborn facticity characteristic of otherness by establishing a somewhat parallel presentation of diremption and immediate return as negation and negation of negation or positive. They would suggest that Hegel has in fact discovered more to the notion of otherness than his speculative and systematic insight would seem to have permitted. They would want to rejoice with Hegel's discovery. They would also want to suggest that his situating of otherness within the wider context of a theory of subjectivity, even intersubjectivity, still establishes the general parameters for any adequate discussion of the question. They would say that this is true, and that Hegel has set up these generally valid overall parameters, to the extent that otherness must somehow, and inevitably, be considered in relation to self and subjectivity. But, those who take a stance vis-à-vis Hegel's system from the perspective of this third attitude, would object to his particular way of anchoring otherness within a movement of self-positing subjectivity. They would, from a more contemporary perspective, claim that his speculatively formulated method seems to have restricted his horizon. For them, this particular way of anchoring otherness would seem to have hemmed in his otherwise enthusiastic sensitivity to the perduring reality and importance of otherness. His particular framing of the question of otherness would not allow one to see the further implications of the perduring reality and importance of otherness for a renewed interpretation of Christ as enriching other within the context of a more open philosophical trinitarianism and a consequent renewal in understanding of the religious metaphor, "kingdom of God."

The history of Hegel interpretation so far would lead us to conclude that these three possible overall attitudes or stances toward Hegel's efforts to interpret incarnation in terms of otherness will coexist for the foreseeable future. These three attitudes are really three views of the nature of otherness and of the relationship between difference and identity. They have immense implications for how we conceive the movement of divine subjectivity. They are, indeed, equally three views of the nature of incarnation. The very fact that we can propose three alternative readings and evaluations of Hegel on incarnation and otherness witnesses to the complexity of Hegel's rich philosophical interpretation of these two realities. Whether we speak of incarnation or of otherness, or of both together, Hegel remains indispensable partner in any truly informed contemporary dialogue.

NOTES

[1] As Peter C. Hodgson points out, Hegel customarily used "Christ" (*Christus*) as name for Jesus of Nazareth. When Hegel intended to use "Christ" as a title he used "the Christ" (*der Christ*). "Hegel's Christology: Shifting Nuances in the Berlin Lectures," *Journal of the American Academy of Religion* 53 (1985) 32 n. 11.

2 See overall Part 3, "Revelatory Religion" ("Die offenbare Religion"), of Chapter 7 of the *Phenomenology of Spirit*, GW 9:400.1-18/ PS 453-478. On incarnation and Trinity in Hegel's *Phenomenology*, see Schlitt, *Hegel's Trinitarian Claim* 146-158 with the various subsectins of this Part 3 indicated in the footnotes and with bibliography p. 146 n. 21. More specifically on incarnation in the *Phenomenology*, see also: Hans Küng, *Menschwerdung Gottes* (Freiburg: Herder, 1970) 243-302; Emilio Brito, *La christologie de Hegel* (Paris: Beauchesne, 1983) 97-172.

Note that Ricardo Ferrara identifies the first phenomenological occurrence of incarnation in Hegel's *Phenomenology* presentation of revelatory religion as more revelatory and the second as more reconciliational. See Ferrara's helpful review of Emilio Brito's *La christologie de Hegel*, in *Hegel-Studien* 22 (Bonn: Bouvier, 1987) 226.

3 "Denn der Geist ist das Wissen seiner selbst in seiner Entäusserung; das Wesen, das die Bewegung ist, in seinem Andersseyn die Gleichheit mit sich selbst zu behalten." GW 9:405.17-19/PS 459.

4 GW 9:405.34/PS 459. Note also GW 9:407.21-22, where Hegel describes the immediately appearing exclusive one as "die noch unaufgelöste Form eines *sinnlichen Andern* hat" ("which has the still unresolved form of a 'sensuous' other" PS 461).

5 GW 9:409.12-21/PS 464. Note that, though Hegel in fact here identifies each of the three elements of consciousness as "a transition into another" ("der Uebergang in den Andern" GW 9:409.21/PS 464), he nevertheless considers the second moment or element specifically that of otherness.

6 GW 9:410.18-20/PS 465. Hegel's wording here would seem to allow for a reading of these lines as applicable both to the second moment in the element of pure thought and to the moment of *für sich* in the movement of his thought more globally considered.

7 See the whole presentation, GW 9:412.1-415.11/PS 467-471. Specifically regarding the death and "resurrection" of the sensuously present self, see GW 9:415.4-10/PS 471.

8 On incarnation within the context of revealed religion, see E §§564-571. For a brief overview, see Schlitt, *Hegel's Trinitarian Claim* 107-120. For a longer discussion and alternative reading, see Brito, *La christologie de Hegel* 495-522. For a convenient parallel presentation of

the first, second, and third original editions of the *Encyclopedia* on revealed religion (published respectively in 1817, 1827, and 1830), see Burbidge, "The Syllogisms of Revealed Religion" 29-42 esp. 32-35.

[9] For a more technically precise presentation of the 1821 manuscript text, the layout of marginal notes to this manuscript and the loose sheets sketched by Hegel in preparation for the working out of this manuscript, see the editorial materials in *Gesammelte Werke*, Vol. 17: *Vorlesungsmanuskripte I (1816-1831)*, ed. Walter Jaeschke (Hamburg: Felix Meiner, 1987). For bibliography on Hegel on the philosophy of religion, but with a special concern for Christology and incarnation, see Küng, *Menschwerdung Gottes* 672-683; James Yerkes, *The Christology of Hegel* (Missoula, Montana: Scholars, 1978) 334-341; Brito, *La christologie de Hegel* 659-681; Jaeschke, *Die Religionsphilosophie Hegels* 91-100. For a helpful study, which places Hegel's philosophical Christology in the context of his philosophy of religion, see Vincent A. McCarthy, *Quest for a Philosophical Jesus. Christianity and Philosophy in Rousseau, Kant, Hegel, and Schelling* (Macon, GA: Mercer University Press, 1986) 109-161.

[10] "Das System ist Darstellung der Menschwerdung Gottes im Sinne der Selbstkonstruction des Absoluten zur Totalität." The wording is that of Jaeschke, *Die Religionsphilosophie Hegels* 92-93, where he cites Hegel GW 4:74f.

[11] Verified in the fact that Hegel, in the Introduction to the 1830 edition of the *Encyclopedia*, says the object of philosophy is God understood as truth (E § 1) and, then, in the presentation of philosophy (E §§ 574-577), summarizes the whole encyclopedic movement of the self-thinking idea in the spheres of logic, nature, finite and absolute spirit with his famous final quote from Aristotle.

[12] Note Hegel's insistence that each moment of the concept of religion is, at least in principle, realized in some way or other in each of the forms of determinate religion. E.g., V 3:28.686-29.690, 103.168-177 (1821); V 3:90.701-91.718 (1827).

[13] Based in Hegel's position that the moments of the concept of religion become the explicit object of religious consciousness in the consummate religion. See Ch. 4 Section 2 above.

[14] See Ch. 2 Subsections 2b and 2c above.

¹⁵ Again, see Ch. 4 Section 2 above. In another study it would be helpful and of value to refer back as well more immediately and explicitly to the concept of the consummate religion in the 1821 and 1827 lectures in the light of Hegel's general view that a specific religion is the dialectical development or self-determination of that religion's concept of God.

¹⁶ On the overall structure of the consummate religion in relation to the concept of religion in the 1821 manuscript and for further literature on the question, see Ch. 4 Subsection 2a above.

¹⁷ E §§ 569-570. The *Encyclopedia* presentation will be treated more indirectly though the analysis of the 1821 lecture series.

¹⁸ V 5:28.779-69.915.

¹⁹ V 5:16.414-24.647.

²⁰ E.g., V 5:5.120-6.142 with 14.371-372 and 15.383-16.413.

²¹ V 5:16.415.

²² E § 567.

²³ V 5:17.433-434.

²⁴ V 5:16.415-442 with 18.470-472.

²⁵ V 5:18 note to text line 480/L 3:79-80 n. 54.

²⁶ "indem wir sagen: 'Gott an sich, nach seinem Begriff, ist die unendliche, sich dirimierende und in sich zurückkehrende Macht', so ist er dies nur als die sich unendlich auf sich selbst beziehende Negativität, d. i. die absolute Reflexion in sich, was schon die Bestimmung des Geistes ist." V 5:21.579-583/L 3:83 (trans. amended).

²⁷ V 5:24.648-28.778. Hodgson gives this concrete sphere the title "The Idea in Diremption: Creation and Preservation of the Natural World." L 3:86. Jaeschke speaks of a threefold sense in which Hegel uses "Son of God": the divinity of Jesus; the theological reading of "world"; and the second moment of the immanent Trinity. See *Die Vernunft in der Religion* 323, where he refers to E § 567. Within the context of a discussion on this threefold sense Hegel gives to the expression "Son of God," Jaeschke criticizes Hegel's various efforts to link the "eternal Son" within the immanent Trinity with the "temporal Son," Christ or Jesus of Nazareth (p. 327, where Jaeschke refers to E § 569).

[28] "Indem nun das Anderssein als Totalität einer Erscheinung bestimmt, so *drückt es an ihm selbst die Idee aus*, und dies ist überhaupt, was mit der *Weisheit* Gottes in der Natur bezeichnet wird." V 5:27.755-758/L 3:27.

[29] V 5:26.729; 5:25.688-690.

[30] See GW 21:69.9-19/GL 82.

[31] See E §§ 247 and 250 on nature and compare them with §§ 381 and 382 on the concept of spirit.

[32] See n. 7 above.

[33] "Objektivität – Entwicklung derselben – d.i. Festhalten der bestimmten Unterschiede – Sohn – *Abstrakte* Bestimmung des *Andersseins* – *Gegensatz* von NATUR und ENDLICHEM Geist." V 5:24 note to line 650/L 3:86 n. 75. See GW 17:230.20-23.

[34] "d.h., unmittelbar oder im Anderssein gesetzte Idee." V 5:28.777-778/L 3:90 (trans. amended).

[35] V 5:28.779-69.915. Hodgson gives this third sphere the title, "Appearance of the Idea in Finite Spirit: Estrangement, Redemption, and Reconciliation," in L 3:90.

[36] "die Objektivität *als endlicher Geist*, die Erscheinung der Idee an und in demselben – Erlösung und Versöhnung – als selbst göttliche Geschichte." V 5:28.780-782/L 3:90-91.

[37] "Dies das Moment der göttlichen, entwickelten Objektivität, in welchem das Göttliche ebensosehr ZU SEINEM HÖCHSTEM *Außersichsein* kommt als es darin seinen *Wendungspunkt* hat, und eben beides – die höchste Entfremdung, die Spitze der Entäusserung – ist dies Moment der Rückkehr selbst." V 5:28.785-789/L 3:91.

[38] V 5:29.809-44.262. Hodgson's title, "Estrangement: Natural Humanity," in L 3:92.

[39] V 5:45.263-69.915. Hodgson's title, "Redemption and Reconciliation: Christ," in L 3:109.

[40] E § 568. As regards the juxtaposition of nature and spirit this text is essentially the same in the 1817, 1827, and 1830 editions of the *Encyclopedia*. See Burbidge, "The Syllogisms of Revealed Religion" 32-33.

41 "ist, in dieser als denkend zugleich auf das Ewige gerichtet." E § 568/PM § 568 (trans. amended). This reference to finite spirit as thinking was added to the 1827 edition of the *Encyclopedia* and maintained in the 1830 edition.

42 E § 566. But, on the other hand, we should also note here Hegel's clear distinction between the second moment of differentiation and the third, namely, that of return. This distinction was introduced with the second original edition of the *Encyclopedia* in 1827. See Burbidge, "The Syllogisms of Revealed Religion" 31.

43 V 5:36.997, 38.65-67.

44 "wesentlich das, was er nicht *sein* und bleiben SOLL." V 5:30.827-828/L 3:92-93.

45 See, e.g., V 5:38.77-39.112 and 40.122-123.

46 For a brief summary of such contradictions see V 5:42.199-43.214.

47 V 5:40.128-131. With reference to good and evil, Hegel writes concisely, "Erkennen heilt die Wunde, die es selber ist." V 5:42.205/ "Knowledge heals the wound that it itself is." L 3:106.

48 "gehört zum göttlichen Leben, das göttlicher Geist ist, sich objektivieren, in freiem zunächst endlichem Geist, der Gott *an sich*." V 5:44.260-262/L 3:108.

49 See V 5:29.790-796. For reflections on possible readings of this text see V 5:327 note to 29.796 and L 3:91 note 89. Here the second side to the history of the divine idea in finite spirit is taken to refer to the second subsection of this third concrete sphere of the consummate religion.

50 For further remarks on the question as to whether, and to what extent, one can use the subdivisions indicated by various sets of Greek letters in the manuscript, see Brito, *La christologie de Hegel* 287 n. 170. Hodgson's outlining of this second subsection to the third concrete sphere follows the five stages indicated in the presentation by Hegel's Greek letters in the margins of the manuscript. Hodgson, in L 3:18-21. Our presentation also follows Hegel's subdivision of the second subsection.

51 See, e.g., V 5:32.900-903.

52 V 5:45.264-46.307.

53 "diese Erhebung des Geistes aus seinem *natürlichen* Willen, aus dem Bösen, aus dem Wollen der Einzelheit." V 5:45.264-265/L 3:109.

54 See, e.g., n. 37 above.

55 "Diese Erhebung besteht darin überhaupt, daß der Mensch zum Bewußtsein des *an und für sich* Allgemeinen kommt, und zwar als *seines* Wesens." V 5:45.267-269/L 3:109.

56 See n. 48 above.

57 V 5:45.264-282 and 45.283-46.307.

58 "Es ist dies das Bewußtsein der Einheit *der göttlichen* und *menschlichen Natur*, daß der Mensch AN SICH die göttliche Idee in sich trage ... dies *seine substantielle Natur* sei, seine Bestimmung sei, er die einzige Möglichkeit derselben – die unendliche *Möglichkeit* –, ist seine Subjektiviät." V 5:45.283-288/L 3:109.

59 See n. 51 above.

60 V 5:46.298-307.

61 V 5:46.308-49.400.

62 V 5:49.401-57.587. On this third and then the fourth stages to Hegel's presentation of redemption and reconciliation see also Ch. 8 Subsection 1a below.

63 "die Erscheinung des Geistes im unmittelbaren Dasein und für die unmittelbare Anschauung." V 5:50.412-413 with 49.401-50.402/L 3:115.

64 V 5:50.413-415.

65 V 5:50.418-51.435.

66 V 5:53.479.

67 V 5:53.490-54.497 with 54.509-510.

68 V 5:53.480.

69 V 5:56.561-564.

70 V 5:57.588-67.841/L 3:122-131. The title is "LEBEN und Tod" V 5:57.588/L 3:122.

71 "ist aus dem Allgemeinen SICH BESTIMMEN, zur *Wirklichkeit* übergehen; diese Bewegung, Prozeß der Bestimmung kommt dem Leben Jesu zu." V 5:58.604-606/L 3:123 (trans. amended).

72 "Diese Darstellung, Objektivität der Anschauung der *Geschichte des Geistes* ist, *daß* der *Geist an sich*, der *sich Anderes, natürlicher Wille* und *Dasein ist*, dies sein Anderssein *aufhebt* und jetzt für sich ist, *in seiner Herrlichkeit* – nämlich durch diese Geschichte Geist zu sein – hervorgeht." V 5:58. 624-59.628/L 3:123-124.

73 "Anderswerden des Göttlichen." V 5:59 marginal note to line 648/L 3:124 n. 161. Note that the death of Christ, "incarnation, as immediate existence in the form of finitude" ("die *Vermenschlichung als unmittelbares Dasein* schon *als Endlichkeit*"), and nature are all described by Hegel in terms of other-being (*Anderssein*). See V 5:59.651-60.661, with the phrase concerning incarnation found at V 5:59.655-656/L 3:124.

74 "Aber die *höchste Endlichkeit ist* nicht das *wirkliche Leben* im *Zeitlichen*, sondern der *Tod*, der Schmerz des todes; er ist die höchste *Negation*, die abstrakteste, *selbst natürliche* – die *Schranke, Endlichkeit* in ihrem höchsten Extrem; das *zeitliche*, vollkommene Dasein der göttlichen Idee in der *Gegenwart* wird nur in seinem TODE angeschaut." V 5:60.662-667/L 3:124-125).

75 V 5:60.669-670.

76 "im Anderen höchstes Aufgeben – eben in diesem *äussersten Anderssein des Todes* . . . Tod Christi Anschauung dieser Liebe selbst – nicht für, um Anderes –, sondern Göttlichkeit eben in dieser allgemeinen Identität mit dem Anderssein, Tod." V 5:60.680-684/L 3:125.

77 V 5:61.687-692.

78 See n. 72 above.

79 "Der Tod ist überhaupt ebenso als die höchste Verendlichung ebenso das *Aufheben* der natürlichen Endlichkeit, des unmittelbaren Daseins, das Aufheben der Entäußerung, die Auflösung der Schranke – das Moment *des Geistes, sich in sich zu fassen*, dem *Natürlichen abzusterben*." V 5:61.705-709/L 3:126.

80 E.g., V 5:62.720-726.

81 V 5:64.781-66.814.

[82] "Dieser in seiner Entwicklung [ist] *der Fortgang der göttlichen Idee* zur *höchsten Entzweiung,* zum *Gegenteil des Schmerzes des Todes,* welcher selbst *die absolute Umkehrung, die höchste Liebe,* in sich selbst das Negative des Negativen, *die absolute Versöhnung* ist, das Aufheben des vorherigen Gegensatzes der Menschen gegen Gott." V 5:68.876-881/L 3:132.

[83] V 5:68.887-69.897.

[84] "oder also zugleich die Vollendung der Äußerlichkeit zur tiefsten Entzweiung, dem gewußten Negativen, und damit die Rückkehr zur ewigen Idee ist." V 5:68.893-69.895/L 3.132-133.

[85] V 3:103.168-170.

[86] For more detail and an overview of the moments of the concept of religion see Ch. 2 Section 2 and Ch. 4 Subsection 2a above.

[87] See, e.g., V 3:106.205-213. See also n. 12 above. The phrase "structured movement congruent with, and parallel to," is based upon remarks in an as yet unpublished paper by Walter Jaeschke, "Hegel's Interpretation of the Non-Christian Religions in Relation to the Concept of Christianity as the Absolute Religion" p. 15. This paper alerted me to several of the questions being treated in the present chapter. I am also indebted to Walter Jaeschke for his remarks on the overall developmental character of the 1821 manuscript and its various marginal notations.

[88] See especially V 3:95.8-105.197. Though we will concentrate on the text of Hegel's manuscript itself, it should be noted that there are quite interesting and often more developed variant or supplemental materials from the second Friends Edition placed in footnotes in V 3 and L 1.

[89] V 3:104.179-186.

[90] "Gott absolute das Positive, also [ist] das von ihm Verschiedene das *Negative.* Dies *Negative* erscheint auf der Seite des *Weltwesens, des Menschen.*" V 3:104.182-184/L 1:194 (trans. slightly amended).

[91] It is quite possible that Hegel gave a considerably more dialectically developed analysis in his oral presentation. See, for example, V 3:103-104 note to text lines 178-186/L 1:194-195 n. 28, where there is explicit reference to finite spirit.

[92] V 3:104.187-105.195.

[93] "Absolutheit, Unendlichkeit des Selbstbewußtseins ist in der Vorstellung und Lehre der *Unsterblichkeit der Seele.*" V 3:105.190-191/L 3:195.

[94] See esp. V 3:130.768-142.974.

[95] "*endliche Welt, Nature und endliches* Bewußtsein ist der Gegensatz, das Andere der Idee; in Gott ist, wie es die Religion *vorstellt,* das Andere Gottes sein *Sohn,* d. i. er *als Anderes,* das in der Liebe, in der Göttlichkeit bleibt – *und der Sohn ist die* Wahrheit der endlichen Welt." V 3:141.967-142.971/L 3:232.

[96] For the text directly on religion itself, see V 3:114.419-115.447.

[97] "Die zwei Momente in ihrem Begriff – des Gegensatzes [next two lines:] a) absolute Allgemeinheit – reines Denken b) absolute Einzelheit – Empfindung." V 3:115.445-447/L 1:207 (trans. amended).

[98] On this resturcturing of spheres and redistribution of thematic content see the especially helpful schematic comparative structural analysis by Hodgson, in L 3:54-55.

[99] See Jaeschke, *Die Vernunft in der Religion* 305.

[100] On the relationship between the elements of the concept of the consummate religion and the moments of the concept of religion see Ch. 4 Subsection 2b above.

[101] The division is found in V 5:196.600-199.688 with the first presentation on V 5:197.608-651 and the second on V 5:198.669-199.688. For an overview of the 1827 lectures on the consummate religion, see Hodgson, in L 3:36-47; Jaeschke, *Die Religionsphilosophie Hegels* 93-97.

[102] On the presentation of the revealed religion in the various editions of the *Encyclopedia* see n. 8 above. Jaeschke provides a strong argument that the restructuring and redistribution in the 1827 lectures cannot be a simple advance or evolution since the *Encyclopedia* editions do not incorporate these shifts. He attributes the shifts more to a desire to establish a trinitarian structure to the overall presentation of the consummate religion, a structure which for Jaeschke then could be seen as conflicting with the structure established by the presentation of the speculative concept of religion. See Jaeschke, Die

Religionsphilosophie Hegels 95; ___ , *Die Vernunft in der Religion* 303-308; ___ , "Hegel's Interpertation of the Non-Christian Religions" 14-16.

[103] "Gott in seiner ewigen Allgemeinheit ist dies, sich zu unterscheiden, zu bestimmen, ein Anderes seiner zu setzen und den Unterschied ebenso aufzuheben, darin bei sich zu sein, und nur durch dies Hervorgebrachtsein ist er Geist." V 5:209.927-930/L 3:284-285 (trans. amended).

[104] Particularly in relation to the notion of personhood (*Persönlichkeit*), "Das Wahre der Persönlichkeit ist eben dies, sie durch das Versenken, Versenktsein in das Andere zu gewinnen." V 5:211.951-953/"The truth of personality is found precisely in winning it back through this immersion, this being immersed in the other." L 3:286. Note that this use of *Versenken* and *Versenktsein* may vaguely reflect Hegel's terminology in discussing the second moment in dialectical method, which he describes as negation or "mediating" (*die Vermittelnde*) and "being mediated" (*die Vermittelte*). See, e.g., GW 12:245.27-28/GL 834.

[105] V 5:201.703-717 with 204.805-810.

[106] E.g., V 5:201.734-202.737.

[107] "Die Idee . . . ist selbst dies, die von ihr gesetzten Widersprüche aufzulösen." V 5:203.777-778/L 3:278. See V 5:203.764-780, where Hegel speaks specifically of the distinctions arising out of the unspeculative affirmation of a series of predicates of God.

[108] Note, e.g., the preliminary 1827 division of the second element in relation to the third element, V 5:197.618-198.651 with 198.671-199.688.

[109] V 5:217.133-149, 218.160-167. See also Hodgson, in L 3:40-41. This would seem to be part of Hegel's overall strategy to refute the accusation of pantheism. See Ch. 2 Subsection 2b above.

[110] See Subsection 2a, under "Incarnation in the Consummate Religion," in the present chapter above.

[111] Hodgson, in L 1:10-12, 15-16.

[112] "Das zweite ist also der Prozeß der Welt an ihr [Liebe], aus dem Abfall, der Trennung, zur Versönung überzugehen." V 5:217.158-159/L 3:293.

113 V 5:217.156-157.

114 And at this same time in the *Encyclopedia* he maintains the general distribution of diremption in the second moment and immediate and further realized reconciliation in the third moment, though there is, even in the *Encyclopedia*, an indication of implicit reconciliation, already in the second moment, with the reference to finite spirit. See again n. 8 above.

115 V 5:215.74-218.178.

116 V 5:218.178-182.

117 See n. 33 above.

118 In V 5:219.191-224.338 Hegel works through the opposition of good and evil, an opposition constitutive of finite spirit. Then in V 5:224.339-228.447 he reviews the story of the fall to introduce again the notion of knowing. See Hodgson, in L 3:300 n. 138. In V 5:228.448-233.621 Hegel pursues the question of finite spirit's knowing this division as occurring within itself.

119 V 5:224.330-338.

120 V 5:228.469-231.549.

121 V 5:232.581-233.621.

122 See n. 112 above.

123 "das Bedürfnis der Wahrheit, das zweite die Art und Weise ihrer Erscheinung." V 5:219.193-194/L 3:295.

124 "dies die Wahrheit ist, durch die Negation des Gegensatzes die Einheit zu erreichen." V 5:233.632-633/L 3:310.

125 E.g., V 5:234.644-646.

126 Succinctly stated in V 5:239.751-755.

127 V 5:234.660-235.691.

128 "Diese Unangemessenheit ist der Ausgangspunkt, der das Bedürfnis ausmacht." V 5:234.669-670/L 3:311.

129 "Daß sie keinen Eintrag tue, sahen wir in der göttlichen Idee. Denn der Sohn ist ein Anderes als der Vater, und das Anderssein ist Verschiedenheit, sonst ist es kein Geist; aber das Andere ist Gott, hat

die ganze Fülle der göttlichen Natur in sich. Dem, daß dieser Andere der Sohn Gottes und somit Gott ist, tut die Bestimmung des Andersseins keinen Eintrag. Dieses Anderssein ist das ewig sich Setzende, ewig sich Aufhebende, und dies sich Setzen und Aufheben des Andersseins ist die Liebe, der Geist." V 5:235.683-691/L 3:311-312.

130 "die abstrakteste Weise der Menschlichkeit, die höchste Abhängigkeit, die letzte Schwäche, die tiefste Stufe der Gebrechlichkeit." V 5:249.957-959/L 3:326.

131 V 5:249.960-250.973.

132 V 5:250.992-994.

133 V 5:251.8-9.

134 On the reference to method in the 1821 manuscript, see V 3:28.671-672 and 106.200-204.

135 "Es kann nur *eine* Methode in aller Wissenschaft, in allem Wissen sein. Methode ist der sich explizierende Begriff, nichts anderes, und dieser ist nur einer. Das erste ist also auch hier der Begriff wie immer. Das zweite ist die Bestimmtheit des Begriffs, der Begriff in seinen bestimmten Formen. . . . . Das erste ist also der Begriff der Religion oder die Religion im allgemeinen, und das zweite, daß wir die bestimmte Religion betrachten. Die Bestimmtheit also nehmen wir nicht von außen her, sondern es ist der freie Begriff, der sich zu seiner Bestimmtheit hintreibt. . . . . Deshalb betrachten wir drittens den Begriff, wie er aus seiner Bestimmtheit, aus seiner Endlichkeit zu sich selbst kommt, sich aus dieser seiner Endlichkeit, Beschränktheit wiederherstellt, und dieser wiederhergestellte Begriff ist der unendliche, wahrhafte Begriff, die absolute Idee, oder die wahrhafte Religion." V 3:83.512-516, 84.539-542 and 552-557/L 3:174-176.

136 For more detail and an overview of the moments of the concept of religion in the 1827 lectures, see Ch. 2 Subsection 2c "The 1827 Lectures," and Ch. 4 Subsection 2b above.

137 See V 3:266.36-277.381.

138 V 3:272.224-229.

139 V 3:277.383-278.396. The long treatment of the second moment of the concept of religion is found on V 3:277.383-329.902. See also V 3:336.54-338.62.

[140] The editorial note to V 3:278.394 refers to GW 12:52-53/GL 623-625.

[141] V 3:278.402.

[142] V 3:278.399-401.

[143] V 3:280.435-281.443. However, with regard to this particular quote it should be noted that Hegel is referring more directly to how we come to affirm the arising of distinction.

[144] On the proofs, see V 3:308.214-329.902.

[145] On identity and difference, see Ch. 5 above.

[146] I am indebted to Walter Jaeschke's remarks concerning Hegel's almost axiomatic working usage of the notion of spirit in the lectures on the philosophy of religion. "Hegel's Interpretation of the Non-Christian Religions" 12. But of course I must take responsability for the ways in which this insight is used here.

[147] See n. 3 above.

[148] On the 1821 lectures, see nn. 90-92 above. On the 1827 lectures, see nn. 139-144 above.

[149] See n. 33 above.

[150] See nn. 40-42 above.

[151] "Daseyn als das Nichts seiner selbst, so daß diß Nichts seiner selbst gleichfalls Daseyn ist. – Oder das daseyn ist wesentlich *Andersseyn.*" GW 11:60.30-31/trans. my own.

[152] "*Anderes* ist *Nichtdiß.*" GW 11:61.8/trans. my own.

[153] See, e.g., GW 21:105.5-29/ GL 117-118.

[154] GW 21:103.10/GL 115.

[155] GW 21:104.7-18/GL 116.

[156] "Das zweyte ist ebenso ein *Daseyendes,* aber als Negatives das Etwas bestimmt, – ein *Anderes.*" GW 21:104.12-13/GL 116.

[157] "übergehen in ein Anderes," E §§ 161, 240; see also GW 21:109.28-110.1/GL 121-122

[158] "übergegangenseyn," e.g., GW 11:44.24, GW 21:69.26/GL 82-83.

159 "scheinen in dem Entgegengesetzten," E §§ 161, 240; see also GW 21:110.1-8/GL 122.

160 E § 161; GW 12:59.9-12/GL 630.

161 E § 160; GW 12:16.16-18, 31.1-7/GL 582, 599.

162 GW 12:57.6-17/GL 627-628.

163 See GW 12:56.25-26/GL 627. On judgement, see esp. the introductory presentation, GW 12:53.1-59.31/GL 623-630.

164 E.g., GW 12:54.35-55.12/GL 625.

165 On method, see GW 12:236.1-253.34/GL 824-845.

166 "Dieses . . . Moment des *Urteils*, wodurch das anfängliche Allgemeine aus ihm selbst als das *Andere seiner* sich bestimmt, ist das *dialektische* zu nennen." GW 12:242.14-16/GL 831 (trans. amended).

167 Hegel constantly reminds us that counting the moments in the dialectical movement of thought is neither useful nor necessary. Yet he himself will speak in terms of sequence and will regularly enough use numerical references to indicate moments in the overall movement of thought. What is crucial is to remember that Hegel is speaking of movement, but especially of structured movement. See Schlitt, *Hegel's Trinitarian Claim* 23 n. 58 for a short bibliography on the question of structured movement. And see p. 28 n. 95 for further remarks on the question of a triply structured movement of thought.

168 "die *gesetzte Dialektik ihrer selbst*." GW 12:245.34-35/GL 835.

169 GW 12:246.1-3/ GL 835.

170 GW 12:246.18-23/GL 835.

171 "das *Dritte* . . . [ist] das Positive durch Aufheben des Negativen, der Begriff, der sich durch das Andersseyn realisirt und durch Aufheben dieser Realität mit sich zusammengegangen." GW 12:248.5-8/GL 837.

CHAPTER EIGHT

THE KINGDOM OF GOD

Trinity and incarnation are the more evident themes or religious representations with which Hegel works in elaborating his understanding of identity and difference in the form of a philosophical interpretation of the consummate religion. However, if we were to single out a third and particularly interesting religious representation which Hegel regularly enough uses, it would have to be the metaphor "kingdom of God" (*Reich Gottes*). This metaphor carries with it a whole host of connotations such as those of inclusiveness and finality. It necessarily includes reference both to God and to finite spirit. So Hegel recognized in it the means to express his understanding of grounding, inclusive identity. Its ready availability in the teaching of Christ gave Hegel the chance to give a religious formulation to his conception of identity as the identity *of* difference. He likewise found in this religious representation a unique opportunity to speak of the more generally statable philosophical problematic of the one and the many. He will present the kingdom of God as the spiritual community's sharing in the presence of the one divine idea. It is, then, especially with this philosophical interpretation of the kingdom of God that Hegel will be able to integrate, on the level of religion, his

271

responses to the problematics involved in the questions of the one and the many and of identity and difference. His overall response takes the form of a movement of spirit as inclusive divine subjectivity.

In his earlier Berlin philosophy of religion lectures Hegel generally first refers to the kingdom of God as the content of Jesus' teaching. He then identifies it with the worshipping and loving community, namely, with the final moment of the consummate religion. By the 1831 lectures he comes explicitly to identify the three moments or elements of the consummate religion as kingdom of the Father, kingdom of the Son, and kingdom of the Spirit.[1] But, already from the 1821 lectures on, he has gone beyond Kant's reductionist reading (at least as found in Kant's later philosophy of religion) of the kingdom of God as the moral kingdom of good opposed to a kingdom of evil.[2] Several factors have allowed Hegel to avoid this reductionist interpretation and overcome Kant's dualist affirmation of two kingdoms. One of these factors is Hegel's starting point in religion as an originary, namely, original and originating, unity of religious consciousness and the object of that consciousness. But we can quickly identify another factor: Hegel's development of the philosophy of religion as a movement of divine subjectivity which, as movement, has taken its starting point in this originary unity. In the course of the dialectical development of that divine subjectivity, and in line with his early abandonment of the notion of a negative dialectical mediation in favor of an always affirmative third moment,[3] Hegel affirms that evil has already been objectively overcome with the death of the particular divine-human individual. In fact, it is his overall dialectical method which allows Hegel to go considerably beyond Kant's more reductive moral interpretation of the kingdom of God.

In line with, and in the light of, these general observations, we will in this final chapter first of all examine in more detail what Hegel actually said about the kingdom of God in his Berlin lectures on the philosophy of religion. We will carry out this review with the presupposition that a good number of twentieth-century interpretations of "kingdom of God" are, in some way, dependent on Hegel's formulations. Once Hegel's thought is given clear exposition, it should be possible for us rather spontaneously to recognize parallels in terminology, structure, and even content between such twentieth-century interpretations and those found in Hegel's philosophy of religion. We will make brief reference to several such parallels at the end of the chapter. These references should help us retroactively to situate this consideration of Hegel on the kingdom of God in a modern philosophical and theological context.

Secondly, we will pursue two more specific, interrelated theses internal to Hegel studies. First, that Hegel's identifying of the consummate religion's three moments as the kingdom of the Father, the kingdom of the Son, and the kingdom of the Spirit is simply the making explicit of what was implicit throughout the development of Hegel's Berlin lectures on the philosophy of religion. Second, that this 1831 expansion of the religious representation "kingdom of God" is fully consistent with Hegel's general approach to the philosophical reinterpretation of religious representations and with the structure and movement of Hegel's overall dialectical method. We will carry out this review of Hegel on the kingdom of God, and will argue these more specific theses, by means of both a more detailed study of selected explicit references by Hegel, in his Berlin philosophy of religion lectures,[4] to "kingdom of God" and by careful consideration of certain key aspects of his thought. We will also carry this review forward, and explore these theses, by noting shifts in emphasis and structure among the four series of philosophy of religion lectures as well as by recalling the differing polemical contexts in which Hegel works out his philosophical interpretation of the consummate religion as the religion of absolute subjectivity.

1. Hegel's Explicit References to "Kingdom of God"

Hegel employs the metaphor "kingdom of God" neither in the *Phenomenology of Spirit*'s Chapter Seven on religion[5] nor in his treatment of revealed religion in the 1817, 1827, or 1830 editions of the *Encyclopedia*.[6] The brief, apparent reference to the kingdom of God in his 1809 *Philosophical Encyclopedia*,[7] prepared for the upper level classes of the Nurnberg gymnasium of which he was for a time rector, is in fact Karl Rosenkranz's mislocation and rewriting of pages sketched by Hegel in preparation for his 1821 philosophy of religion lectures.[8] The texts that will prove of most interest, and that present at some length Hegel's philosophical reading of "kingdom of God," are, as we would expect, found in his four series of Berlin lectures on the philosophy of religion. By way of anticipation we can say that, in the earlier lecture series, the texts of particular interest appear chiefly in the later sections of what can generally be referred to as the second moment in the development of the consummate religion, and in that religion's third moment, namely, cultus or community. By the 1831 lectures, references to the "kingdom of God" will be found more widely distributed throughout what is still available of Hegel's 1831 presentation of the consummate religion.

1.a. The 1821 Manuscript and Its Preparation

Before writing out the 1821 lecture manuscript, which itself often consisted more of sketchings than fully developed sentences and paragraphs, Hegel apparently sketched some first thoughts, a few reminders, and then additional ideas on a series of loose sheets. Some of these loose sheets are still available, and sheets 155a-155b, 162a-165b let us glimpse his preliminary work on the consummate religion.[9] In these loose sheets Hegel refers four times to "kingdom of God." After a brief segment on love he mentions the kingdom of God for the first time and places it as a first subdivision of the segment headed by the words, "Holy Spirit" (*Heiliger Geist*). In this segment on the Holy Spirit[10] he simply lists "Holy Spirit" with two subdivisions: "(a) God's kingdom, an invisible church – from all areas, different religions (b) The outward church – Protestants and Catholics . . . "[11] From this first sketching on throughout his philosophy of religion Hegel maintains this linkage of Holy Spirit, kingdom of God, church, and community. Unfortunately, what seems, from the 1821 manuscript itself on, to drop more by the wayside is the explicit reference made here to the kingdom as coming out of all areas and different religions.

Hegel refers three more times to the kingdom of God in the preparatory loose sheets. It is as if the previously cited mention of kingdom of God has occurred in the context of a first sketching of thoughts on the consummate or Christian religion. Now he seems, in continuing the loose sheet sketchings, to resketch a loosely knit outline of the consummate religion. He develops the outline in more detail and in a series of forms we can recognize as closer to that which will appear in the 1821 manuscript.[12] It is in the context of this second sketching that Hegel gives the slightest initial evidence of his future doubled treatment of the kingdom of God: first, as the content of Christ's teaching and, then, as worshipping and loving community. Hegel lists "kingdom of God" as third subdivision under "doctrine" (*Lehre*) and links the phrase by a dash with "human intelligence in the highest degree."[13] In a second reference to "kingdom of God" a few lines later, he writes, "Doctrine the universal soil – kingdom of God – love – complete severance from the world."[14] In his third reference to the kingdom of God it is clear that Hegel is explicitly treating of the community itself as the "actual kingdom of God – God as spirit in his community – Region of the *Holy Spirit*."[15] It is as if in this second sketching, with its three references to the kingdom of God, Hegel has caught the spirit of what he is about. We can also already here discern the doubled triple division characteristic of the 1821 presentation of the consummate religion.[16] Of particular interest, we should note that Hegel describes the community and spirit as "Individuality as such."[17]

Now we can best appreciate Hegel's doubled presentation of the kingdom of God in the 1821 manuscript itself when we situate it within the overall framework of Hegel's presentation of the consummate religion. Hegel develops this presentation in an outer triple division of three moments: abstract concept, concrete representation, and community or cultus. He again triply subdivides the second moment, namely, concrete representation into three inner spheres: first, the idea effectively as "immanent" Trinity; second, the divine idea as diremption into nature; and, third, the idea as appearance in finite spirit. He further subdivides this treatment of appearance in finite spirit, practically speaking, first into estrangement and then redemption and reconciliation.[18] It is in the further subsections three and four under "redemption and reconciliation" that Hegel makes his first presentation of the kingdom of God as the content of the teaching of Christ (subsection three)[19] and then more explicitly in relation to Christ's life and death (subsection four).[20]

In subsection three under "redemption and reconciliation" Hegel is concerned to explore how Christ, this individual, attests to being the divine idea, "the appearance of spirit in immediate existence and for immediate intuition."[21] Almost instinctively he zeros in on Christ's teaching as that which integrates Christ's life and destiny insofar as these two are themselves for Hegel manifestations of the divine idea. Here we see Hegel creatively bring together, and interrelate, his loose-sheet sketchings on the themes of teaching, a "universal soil," the kingdom of God, and love.[22] In a tightly knit paragraph,[23] he describes teaching as that which contains the universal and is, itself, the universal soil (der allgemeine Boden). It is the soil in which spirit must know itself to be at home. "The universal soil is the heavenly kingdom, the kingdom of God – a substantial, intelligible world in which all values that are sought in earthly, mundane things are cast away."[24] As if to pick up on his insistence that religion is concerned neither with merely subjective religious states nor with the object of religious consciousness alone, Hegel insists he is not speaking here of God alone. Rather, he is referring to the kingdom of God, in which spirit finds its homeland. He then, in effect, ties Christ's teaching on the kingdom in with the question of determinate religions. He does this when he indicates the Roman and Jewish contexts, respectively, of the this-worldly rulership and the empty universality[25] within which Christ's proclamation occurs.

Hegel completes this philosophical interpretation of the kingdom of God as the content of Christ's teaching[26] by distinguishing three aspects to that teaching.[27] In the first and second of these aspects he regularly refers to texts from the Gospel of Matthew.[28] He underscores, first of all, the inward and world-shunning character of the kingdom of God as homeland for spirit. Hegel notes the moral implications of this higher and inward kingdom. But, as if to underscore again, in going beyond Kant, that Christ is not a mere moral teacher,[29] he rushes on to stress that Christ's comprehensive teaching is love of neighbor. Followers of Christ are to make the unity of a dialectically interpreted movement of love, namely, the community in and for itself, their only goal.[30] Hegel sees the call to stand in "revolutionary" opposition to all established orders as the second aspect of Christ's teaching, and, consequently, as second aspect of the kingdom of God.[31] It is especially in his seeing these first two aspects of Christ's teaching on the kingdom of God as offering a challenge to the disciples that Hegel has sensed something of what scholars in recent studies would call the functioning of kingdom as tensive symbol.[32] Yet Hegel will also go on beyond the indication of such a functioning to insist that there is a speculative content to the religious metaphor "kingdom of God."

It is in the third, quite briefly presented[33] aspect of Christ's teaching on the kingdom of God that Hegel, with predominant reference to the Gospel of John, touches on "the more precise definition or the proper definition and determinacy of the kingdom of God, i.e., with the relationship of Christ himself to God and of humanity to God and Christ."[34] With, and yet despite, an acknowledgement of certain more difficult exegetical questions, he sees the Johannine insight into the elevation of Christ's spirit to the Father as being very important. He understands this elevation as the affirmation of the identity of divine and human, namely, the presentation of the idea which Christ has become for the community. This third aspect to the content of the teaching of Christ clearly involves a moment of speculative reinterpretation of "kingdom of God." Already with this third aspect Hegel has presented the kingdom as the universal homeland of spirit. In a very general way, he has hinted that the kingdom of God is to be conceived in the form of inclusive totality when he writes of it in terms of the relationship between God and humanity in and through Christ.

Hegel continues with the fourth subdivision of redemption and reconciliation, which he entitles "Life and Death." He briefly refers[35] to a non-speculative, or even external and abstract, understanding of the normally expected conformity of the life and death of a teacher to his or her teaching. Then, in a paragraph[36] worth quoting from at greater length, he affirms, on the basis of the nature of the content of Christ's teaching, an internal and intrinsic relationship between that teaching and Christ's death.

> But here life and death have another, quite different relation to the teaching [of Christ]. Its content is the kingdom of God – not a universal essence but a living, spiritual life, a divine community. (aa) The teaching as such [is] the universal form of the content – the kingdom of God, the first, eternal idea itself, but in concrete terms. (bb) The kingdom of God – or spirit – is to move from the universal to determinacy, to pass over into actuality. This movement, the process of determining, takes place in the life of Jesus.[37]

The rest of this important paragraph, made up mostly of attached margin notes, is in effect the explication of the juxtaposition of "kingdom of God" and of spirit as a process taking place in the life of Jesus. As teaching, the kingdom of God remains universal idea of that into which individuals are to enter. It becomes actual as community only through the individual, Jesus. Equally, the divinity of Christ is at first only implicit and, in fact, comes into being as the self-constituting process of spirit. Thus Hegel can go on beyond what he wrote in this paragraph to affirm that it is the divine idea which courses through the history or self-constituting process of spirit in the life and death of Christ.[38] As he begins to concentrate on the death of Christ, Hegel has already effectively identified the kingdom of God with that movement of self-diremption of spirit which, as initial moment of reconciliation, is equally the first moment of return. He sees this moment religiously represented in the life and death of Christ. "Thus the kingdom of God has its representative (i.e., the mode of its existence) initially in this existing human being."[39]

Hegel proceeds with a long and impressive analysis of the natural and real death of one specific individual as the necessary moment of absolute love. He presents love as self-diremption and self-giving to the ultimate moment or pinnacle of finitude such that death is equally the moment of spirit as the sublation of natural finitude.[40] After this analysis he calls this death the death of God, a death which presents the absolute history of the divine idea.[41] When the condition of the then contemporary world is taken into consideration as context for this death of Christ, it becomes clear for Hegel that such a total self-surrender introduces "a revolutionary element to the extent that it gives the world another shape. All things great and of worldly value [are] as nothing; [all these things are] buried in the grave of spirit."[42] When the movement of love is expressed in terms of the exaltation of a despicable death on the cross, when other-being which is ignominious and counted the lowest is now exalted, then "we find here the direct expression of a complete revolution against all that is established and regarded as valuable."[43] Thus, in the context of his criticism of the Roman world, Hegel interprets the kingdom of God as the positive content of the cross now raised up as a banner.[44] For Hegel Christ's death on the cross is the immediate actualization of the kingdom of God. It has challenged and, in the deepest possible revolutionary way, subverted the Roman world with its degrading imperial state, authority, and power.[45]

Following a brief, transitional consideration of resurrection and ascension in the fifth and final subdivision of his treatment of redemption and reconciliation, Hegel turns to the last of the three overall moments constituting his 1821 manuscript presentation of the consummate religion, namely, "Community, Cultus."[46] He introduces this third moment with a longer presentation[47] of the consummate religion, clearly identified in historical realization as the Christian religion.[48] The consummate religion is now, in this third moment, explicitly the religion of the spirit.[49] It is the community of the spirit as the gathering of those who have in themselves subjectively present the speculative concept of love.[50] Likewise, the members of this community have this same concept of love objectively and representationally available in the life, death, resurrection and ascension of Christ.[51] "Accordingly, this sphere of infinite love [is] the kingdom of the Spirit."[52] Each individual bears the call to be citizen of the kingdom of God.[53] The divine idea is spirit, "Holy Spirit" Hegel says, insofar as the movement of speculative love occurs in these individuals as their elevation to God, the actual presence of God here and now. "This [is] the Spirit of God, or God as the present, actual Spirit, God dwelling in his community."[54] At the end of this introductory section Hegel places the community parallel with the kingdom of God when he writes that the disciples went out to elevate their community to the universal community "and to spread abroad the kingdom of God."[55]

So often Hegel ties things together in brief summaries. And that is just what he has done here in such a brief resume of his presentation of the consummate religion to this point. He boldly proclaims that the very becoming immanent of the appearance of the concept of God in the community of the spirit is "the kingdom of the Spirit. The kingdom of God *is* the Spirit."[56]

After a brief but important general remark on love, Hegel divides the presentation of "community and cultus" or the overall third moment into the origin of the community, the being of the community and cultus, and, in a formulation peculiar to the 1821 lectures, the passing away of the community. It is in the second and third of these moments of community and cultus that he continues his speculative reinterpretation of "kingdom of God." He develops the second moment of community and cultus in three main steps. In the first of these he discusses faith, teaching or doctrine, and feeling. But it is in the second and third steps, where he treats respectively of the developed community as a church and then as cultus or worship proper, that Hegel brings up the kingdom of God. In the second step he speaks of the developed church as being inwardly at peace and enduring through time.[57] And, without picking up on the distinction between invisible and external church which he had sketched earlier in the loose sheets,[58] he announces: "The church is the kingdom of God, the achieved presence, life, preservation, and enjoyment of the Spirit."[59] In line with this stress on achieved presence and enjoyment of the spirit, he goes on, with some at least at times suspicious argumentation, to say that the earlier polemical tendency against any external worldly presence now naturally falls away.[60] His concern is that there be formed out of the womb of the church "a rational, worldly kingdom in accord with the idea of freedom and the absolute character of rights."[61]

In the last of these steps, cultus, it is Hegel's discussion of sacraments which is of particular present interest. The sacraments are seen as the means by which the spirit, which fills the community, provides "the immediate certainty of the kingdom, that of being received into it, of being [its] citizens."[62] This certainty is one of partaking (Genuß).[63] The sacraments, and especially the main sacrament (Communion) are the immediate enjoyment of the unity of the subject with its absolute object, with the kingdom of God.[64]

Hegel ends the 1821 manuscript with a rather brief, enigmatic third subdivision or moment to "Community, Cultus," namely, "The Passing Away of the Community."[65] He opens the presentation of this moment with the paradoxical statement that all things historical share in the rhythm of origin, preservation, and perishing (Untergehen), and yet the kingdom of God is to have been established eternally. If the kingdom of God is eternal, "then perishing or going under would [in fact] be a passing over to the kingdom of heaven [and would apply] only for single subjects, not for the community; the Holy Spirit as such has eternal life in its community."[66] Apparently this difficulty in reconciling the all-too-ordinary perishing of historical entities with the eternity of the kingdom of God was a problem for Hegel himself and not just for those trying to interpret the manuscript text.[67] To end merely with such a passing away would be to end on a discordant note (Mißton).[68] And then, as if at this point his polemical concerns overwhelm him, Hegel dedicates a paragraph[69] to underscoring the collapse of the Roman world. He does this in order, by allusion, to criticize Schleiermacher[70] and, by more direct reference, to reject the opinion of those who say we can know nothing of God but can only have a type of historical knowing.[71] He manifests great concern that the Gospel is not being preached to the poor, that the clergy are shirking their responsibility to stimulate religion, and that moral people are satisfied with reflection and limiting their concerns to the finite. With the expression of this concern he underscores his fear that religion will continue to decline. He fears that reason and religion will be allowed to contradict one another.[72]

This proposed contradiction between reason and religion seems to jolt Hegel's attention back to the question of the passing of all things historical and of the eternal character of the kingdom of God. In what comes across as a sense of resignation, he, now in immediate reference to this contradiction between reason and religion, uses the same word, namely, "discordant tone" (*Mißton*), that he had used to indicate the tension between the passing away of all things historical and the eternity of the kingdom of God. At the very end of this 1821 lecture manuscript Hegel writes that the present day must be left to solve its own problems.[73] "Religion must take refuge in philosophy."[74] It is as if he is saying that what is eternal in the kingdom of God as community of the spirit will remain. That which is eternal, that which is common to individual and community, namely, the certainty of truth, is expressed in and as the identity of self and concept. The last vestiges of the otherness of religiously represented reconciliation as kingdom of God are now for Hegel overcome in philosophical thought as the true form of the content religiously expressed by "kingdom of God."

By the end of the 1821 lecture manuscript Hegel has given a speculative philosophical content to "kingdom of God." By now he has equated it, in its realization, with the consummate religion as community and cultus. He first introduced this religious representation as the content of Christ's teaching. There, in a philosophical reading limited to the sphere of reconciliation in Christ, he spoke of the kingdom of God as the universal to be made actual in the life and death of Christ. In the most fundamental sense possible of the term "revolutionary," this death and its positive content, the actualization of the kingdom of God, turn the world upside down. Then, toward the end of this sphere of reconciliation in Christ, and especially in the moment of community or cultus, the kingdom of God finds its concrete universal expression in and as the community of the spirit. Here Hegel directly identified church and kingdom. He likewise thematized the sacraments, and particularly the principal sacrament (Communion), as sacraments of the kingdom and moments of immediate certainty of the presence of God. In the course of his treatment of community or cultus he comes to speak of kingdom of God as presence of God and enjoyment of that presence. But that presence, and the enjoyment of it, go over into philosophical thought as the immediate certainty of truth. Already on the level of religious representation Hegel had philosophically reinterpreted kingdom of God as spirit and, more specifically, as the community of the spirit. In "kingdom of God" he saw reconciliation, representationally expressed, occurring objectively in Christ and, then, subjectively as spirit present in the community of Christ's disciples. The kingdom of God, this otherness of reconciliation in Christ and in the spirit, is detemporalized. For Hegel it is given its true speculative expression as the very overcoming of such otherness in the eternal, and true, form of philosophical thought, which is self-mediation and inclusive totality.

1.b. The 1824 Lectures

Hegel's 1824 series of lectures on the philosophy of religion, as available in the corrected and supplemented Griesheim transcript, is the longest of the four. However, in these 1824 lectures Hegel makes considerably less reference to "kingdom of God" than in any of his other series of lectures on the philosophy of religion. When he is cited as having spoken of the kingdom of God, the kingdom of heaven, or the kingdom of the spirit, it is in places in the 1824 lectures corresponding to similar locations in the 1821 manuscript.[75] There would seem to be at least two reasons for Hegel's having given so much less attention to the religious representation "kingdom of God" in the 1824 lectures. The first would appear to be that there was less time left for the last half of the presentation on the consummate or absolute religion because of his significantly lengthened presentation of determinate religion in the second part of the lectures. The second, and more interesting, reason would seem to be the polemical context of the 1824 lectures. Hegel is particularly concerned to stress the objective and absolute, speculatively justified content of religion, and particularly of the consummate religion, over against those who would deny the possibility of a conceptual knowledge of God. He saw such a denial as leading on to a merely historicist position in that, according to him, those who denied a true conceptual knowledge of God often, consequently, found themselves left with the option of studying only what has been said in the past. Ultimately he was combatting what he perceived to be a merely subjectivist position.[76] Though he would continue to stress that the life and death of Christ constitute moments in the history of God and in the history of spirit,[77] in the 1824 lectures Hegel is neither inclined toward, nor concerned about, dwelling on what might be considered historical warrant for the community's affirmations concerning Christ. Now the only adequate warrant is the witness of the spirit.[78] So Hegel merely mentions Christ's life and passes quickly over Christ's teaching as such and its announcement of the kingdom of God. He does little explicitly to link the death of Christ with the religious representation, "kingdom of God." Rather, he is taken up with the effort to see the death of Christ as transitional moment in the history of God. He stresses the need for a transition from the sensible presence of Christ to Christ's spiritual presence which founds the community.[79] This initial tendency for Hegel to downplay reference to "kingdom of God" then carries over quite naturally into what has come, in 1824, to be his presentation of the third element in the consummate religion's concrete representation.

But now to turn briefly to those occasions on which Hegel does make explicit reference to the kingdom of God. Toward the end of the presentation of the overall second element under "concrete representation,"[80] he indicates that he has proceeded in this second element in three steps: from the general consideration of the concept of this standpoint for consciousness (reconciliation), to what is present to consciousness, and to the transition to the community. In the second of these steps he distinguishes between the teaching of the church or the community, namely, a teaching which begins with assertions as doctrines, and the teaching of Christ, which is to evoke sensations and has a content.[81] But he discusses the teaching of Christ from a loftier perspective than in 1821. He does this in so far as he jumps on the notion of content in order to present in considerably briefer, but also much more speculative, fashion the position he had worked out in the 1821 manuscript on Christ's teaching. Now Hegel is recorded as saying, "First there [is] the universal soil, and second there is what is particular, determinate, and concrete."[82] Then he launches off into a speculative assertion that, for representational thinking, these two remain opposed whereas for comprehending thought the universal posits itself as the particular.[83] In 1821 Hegel had insisted that the universal in Christ's teaching was not God as such but the more inclusive representation of the kingdom of God.[84] Now, in 1824, he speaks of this same inclusiveness, but in a more integrated way. He more directly identifies God and kingdom:

> So what can initially be produced here by teaching is the universal soil for the concept of God. This can be expressed briefly as the *kingdom of God*. This has been taught: it is the real divinity, God in his *determinate being* [*Dasein*], in his *spiritual actuality*, the kingdom of heaven. This divine reality contains already within itself God and his kingdom, the community – a concrete content. This is the main content.[85]

Hegel's further observations, during the rest of his presentation of the second element, on the development of the consummate religion continue to reflect his more speculative and integrating 1824 stance. One example will suffice to illustrate this more speculative perspective. As in the 1821 lectures, here Hegel again speaks of the revolutionary in Christ's teaching, but now he speaks of the abstract universal in the determination of negation over against all that is at hand.[86]

Throughout the 1824 lectures Hegel has elaborated his philosophy of religion particularly in terms of consciousness and, in the third element of the consummate religion, in terms of self-consciousness. Nowhere is this clearer than in his treatment of the first moment of the third element of consummate religion, where he asks, "Who are 'we'?"[87] In this first moment, namely, the origin of the community, in a manner somewhat reminiscent of his procedure in the *Phenomenology of Spirit*, Hegel refers to an initial unitary notion of faith.[88] Then, by means of a recurrent pattern of reversal, he stresses the varied objective presence of the spirit to subjectivity, to the community of the spirit.[89] For example, teaching, which would be expected to arise out of the community, is also presented here as the doctrine of the church (concerning Christ as son of God), but now equally giving rise to the community.[90] Throughout this triply staged movement of the community as faith coming to consciousness of itself, but especially in the second moment as the subsistence of the community and in the third moment, namely, the realization of faith as the transition to philosophy, Hegel only refers twice to the kingdom of God and once to the kingdom of spirit. In the first reference to the kingdom of God he treats of sacrament as moment of the consciousness of being a citizen of God's kingdom:

> 3. The third [moment] in regard to this rebirth is that of *partaking* [*Genuß*] – the consciousness of this divine grace, the consciousness of being a "citizen" . . . of God's kingdom – what is called mystical union, the sacrament of the Lord's Supper, where human beings are vouchsafed the consciousness of their reconciliation with God in a sensible, intuitable form, the indwelling and lodging of the Spirit within them.[91]

The second, and more enigmatic, reference to the kingdom of God is found toward the beginning of the final moment, the realization of faith. Hegel had, in line with his working more with consciousness, just spoken of "the 'now' of communion [which] dissolves in its representation, partly into a beyond, an otherworldly heaven, partly into the past, and partly into the future."[92] In what is perhaps part of his attempt to maintain a sense of otherness and also only the looser transcript wording, he stated, "Thus over against the community, and the kingdom of God in the community, there stands an *objective reality*."[93] Hegel is concerned to overcome the two forms of this objective reality or, better, objectivity. These are forms which still stand over against the community. They are the immediate world and reflection or abstract thought. These forms must be overcome in order to arrive at the *true* objectivity of the concept.[94] It is in and through these three elements or forms of objectivity that faith, or even religion as such, realizes itself.[95] It is this reference to objectivity which, then, leads to Hegel's only use of "kingdom of spirit." At the very end of these 1824 lectures Hegel interprets the triple movement of the realization of faith as three stages which "take shape in regard to the kingdom of the Spirit."[96] It is as if for him the immediate religion of faith, then reflection and the Enlightenment, and finally the community of philosophy[97] constitute the kingdom of the spirit. He has expanded the notion of "kingdom of God" to cover as well that into which it is sublated.

Hegel's quite sparing use of the phrase "kingdom of God" in the 1824 lectures would seem to be the result of his wanting, as previously mentioned, to avoid giving historical warrant to what he now insists can only be justified by and in the spirit. Stated more positively, this more restrained use seems equally to be the result of his total absorption in a more speculative interpretation of the philosophy of religion. It is indeed Hegel's breakthrough to a certain clarity concerning the speculative definition of religion, in Part One of the 1824 lectures, which can be seen to structure his speculative interpretation of the consummate religion and, to the extent that they are used, his readings of "kingdom of God" and "kingdom of the spirit." There in Part One, The Concept of Religion, Hegel had described religion as "this idea, the idea of spirit, which relates itself to itself, the self-consciousness of absolute spirit."[98] The few references he does make to the kingdom of God and the kingdom of the spirit indicate that he has not so much rejected what he had said concerning the kingdom of God in the 1821 manuscript as put the term itself on the back burner. In one sense its use has, for the time being, become a casualty of his war with historicism and subjectivism. But in another sense, with his pursuit of the speculative definition of religion Hegel has laid the foundation for a more integrated philosophical reinterpretation of the kingdom of God. The unfortunate side to his having put the phrase, "kingdom of God," somewhat aside in the 1824 lectures is that he missed a golden opportunity further to explore riches discoverable in that phrase through a more prolonged elaboration of logical, phenomenological, spatial, and temporal frameworks that he had laid out earlier in introductory remarks to the 1824 presentation of the consummate religion.[99]

1.c. The 1827 Lectures

In the 1827 lectures, as available primarily in the Lasson text, Hegel makes explicit reference both to "kingdom of God" and "kingdom of heaven," but surprisingly not to "kingdom of the spirit."[100] He does this in places corresponding to those in the 1821 and 1824 lectures, namely, where he discusses the teaching of Christ and where he presents the consummate religion as community. He elaborates, in greater detail, on Christ's teaching here in the 1827 lectures than he did in 1824. He uses some argumentation similar to what he employed in 1821. It would seem that, at least at this point in his lectures, he is again working from the 1821 manuscript.[101] Apparently, then, this return to the manuscript presentation of Christ's teaching also helps explain Hegel's more frequent reference to "kingdom of God" in the 1827 discussion of Christ's teaching than in that of 1824. An additional reason for this greater reference to "kingdom of God" may lie in the fact that the polemical context of the 1827 lectures has shifted. Hegel is now struggling against an antispeculative neo-pietism and more on the defensive in response to various attacks that his thought is Spinozist and pantheistic, if not downright atheistic. Surely in response to these attacks, now in 1827 he begins the lectures on the philosophy of religion with the concept of God.[102] The best defense is a good offense. This is a beginning which reflects both these lectures' particular polemical context and their more directly speculative interpretation of religion. The philosophy of religion is now the scientific development and knowing of what God is.[103]

It is important to take into consideration that the 1821 manuscript comes directly from Hegel's own hand and the 1827 Lasson text is a construction from several auditors' transcripts. Nevertheless, a comparison of the two and a glance at the 1824 text on Hegel's presentation of Christ's teaching, including reference to Christ's life and death,[104] reveal that in 1827 Hegel is working in a very particular way. He is surely taking ideas from the 1821 manuscript. Now, however, he is trying to develop them within the 1827 polemical context and in line both with his more speculative 1824 definition of religion and with the notion of consciousness stressed in the 1824 lectures. In a way vaguely reminiscent of his earlier attempt in the *Phenomenology of Spirit*, he tries to integrate history into a movement of consciousness. He proposes to reinstate historical concerns, but without attributing to them the value of warrant. He does this by distinguishing, though only partially successfully,[105] between non-religious[106] and religious[107] perspectives on Christ. Hegel refers to the kingdom of God in his discussion of each perspective.

We can illustrate these references and this discussion by turning directly to, but without needing to summarize in every detail, Hegel's explicit references to kingdom of God in this 1827 treatment of Christ's teaching.

Hegel seems as if he cannot resist jumping ahead of himself in his discussion of the non-religious perspective on Christ. As he clearly did in 1824,[108] and in fact but not explicitly in 1821,[109] he distinguishes right away between the teaching of Christ and that of the Church. He remarks that certain elements of the former will necessarily drop away. He is recorded as saying, in language reminiscent of the 1821 manuscript, "Once the community is established, once the kingdom of God has attained its determinate being and its actuality, these teachings are either interpreted in other ways or else they fall by the wayside."[110] Hegel seems to find himself in a constant "back and forth" between what we would expect to find him treating in the third element of consummate religion, namely, "Community," and what we would expect to find here in the second element.

During this "shifting back and forth" Hegel makes a number of observations on the kingdom of God. He says that here, with the life and death of Christ, we are dealing with a question of the consciousness of absolute reconciliation. We are facing a new human consciousness, which, therefore, conditions a new world. With Christ there arises a new religion,[111] namely, a new consciousness of reconciliation of humanity with God. Then Hegel makes a sort of preliminary philosophical interpretation of the polemical aspects to Christ's teaching. He sees this new consciousness as being opposed, in negative fashion, to the continuing subsistence of externality in human consciousness. He will return to this point in his presentation of community.

What is of particular present interest is the fact that Hegel both asserts "this reconciliation, expressed as a state of affairs, is the kingdom of God, an actuality,"[112] and juxtaposes the kingdom of God and this new religion.[113] In effect, all that he says here about the new religion is being said as well about the kingdom of God. This new religion, and consequently the kingdom of God, is still not present as community, but only in a "concentrated" (*konzentriert*) form.[114] Apparently here Hegel means in the life, teaching, and death of Christ.

He then picks up on the notion of "immediacy" to continue his more speculative interpretation of "kingdom of God" as truth. He insists that one is called to place oneself directly and without mediation "into the truth, into the kingdom of God. It is to this kingdom, to this intellectual, spiritual world, that humanity ought to belong."[115]

During the presentation of the last part of this second element of the consummate religion in the 1827 lectures Hegel claims he is taking up the religious perspective on Christ. "It is this second view that leads us for the first time into the religious sphere as such, where the divine itself is an essential moment."[116] Here Hegel, in line with his continuing emphasis on consciousness, speaks of a relation to God similar to the way in which he had spoken, in 1821, of the more specific relationship of Christ to God. But we should note that now he speaks of an infinite relationship.[117] Nevertheless, here in this discussion concerning an infinite relationship Hegel emphasizes certainty. He expresses this emphasis on certainty in such a way that he clearly reaffirms, in the present context, that the kingdom of God is the very relationship to God self.[118]

Hegel is recorded here as asserting, more forcefully than in 1821, that "the defining characteristic of this kingdom of God is the *presence of God*."[119] We can take this insistence as an instance of his ongoing interpretation of the consummate religion as the self-development of God in and through religious consciousness. He argues that the kingdom of God, or God's being present, is the very determination of one's feeling as the certainty of this divine presence. But this determination of one's feeling, this response to the subject's need, itself creates for Hegel, in his typical phenomenological dialectic of consciousness, a double need. This determination and response creates the need both to assert a distinction from that kingdom, in so far as it is sensibly present, and to come to the realization that this distinction is overcome in the death of Christ. This speculative religious realization that the distinction is overcome is the point at which the community begins to come into being.[120]

In the tightly, but logically quite rigorously, developed presentation of the 1827 third element of the consummate religion, Hegel is presented as mentioning the kingdom of God explicitly only three times. He refers to the kingdom of God once in the introduction to the triply divided third element, once in the first subsection presenting the origin of the community, and once at the beginning of the third subsection, "The Realization of the Spirituality of the Community."[121] In traversing from the sensible realization of reconciliation to reconciliation's spiritual realization, the individual subject "becomes spirit, and thus a citizen of the kingdom of God."[122] Secondly, at the beginning of his discussion of the origin of the community and in the context of a review of what he has done so far in the presentation of the consummate religion, Hegel identifies, in logical terms, the first element of the consummate religion, namely, "immanent" Trinity, with simple universality. He identifies the second element of the consummate religion with particularity. He goes on to speak of the third element in a way that could only be interpreted as individuality.[123]

In then discussing the third element Hegel says that the community begins with the truth being at hand, that is, knowing that God is triune. And the second side to this truth is that it has appeared and given certainty of reconciliation so that "the subject is essentially related to it, and is meant to be a citizen of the kingdom of God."[124] Hegel is bringing the religious representations of Trinity and kingdom of God into a closer relationship. Thirdly, at the beginning of the last subsection he mentions in very brief but seminal fashion that, though the heart is now reconciled, there stands over against it a world yet to be reconciled:[125]

> The self that exists in this reconciliation, in this religious communion, is the pure heart, the heart as such, universal spirituality; but at the same time the self or subject constitutes that aspect of spiritual presence in accord with which there is a developed worldliness present in it, and thus the kingdom of God, the community, has a relationship to the worldly. In order that reconciliation may be real, it is required that it should be known in this development, in this totality; it should be present and brought forth [into actuality].[126]

Hegel then introduces the idea that freedom is rationality. He insists that this freedom, or reconciliation, should be realized as well in the worldly realm.[127] He observes that there are three ways in which this reconciliation, the community, the kingdom of God, can be related to worldliness: first in the unacceptable way of immediacy; second, in the equally unacceptable way of an external relation between Church and world; and, third, the only true way, namely, by means of ethical living (*Sittlichkeit*).[128] It is fascinating to see Hegel again, even if only in the briefest of fashions, reaffirming now, as expressions of ethical living, many of those things he had earlier seen to be denied in the initial and polemical teaching of Christ about the kingdom of God. And many of these things are here gathered rather cleverly into three to form a critique of religious vows. Celibacy is not to be valued over family life, nor poverty over self-enrichment through personal effort, nor blind obedience over obedience of the subject to the rational and the ethical. Family life, self-enrichment, and rational ethical living are to be the means by which the kingdom of God enters, as principle of freedom, into worldliness.[129] For Hegel the kingdom of God is actualized in the world through rational and free ethical living. Here we can indeed see Hegel bringing Trinity and "kingdom of God" into a closer and more conceptually expressed relationship. But more than this, he has related "kingdom of God," and consequently through "kingdom of God" also Trinity, to worldliness through ethical living. This he has done precisely in as the kingdom of God is the realm of rationality as freedom.

Taking a step back from the 1827 text itself will allow us to make several more general and summary observations. It is interesting, for example, to note that now, in 1827, Hegel is at least no longer recorded as making any distinction between Christ's teaching and the content of that teaching. The teaching and its content are now effectively interchangeable. Consequently, Hegel would no longer seem to need to distinguish clearly and explicitly, within his presentation of Christ's teaching itself, between the kingdom of God as universal moment and that moment's needing to be particularized. In fact, in 1827 he pretty well coopts these logical thought determinations, in a particularly explicit way, to describe the consummate religion's first element as universality, its second as particularity, and its third as individuality.[130]

This renewed, wider, and quite explicit application of these thought determinations to the three elements of the consummate religion surely forms part of Hegel's strategic defense against attacks that his thought is either pantheistic or atheistic. Furthermore, the dialectical movement of the consummate religion from universality to particularity to individuality confirms, on its own level and in its own way, Hegel's insistence that God is not merely substance but also, and especially, subject.[131] It is with particular clarity that Hegel, in these 1827 lectures, interprets what can be termed "immanent" Trinity, or God "before" the creation of the world, as the moment of universality. The kingdom of God, now treated as equivalent to the teaching of Christ, shares in the overall logical characterization of the consummate religion's second element, namely, particularity. In the consummate religion's third element "kingdom of God" comes to be used interchangeably with community and spirit. There it bears the characteristic of inclusive individuality. The kingdom of God is the communitarian reconciliation of the individual subject with the infinite or God. However, until the moment of true mediation in philosophical thought it remains this reconciliation still expressed in the form of otherness characteristic of religious representation. Hence, the kingdom of God is the presence of God and the enjoyment of that presence.[132] It is for Hegel the religious realm of truth and freedom, both of which are to be actualized in the rational state. When we consider these presentations in the second and third elements together, we can see that, for Hegel, the kingdom of God comes to be interpreted philosophically as a whole movement. It is a movement from reconciliation, which is initially sensibly present, on to the ever more intense identification of consciousness with realized reconciliation in the community as self-consciousness and, through the realization of that reconciliation in ethical living, finally on to philosophical thought. Philosophical thought is the true and, therefore, final form of mediation.

1.d. The 1831 Lectures

Hegel gave the 1831 lectures on the philosophy of religion during the last summer of his life. These lectures, and particularly the presentation of the consummate or, historically speaking, the Christian religion, no longer give evidence of polemical struggles with concerns over Schleiermacher's competing position as in 1821, nor with subjectivism as in 1824, nor again with accusations of being pantheist or atheist as in 1827.[133] Still, the introduction of a longer treatment of the relationship between religion and the state[134] does reflect Hegel's general political concerns during his last year of teaching in Berlin.[135]

In addition to Hegel's longer reflection on the relationship between religion and state, from the perspective of this study four points are particularly striking in the 1831 lectures. The first three of them are already present in one way or another in the earlier lecture series. The first of these is Hegel's further qualification of his speculative definition of religion. Hegel had worked out the definition in 1824, when he spoke of religion as the idea of spirit which relates itself to itself, the self-consciousness of absolute spirit.[136] Then, in 1827, he spoke of religion as the self-development of the concept of God.[137] Now, in 1831, he continues to bring together his conceptions of spirit, of consciousness, and of God. We can see this at two points. First, when Hegel is presented as speaking of religion in general: "This is the concept of religion, that God knows God self in spirit and that spirit knows itself in God."[138] And, second, when he elaborates on this definition in speaking of the consummate religion as that within which the finite subject, in being conscious of God, is a moment in God's consciousness of God self:

> We have defined religion more precisely as the *self-consciousness of God* .... God is self-consciousness; he knows himself in a consciousness that is distinct from him, which is implicitly the consciousness of God, but is also the divine consciousness explicitly since it knows its identity with God, an identity that is mediated, however, by the negation of finitude. It is this concept that constitutes the content of religion.[139]

The second of these particularly striking points concerning the 1831 lectures is the way in which Hegel comes back, time and again, to the notion of freedom as a primary concern. Freedom is effectively identified with the movement of divine self-development, a self-determination in which there is no final externality. And it is, historically, from the Christian standpoint and in the Christian religion that we have the concept of God in all its freedom.[140]

The third point is the way in which Hegel can be seen working to identify, in "immanent" and "economic" trinitarian terms, the movement of divine self-consciousness and freedom as the very structure of the consummate religion, which develops from universality to particularity to individuality.

The fourth, and for present purposes most important, of these points is the fact that he for the first time identifies the three spheres of the consummate religion, namely, pure ideality, diremption, and reconciliation respectively as "the kingdom of the Father," "the kingdom of the Son," and "the kingdom of the Spirit."[141]

The presently available more limited sources for the 1831 lectures do not permit as detailed a scrutiny of Hegel's 1831 presentations as was possible either with the 1821 manuscript or with the quite reliable auditors' transcripts for the 1824 and 1827 lectures. Nevertheless, the excerpts on the consummate religion, from a transcript by David Friedrich Strauss,[142] do seem to provide an accurate view of the order Hegel followed in the 1831 lectures. In fact, for the consummate religion he generally followed the order of 1827. But we should note that Hegel, in a way similar to what he had done in 1824, reintroduces a preliminary treatment of the ontological proof for the existence of God before he develops the three spheres of the consummate religion. This order and the content, which have been recorded by Strauss, are both corroborated and complemented by passages from the first and second Friends Editions of Hegel's collected works. The Friends Editions passages are easily available, since they are either footnoted to the 1827 lectures on the consummate religion[143] or printed as a separate study on the ontological proof for the existence of God.[144] The following summary presentation of the three kingdoms will, then, follow the order of the Strauss excerpts and make reference to the often more interestingly and more fully articulated phrasing in the passages from the Friends Editions.[145]

Hegel divides the consummate religion into three spheres constituting the kingdoms of Father, Son, and Spirit. It is characteristic of Hegel's thought that his division is meant neither to be static nor merely formal. Rather, his tripartite division gives expression to three dialectically developing stages or modes of divine self-revelation.[146] The first sphere,[147] the kingdom of the Father (*das Reich des Vaters*), is the realm of free universality. It is the course and process of God's own self-explication. Thus it is revelation of the divine idea in thought

(*Denken*). "This is the first relationship, which is only for the thinking subject, and is occupied only with the pure content. This is *the kingdom of the Father*."[148] It is here that Hegel, as in the previous lecture series, presents his philosophical reinterpretation of "immanent" Trinity as self-othering and overcoming of that otherness. In comparison with the otherness posited in the next sphere, the otherness here in question is one not yet come to externality. As such it is not yet contradiction.[149] Hegel has come so far now as to give a certain preference to the phrase "kingdom of the Father" in indicating this first sphere: "Thus the *doctrine of the Trinity* pertains to this sphere, although it is preferentially termed the *kingdom of the Father*."[150]

The second sphere is that of diremption, indeed a diremption which occurs no longer merely in the form of thought but now in the form of representation (*Vorstellung*). This sphere is the kingdom of the Son (*das Reich des Sohnes*).[151] In the first part of this presentation, where Hegel treats what we more classically speak of as creation, he strongly insists on the difference between differentiation internal to the first sphere, in which otherness arises only in the momentary form of the Son, and differentiation as real externalization into this second sphere where "the Son obtains the determination as other."[152] Consistent with the overall structure of Hegel's dialectic, the other in this second sphere appears in the doubled form of nature and finite spirit,[153] both of which are, in their own ways, the revelation of God.[154] In what is the second and longer part of this presentation, this doubled divine self-othering climaxes in a single finite subject, Christ, and in his teaching, but especially in his death. In a way parallel to the 1827 distinction between what can be historically known concerning Christ and what is the witness of the spirit, here, in the 1831 lectures, Hegel works with the distinction between unfaith (*Unglauben*) and faith (*Glauben*).[155] Christ's teaching concerning love, the proclamation of the kingdom of heaven as the awakening of consciousness to interiority, and the natural relating of Christ's death to his teaching can be perceived even by unfaith. However, they then form a sort of basis for the spiritual interpretation of Christ's death.[156] In this spiritual interpretation of the death of Christ, one, in faith, sees reenacted the very dialectic from immediacy to differentiation to overcoming of that differentiation. This is a dialectic which has occurred as Trinity in the first sphere but which now, from the perspective of the second sphere, is regarded both as presupposition to, and yet as revealed in, Christ's life and death.[157] For Hegel, in the death of Christ it is God or, again, the Father who dies. More philosophically expressed, it is the abstractness of the Father[158] as universality that is now sublated in the Son, in the realm of particularity.[159] It is with this spiritual interpretation of the death of Christ as the negation of negation, namely, as love or the unity of Father and Son, that there occurs the transition to the community of finite subjects who are bound together in faith. This community is the kingdom of the Spirit (*das Reich des Geistes*).[160]

"The distinctive element of this [the kingdom of the Spirit] is the self-conscious awareness of human beings that they are reconciled with God, and the fulfillment of this consciousness in church and cultus."[161] If at the end of this, quote taken from Strauss's excerpts, we add the further observations that this fulfillment also takes place in worldliness and in philosophical thought, the rest of the still extent 1831 materials can be read essentially as an elaboration of this statement.

In a way reminiscent of his observation concerning Christ's life and death as being the same overall dialectical movement as that which had occurred earlier in the kingdom of the Father, now Hegel insists that the members of the community are to live this same dialectic of immediacy, the sublation of immediacy, and the enjoyment of reconciliation. The Strauss excerpts show him interweaving the necessary passage of each individual from the consciousness of not being what that individual ought to be on to participation in the kingdom of reconciliation with the threefold development of the community.[162]

To abbreviate somewhat the process as found in the Strauss excerpts, we can say that finite subjects are, first of all, members of the community in the immediacy of their faith and their baptism.[163] Then they are to live this faith as the overcoming of that evil which has already been overcome in Christ. This they are to do even with repentance and penance.[164] Here we can see that, as part of his effort to establish the same dialectical rhythm in the third sphere as had occurred in the first and second spheres, Hegel has transferred his consideration of estrangement and evil from the consummate religion's second element to this third sphere or the kingdom of the Spirit. More precisely, he has shifted this consideration to the second moment of the realization of reconciliation in the finite subject as member of the community. However, as was just mentioned, this transfer was done with the important proviso that evil has, in itself, already been overcome with the death of Christ. Therefore the situation is now easier for the members of the community.[165] In overcoming evil, a process which is really that of sublating immediacy as well, the finite subject enjoys, in community, the assurance of reconciliation in the reception of the sacrament of Holy Communion.[166] These three steps are the development of God self in and as community.[167] They constitute the first of three realizations of the kingdom of the Spirit, what we can call the inner-ecclesial actualization of spirit.

Hegel then elaborates, more forcefully than in 1827, a second actualization of the kingdom of the Spirit. This actualization is that of the truth and the freedom of the community in worldliness as ethical living and, primarily, as the ethical, rational organization of the life of the state. In a short passage from the Friends Editions he is presented as saying:

> It is in the organization of the state that the divine has broken through [*eingeschlagen*] into the sphere of actuality; the latter is permeated by the former, and the worldly realm is now justified in and for itself, for its foundation is the divine will, the law of right and freedom. The true reconciliation, whereby the divine realizes itself in the domain of actuality, consists in the ethical and juridical life of the state: this is the authentic discipline [*Subaktion*] of worldliness.[168]

And, finally, he sees the fulfillment of the kingdom of the Spirit in a third direction, in the transition to philosophy. This transition is an enriched return to the first sphere in so far as that first sphere was the presentation of reconciliation in abstract formulation. But, now, that reconciliation is mediation realized in self-positing and self-developing thought where concept and self are identical. More so than previously, Hegel here in 1831 insists that this move to philosophy is not a replacement either for religion or for feeling, which is so characteristic of religion. Rather, here philosophy is the expression of the true content of religion and feeling.[169]

To recapitulate, Hegel has laid out the final presentation of his philosophical reinterpretation of "kingdom of God" as the kingdom of the Spirit in three directions: as the inner-ecclesial dialectic of the realization of reconciliation; as the going over of this inner-ecclesial communitarian dialectical reconciliation into its own actualization as the ethically organized life of the state; and, as the explication of the true content of religiously represented reconciliation, namely, the self-mediation of philosophical thought. With this tri-directional reinterpretation of the development of the kingdom of the Spirit, but especially with the move to self-mediating philosophical thought, Hegel has effectively shown that, and explained why, for him the kingdom of God is the goal of the whole history of reconciliation, of mediation, and of freedom. The kingdom of God is the goal of world history.[170]

As a general observation we can say that, here in the 1831 lectures on the consummate religion, Hegel has, with his identification of the three spheres of the self-development of God as the kingdoms of the Father, of the Son, and of the Spirit, managed further to integrate among themselves, and to relate directly to the kingdom of God, many of the themes fundamental to, or at least characteristic of, Christianity. He has explicated the consummate religion as a movement of divine self-revelation in three spheres and three corresponding ways of God's being present to religious consciousness, namely, thought, representation, and self-consciousness. These three spheres become, each in its own way, three realms of freedom because externality occurs varyingly *within* each of them. Each of these realms is characterized by a variously developed, and dialectically structured, internal movement. Of course, externality also arises as the second moment, but still within the overall movement of divine self-development. Given his own understanding of freedom, we can with certainty say that Hegel interprets the consummate religion, in its various elements and as a whole, as religion of freedom and liberation.[171]

With more particular reference to the first sphere of consummate religion, we can say that Hegel has identified "immanent"

Trinity and the kingdom of the Father. He has even indicated a certain preference for referring to the first sphere as the kingdom of the Father. In asserting that the overall dialectical movement constitutive of the kingdom of the Father occurs again in the kingdom of the Son and in the kingdom of the Spirit, Hegel has effectively foreseen, though his position may not be reduced to, the popular twentieth-century theological thesis that the "immanent" Trinity is, in some sense, the "economic" Trinity. He has interpreted creation, incarnation, and redemption in terms of the kingdom of the Son. He has, in the process, foreshadowed the distinction between the Christ of history and the Christ of faith as well as given a serious presentation of the theme of the death of God. Especially from the moment of realization, in faith, of the divine significance of the death of Christ, he speaks of the history of God.[172] This is a theme apparently more predominant in the earlier lectures, but here clearly associated with the kingdom of the Son. With the kingdom of the Spirit Hegel has, in identifying the Spirit with the presence of God in the community of finite subjects, in fact brought together or, better, identified the religious themes of revelation and grace. Furthermore, he has presented the church as the concrete existence of the kingdom. He has provided a context within which to consider evil and penance, and within which he can effectively speak of the Lord's Supper as the sacrament of the kingdom. With the community seen as the kingdom of the Spirit, Hegel has affirmed a kingdom of truth and love and freedom. He has related this kingdom of the Spirit to everyday life in his assertion that the community finds its actualization in the ethically organized life of the state. Finally, he has given a particularly challenging interpretation to the kingdom of God as interiority. He does this when he sees the enjoyment of the peace of God[173] finding true expression in the renewed immediacy of philosophical thought.

2. *Further Reflections*

Prior to Hegel's efforts, Kant had already given a philosophically formulated moral interpretation to the religious representation "kingdom of God" when he spoke of it as the kingdom of the good. However, already with the first of the Berlin philosophy of religion lectures in 1821 Hegel had gone beyond Kant. He did this by integrating the ethical and the "ontological" in his presentation of the community of spirit. Hegel insisted that it was a question neither of the kingdom alone, nor of God alone, but of both together.

Moreover, the dynamic movement indicated by the notion of the kingdom of God as that to, and into, which one is called provided him with an excellent means of giving religious expression to the concept of inclusive identity as the true infinite. He interpreted this "to" and "into" as the movement or sublation of finite into infinite, the reconciliation of finite and infinite in the as yet religiously expressed true or inclusive infinite. Hegel presented the kingdom of God as inclusive totality, and not any sort of oppressive or smothering totality. Rather, the kingdom of God was totality in the sense that it was the identity *of* difference. It was the infinity *of* finitude. It was the one meant to be respectfully inclusive of the many. Hegel wrapped all these formulations concerning the many and the one, difference and identity, and finitude and infinity up into one when he interpreted the metaphor "kingdom of God" as the movement of spirit as inclusive divine subjectivity.

We can also focus more specifically on Hegel's use of the metaphor during the Berlin years. By the 1831 lectures "kingdom of God" has, in its threefold formulation as the kingdom of the Father, the kingdom of the Son, and the kingdom of the Spirit, proven to be that flexible and overarching religious representation with which Hegel could give religious expression to an interrelationship among the three elements or spheres of the consummate religion. The movement of his thought from 1821 to this position in 1831 should be seen both in terms of shifts and in terms of development. First of all, and especially from the point of view of actual content,[174] the movement needs to be described in terms of shifts. It was above all in 1824 that his various polemical concerns directed his attention away from the richer content and longer presentation of the kingdom of God found in the 1821 manuscript. Presently available sources would indicate that Hegel returned in 1827, and probably more so in 1831, to some of that richer content, but never to so full a development of certain specific aspects as in 1821. In the movement from 1821 to 1831 it would seem he simply left some material behind. But secondly, and particularly from the perspective of structure and integration, the movement of his thought on the kingdom of God from 1821 to 1831 must be seen in terms of a basic and, finally, evident continuity expressible as development. After his 1821 presentation, he goes on, in 1824, to state clearly his speculative definition of religion, and, in 1827, to speak of religion as the development of the concept of God. It is these two steps which allow him, in 1831, to speak of the consummate religion as a dialectical movement of three kingdoms. And it is especially these two advances which make clear that the overall movement in his thought on the kingdom of God from 1821 to 1831 was a making explicit of that which was implicitly presented from 1821 on. His earlier, 1821 affirmation that the kingdom of God finds its objective presentation in the life, teaching, and death of Christ, and its subjective realization in the community of the spirit, comes to a fuller and more developed expression when extended, by means of the more explicit speculative 1824 and 1827 definitions of religion, into the three kingdoms.

A more or less micro-reading of specific philosophy of religion texts has shown the development in Hegel's philosophical interpretation of "kingdom of God." Now a macro-reading by means of brief reference to Hegel's dialectical method will help to indicate that this development is fully consistent with Hegel's general approach to the philosophical reinterpretation of religious representations and with that dialectical method itself.

Hegel's overall philosophical concern is, of course, to overcome alienation in its many forms. We see this in his characteristic, and quite incessant, efforts to bring together or integrate what is often treated separately either in philosophy or in theology. This seemingly innate tendency in Hegel to relate internally, and dialectically to identify, what has previously been maintained more or less only in separation is the essence of what he is about in his philosophical reinterpretation of religion, of religions, and of the consummate religion. This tendency and effort of his finds no clearer expression than in the development of his, we would propose, ever more integrated presentation of the kingdom of God.

Hegel's general, integrative approach to the philosophical reinterpretation of religious representations, and specifically of "kingdom of God," can in fact be recognized as a particular manifestation of his dialectical method at work in the religious realm. In this realm the rhythm of the dialectical method comes to expression as a dialectically developing movement of subjectivity in the form of self-relationality.[175] This method, as we have indicated in previous chapters, is a structured, self-positing, and self-developing movement from beginning through progression to result. The movement constituting this dialectical method is finally, from the perspective of the result, a truly internal one since it is the result as inclusive of beginning and progression. This brief recall of, and summary statement on, Hegel's dialectical method, and its expression in the realm of religion, can help us to see why Hegel's 1821 elaboration of the subjective realization of reconciliation as the community of spirit and the kingdom of God opens the way to a more explicit and inclusive presentation of the kingdom of God in terms of three kingdoms. Hegel has positioned the subjective realization of reconciliation, namely, the kingdom of God, as third and final moment in the triadically structured movement of the consummate religion as beginning, progression, and result. In effect, then, the 1831 lecture presentation of the three kingdoms has, on the level of religion, taken seriously and given appropriate formulation to the dialectic of beginning, progression, and result.

In this review of Hegel on the kingdom of God in the Berlin lectures on the philosophy of religion, we have proceeded under the presupposition that many aspects of twentieth-century interpretations of the religious metaphor "kingdom of God" show parallels in terminology, structure, and even content with Hegel's efforts. Some twentieth-century interpretors, in either direct or perhaps more indirect response to the eschatological challenge in fact, if not in intention, posed by Johannes Weiss and Albert Schweitzer at the turn of the century, focus on explaining the meaning and significance of the metaphor either for Jesus or in the various biblical traditions. There are, again, interpretors who attempt to give a more constructive sociological, philosophical, or theological interpretation of "kingdom of God." From our present perspective these would be of more direct interest. However, some of these refer to, and use, the metaphor very sparingly. We might think of such interpretors as Harvey Cox, Josiah Royce, and Teilhard de Chardin. Others, and these are of particular interest here, continue to use the metaphor while also giving it a certain conceptually expressible content. These range from Gustavo Gutierrez to Walter Rauschenbusch, Karl Barth, Paul Tillich, Ernst

Bloch, Jürgen Moltmann and Wolfhart Pannenberg, Marjorie Suchocki and tens if not hundreds of others. Again, among these we could identify those who tend to speak, in a more particular and almost Kantian way, of the kingdom of God in relation to the good and the moral community. Others, who are of most interest in view of our concern for Hegel's thought, take what could very generally be called a somewhat more Hegelian route and tend to speak of the very being of God when they speak of the kingdom of God.[176] These interpreters can, at least in principle, more easily maintain Hegel's integration of the ethical and the ontological in their interpretations of "kingdom of God." Among those who would follow this more inclusive Hegelian route we could name Karl Barth, who, in a general way followed by Pannenberg, has identified God's rule or kingdom with God's being.[177] And, given Barth's trinitarian interpretation of revelation, would we not need to say Barth has brought together Trinity, revelation, divine being, and kingdom? Moltmann speaks particularly of Joachim of Fiore, but Moltmann's own kingdom of freedom certainly finds at least linguistic parallels in Hegel as well.[178] Without wanting to read Pannenberg in an overly Hegelian direction, we still find it hard not to think of Hegel when Pannenberg speaks of history and the God of the kingdom.[179] Paul Tillich's densely stated formulation of a correlational kingdom would require more attention before anything definitive could be said concerning him in relation to Hegel on the kingdom of God. But Tillich did lecture at length on Hegel's thought.[180]

The presupposition of a certain dependence, on the part of a good number of twentieth-century thinkers, on Hegel for their interpretations of "kingdom of God" seems, intuitively speaking, quite correct. Such a dependence simply contributes to the documentation witnessing to the ongoing twentieth-century Hegel Renaissance. However, despite the evident growth of interest in Hegel during the twentieth century, it often remains difficult to formulate and argue intellectual dependence upon Hegel more precisely. This would seem to be the case for several reasons. First of all, because the dependence would seem to take on a different form in each instance. Second, because there is always Joachim of Fiore, with his thought on the three *status* of the Father, the Son, and the Holy Spirit, lurking in the background as an alternative or, perhaps, additional but more remote influence on twentieth-century thinking.[181] Third, and perhaps the most obvious reason why it is difficult to document direct dependencies, there is the fact that so many twentieth-century thinkers on the kingdom of God do not, despite the overall renewal of interest in Hegel, seem to want to admit any direct dependence on Hegel.

Whatever Hegel's influence may have been on such thinkers, his own efforts philosophically to interpret "kingdom of God" have highlighted many of the issues and questions still being wrestled with in various late twentieth-century approaches toward the reinterpretation of that religious and, more specifically, biblical metaphor "kingdom of God."

NOTES

1 On Hegel on the kingdom of God, note Christian Walther, *Typen des Reich Gottes-Verständnisses* (Munich: Chr. Kaiser, 1961) 60-87; Walter Jaeschke, *Die Suche nach den eschatologischen Wurze ln der Geschichtsphilosophie* (Munich: Chr. Kaiser, 1976) esp. 304-307 in discussion with Michael Theunissen, *Hegels Lehre vom absoluten Geist als theologisch-politischer Traktat* (Berlin: Walter de Gruyter, 1970) and Peter Cornehl, *Die Zukunft der Versöhnung* (Göttingen: Vandenhoeck and Ruprecht, 1971); Wolfgang Röd, "Die Säkularisierung der Reich-Gottes Idee bei Hegel und Marx," in P. Thomas Michels, ed., *Reich Gottes, Kirche, Civitas Dei* (Salzburg: Anton Pustet, 1980) 183-200, esp. on Hegel and with a particular interest in the younger Hegel, pp. 185-192, with discussion pp. 201-214; Michael Beintker, "Herrschaft Gottes/Reich Gottes, VI/2, Neuzeit (ab 1789)," in *Theologische Realenzyklopädie*, vol. 15 (Berlin: Walter de Gruyter, 1986) 226-228. Concerning Hegel's use of the terminology of three kingdoms see Walter Jaeschke, *Die Religionsphilosophie Hegels* 81-83.

2 See Immanuel Kant, *Kants Werke, Akademie-Textausgabe*, vol. 6: *Die Religion innerhalb der Grenzen der bloßen Vernunft, Die Metaphysik der Sitten* (Berlin: Walter de Gruyter, 1968) 1-202/*Religion within the Limits of Reason Alone*, trans. Theodore M. Greene and Hoyt H. Hudson (Chicago: Open Court, 1934). On Kant on the kingdom of God, see Johannes Weiss, *Die Idee des Reiches Gottes in der Theologie*

(Gießen: J. Ricker, 1901) 82-94; Walther, *Typen des Reich-Gottes Verständnisses* 20-41. For brief remarks on the comparison between Kant and Hegel on the kingdom of God, see Brito, *La christologie de Hegel* p. 364 n. 342, p. 365 n. 345, pp. 370-371.

3 Henri Niel, *De la médiation dans la philosophie de Hegel* (Paris: Aubier, 1945) 70 n. 10.

4 It might be helpful to recall that page references to the English translation will be given only when that translation is being directly quoted or when reference is made to footnoted 1831 lecture materials from the first and second Friends Editions. This footnoted material is placed somewhat differently in the new German edition and in the English translation. Concerning Hegel's philosophy of history lectures, see n. 170 below.

5 GW 9:363-421/PS 410-478.

6 *Sämtliche Werke. Jubiläumsausgabe in zwanzig Bänden*, ed. Hermann Glockner, vol. 6: *Enzyklopädie der philosophischen Wissenschaften im Grundrisse und andere Schriften aus der Heidelberger Zeit*, first original edition 1817 (Stuttgart: Frommann, 1927) §§ 465-471; *Encyclopädie der philosophischen Wissenschaften im Grundrisse*, second original edition 1827 (Heidelberg: Oßwald, 1827) §§ 564-571; *Enzyklopädie der philosophischen Wissenschaften im Grundrisse*, third original edition 1830, Philosophische Bibliothek, vol. 33, eds. Friedhelm Nicolin and Otto Pöggeler (Hamburg: Felix Meiner, 1969) §§ 564- 571.

7 *Dritter Cursus. Oberclasse. Begriffslehre und philosophische Encyklopädie*, in G. W. F. Hegel, *Sämtliche Werke. Jubiläumsausgabe in zwanzig Bänden*, ed. Hermann Glockner, vol. 3: *Philosophische Propädeutik, Gymnasialreden und Gutachten über den Philosophie=Unterricht* (Stuttgart: Fr. Frommanns Verlag, 1940) § 207, 2nd paragraph on/*The Philosophical Propaedeutic*, trans. A. V. Miller, eds. Michael George and Andrew Vincent (New York: B. Blackwell, 1986) § 207, 2nd paragraph on.

On Hegel's earlier references to "kingdom of God," including his Tübingen sermon as a theology student, see Brito, *La christologie de Hegel* 26-27, 362-363. In his earliest systematic presentation of religion (1805-1806) Hegel makes several brief references to the kingdom of heaven (*Himmelreich*). See "Naturphilosophie und Philosophie des

Geistes," in *Gesammelte Werke*, vol. 8: *Jenaer Systementwürfe III*, ed. Rolf-Peter Horstmann (Hamburg: Felix Meiner, 1976) 281:23 and 284:19 and 21. On the early Hegel's more "Kantian" interpretation of the kingdom of God and on Hegel's break with this interpretation, see Masakotsu Fujita, *Philosophie und Religion beim jungen Hegel* (Bonn: Bouvier, 1985) 38, 43-44, 92.

8 See Walter Jaeschke, *Die Religionsphilosophie Hegels* 70-71.

9 V 5:291.1-303.402/L 3:375-385. For further detail on these loose sheets see Jaeschke, in V 3:xxix-xxx, and Hodgson, in L 3:6-7.

10 Top of loose sheet 155b in V 5:292.57-62/L 3:377.

11 "Reich Gottes, eine unsichtbare Kirche – aus allen Zonen, verschiedenen Religionen b) äußerliche Kirche; Protestanten und Katholiken; . . . " V 5:292:59-61/L 3:377.

12 Tentatively to be demarcated as loose sheets 162a-165a as reorganized in V 5:294.118-303.402/L 3:378-385.

13 "Aber – Reich Gottes – Intelligenz des Menschen am Höchsten." V 5:300.309-310/L 3:383.

14 "Lehre allgemeiner Boden – Reich Gottes – Liebe – gegen die Welt gänzliche Abrißung." V 5:300.321-322/L 3:383.

15 "Wirkliches Reich Gottes – Gott als Geist in seiner Gemeinde – Region des *Heiligen Geistes*." V 5:301.339-340/L 3:383.

16 E.g., V 5:299.290-294 with 301.336ff/L 3:382 with 383ff.

17 "Einzelheit als solche – Gemeinde, *Geist*." V 5:300.303/L 3:383.

18 On these divisions and subdivisions, see the excellent overview by Hodgson, in L 3:10-23.

19 V 5:49.401-57.587. For a longer commentary on this section of Hegel's manuscript and on the section mentioned in n. 20 immediately below, with special reference to "kingdom of God," see Brito, *La christologie de Hegel* 351ff.

20 V 5:57.588-67.841.

21 "die Erscheinung des Geistes im unmittelbaren Dasein und für die unmittelbare Anschauung." V 5:50.412-413 with 49.401-50.402/L 3:115.

22 E.g., V 5:300.321-322.

23 V 5:50.418-51.435.

24 "Der allgemeine Boden ist das *Himmlische Reich*, das *Reich Gottes*, substantielle, *intellektuelle Welt*, mit *Hinwegwerfung alles Wertes*, der in irdischen, weltlichen Dingen gesucht wird." V 5:50.427-51.430/L 3:116.

25 V 5:51.436-450.

26 V 5:57.600.

27 In this summary I have profited from the overview by Hodgson, in L 3:19.

28 Hodgson speaks of a "fairly detailed exegesis, which has its own rigor, though certainly not of a historical-critical kind." In L 3:19.

29 V 5:47.325.

30 V 5:54.496-497.

31 V 5:54.509-56.560, esp. 54.509-516.

32 See, for example, Norman Perrin, *Jesus and the Language of the Kingdom* (Philadelphia: Fortress, 1976) 29-34, 197-199. On another occasion and from a different perspective one could well begin a study of Hegel's interpretation and use of biblical references with and from an analysis of Hegel's scriptural citations concerning Jesus' proclamation of the coming of the kingdom of God.

33 V 5:56.561-57.587.

34 "die nähere Bestimmung oder eigentliche Bestimmung und Bestimmtheit des Reiches Gottes, nämlich der Zusammenhang seiner selbst mit Gott und der Menschen mit demselben und mit ihm." V 5:56.561-564/L 3:121.

35 V 5:57.588-598. The title is "Leben und Tod," V 5:57.588/L 3:122.

36 V 5:57.599-58.623.

37 "Aber Leben und Tod hat hier noch ein ganz anderes *Verhältnis an der Lehre*; dieser Inhalt ist das *Reich Gottes* – nicht ein Allgemeines Wesen, sondern ein lebendiges *geistiges Leben, eine göttliche Gemeinde*. aa) Lehre als solche das Allgemeine des Inhalts – Reich

Gottes, die erste ewige Idee selbst, aber konkret; bb) Reich Gottes – Geist – ist aus dem Allgemeinen SICH BESTIMMEN, zur *Wirklichkeit* übergehen; diese Bewegung, Prozeß der Bestimmung kommt dem Leben Jesu zu." V 5:57.599-58.606/L 3:123.

38 V 5:59.631-632.

39 "Das Reich Gottes hat also seinen Repräsentanten, d. i. die Weise seiner Existenz zunächst an diesem existierenden Menschen." V 5:59.642-643/L 3:124.

40 V 5:59.648-62.726.

41 V 5:62.727-730.

42 "Revolutionäres Element, insofern es der Welt eine andere Gestalt gegeben. Nichts alle Größe, alles Geltende der Welt – mit hinab in das Grab des Geistes versenkt." V 5:64.778-780/L 3:128-129.

43 "Hier liegt der unmittelbare *Ausdruck der vollkommenen Revolution* gegen das *Bestehende*, in der Meinung Geltende." V 5:65.798-800/L 3:129.

44 V 5:65.805-66.808.

45 V 5:66.808-67.841.

46 V 5:69.916-97.649.

47 V 5:69.916-78.149. See further remarks by Hodgson, in L 3:133-134 n. 185.

48 E.g., V 5:69.921-70.922, 72.976, 76.104-105.

49 V 5:69.921-70.922.

50 V 5:78.142-145.

51 E.g., V 5:76.91-93.

52 "*Diese Sphäre* der unendlichen Liebe *deswegen das Reich des Geistes.*" V 5:71.953-954/L 3:135.

53 V 5:74.26-28.

54 "*Dies der Geist Gottes oder Gott als* gegenwärtiger, wirklicher Geist, *Gott in seiner Gemeinde wohnend.*" V 5:76.96-98, with the whole of p. 76/L 3:140 with 140-141.

55 "und das *Reich Gottes auszubreiten.*" V 5:77.134-135/L 3:142.

56 "das Reich des Geistes; Reich Gottes ist der Geist." V 5:78.142 with 77.135-78.142/L 3:142.

57 V 5:87.399-400.

58 V 5:292.58-60.

59 "Sie ist das Reich Gottes, *die errungene* Gegenwart, *Leben und Erhalten* und Genuß des Geistes." V 5:87.401-402/L 3:151.

60 V 5:87.403-414.

61 "[ein] *vernünftiges* weltliches Reich, *der Idee der Freiheit*, Absolutheit des Rechts gemäß." V 5:87.417-419/L 3:152.

62 "der inneren Gewißheit der Wahrheit die *unmittelbare* Gewißheit des Reiches, aufgenommen, Bürger sein." V 5:88.434-436/L 3:153.

63 V 5:88.441.

64 V 5:89.465-469 with 90.483-484.

65 "Vergehen der Gemeinde." V 5:93.575/L 3:158. Subdivision found in V 5:93.575-97.649/L 3:158-162.

66 "das Untergehen ein übergang zum Himmelreich nur für die einzelnen Subjekte, nicht für die Gemeinde; heiliger Geist als solcher lebt ewig in seiner Gemeinde." V 5:93.578-94.580/L 3:158.

67 Perhaps in the oral presentation Hegel tried to soften this question of the passing of the community by speaking of a "realizing" (*Realisierung*) of the community, which he goes on to say would seem to have to be a "passing away" (*Vergehen*). See the parallel second Friends Edition text as footnoted in V 5:93 to lines 576-581.

68 V 5:94.582.

69 V 5:94.583-95.600.

70 See the second endnote (V 5:338) to the footnote to V 5:94.583-641, where Jaeschke indicates Hegel's apparent reference to Schleiermacher. See also the endnote (V 5:339) to V 5:95.612.

71 V 5:95.599-600. See further in the editor's n. 253 in L 3:159.

72 V 5:95.601-96.640.

73 V 5:96.641-642, 97.647-648.

74 "Religion in die Philosophie sich flüchten." V 5:96.644/L 3:162.

75 For an overview of structural shifts from the 1821 manuscript to the 1824 Griesheim lecture transcript, see the schema by Hodgson, in L 3:54, and for an outline of the 1824 text, Hodgson, in L 3:24-35.

76 By way of entry into these questions see Hodgson, in L 3:24-25 with n. 25.

77 E.g., V 5:147.553-557, 151.682-687.

78 V 5:151.694-700. See Hodgson, in L 3:31-32.

79 Hodgson, in L 3:32.

80 V 5:152.731-734. See Hodgson, in L 3:221, n. 156.

81 V 5:147.564-573. This stress on the content of Christ's teaching can be seen as an exemplification of Hegel's general understanding that religion presents the true content still in an inadequate form. See, e.g., E § 573R.

82 "Die erste [ist] der allgemeine Boden, die zweite ist dann das Besondere, Bestimmte, Konkrete." V 5:147.577-578/L 3:216. This distinction, rooted in the structure of consciousness, reflects Hegel's tendency in the 1824 lectures to highlight and work with a sort of phenomenology of consciousness.

83 V 5:147.578-148.584.

84 V 5:50.427-51.435.

85 "Was durch Lehre also hier zunächst hervorgebracht werden kann, ist der allgemeine Boden für den Begriff Gottes. Dieser kann kurz ausgedrückt werden als das Reich Gottes. Dies ist gelehrt worden; es ist die reale Gottheit, Gott in seinem Dasein, seiner geistigen Wirklichkeit, das Himmelreich. Diese göttliche Realität hat in sich schon Gott und sein Reich, die Gemeinde – ein konkreter Inhalt. Dies ist der Hauptinhalt." V 5:148.584-591/L 3:217.

86 V 5:148.592-595.

87 "Wer sind wir?" V 5:155.807/L 3:224.

88 E.g., V 5:156.858-157.871.

89 E.g., V 5:160.974-161.5.

[90] V 5:155.830-831.

[91] "3. Das dritte zu dieser Wiedergeburt ist der Genuß, das Bewußtsein dieser göttlichen Gnade, das Bewußtsein, Bürger im Reiche Gottes zu sein – das, was mystische Union genannt ist, das Sakrament des Abendmahls, wo auf sinnliche, anschauliche Weise dem Menschen gegeben wird das Bewußtsein seiner Versöhnung mit Gott, das Inwohnen und Einkehren des Geistes in ihm." V 5:166.127-132/L 3:235-236.

[92] "Das Jetzt des Genusses zerrinnt in der Vorstellung teils in ein Jenseits, in einen jenseitigen Himmel, teils in Vergangenheit, teils in Zukunft." V 5:167.180-182/L 3:237. And see the reference in n. 99 below.

[93] "So steht der Gemeinde, dem Reiche Gottes in der Gemeinde, eine Objektivität überhaupt gegenüber." V 5:167.185-187/L 3:237.

[94] V 5:167.185-191.

[95] V 5:167.191-168.192.

[96] "so bilden sich in Rücksicht auf das Reich des Geistes drei Stufen." V 5:176.439-440/L 3:247.

[97] V 5:176.440-443.

[98] "diese Idee, die Idee des Geistes, der sich zu sich selbst verhält, das Selbstbewußtsein des absoluten Geistes." V 3:222.667-668/L 1:318 (trans. amended).

[99] V 5:119.650-122.761. For an excellent schematic presentation of these four frameworks, see Hodgson, in L 3:26-27.

[100] It may simply be that the Lasson text and the three student transcripts have not retained such a reference made by Hegel during the lectures.

[101] Hodgson, in L 3:43. On the 1827 lectures see Hodgson, in L 3:36-47.

[102] E.g., V 3:266.37-41 with lines 48-50 and V 3:277.383-385.

[103] V 3:266.42-47.

[104] The 1821 text, V 5:50.410-69.915; the 1824 text, V 5:147.552-153.762; the 1827 text, V 5:239.769-251.24.

105 Hodgson, in L 3:43.

106 Approximately V 5:239.769-244.895.

107 Approximately V 5:245.896-251.24.

108 V 5:147.564-573.

109 V 5:83.404-414.

110 "Wenn die Gemeinde erst etabliert ist, wenn das Reich Gottes sein Dasein, seine Wirklichkeit erlangt hat, so haben diese Lehren mehr andere Bestimmungen oder man läßt sie auf der Seite liegen." V 5:240.800-804/L 3:317.

111 V 5:241.804-812.

112 "Diese Versöhntheit, als Zustand ausgesprochen, ist das Reich Gottes, eine Wirklichkeit." V 5:241.812-813/L 3:318.

113 V 5:241.816.

114 V 5:241.822-824.

115 "in die Wahrheit, in das Reich Gottes . . . Diesem Reiche, dieser intellektuellen, geistigen Welt ist es, da der Mensch angehören soll." V 5:243.858-860/L 3:319.

116 "Diese zweite Betrachtung erst führt auf das Religiöse als solches, wo das Göttliche selbst wesentliches Moment ist." V 5:245.896-897/L 3:322.

117 V 5:245.910. Regarding 1821, see V 5:56.561-564, where Hegel speaks more generally of *Zusammenhang*, whereas here the word for relation is *Verhältnis*.

118 V 5:245.909-917.

119 "Die Grundbestimmung in diesem Reiche Gottes ist die Gegenwart Gottes." V 5:245.918-919/L 3:322.

120 V 5:246.921-248.936 with 248.937-251.24.

121 "Die Realisierung des Geistigen der Gemeinde." V 5:262.293/L 3:339.

122 "das Subjekt selbst Geist and damit Bürger des Reiches Gottes wird." V 5:252.38/L 3:329.

123 V 5:254.82-89.

124 "das Subjekt wesentlich Beziehung darauf hat und Bürger des Reiches Gottes sein soll." V 5:254.95-96/L 3:331.

125 V 5:262.294-303. For an overview of this third subsection, see Schlitt, *Hegel's Trinitarian Claim* 217-223.

126 "das Selbst, das Subjekt ist dann zugleich die Seite dieser geistigen Gegenwart, nach der eine entwickelte Weltlichkeit in ihm vorhanden ist, und das Reich Gottes, die Gemeinde hat so ein Verhältnis zum Weltlichen. Da nun die Versöhnung real sei, dazu gehört, da in dieser Entwicklung, in dieser Totalität ebenso die Versöhnung gewußt werde, vorhanden, hervorgebracht sei." V 5:262.303-308/L 3:339.

127 V 5:262.322-263.329.

128 V 5:263.330-265.389.

129 V 5:264.374-265.386. In order to qualify further this rather bourgeois reading of "kingdom of God" it would be necessary to explore Hegel's remarks in other areas of thought such as in his *Philosophy of Right*. By way of entry into this question, see Paul Lakeland, *The Politics of Salvation: The Hegelian Idea of the State* (Albany: State University of New York Press, 1984). And note Hegel's further discussion of the relationship between religion and state in the 1831 lectures, which are briefly reviewed below. See, e.g., n. 168 below.

130 V 5:254.82-89 with 198.660-662.

131 See, e.g., V 3:269.129-273.243.

132 V 5:260.268-272, 261.290-262.292

133 For a helpful overview of the consummate religion in the 1831 lectures, see Hodgson, in L 3:47-53, 56-57.

134 V 3:339.1-347.318 with V 5:289.380-398.

135 See Walter Jaeschke, "Hegel's Last Year in Berlin," in *Hegel's Philosophy of Action*, eds. Lawrence S. Stepelevich and David Lamb (Atlantic Highlands, NJ: Humanities, 1983) 31-48.

136 V 3:222.667-668, cited in n. 98 above.

137 In V 3:266.42-47 Hegel says this, technically speaking, in relation to the philosophy of religion. However, it can be said of

religion as such when this text is taken in conjunction with V 3:277.382-281.443.

138 "Dies ist der Begriff der Religion, da Gott sich weiß im Geiste und der Geist sich in Gott." V 3:354.130-131/L 1:465 (trans. slightly amended).

139 "Wir haben die Religion näher bestimmt als Selbstbewußtsein Gottes; . . . Gott ist Selbstbewußtsein; er weiß sich in einem von ihm verschiedenen Bewußtsein, das an sich das Bewußtsein Gottes ist, aber auch für sich, indem es seine Identität mit Gott weiß – eine Identität, die aber vermittelt ist durch die Negation der Endlichkeit. – Dieser Begriff macht den Inhalt der Religion aus." V 5:177 note to lines 3-14/L 3:249-250 n. 3.

140 Note, for example, Hegel's initial description of the freedom of the concept: "Die Freiheit des Begriffs ist selbst die absolute Beziehung auf sich, die Identität, die auch die Unmittelbarkeit ist, vermittlungslose Einheit." V 5:274.128-130/"The freedom of the concept is itself absolute self-relatedness, the identity that is also immediacy, unity devoid of mediation." L 3:355. On Christianity, see V 5:275.154-177.

141 Hodgson, in L 3:50-51. On Hegel's tripartite division, see V 5:280.67-281.96, 199-200 note to line 688.

142 V 5:279.1-289.398.

143 V 5:177-270.

144 V 5:271.1-276.209.

145 The footnoting of materials in the German edition and explicit correlations indicated in the English translation, L 3, greatly facilitate relating the various texts.

146 V 5:280.67-281.75.

147 Note especially the following texts: V 5:280.68-69, 281.76-82, 281.97-282.131, p. 199 note to line 688, pp. 208-210 note to lines 916-925, p. 247 n./L 3:362-364, p. 274 n. 67, pp. 283-285 n. 93, p. 324 n. 199. When referring to the various spheres, the Strauss and Friends Editions texts speak, seemingly without any particularly important nuance, in various ways of "sphere" (*Sphäre*), "part" (*Teil*), "determination" (*Bestimmung*), and "element" (*Element*).

148 Dies ist das erste Verhältnis, das nur für das denkende Subjekt ist, welches von dem reinen Inhalt allein eingenommen ist. Dies ist das Reich des Vaters." V 5:199 note to line 688/L 3:274 n. 67.

149 V 5:199 note to line 688 with p. 210 continuation of the note to V 5:208.916-925.

150 "Hierher, obgleich es das Reich des Vaters vorzugsweise heißt, fällt also dennoch die Lehre von der Dreieinigkeit." V 5:281.80-82/L 3:362. Walter Jaeschke sees in this phrase Hegel's own admission that the term "kingdom of the Father" does not fit exactly this first element. *Die Vernunft in der Religion* 318. Note also Hodgson's qualifying statement in L 3:362-363 n. 8. It might be helpful as well to recall that we are here dealing with Strauss's summary wording.

151 On representation, see V 5:281.83-84, pp. 199-200 note to line 688/L 3:363, p. 274 n. 67). On this second sphere as a whole, note especially the following: V 5:199-200 note to line 688, pp. 218-219 note to line 190, pp. 235-237 note to lines 701-755, pp. 240-241 note to line 803, pp. 244-245 note to lines 893-895, pp. 246-248 note to lines 929-17, V 5:280.70-71, 281.83-94, 282.132-287.316/L 3:274-275 note 67, pp. 294-295 note 128, pp. 314-315 note 173, p. 317 note 183, p. 321 note 196, pp. 362-363, pp. 365-371. Strauss's more generous excerpts of this second sphere surely reflect his Christological interests. For a helpful summary of this second sphere, see Hodgson, in L 3:51-53 and 56, with a comparison of the structure of the 1831 lectures on the consummate religion to the structures of the earlier lectures on pp. 54-55.

152 "erhält . . . der Sohn die Bestimmung als Anderes." V 5:200 note/L 3:274 n. 67. See also, e.g., V 5:282.132-140/L 3:365.

153 V 5:281.84-86, 282.135-139, 200 note/L 3:363, 365, 274-275 n. 67.

154 V 5:219 note with pp. 235-237 note to lines 201-755/L 3:294 n. 128 with pp. 314-315 n. 173.

155 E.g., V 5:285.221-232/L 3:368.

156 V 5:284.184-285.228 with 285.244-248/L 3:367-368 with 369. See Hodgson, in L 3:53. We might note as well that Hegel maintains his earlier distinction between the teaching of Christ and the doctrine of the church. E.g., V 5:240-241 note to line 803/L 3:317 n. 183. The

limited materials available on the 1831 lectures present Hegel as referring explicitly to kingdom of God only once, and then with reference to the force with which Christ's teaching strikes one. See V 5:284.207-210.

157 V 5:285.238-244 with pp. 244-245 note to lines 893-895 and pp. 246-248 note to lines 929-17/L 3:369 with p. 321 n. 196 and pp. 323-325 n. 199. It is, however, not necessary at this point to enter into the differing syllogistic formulations of this dialectical movement in the various spheres.

158 V 5:286.290-291/L 3:370.

159 V 5:281.76-77 and lines 83-84 with p. 247 note/L 3:362-363 with pp. 323-324 n. 199.

160 V 5:286.291-292 with 281.92-94/L 3:370 with 363.

161 "Dessen element ist das Selbstbewußtsein des Menschen, mit Gott versöhnt zu sein und die Vollbringung dieses Bewußtseins in Kirche und Kultus." V 5:281.94-96/L 3:363. On the 1831 lectures note particularly the following texts: V 5:281.72-73, 281.94-96, 287.317-289.398, p. 200 note, p. 259 note to line 242, p. 260 note to line 267, pp. 260-261 notes to lines 275, 278, 284, and 289, p. 264 note to line 378, p. 266 note to line 444, pp. 268-269 note to line 497/L 3:362, 363, 371-374, p. 275 n. 67, p. 336 n. 235, p. 337 n. 239, p. 338 nn. 240, 243, and 244, p. 342 n. 250, p. 344 n. 258, p. 346 n. 265.

162 V 5:289.366-368 with 287.318-329, 288.330-332 and 289.373-379.

163 V 5:287.325-329.

164 V 5:288.346-348.

165 V 5:288.331.

166 V 5:288.345-346 and 348-351.

167 V 5:289.366-368.

168 "In der Organisation des Staates ist es, wo das Göttliche in die Wirklichkeit eingeschlagen, diese von jenem durchdrungen und das Weltliche nun an und für sich berechtigt ist, denn ihre Grundlage ist der göttliche Wille, das Gesetz des Rechts und der Freiheit. Die wahre Versöhnung, wodurch das Göttliche sich im Felde der

Wirklichkeit realisiert, besteht in dem sittlichen und rechlichen Staatsleben: Dies ist die wahrhafte Subaktion der Weltlichkeit." V 5:264 note to line 378/L 3:342 n. 250. On the relationship between religion and state in Hegel, in addition to Lakeland, *The Politics of Salvation*, see, for example: James Yerkes, *The Christology of Hegel* 132-142, 158-160; Walter Jaeschke, "Staat aus christlichem Prinzip und christlicher Staat: Zur Ambivalenz der Berufung auf das Christentum in der Rechtsphilosophie Hegels und der Restauration," in *Der Staat: Zeitschrift für Staatslehre, öffentliches Recht, und Verfassungsgeschichte* 18 (1979) 349-374; _____, "Christianity and Secularity in Hegel's Concept of the State," *The Journal of Religion* 61 (1981) 127-145; _____, *Die Vernunft in der Religion* 271-273 and 356-358. Note Hegel's longer 1831 treatment of the relationship between religion and state in V 3:339.1-347.318, 360.339-363.426. On the ethical (*Sittliche, Sittlichkeit*), see further references and brief remarks in L 3:341 n. 249.

[169] V 5:289.393-398, pp. 268-269 note to line 497/L 3:374, 346 n. 265.

[170] Beintker observes, "Als Zielpunkt umfassender Versöhnung zwischen Subjekt und Objekt, Göttlichem und Menschlichem, Glaube und Denken, Individuum und Gesellschaft bildet das Reich des Geistes bei G. W. F. Hegel den unauffälligen Motor aller Entwicklungen in der Geschichte der Menschheit." "Neuzeit," in *Theologische Realenzyklopädie* vol. 15 p. 226.

On Hegel's interpretation of the kingdom of God in the philosophy of world history lectures, see Walther, *Typen des Reich-Gottes-Verständnisses* 60- 61, 69-87. And note Hegel's reference to the three historical periods of the Germanic world respectively as the kingdom of the Father, the kingdom of the Son, and the kingdom of the Spirit in *Vorlesungen über die Philosophie der Weltgeschichte*, vol. 4: *Die germanische Welt*, Philosophische Bibliothek, vol. 171 d (Hamburg: Felix Meiner, 1976) 766, and on world history in general, see p. 881.

[171] V 5:279.15-16 and 22. As Henri Niel correctly observes concerning religion in general, "On ne saurait trop insister sur ce fait que, pour Hegel, la catégorie fondamentale du religieux est la catégorie de libération." *De la médiation dans la philosophie de Hegel* 340.

[172] V 5:286.287-287.294.

[173] "Peace of God" (*der Friede Gottes*) is a term here borrowed from Hegel's 1827 lectures. See V 5:269.507.

[174] "Content" is used here in a very general sense and not with any specifically Hegelian meaning in mind.

[175] On Hegel's dialectical method, see especially GW 12:236.1-253.34/GL 824-845.

[176] This is not to say that one group is Kantian and the other Hegelian in the sense that the groups are, respectively, necessarily directly dependent on Kant or Hegel, but only that we can begin to discern two basic approaches distinguishing these twentieth-century thinkers' orientations. Furthermore, for present purposes the Kant here spoken of can be restricted more specifically to the Kant of *Religion within the Limits of Reason Alone*. See n. 2 above.

[177] This identification of God's rule and God's being is intimated by Karl Barth already in the second edition of *The Epistle to the Romans* (New York: Oxford University Press, 1968), e.g., 215-216 with 525. Wolfhart Pannenberg speaks of this identification in *Theology and the Kingdom of God* (Philadelphia: Westminster, 1969) 55-56.

[178] Jürgen Moltmann, *The Trinity and the Kingdom* (New York: Harper and Row, 1981).

[179] Pannenberg, *Theology and the Kingdom of God*.

[180] Paul Tillich, *Systematic Theology*, vol. 3 (Chicago: The University of Chicago Press, 1963) 297-423. Note that Hodgson, in "Hegel's Christology" 38 n. 15, cites Tillich, *Systematic Theology* vol. 3 pp. 400ff, in pointing out that Tillich does employ the Hegelian expression "spiritual community."

[181] On Joachim of Fiore see, for example, the very helpful study by Bernard McGinn, *The Calabrian Abbot* (New York: Macmillan, 1985) 161-203.

CONCLUSION

Understanding Hegel, his philosophy in general and his philosophy of religion in particular, is no easy task. Though we today find ourselves at some time and mental distance from his day and age, we still find ourselves referring back to him time and again as we struggle to discover and articulate meaning in a quickly changing world. Hegel seems to serve as a particularly important point of reference. He is a convenient point of reference because he is perhaps the last of those great philosophers who managed to find every aspect of the human phenomenon significant. He studied what we would today divide up into the natural sciences, the humanities, and the social and political sciences. As we have seen, he found religion very significant.

Our century's renewed interest in Hegel, what we have called the twentieth-century Hegel Renaissance has surely helped to bridge the gap between his day and ours, between his way of thinking and ours. In the light of so many studies we are surely coming to something of a consensus on what Hegel was about. It would seem that, as we head toward the twenty-first century, we are better able to place Hegel in a certain philosophical context. There would seem to be growing agreement on the overall nature of his philosophy. We more clearly appreciate that he struggled with universal questions which are still ours today. In fact, it becomes clearer and clearer that his is a philosophy of subjectivity. He is concerned with what it means to be subject. He is preoccupied with the question of how to be whole and real in what comes across as a splintered and suffering world.

Hegel saw that wholeness and unity, identity and oneness, come into being out of that very splintering and suffering. He looked at difference and at multiplicity, and spoke of contradiction. But he took a second look and saw that wholeness arises out of disparateness. To be more exact, he thought contradiction through until the unity latent in it came to mind. This was the essence of his notion of the speculative. For speculative thinking was the grasping of the unity of those things which were opposed.[1] In his 1821 lectures on the philosophy of religion Hegel wrote of the speculative as the true and as the awareness that God is the self-determining unity of all which is opposed or contradictory.[2] He sketched out a theory of religion as the sphere in which the universal and the individual are no longer merely opposed, but also reconciled. In 1824 he spelled out more explicitly what a full theory of the truly speculative implied.[3] He argued that any reconciliation of individual and universal would come about within a more inclusive movement. It must occur within a movement of spirit which knows itself and is conscious of itself. Spirit conscious of itself is the speculative concept, Hegel said. Religion and philosophy, each in its own way, are instantiations of this speculative concept. Each of these instances of spirit is, again in its own way, first, the moment of pure thought without differentiation. Then, especially with reference to religion but also, in a sense, regarding philosophy, each enters into the distinction of subject and object. Distinction arises because we are speaking of one or another form of consciousness. But this distinction is internal to the concept and is the realization of the concept. The speculative comes to the fore in the sense that the first moment, and its realization, are thought in their identity. This is the overall structure and movement of spirit with which Hegel worked as he gave his various Berlin lectures on the philosophy of religion. This integrating speculative movement of spirit is, for Hegel, inclusive divine subjectivity.

Hegel's philosophy, and especially his philosophy of religion, is an effort at comprehensive presentation. His understanding of spirit as a movement of self-relationality in the form of an inclusive divine subjectivity was an effort to leave nothing aside. He wanted his philosophy to include every aspect of spirit. This intention toward inclusivity, and the fervor with which Hegel pursued it, render the study of his philosophy most rewarding. They also make the study very difficult. But coming to terms with Hegel's philosophy as a philosophy of subjectivity, and with his philosophy of religion as a movement of inclusive divine subjectivity, should help us understand his project and its greatness. Seeing his philosophy in this light should help us understand what he is about.

It is one thing to come to an understanding of Hegel's philosophy – and here in the present context we are thinking primarily of his philosophy of religion. But it is quite another to come to an understanding *with* that philosophy. Hegel's intention toward inclusion is also a claim. Many aspects of this claim and of its interpretation are highly disputed. This is, of course, the case with so much of what Hegel said, or might not have said. There are bound to be vague, or at least differently interpreted, points in such a massive project as Hegel's. Be this as it may, there is a certain minimum which I would think we must admit if we want to remain faithful to the Hegelian corpus and to the spirit of Hegel's thought. That minimum would be the need to admit that Hegel proposed an overall understanding of the speculative movement of spirit, an understanding which he considered of permanent value. Hegel will not let the informed reader simply set aside this understanding of spirit. For him the movement of spirit is, in principle, inclusive and does not permit end-run appeals to other experiences. Given Hegel's claim, it is not possible simply to appeal to other experiences out of which one can then philosophize in a new way.

Hegel's inclusive intention, and claim, is such that the informed reader must find a way of coming to an understanding with that claim. If I might be permitted to pick up again on remarks made at the end of Chapter Seven above, I would suggest that there are at least three attitudes or stances which we can take vis-à-vis Hegel's philosophy, and especially his philosophy of religion. The first of these is a more sympathetic and positive reading of that philosophy. Hopefully, then, an enthusiastic reading as well. If we see in Hegel's overall understanding of the dynamic of spirit the appropriate, and arguable, expression of what it means to be subject, and of how that dynamic plays itself out, then we can come to terms with various deficiencies of his thought and with its historical contingencies.

The second of these possible attitudes or stances would be a more negative reading and, consequently, a rejection both of Hegel's project and of the general way in which he thought it needed to be carried it out. Hegel can be rejected for a variety of reasons. But he really will not permit us to reject him merely for extrinsic reasons. He insists that there is nothing finally extrinsic to his understanding of spirit. And he usually is comprehensive and clever enough already to have foreseen, at least in principle, most extrinsic argumentation with which we might challenge his position. So the informed reader will effectively be forced to check out the internal dynamics of Hegel's presentation of spirit and make his or her rejection of Hegel stand on the basis of that critical analysis. On the basis of an internal critique one might want to say that Hegel's understanding of spirit simply does not work. Then one could simply set Hegel aside. There are other thinkers and other approaches to which one can turn.

There is a third attitude, or stance, possible vis-à-vis Hegel, his philosophy, and his overall understanding of spirit. This attitude consists in a reading of Hegel which is both sympathetic and critical. Sympathetic to his project and yet critical to the way in which it was actually carried out. Sympathetic in principle to his notion of spirit as speculative movement of inclusion and integration, but critical with regard to the specific formulation of certain basic aspects of that process. I would personally tend to identify with this way of coming to an understanding with Hegel. Perhaps I could be permitted to conjure up several aspects of one of several possible profiles of someone who would read Hegel from this perspective. Such a reader might insist that Hegel was concerned with, and discussed, many issues which remain important today. This reader would suggest that we, in our own day, remain conditioned, and even constituted in our self-awareness, by a quest for social and personal meaning similar to the one on which Hegel embarked. Liberation, freedom, and the longing for a richer life remain our fundamental social and personal goals. Furthermore, one who reads Hegel from this perspective might well be convinced that meaning, freedom, and enrichment must be understood in terms of an appropriate theory of subjectivity. She or he would appreciate Hegel's stress on wholeness and his interest in understanding the dynamic movement of spirit in terms of inclusive divine subjectivity. Such a reader would, nevertheless, hesitate to accept certain aspects of Hegel's understanding of the dynamic of spirit. To this extent the reader would identify him or herself with the second, more negative attitude or stance indicated above. On the one hand, it would seem that fundamental aspects of the way in which Hegel envisions the dynamic of spirit need to be revamped in order better to express inclusion and wholeness. Yet, on the other hand, such a reader would not want simply to pick and choose piecemeal from the many insights Hegel has gathered. In light of these two considerations, if one were to take up some form of this critically appreciative attitude toward Hegel and his project, one would have to propose another understanding of the dynamic of spirit as a movement of subjectivity. One would want to propose an understanding of spirit which would allow one to work coherently and in a systematic way with the riches of Hegel's thought. The "one" we are referring to here remains ambiguous. Such a project will surely have to be the result of the cooperative work of many. The challenge for such readers would seem to be to find an understanding of spirit which would allow them to do three things. They would need to develop an understanding of spirit which would permit them to maintain Hegel's speculative insight, to respond to what they find untenable in his formulation of the movement of spirit, and systematically to incorporate the ever-surprising richness of his insights.

It may well be that we could delineate further possible attitudes or stances one could adopt vis-à-vis Hegel, his philosophy, and his philosophy of religion. But, whatever they might be, we cannot simply remain neutral, we cannot stand indifferent before Hegel's philosophy or divine subjectivity.

NOTES

1 E § 82.

2 V 3:114.119-116.452.

3 V 3:55.614-56.646.

BIBLIOGRAPHY OF WORKS CITED

1. G. W. F. Hegel's Works

Early Writings

Hegels theologische Jugendschriften. Edited by Hermann Nohl. Tübingen: Mohr, 1907.

Early Theological Writings. Translated by T. M. Knox. Chicago: University of Chicago Press, 1948.

Jena Writings

Differenz des Fichte'schen und Schelling'schen Systems der Philosophie. In *Gesammelte Werke.* Vol. 4: *Jenaer kritische Schriften.* Pp. 1-92. Edited by Hartmut Buchner and Otto Pöggeler. Hamburg: Felix Meiner, 1968.

The Difference between Fichte's and Schelling's System of Philosophy. Translation by H. S. Harris and Walter Cerf. Albany: State University of New York Press, 1977.

Glauben und Wissen. In *Gesammelte Werke.* Vol. 4: *Jenaer kritische Schriften.* Pp. 313-414. Edited by Hartmut Buchner and Otto Pöggeler. Hamburg: Felix Meiner, 1968.

Faith and Knowledge. Translation by Walter Cerf and H. S. Harris. Albany: State University of New York Press, 1977.

"Naturphilosophie und Philosophie des Geistes." In *Gesammelte Werke*. Vol. 8: *Jenaer Systementwürfe III*. Edited by Rolf-Peter Horstmann. Hamburg: Felix Meiner, 1976.

Nürnberg

Dritter Cursus. Oberclasse. Begriffslehre und philosophische Encyklopädie. In *Sämtliche Werke. Jubiläumsausgabe in zwanzig Bänden*. Edited by Hermann Glockner. Vol. 3: *Philosophische Propädeutik, Gymnasialreden und Gutachten über den Philosophie=Unterricht*. Stuttgart: Fr. Frommanns Verlag, 1940.

The Philosophical Propaedeutic. Translated by A. V. Miller. Edited by Michael George and Andrew Vincent. New York: B. Blackwell, 1986.

Phenomenology of Spirit

Gesammelte Werke. Vol. 9: *Phänomenologie des Geistes*. Edited by Wolfgang Bonsiepen and Reinhard Heede. Hamburg: Felix Meiner, 1980.

Phenomenology of Spirit. Translated by A. V. Miller. New York: Oxford, 1977.

Science of Logic

Gesammelte Werke. Vol. 11: *Wissenschaft der Logik. Erster Band: Die objektive Logik (1812-1813)*; Vol. 12: *Wissenschaft der Logik. Zweiter Band: Die subjektive Logik (1816)*; Vol. 21: *Wissenschaft der Logik. Erster Band: Die objektive Logik (1832)*. Edited by Friedrich Hogemann and Walter Jaeschke. Hamburg: Felix Meiner, 1978, 1981, 1985.

Hegel's Science of Logic. Translated by A. V. Miller. New York: Humanities, 1969.

Outline of the Philosophy of Right

Grundlinien der Philosophie des Rechts. Philosophische Bibliothek. Vol. 124a. Edited by Johannes Hoffmeister. Hamburg: Felix Meiner, 1967.

Outline of the Philosophy of Right. Translated by T. M. Knox. Oxford: Oxford University Press, 1952.

Encyclopedia

Sämtliche Werke. Jubiläumsausgabe in zwanzig Bänden. Edited by Hermann Glockner. Vol. 6. *Enzyklopädie der philosophischen Wissenschaften im Grundrisse und andere Schriften aus der Heidelberger Zeit.* First original edition 1817. Stuttgart: Frommann, 1927.

Encyclopädie der philosophischen Wissenschaften im Grundrisse. Second original edition 1827. Heidelberg: Oßwald, 1827.

Enzyklopädie der philosophischen Wissenschaften im Grundrisse. Third original edition 1830. Philosophische Bibliothek. Vol. 33. Edited by Friedhelm Nicolin and Otto Pöggeler. Hamburg: Felix Meiner, 1969.

Hegel's Logic. Translation of E, Part One, by William Wallace. Oxford: Clarendon, 1975.

Hegel's Philosophy of Nature. 3 vols. Translation of E, Part Two, by M. J. Petry. New York: Humanities, 1970.

Hegel's Philosophy of Mind. Translation of E, Part Three, by William Wallace. Oxford: Clarendon, 1975.

Hegel's Philosophy of Subjective Spirit. Translation of E, the first section of Part Three, by M. J. Petry. Dordrecht: Riedel, 1979.

Review Articles

Review of "Über die Hegelsche Lehre oder: absolutes Wissen und moderner Pantheismus," 2. "Über Philosophie überhaupt und Hegels Enzyklopädie der philosophischen Wissenschaften insbesondere. Ein Beitrag zur Beurteilung der letzteren. Von Dr. K. E. Schubarth und Dr. L. Cargonico." In *Berliner Schriften 1818-1831.* Philosophische Bibliothek. Vol. 240 pp. 339-402. Edited by Johannes Hoffmeister. Hamburg: Felix Meiner, 1956.

Lectures on the Philosophy of History

Vorlesungen über die Philosophie der Weltgeschichte. Auf Grund der Handschriften herausgegeben. Philosophische Bibliothek. Vol. 171a. Edited by Johannes Hoffmeister. Vol. 171b-d. Edited by Georg Lasson. Hamburg: Felix Meiner, 1970, 1976.

Lectures on the Philosophy of Religion

Werke. Vollständige Ausgabe durch einen Verein von Freunden des Verewigten. Vols. 11-12: *Vorlesungen über die Philosophie der religion. Nebst einer Schrift über die Beweise vom Daseyn Gottes.* Edited by Philipp Marheineke. Berlin: Duncker und Humblot, 1832.

Werke, Vollständige Ausgabe durch einen Verein von Freunden des Verewigten. Second edition. Vols. 11-12: *Vorlesungen über die Philosophie der Religion. Nebst einer Schrift über die Beweise vom Daseyn Gottes.* Edited by Philipp Marheineke [and Bruno Bauer]. Berlin: Duncker und Humblot, 1840.

Vorlesungen über die Philosophie der Religion. Philosophische Bibliothek. Vols. 59, 60, 61, 63 bound in two volumes. Edited by Georg Lasson. Hamburg: Felix Meiner, 1925, reprinted 1974.

Religionsphilosophie. Edited by Karl-Heinz Ilting. Vol. 1: *Die Vorlesung von 1821.* Naples: Bibliopolis, 1978.

Vorlesungen. Ausgewählte Nachschriften und Manuskripte. Vol. 3: *Vorlesungen über die Philosophie der Religion. Teil 1: Einleitung. Der Begriff der Religion.* Vol. 4: *Vorlesungen über die Philosophie der Religion. Teil 2: Die bestimmte Religion. a: Text. b: Anhang.* Vol. 5: *Vorlesungen über die Philosophie der Religion. Teil 3: Die vollendete Religion.* Edited by Walter Jaeschke. Hamburg: Felix Meiner, 1983, 1985, 1984.

Gesammelte Werke. Vol. 17: *Vorlesungsmanuskripte I (1816-1831).* Edited by Walter Jaeschke. Hamburg: Felix Meiner, 1987.

The Christian Religion: Lectures on the Philosophy of Religion, Part III: *The Revelatory, Consummate, Absolute Religion.* Edited and translated by Peter C. Hodgson. Missoula, Mont.: Scholars Press, 1979.

Lectures on the Philosophy of Religion. Vol. 1: *Introduction and The Concept of Religion;* Vol. 2: *Determinate Religion;* Vol. 3: *The Consummate Religion.* Edited by Peter C. Hodgson. Translation by R. F. Brown, P. C. Hodgson, and J. M. Stewart with the assistance of J. P. Fitzer (L 1) and H. S. Harris. Berkeley: University of California Press, 1984, 1987, 1985.

2. Secondary Litterature

Ahlers, Rolf. Review of *Die Idee als Ideal: Trias und Tripliziät bei Hegel*, by Katharina Comoth. In *The Owl of Minerva* 19 (1988) 194-200.

Atherton, J. Patrick. "The Neoplatonic 'One' and the Trinitarian 'APXH.'" In *The Significance of Neoplatonism*. Pp. 173-185. Edited by R. Baine Harris. Norfolk, VA: International Society for Neoplatonic Studies, Old Dominion University, 1976.

Barth, Karl. *The Epistle to the Romans*. New York: Oxford University Press, 1968.

Beintker, Michael. "Herrschaft Gottes/Reich Gottes, VI/2, Neuzeit (ab 1789)." In *Theologische Realenzyklopädie*. Vol. 15 pp. 226-228. Berlin: Walter de Gruyter, 1986.

Beyer, Wilhelm Raimund, ed. *Hegel Jahrbuch 1979*. Cologne: Pahl-Rugenstein, 1980.

_____. *Hegel Jahrbuch 1980*. Cologne: Pahl-Rugenstein, 1981.

Brito, Emilio. *La christologie de Hegel*. Paris: Beauchesne, 1983.

_____. Review of *Hegel's Trinitarian Claim*, by Dale M. Schlitt. In *Revue théologique de Louvain* 17 (1986) 368-369.

Brown, Robert F. "Hegel's Lectures on the Philosophy of Religion: A Progress Report on the New Edition." *The Owl of Minerva* 14, 3 (1983) 1-6.

Bubner, Rüdiger. *Zur Sache der Dialektik*. Stuttgart: Reclam, 1980.

Burbidge, John. *On Hegel's Logic. Fragments of a Commentary*. Atlantic Highlands, NJ: Humanities Press, 1981.

_____. "The Syllogisms of Revealed Religion, or the Reasonableness of Christianity." *The Owl of Minerva* 18 (1986) 29-42.

Butler, Clark. "Commentary." In G. W. F. Hegel. *Hegel: The Letters*. Translated by Clark Butler and Christiane Seiler with commentary by Clark Butler. Bloomington: Indiana University Press, 1984.

Comoth, Katharina. "Hegels 'Logik' und die spekulative Mystik." In *Hegel Studien*. Vol. 19 pp. 65-93. Bonn: Bouvier, 1984.

_____. *Die Idee als Ideal. Trias und Triplizität bei Hegel.* Heidelberg: Carl Winter Universitätsverlag, 1986.

Cornehl, Peter. *Die Zukunft der Versöhnung.* Göttingen: Vandenhoeck and Ruprecht, 1971.

Croce, Benedetto. *Ciò che è vivo e ciò che è morto della filosofia di Hegel.* Bari: Laterza, 1907.

_____. *What Is Living and What Is Dead in the Philosophy of Hegel.* Translated by Douglas Ainslie. London: Macmillan, 1915.

Dilthey, Wilhelm. *Die Jugendgeschichte Hegels.* Berlin: Reimer, 1905.

Doniela, William V. "Identity and Difference: Social Source of Hegel's Logic." In *Hegel-Jahrbuch* 1980. Pp. 39-43. Edited by Wilhelm Raimund Beyer. Cologne: Pahl-Rugenstein, 1981.

Düsing, Klaus. "Hegels Begriff der Subjektivität in der Logik und in der Philosophie des subjektiven Geistes." In *Hegels philosophische Psychologie. Hegel-Tage Margherita. Hegel-Studien.* Beiheft 19 pp. 201-214. Edited by Dieter Henrich. Bonn: Bouvier, 1979.

_____. *Das Problem der Subjektivität in Hegels Logik. Hegel-Studien.* Beiheft 15. Bonn: Bouvier, 1976.

Ferrara, Ricardo. Review of *La christologie de Hegel*, by Emilio Brito. In *Hegel-Studien*. Vol. 22 pp. 225-228. Bonn: Bouvier, 1987.

Findlay, John N. *Hegel. A Re-examination.* London: George Allen and Unwin, 1958.

_____. "Hegel's Concept of Subjectivity." In *Hegels philosophische Psychologie. Hegel-Tage Santa Margherita. Hegel-Studien.* Beiheft 19 pp. 13-26. Edited by Dieter Henrich. Bonn: Bouvier, 1979.

Fink-Eitel, Hinrich. *Dialektik und Socialethik. Kommentierende Untersuchungen zu Hegels "Logik."* Meisenheim am Glan: Hain, 1978.

Fujita, Masakotsu. *Philosophie und Religion beim jungen Hegel.* Bonn: Bouvier, 1985.

Gauvin, Joseph. *Wortindex zu Hegels "Phänomenologie des Geistes."* In *Hegel-Studien.* Beiheft 14. Bonn: Bouvier, 1977.

Haag, Karl Heinz. "Die Seinsdialektik bei Hegel und in der scholastischen Philosophie." Ph.D. dissertation, Johann Wolfgang Goethe Universität, Frankfurt am Main, 1951.

Harris, H. S. *Hegel's Development. Toward the Sunlight, 1770-1801.* Oxford: Clarendon, 1972.

Harris, H. S. *Hegel's Development. Night Dreams, Jena 1801-1806.* Oxford: Clarendon, 1983.

Heede, Reinhard. "Die göttliche Idee und ihre Erscheinung in der Religion. Untersuchungen zum Verhältnis von Logik und Religionsphilosophie bei Hegel." Ph.D. dissertation, Philosophical Faculty of the Westfälischen Wilhelms-Universität zu Münster/Westfalen, 1972.

_____. "Hegel-Bilanz: Hegels Religionsphilosophie als Aufgabe und Problem der Forschung." In *Hegel-Bilanz. Zur Aktualität und Inaktualität der Philosophie Hegels.* Pp. 41-89. Edited by Reinhard Heede and Joachim Ritter. Frankfurt am Main: Klostermann, 1973.

Heidegger, Martin. *Identität und Differenz.* Pfullingen: Neske, 1957.

_____. *Identity and Difference.* New York: Harper, 1969.

Henrich, Dieter. "'Identität' – Begriffe, Probleme, Grenzen." In *Identität.* Pp. 133-186. Edited by Odo Marquard and Karlheinz Stierle. Munich: Fink, 1979.

Hirsch, Emanuel. Review of *Vorlesungen über die Philosophie der Religion.* Philosophische Bibliothek. Vols 59, 60, 61, 63, by G. W. F. Hegel. Edited by Georg Lasson. In *Theologische Literaturzeitung* (1925) cols. 421-423, (1928) cols. 376-379, (1930) cols. 425-427.

_____. *Geschichte der neueren evangelischen Theologie.* 5 vols. Gütersloh: Gerd Mohn, 1953.

Hodgson, Peter C. "Editor's Introduction." In G. W. F. Hegel. *The Christian Religion: Lectures on the Philosophy of Religion*, Part Three: *The Revelatory, Consummate Absolute Religion*. Pp. vii-xxix. Edited and translated by Peter C. Hodgson. Missoula: Scholars Press, 1979.

_____. "Editorial Introduction." In G. W. F. Hegel. *Lectures on the Philosophy of Hegel*. Vol. 1: *Introduction and The Concept of Religion*. Pp. 1-81. Edited by Peter C. Hodgson. Berkeley: University of California Press, 1984.

_____. "Editorial Introduction." In G. W. F. Hegel. *Lectures on the Philosophy of Hegel*. Vol. 2: *Determinate Religion*. Pp. 1-90. Edited by Peter C. Hodgson. Berkeley: University of California Press, 1987.

_____. "Editorial Introduction." In G. W. F. Hegel. *Lectures on the Philosophy of Hegel*. Vol. 3: *The Consummate Religion*. Pp. 1-57. Edited by Peter C. Hodgson. Berkeley: University of California Press, 1985.

_____. "Editorial Introduction." In G. W. F. Hegel. *Lectures on the Philosophy of Hegel*. One-volume edition. *The Lectures of 1827*. Pp. 1-71. Edited by Peter C. Hodgson. Berkeley: University of California Press, 1988.

_____. "Hegel's Approach to Religion: The Dialectic of Speculation and Phenomenology." *The Journal of Religion* 64 (1984) 158-172.

_____. "Hegel's Christology: Shifting Nuances in the Berlin Lectures." *Journal of the American Academy of Religion* 53 (1985) 23-40.

_____. "Logic, History, and Alternative Paradigms in Hegel's Interpretation of the Religions." *The Journal of Religion* 68 (1988) 1-20.

_____. "Plans for Completing the English Study Edition of Hegel's Lectures on the Philosophy of Religion." *The Owl of Minerva* 11, 4 (1980) 6-7.

_____. Review of *Religionsphilosophie*. Vol. 1: *Die Vorlesung von 1821*, by G. W. F. Hegel. Edited by Karl-Heinz Ilting. In *The Owl of Minerva* 11, 2 (1979) 4-7.

Hogemann, Friedrich and Jaeschke, Walter. "Die Wissenschaft der Logik." In *Hegel. Einführung in seine Philosophie.* Pp. 75-90. Edited by Otto Pöggeler. Munich: Karl Alber, 1977.

Homann, Karl. "Zum Begriff 'Subjektivität' bis 1802." *Archiv für Begriffsgeschichte* 11 (1967) 184-205.

Huber, Herbert. *Idealismus und Trinität, Pantheon und Götterdämmerung. Grundlagen und Grundzüge der Lehre von Gott nach dem Manuscript Hegels zur Religionsphilosophie.* Weinheim: Acta humaniora, 1984.

_____. "Zum Vorlesungsmanuskript von 1821. Bemerkungen zur Edition von K.-H. Ilting." In *Die Flucht in den Begriff.* Pp. 159-162. Edited by Friedrich Wilhelm Graf and Falk Wagner. Stuttgart: Klett-Cotta, 1982.

Hyppolite, Jean. *Genèse et structure de la "Phénomenologie de l'Esprit" de Hegel.* Paris: Aubier, 1946.

_____. *Genesis and Structure of the Hegel's "Phenomenology of Spirit."* Translated by Samuel Cherniak and John Heckman. Evanston, IL: Northwestern University Press, 1974.

Ilting, Karl-Heinz. "Zur Edition." In G.W.F. Hegel. *Religionsphilosophie.* Vol. 1: *Die Vorlesung von 1821.* Pp. 737-765. Edited by Karl-Heinz Ilting. Naples: Bibliopolis, 1978.

Jaeschke, Walter. "Absolute Idee – absolute Subjektivität. Zum Problem der Persönlichkeit Gottes in der Logik und in der Religionsphilosophie." *Zeitschrift für philosophische Forschung* 35 (1981) 385-416.

_____. "Der Aufbau und die bisherigen Editionen von Hegels Vorlesungen über Philosophie der Religion." M.A. dissertation, Die freie Universität Berlin, 1970-1971.

_____. "Äußerliche Reflexion und immanente Reflexion. Eine Skizze der systematischen Geschichte des Reflexionsbegriffs in Hegels Logikentwürfen." In *Hegel-Studien.* Vol. 13 pp. 85-117. Bonn: Bouvier, 1978.

_____. "Christianity and Secularity in Hegel's Concept of the State." *The Journal of Religion* 61 (1981) 127-145.

_____. "Die Flucht vor dem Begriff: Ein Jahrzehnt Literatur zur Religionsphilosophie (1971-1981)." In *Hegel-Studien*. Vol. 18 pp. 297-309. Bonn: Bouvier, 1983.

_____. "Hegel's Interpretation of the Non-Christian Religions in Relation to the Concept of Christianity as the Absolute Religion." Paper presented to the annual conference of the Hegel Society of Great Britain, Oxford, September, 1987.

_____. "Hegel's Last Year in Berlin." In *Hegel's Philosophy of Action*. Pp. 31-48. Edited by Lawrence S. Stepelevich and David Lamb. Atlantic Highlands, NJ: Humanities, 1983.

_____. "Zur Logik der Bestimmten Religion." In *Hegels Logik der Philosophie. Religion und Philosophie in der Theorie des absoluten Geistes*. Pp. 172-188. Stuttgart: Klett-Cotta, 1984.

_____. "Between Myth and History: On Hegel's Study of the History of Religion." In "Papers of the Nineteenth Century Theology Working Group." Vol. 13 pp. 59-70. American Academy of Religion 1987 Annual Meeting. Edited by Walter H. Conser and James Yerkes. Duplicated at the Graduate Theological Union, Berkeley, California, 1987.

_____. "Philosophy of Religion: The Quest for a Critical Edition." *The Owl of Minerva* 11, 3 (March 1980) 4-8, and 11, 4 (June 1980) 1-6.

_____. "Probleme der Edition der Nachschriften von Hegels Vorlesungen." *Allgemeine Zeitschrift für Philosophie* 3 (1980) 51-63.

_____. *Die Religionsphilosophie Hegels*. Darmstadt: Wissenschaftliche Buchgesellschaft, 1983.

_____. "Staat aus christlichem Prinzip und christlicher Staat: Zur Ambivalenz der Berufung auf das Christentum in der Rechtsphilosophie Hegels und der Restauration." *Der Staat: Zeitschrift für Staatslehre, öffentliches Recht, und Verfassungsgeschichte* 18 (1979) 349-374.

_____. *Die Suche nach den eschatologischen Wurzeln der Geschichtsphilosophie*. Munich: Chr. Kaiser, 1976.

_____. *Die Vernunft in der Religion*. Stuttgart-Bad Cannstatt: Frommann-holzboog, 1986.

_____. "Vorwort des Herausgebers." In G. W. F. Hegel. *Vorlesungen. Ausgewählte Nachschriften und Manuskripte*. Vol. 3: *Vorlesungen über die Philosophie der Religion. Teil 1: Einleitung. Der Begriff der Religion*. Pp. ix-lxxxvi. Edited by Walter Jaeschke. Hamburg: Meiner, 1983.

Kant, Immanuel. *Kants Werke, Akademie-Textausgabe*. Vol. 6: *Die Religion innerhalb der Grenzen der bloßen Vernunft, Die Metaphysik der Sitten*. Berlin: Walter de Gruyter, 1968. Pp. 1-202.

_____. *Religion within the Limits of Reason Alone*. Translated by Theodore M. Greene and Hoyt H. Hudson. Chicago: Open Court, 1934.

Küng, Hans. *Menschwerdung Gottes*. Freiburg: Herder, 1970.

Kimmerle, Heinz. "Hegels "Wissenschaft der Logik" als Grundlegung seines Systems der Philosophie. Über das Verhältnis von 'Logik' und 'Realphilosophie.'" In *Die Logik des Wissens und das Problem der Erziehung*. Pp. 52-60. Edited by Wilhelm Raimund Beyer. Hamburg: Meiner, 1982.

Kojève, Alexandre. *Introduction à la lecture de Hegel*. Paris: Gallimard, 1947.

_____. *Introduction to the Reading of Hegel*. Translated by James H. Nichols. New York: Basic Books, 1969.

Labarrière, Pierre-Jean. *Structures et mouvement dialectique dans la "Phénoménologie de l'Esprit" de Hegel*. Paris: Aubier-Montaigne, 1968.

_____. Review of *Hegel's Trinitarian Claim*, by Dale M. Schlitt. In *Archives de Philosophie* 50 (1987) 318-319.

Lämmermann, Godwin. "Redaktion und Redaktionsprinzipien der Vorlesungen über Religionsphilosophie in ihrer zweiten Ausgabe." In *Die Flucht in den Begriff*. Pp. 140-158. Edited by Friedrich Wilhelm Graf and Falk Wagner. Stuttgart: Klett-Cotta, 1982.

Lakeland, Paul. *The Politics of Salvation: The Hegelian Idea of the State*. Albany: State University of New York Press, 1984.

Léonard, André. *Commentaire littéral de la logique de Hegel* Paris: J. Vrin, 1974.

Leuze, Reinhard. *Die außerchristlichen Religionen bei Hegel.* Göttingen: Vandenhoeck und Ruprecht, 1975.

von der Luft, Eric. *Hegel, Hinrichs, and Schleiermacher on Feeling and Reason in Religion*, Lewiston: Edwin Mellen, 1987.

_____. "Hegel vs. (?) Judaism: A Reassessment." In "Papers of the Nineteenth Century Theology Working Group." Vol. 13 pp. 112-123. American Academy of Religion 1987 Annual Meeting. Edited by Walter H. Conser and James Yerkes. Duplicated at the Graduate Theological Union, Berkeley, California, 1987.

Lukács, Georg [György]. *Der junge Hegel. Über die Beziehungen von Dialektik und Ökonomie.* Zürich: Europa-Verlag, 1948; 2nd ed., *Der junge Hegel und das Problem der kapitalistichen Gesellschaft.* Berlin: Aufbau-Verlag, 1954.

_____. *The Young Hegel. Studies in the Relations between Dialectics and Economics.* Translated by Rodney Livingston. Cambridge, MA: Massachussetts Institute of Technology Press, 1976.

McCarthy, Vincent A. *Quest for a Philosophical Jesus. Christianity and Philosophy in Rousseau, Kant, Hegel, and Schelling.* Macon, GA: Mercer University Press, 1986.

McGinn, Bernard. *The Calabrian Abbot.* New York: Macmillan, 1985.

Marheineke, Philipp. *Die Grundlehren der christlichen Dogmatik.* Berlin: F. Dümmler, 1819.

_____. *Die Grundlehren der christlichen Dogmatik als Wissenschaft.* Berlin: Duncker und Hümblot, 1827.

Marquard, Odo and Stierle, Karlheinz, eds. *Identität.* Munich: Fink, 1979.

Mensching, Gustav. "Typologie außerchristlichen Religion bei Hegel." *Zeitschrift für Missionskunde und Religionswissenschaft* 46 (1931) 329-340.

Moltmann, Jürgen. *The Trinity and the Kingdom.* New York: Harper and Row, 1981.

Moritz, Karl Philipp. *Anthousa oder Roms Alterthümer. Ein Buch für die Menschheit. Die heiligen Gebräuche der Römer.* Berlin: F. Mauer, 1791.

Nicolin, Günther. *Hegel in Berichten seiner Zeitgenossen.* Hamburg: Felix Meiner, 1970.

Niel, Henri. *De la médiation dans la philosophie de Hegel.* Paris: Aubier, 1945.

Nohl, Hermann, ed. *Hegels theologische Jugendschriften.* Tübingen: Mohr, 1907.

_____. *Early Theological Writings.* Translated by T. M. Knox. Chicago: University of Chicago Press, 1948.

Pannenberg, Wolfhart. *Basic Questions in Theology. Collected Essays.* Vol. 2. Philadelphia: Fortress, 1971.

_____. *Theology and the Kingdom of God.* Philadelphia: Westminster, 1969.

Perrin, Norman. *Jesus and the Language of the Kingdom.* Philadelphia: Fortress, 1976.

Puntel, L. Bruno. *Darstellung, Methode und Struktur. Untersuchungen zur Einheit der systematischen Philosophie G. W. F. Hegels.* Hegel-Studien. Beiheft 10. Bonn: Bouvier, 1973.

Rahner, Karl. *The Trinity.* London: Burns and Oates, 1970.

Rendtorff, Trutz. *Kirche und Theologie. Die systematische Funktion des Kirchenbegriffs in der neueren Theologie.* Gütersloh: Mohn, 1966.

Reynolds, Frank E. "Hegel Revisited: A History of Religions/Buddhist Studies Perspective." In "Papers of the Nineteenth Century Theology Working Group." Vol. 13 pp. 100-111. American Academy of Religion 1987 Annual Meeting. Edited by Walter H. Conser and James Yerkes. Duplicated at the Graduate Theological Union, Berkeley, California, 1987.

Ricoeur, Paul. "The Status of Vorstellung in Hegel's Philosophy of Religion." In *Meaning, Truth, and God*. Pp. 70-88. Edited by Leroy S. Rouner. Notre Dame: University of Notre Dame Press, 1982.

Rocker, Stephen. "Hegel's Rational Religion. The Identity of Content between Philosophy and Religion." Ph. D. dissertation, Department of Philosophy, The University of Ottawa, 1989.

Röd, Wolfgang. "Die Säkularisierung der Reich-Gottes Idee bei Hegel und Marx." In *Reich Gottes, Kirche, Civitas Dei*. Pp. 183-200 [discussion pp. 201-214]. Edited by P. Thomas Michels. Salzburg: Anton Pustet, 1980.

Rohrmoser, Günther. *Subjektivität und Verdinglichung. Theologie und Gesellschaft im Denken des jungen Hegels*. Gütersloh: Mohn, 1961.

Rohs, Peter. *Form und Grund, Hegel-Studien*. Beiheft 6. Bonn: Bouvier, 1969.

Rondet, Henri. "Hégélianisme et Christianisme: Réflexions théologiques." *Recherches de Science Religieuse* 26 (1936) 257-296, 419-453.

Schadel, Erwin, ed., with the co-operation of Dieter Brünn and Peter Müller. *Bibliotheca Trinitariorum. International Bibliography of Trinitarian Literature*. Vol. 1: *Author Index*. Vol. 2: *Indices and Supplementary List*. Munich: K. G. Saur, 1984, 1988.

Schleiermacher, Friedrich, D. E. *Der christliche Glaube nach den Grundsätzen der evangelischen Kirche im Zusammenhange dargestellt*. Vol. 1. Berlin: G. Reimer, 1821.

_____. *Über die Religion. Reden an die Gilbildeten unter ihren Verächtern*. Berlin: Bei Johann Friedrich Unger, 1799.

_____. *On Religion. Speeches to Its Cultured Despisers*. New York: Harper and Row, 1958.

Schlitt, Dale M. *Hegel's Trinitarian Claim. A Critical Reflection*. Leiden: Brill, 1984.

Schmidt, Erik. "Hegel und die kirchliche Trinitätslehre." *Neue Zeitschrift für systematische Theologie und Religionsphilosophie* 24 (1982) 241-260.

Schmidt, J., Review of *Idealismus und Trinität*, by Herbert Huber. In *Theologie und Philosophie* 61 (1986) 131-133.

Schmitz, Hermann. *Hegel als Denker der Individualität*. Meisenhan/Glan: Hain, 1957.

Schoeps, Hans-Joachim. "Die außerchristlichen Religionen bei Hegel." In *Studien zur unbekannten Religons-und Geistesgeschichte*. Pp. 255-284. Göttingen: Musterschmidt Verlag, 1963.

Splett, Jörg. *Hegel's Trinitarian Claim*, by Dale M. Schlitt. In *Theologie und Philosophie* 61 (1986) 133-135.

_____. *Die Trinitätslehre G.W.F. Hegels*. Munich: Alber, 1965.

Steinhauer, Kurt. *Hegel Bibliography. Background Material on the International Reception of Hegel within the Context of the History of Philosophy*. Munich: Saur, 1980.

Theunissen, Michael. *Hegels Lehre vom absoluten Geist als theologisch-politischer Traktat*. Berlin: Walter de Gruyter, 1970.

Tillette, Xavier. "Bible et philosophie. La bible des philosophes." Photoreproduced course notes. Paris: Institut Catholique de Paris, 1983.

Tillich, Paul. *Systematic Theology*. 3 vols. Chicago: The University of Chicago Press, 1951, 1957, 1963.

Viyagappa, Ignatius. *G. W. F. Hegel's Concept of Indian Philosophy*. Rome: Università Gregoriana Editrice, 1980.

Wagner, Falk. "Bibliographie zu Hegels Religionsphilosophie." In *Die Flucht in den Begriff. Materialien zu Hegels Religionsphilosophie*. Pp. 309-345. Edited by Friedrich Wilhelm Graf and Falk Wagner. Stuttgart: Klett-Cotta, 1982.

Walther, Christian. *Typen des Reich Gottes-Verständnisses*. Munich: Chr. Kaiser, 1961.

Webster's Seventh New Intercollegiate Dictionary. Springfield, MA: G. and C. Merriam, 1971.

Weiss, Johannes. *Die Idee des Reiches Gottes in der Theologie*. Gießen: J. Ricker, 1901.

Westphal, Merold. "Hegel, Hinduism, and Freedom." *The Owl of Minerva* 20 (1989) 193-204.

Williamson, Raymond Keith. *Introduction to Hegel's Philosophy of Religion*. Albany: State University of New York Press, 1984.

Yerkes, James. *The Christology of Hegel*. Missoula, Montana: Scholars, 1978; Albany: State University of New York Press, 1983.

Zeller, Eduard. "Hegel's Vorlesungen über die Philosophie der Religion (Zweite Auflage, Berlin, 1840)." In *Die Flucht in den Begriff*. Pp. 114-139. Edited by Friedrich Wilhelm Graf and Falk Wagner. Stuttgart: Klett-Cotta, 1982.

INDEX

Ahlers, Rolf, 197
Ainslie, Douglas, 22
Aristotle, 257
Atherton, J. Patrick, 158, 161
Barth, Karl, 302, 303, 318
Bauer, Bruno, 6, 23
Beintker, Michael, 304, 317
Beyer, Wilhelm Raimund, 158, 163
Bloch, Ernst, 303
Boener, Ignacy, 13
Bonsiepen, Wolfgang, ix
Brito, Emilio, 190, 191, 256, 257, 260, 305, 306
Brown, Robert. F., x, 3, 15, 24, 59
Brünn, Dieter, 189
Bubner, Rüdiger, 158
Buchner, Hartmut, ix
Burbidge, John, 64, 160, 191, 257, 259, 260
Butler, Clark, 91
Cargonico, L., 190
Cerf, Walter, ix, 161
Cherniak, Samuel, 22
Comoth, Katharina, 158, 189, 197
Conser, Walter H., 97
Cornehl, Peter, 304
Cox, Harvey, 302
Coyle, J. Kevin, 24
Croce, Benedetto, 4
Deiters, P. F. (F. P.?), 13
Dilthey, Wilhelm, 4
Doniela, William V., 163
Düsing, Klaus, xix
Ferrara, Ricardo, 5, 256
Fichte, Johann Gottlieb, ix, xiv, 38, 139, 161
Findlay, John N., xix, 4
Fink-Eitel, Hinrich, 160, 162
Fitzer, J. P., x, 3, 15
Freud, Sigmund, 58
Fujita, Masakotsu, 306

Gadamer, Hans-Georg, 60
Gauvin, Joseph, 159
George, Michael, 305
Glockner, Hermann, 124, 305
Göschel, Carl Friedrich, 6
Goethe, Johann Wolfgang von, 91
Graf, Wilhelm, 23
Greene, Theodore M., 304
Griesheim, Karl Gustav von, 12, 13, 76, 231, 282, 310
Gutierrez, Gustavo, 302
Haag, Karl Heinz, 196
Harris, Errol E., 26
Harris, H. S., ix, x, 3, 15, 161, 197
Harris, R. Baine, 158
Hausen, Gitta, 22
Heckman, John, 22
Heede, Reinhard, ix, 24, 96, 97, 166, 196
Heidegger, Martin, 196
Henning, Leopold von, 12
Henrich, Dieter, xix, 159
Hinrichs, H. F. W., 26, 27, 41, 61
Hirsch, Emmanuel, 23, 92
Hodgson, Peter C., vii, x, xix, xx, 3, 5, 7, 9, 10, 14-16, 20, 22-24, 26, 59-63, 65, 89, 91-98, 120, 123-126, 165-168, 193, 255, 258-260, 264-266, 306-308, 310-315, 318
Hoffmeister, Johannes, 190, 197
Hogemann, Friedrich, ix, 28
Homann, Karl, xix
Horstmann, Rolf-Peter, 306
Hotho, Heinrich Gustav, 13, 25, 79
Hube, Joseph, 13
Huber, Herbert, 24, 128, 189

Hudson, Hoyt H., 304
Hurtubise, Denis, vii
Hyppolite, Jean, 4
Ilting, Karl-Heinz, 11, 24
Jaeschke, Walter, vii, ix, xi, xix,
  3, 6, 7, 10, 11, 14, 19-25, 27, 28,
  60, 61, 63-65, 87, 89-93, 95-98,
  120, 123-129, 159, 189, 192,
  195, 196, 257, 258, 263-265,
  268, 304, 306, 309, 313, 315,
  317
Joachim of Fiore, 303, 318
Kant, Immanuel, xiv, 38, 67, 68,
  71, 72, 257, 272, 299, 303,
  304, 306, 318
Kehler, F. C. H. von, 13
Kimmerle, Heinz, 163
Knox, T. M., 21
Koch, Traugott, vii
Kojève, Alexandre, 4
Küng, Hans, 256, 257
Labarrière, Pierre-Jean, 27, 164,
  193-195
Laberge, Léo, viii
Lämmermann, Godwin, 23
Lakeland, Paul, 313, 317
Lamb, David, 95, 313
Lasson, Georg, 6, 7, 13, 14, 23,
  79, 197
Léonard, André, 64, 160
Leuze, Reinhard, 87, 91, 92, 96,
  97
Livingston, Rodney, 22
von der Luft, Eric, 26, 27, 60, 61,
  97
Lukács, Georg, 4, 22
Marheineke, Phillip, 5, 6, 11, 23,
  122, 129
Marquard, Odo, 158
Marx, Karl, 6, 304
McCarthy, Vincent A., 257
McGinn, Bernard, vii, 158, 318
Mensching, Gustav, 92, 97
Michelet, Carl Ludwig, 100, 123
Michels, P. Thomas, 304

Miller, A. V., ix, x, 305
Moltmann, Jürgen, 303, 318
Moritz, Karl Philipp, 75, 93
Mühlenberg, Ekkehard, vii
Müller, Peter, 189
Nichols, James H., 22
Nicolin, Friedhelm, ix, 305
Nicolin, Günther, 91
Niel, Henri, 305, 317
Nietzsche, Friedrich Wilhelm,
  58
Nohl, Hermann, 4
Pannenberg, Wolfhart, 90, 97,
  303, 318
Pasternaci, Carl, 13
Perrin, Norman, 307
Petry, M. J., x, 163
Pöggeler, Otto, ix, 28, 305
Prabhu, Joseph, 98
Puntel, L. Bruno, 160
Rahner, Karl, 189
Rauschenbusch, Walter, 302
Rendtorff, Trutz, 165
Reynolds, Frank E., 97
Ricoeur, Paul, 158, 159
Ritter, Joachim, 24
Rocker, Stephen, 65, 168
Röd, Wolfgang, 304
Rohrmoser, Günther, 163, 198
Rohs, Peter, 162
Rondet, Henri, 24
Rosenkranz, Karl, 273
Rouner, Leroy S., 158
Rousseau, Jacques, 257
Royce, Josiah, 302
Schadel, Erwin, 189
Schelling, F. W. J., ix, xiv, 38,
  72, 161, 257
Schiller, J. C. F., 91
Schleiermacher, Friedrich, 26,
  27, 40, 41, 46, 60, 61, 68,
  71, 75, 76, 78, 83, 93, 309

Schlitt, Dale M., viii, xix, 27, 60, 62, 63, 126, 158, 159, 162, 165, 168, 189-193, 256, 269, 313
Schmidt, Erik, 189
Schmidt, J., 129
Schmitz, Hermann, 190, 196
Schoeps, Hans-Joachim, 87, 91, 97
Schubarth, K. E., 190
Schweitzer, Albert, 302
Spinoza, Benedict (Baruch) de, 41, 42
Splett, Jörg, 129, 189, 196
Stahl, Friedrich Julius, 6
Steinhauer, Kurt, 4, 22, 158
Steplevich, Lawrence, viii, 95, 313
Stewart, J. M., x, 3, 15
Stierle, Karlheinz, 159

Strauss, David Friedrich, 6, 8, 14, 72, 82-84, 314, 315
Suchocki, Marjorie, 303
Teilhard de Chardin, Pierre, 302
Theunissen, Michael, 304
Tillette, Xavier, 129
Tillich, Paul, 302, 303, 318
Viyagappa, Ignatius, 87, 91, 92, 94, 97
Vincent, Andrew, 305
Wagner, Falk, xix, 23
Wallace, William, x, xi
Walther, Christian, 304, 305, 317
Weiss, Johannes, 302, 304
Westphal, Merold, 97, 98
Williams, Raymond Keith, 165
Yerkes, James, 97, 257, 317
Zeller, Eduard, 23